The Complete Guide
to Automotive
Refinishing

The Complete Guide to Automotive Refinishing

Second Edition

Harry T. Chudy

Formerly
Automotive Paint Instructor
Ferris State College
and
Fisher Body Division
General Motors Corporation

PRENTICE HALL, Englewood Cliffs, N.J. 07632

Library of Congress Cataloging-in-Publication Data

Chudy, Harry T.,
 The complete guide to automotive refinishing.

 Includes index.
 1. Automobiles—Painting. I. Title.
TL154.C54 1988   629.2′6   87-1330
ISBN 0-13-159807-4

Editorial/production supervision: *Raeia Maes*
Cover design: *Diane Saxe*
Manufacturing buyer: *Lorraine Fumoso*

Cover photo courtesy of Ditzler
Automotive Finishes, PPG Inc.

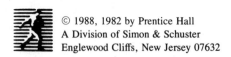 © 1988, 1982 by Prentice Hall
A Division of Simon & Schuster
Englewood Cliffs, New Jersey 07632

Printed in the United States of America

10 9 8 7 6 5 4 3

ISBN 0-13-159807-4   025

Prentice-Hall International (UK) Limited, *London*
Prentice-Hall of Australia Pty. Limited, *Sydney*
Prentice-Hall Canada Inc., *Toronto*
Prentice-Hall Hispanoamericana, S.A., *Mexico*
Prentice-Hall of India Private Limited, *New Delhi*
Prentice-Hall of Japan, Inc., *Tokyo*
Simon & Schuster Asia Pte. Ltd., *Singapore*
Editora Prentice-Hall do Brasil, Ltda., *Rio de Janeiro*

This book is dedicated to my wife, Connie;
to my children, Rick and Sharon; daughter-in-law, Cindy;
to Jason and Benjamin Chudy, grandsons;
and to all young persons who aspire to become
automotive refinishing specialists.

Contents

Contents   xvii

Preface

Major changes have taken place in paint technology and factory methods of paint application since this book was published in 1982. These changes affect all painters and paint shops, all apprentices, all insurance companies, and all paint training schools.

Recent factory methods of applying color finishes, together with completely new paint technologies, particularly the basecoat/clearcoat and tri-coat finishes, are gradually replacing traditional paint systems and refinish products. The use of standard acrylic lacquers and enamels is gradually diminishing. All major car companies are striving to use basecoat/clearcoat finishes as soon as the new paint systems can be installed. Chrysler is the first American car company to become 100% basecoat/clearcoat.

Part of the reason for the new finishes is that basecoat/clearcoat and tri-coat finishes are much cleaner and result in less detrimental effect on our environment. This fits in beautifully with our EPA requirements. Other reasons are that:

1. The finishes are more durable.
2. The finishes have more gloss and greater sales appeal.
3. The finishes are easier to maintain.

Basecoat/clearcoat finishes are repairable in service as explained in this book. Special service repair materials and procedures are required as outlined in Table 9-1 and in applicable chapters. Basecoat and standard colors must never be intermixed or one system used to repair the other system. These are entirely different paint systems and they are designed to be kept that way.

Because of variables in factory paint application, which the factories advise cannot be fully controlled, and due to the new paint technologies, the painter of today and of the future is called on to do more adjusting of colors and more tinting than ever before. For this reason, and with the aid of General Motors Product Service Training, Chapter 14 has been rewritten completely.

The best color-matching fundamentals and information from leading paint suppliers, artists, and automotive color specialists have been assembled in Chapter 14 and cover how to evaluate automotive colors accurately and how to tint a color in the best manner to achieve a successful color match. Chapter 14 lays a solid groundwork for the person who desires to learn the art of tinting. All painters are urged to review and practice the fundamentals explained in Chapter 14 as often as possible until the art of tinting becomes a simple habit.

Chapter 14 provides the theory and practical step-by-step procedure that guides the painter on a known and confident path to successful color matching. The chapter explains how painters can keep a file of successfully color-matched spray-out test panels with specific tinting instructions recorded on the reverse side as an aid for future repair work.

To do acceptable paint repairs on a competitive basis, each paint shop must be in a position to adjust or to tint a color at the time a car is being painted. Time is of the essence. For this purpose, each paint shop should be equipped with a complete set of tinting colors, a color tinting guide, and color-mixing equipment from one of the leading paint suppliers.

Chapter 14 explains why factory pack colors, used alone, may not achieve an acceptable color match in every instance on basecoat/clearcoat and tri-coat finishes. All car companies are relying on qualified painters to have a good knowledge of color adjustment and tinting to achieve successful color matches. In addition to tinting, the book advises the adjustment of a color through tinting or application technique to a ballpark color match, and then blending the color into the adjacent panels. A color that cannot be spot repaired cannot be blended into adjacent panels satisfactorily.

A repair procedure for the repair of gouge-type damage on flexible plastic parts, like bumper covers, has been added to Chapter 16. A repair procedure for the replacement of chip-resistant coatings due to collision damage has been added to Chapter 18. An easy to follow repair procedure for the replacement of OEM single or multiple paint striping has been added to Chapter 12.
This book may be used for a number of purposes:

1. For the beginner or apprentice entering the automotive refinishing trade.
2. For paint instructors in high schools, trade schools, and colleges.
3. For experienced painters who desire to be updated with lasting paint information and to advance their ability to earn a better living.
4. For all personnel connected with automotive refinishing in any way, be it claims department and/or service training, who desire to broaden their background.
5. To familiarize all in the automotive refinishing trade with OSHA regulations concerning paint shops, paint equipment, and the safety of the painter.

This paint guide emphasizes not only *what* to do, but *how* to do each fundamental operation in automotive refinishing, such as cleaning, sanding, spot repairing, color matching the metallics, guaranteeable-type rust repairs, rust prevention, and care of a paint finish. The book is fully illustrated to aid the reader.

Automotive refinishing is made up of two parts: (1) theory, which covers *why* and *how* things happen as they do, and (2) skill development, which requires practicing and doing the skill operations correctly until they become a habit.

A *qualified painter* is a person who is able to do all operations as described and illustrated in this book—safely—and can understand and answer the questions at the end of each chapter. A qualified painter can do paint work for any conventional paint shop or car factory with the automotive refinish products available in the field.

The chapter on the paint spray gun covers the purpose and description of each part of the spray gun.

The chapter on spraying techniques tells how to use all forms of spray fans, from the smallest to the wide-open spray fan.

All popular refinish systems are covered, with emphasis on standard acrylic lacquer and acrylic enamel repair and on basecoat/clearcoat finish repair. The paint repair systems include full chapters on spot repair, panel and sectional panel repair, and complete refinishing.

The book consists of a wide range of updated paint information. Paint repair systems included are exterior car color repairs, exterior flexible plastic parts finishing, interior plastic parts finishing, and vinyl top painting. All these paint repair systems follow factory guidelines and are the best that can be done in the repair trade.

The chapter on rust repair describes how to remove *all* rust from exterior surfaces fast. Together with the best primer system available, rust repairs can be guaranteed for any number of years.

Each applicable chapter contains a summary table of refinish products from five leading paint suppliers. Each product can be ordered from applicable paint jobbers by stock number and description as shown. To see all the primary solvents, undercoat materials, color systems, and clear systems in a single chart is a surprisingly welcome sight for any painter. A knowledge of equivalent competitive products is also of advantage to the painter. The author is thoroughly familiar with the products listed, and they are generally approved by most car factories. There are, no doubt, many equivalent products available in the field that are equal to or superior to the products charted and discussed in this book. It is virtually impossible for any author to test and keep abreast of all paint products on the market. Products listed in this book were in effect at the time of publication. Paint suppliers and car factories reserve the right to make product changes as improvements are developed.

The chapter on paint conditions and remedies is fully illustrated and describes how to identify, repair, and prevent common paint problems. All qualified painters must be thoroughly familiar with this chapter.

For easy reference, each chapter title is self-explanatory. Examples are "Surface Preparation," "Automotive Colors: Description and Behavior," "Automotive Colors: Preparation and Application," "Spot Repair Techniques," "Color Matching Fundamentals and Techniques," and "Compounding and Polishing."

Emphasis is placed on the use of undercoats that provide the best durability. The best primer systems available in refinishing are described and listed in Chapter 8.

OSHA regulations and the role of NIOSH concerning paint shops and the health of the painter are covered in Chapter 5.

References made to OSHA in this book are not intended to be a complete study of OSHA with respect to the automotive refinishing trade. The purpose of covering OSHA regulations in this book is to show painters and painter helpers the government's role in the automotive refinishing trade. References in the book cover OSHA regulations that were in effect as of November 1978.

The Glossary has been expanded and revised to include many common refinish terms associated with the refinish trade. The Glossary should be used by painters and students of automotive refinishing to broaden their scope and understanding of items that are a component part of the trade.

Harry T. Chudy

Acknowledgments

The author wishes to express his sincere thanks to Clifford L. Samuels, Associate Professor, Automotive Department, Ferris State College, whose continuing help and encouragement made this book possible. Also, special thanks to Michael Balga, Robert Allinder, Ken Davis, Brad Thacher and William Mattingly, whose help was instrumental in the rewriting of this book.

The author wishes to acknowledge the help and encouragement of the many companies and individuals that helped make this book possible. A special credit is due to the following companies:

American Motors Corporation, Southfield, Michigan
James G. Biddle Company, Plymouth Meeting, Pennsylvania
Binks Manufacturing Company, Franklin Park, Illinois
Black & Decker, Inc., Willowdale, Ontario, Canada
Chrysler Corporation, Centerline, Michigan
C.I.L. Paints, Inc., Willowdale, Ontario, Canada
The DeVilbiss Company, Toledo, Ohio
Ditzler Automotive Finishes/PPG Industries, Troy, Michigan
The Du Pont Company, Wilmington, Delaware
Ford Motor Company, Dearborn, Michigan
General Electric Company, West Lynn, Massachusetts
General Motors Corp., Product Service Training, Warren, Michigan
Phillips Petroleum Company, Pasadena, Texas

R-M Automotive Products, BASF Inmont Corp., Detroit, Michigan
Sherwin-Williams & Acme Automotive Finishes, Cleveland, Ohio
Survivair U.S.D. Corp., Santa Ana, California
J. L. Terrels & Son, West Chester, Pennsylvania
3M Automotive Trades Division, Farmington, Michigan
U.S. Body Products, Troy, Michigan

About the Author

Harry T. Chudy is a graduate of Wayne State University, where he earned a B.S. Degree in Education in 1938. He taught in the Detroit Public School System.

The author was a member of the Ferris State College Autobody Advisory Board from 1965 to 1983. He also served as an instructor of automotive refinishing at Ferris State College in 1975 and 1976.

Although the author has held several positions with Fisher Body over a 33-year period, his primary duties consisted of teaching automotive refinishing to newly hired body repair persons who were to become instructors to teach in the General Motors Training Centers. The author also served as instrutor at several General Motors Training Centers, conducting various paint schools for GM dealer painters and apprentices.

The author is well aware of the needs of the experienced painter as well as the needs of the apprentice.

The Complete Guide

to Automotive

Refinishing

1

Description of the Automotive Refinishing Trade

NEED FOR THE TRADE

America is a nation on wheels (Fig. 1-1). Every part of our society and all our industries are dependent on wheels of one form or another. There are hundreds of millions of cars, vans, and trucks on American roads. There are additional millions of recreational vehicles, house trailers, and motorcycles, and the total number of vehicles grows each year. If for some unknown reason all automotive transportation, including cars, trucks, vans, buses, motor homes, and motorcycles, were removed permanently from the roads, our economy would come to a screeching halt.

The **appearance** of a car is important to every car owner. The single most important thing that makes a car appealing to the owner is the **beauty** and **gloss** of the paint finish. A paint job in good repair makes a car look its very best. The appearance of every factory-produced car, van, and truck is vital to the sale of that vehicle. The appearance of every used car is also vitally important to the sale of that car. People know that a **good paint finish** is essential to the **lasting beauty and durability** of a car.

Between 30 and 40 million cars pass through collision and paint repair shops each year for major repairs. Additional millions of vehicles pass through bump and paint shops for minor collision damage and general paint repairs. According to insurance companies, the total cost for all this repair work runs into billions of dollars.

An unknown number of cars, unquestionably in the millions, require **rust** repairs each year. Many cars with rust problems are repairable. But rust is like cancer. More than a million cars are scrapped each year because of rust problems that are beyond repair.

Approximately 10 million cars are added to the roads each year. Also, approxi-

Figure 1-1 America—a nation on wheels. (Courtesy of Ditzler Automotive Finishes, PPG Industries, Inc.).

mately 4 million cars are removed from the roads because they are **totally wrecked** or **rusted out** beyond repair. This results in a net increase of approximately 6 million cars to our roads each year. The need for automotive painters and metal repair persons never was so great, and the need grows each year.

GENERAL DESCRIPTION OF THE TRADE

The purpose of the automotive refinishing trade is to keep the paint finish of all cars on the road in good repair. To accomplish this purpose requires many thousands of painters and automotive-related businesses, such as:

1. Paint shops
2. Paint suppliers
3. Paint equipment suppliers
4. Miscellaneous paint material suppliers

While all automotive-related businesses and the people working in them play a vital role in the refinish trade, the painter is the single most important person.

By design, the automotive refinishing trade is so widespread all over the country that a person traveling in any state, in any type of production car, can have paint repairs done on any color by a qualified painter and the color match will be commercially acceptable. To make such a condition possible requires a great amount of teamwork and cooperation among many thousands of people in the refinishing trade. Millions of cars are being painted every day all over the country as a result of collision damage repair or for other reasons. The auto production and auto repair industries are among the largest in the nation. Paint companies provide the necessary paint colors and other essential refinish materials. Paint equipment companies supply the necessary paint spray equipment. Miscellaneous paint material suppliers make available other essential materials, such as masking tape, masking paper, many forms of sandpaper, power sanding tools, sanding blocks, tack rags, and other essential items. The job of the painter is to combine refinish **know-how** and experience:

1. To make all necessary paint repairs flawlessly.
2. To achieve good color matches.

To a bystander, watching a painter at work may appear to be an easy, routine operation. What the bystander is really seeing is a qualified painter with artistic skills developed after countless hours of patient work and practice at his or her trade. To be qualified, a painter must:

1. Be expert at **handling a paint spray gun.**
2. Be expert at **refinish fundamentals,** including **paint problems and repairs.**
3. Be thoroughly familiar with **all production paint systems.**
4. Be thoroughly familiar with **all refinish paint systems.**
5. Be expert at **color matching in all paint systems.**

It takes a certain amount of teamwork among all the people in the refinishing trade to achieve quality results. If the paint color is not right, if the paint equipment is faulty, or if the painter is not qualified, paint repairs will not be commercially acceptable.

The center of the refinishing trade is the paint shop. Three types of paint shops are most prominent in the trade:

1. **Conventional paint shops** do most of the paint work in the refinish trade because they greatly outnumber all other paint shops.
2. **High-volume, low-cost paint shops** do a good share of the refinish business nationally.
3. **Custom paint shops** have the ability to do the best quality work. They are also the most expensive.

An important factor that affects the entire refinishing trade is local safety ordinances and state and federal safety and antipollution regulations. All paint shops must be properly licensed and must follow prescribed guidelines to do paint repair work.

HOW A CONVENTIONAL PAINT SHOP OPERATES

When a person drives into a paint shop for repairs, a qualified person, usually a painter or estimator, writes up the **repair order.** The estimator inspects the car thoroughly for work to be done and writes up each paint operation. In one column on the repair order, the amount of time (in tenths of an hour) is noted opposite each operation. This is known as **labor.** All **labor** time is totaled at the bottom of the column. The total labor time is then multiplied by the flat-rate hourly scale for the area. This is the total labor charge. In another column, the amount of cost for each item of material used on the car is listed. This includes all paint, sandpaper, masking tape, and other items used in painting the car. All **material** costs are totaled at the bottom of the column. The total of the **labor** charges and **material** costs represents the total cost of a paint job. When extra work must be done on a car before painting, such as **rust repairs** and **dent repairs**, the charge is determined on a **straight-time** hourly basis and the extra charge is added to the cost of the paint job.

A common rule to determine the cost of a paint job in the trade is the one-third plus two-thirds formula. The first third represents the total cost of **all materials** for the paint job. The two-thirds represents the total cost of **labor.** Thus, if the total cost for materials is $50, the total cost for labor would be $100, and the total cost of the paint job would be $150. Rust repairs and dent repairs are determined on a straight-time basis, and the costs are added to determine the final cost of the paint job.

Generally, the responsibilities of a painter in a paint shop are:

1. To **write repair orders.**
2. To **order all necessary paint materials.**
3. To **supervise painter's helpers and apprentices** to prepare each car for paint.
4. To **supervise and help complete all masking.**
5. To **prepare paint materials as required.**
6. To **apply paint materials on cars as required.**
7. To **supervise all masking removal and final car cleanup.**
8. To **supervise car delivery to owner.**
9. To **file repair orders.**

Generally, the responsibilities of a painter's helper or apprentice are:

1. To **move cars into and out of the shop.**
2. To **wash and clean up cars** before and after paint operations.
3. To **help with car parts removal and installation.**
4. To **clean and sand paint surfaces as required.**
5. To **apply plastic filler and metal finish** as required when qualified to do so.
6. To **clean and mask cars** before the painting operation.
7. To **apply undercoats when qualified to do so.**
8. To **help sand undercoats** as required.

9. To **have the painter check all completed surface preparation operations.**

10. To **help to clean up the shop** at end of each day, or more often as required.

STRUCTURE OF THE TRADE

Car Factory Paint Organizations

To understand how the refinish trade is organized and how it operates, it is important to understand first how automotive paint suppliers, equipment suppliers, and car factories are organized (Fig. 1-2).

1. The job of paint suppliers is to furnish all necessary paint materials to factories for production-line application. Factory materials usually require a **high bake** for fast curing. Factory paint suppliers are thoroughly familiar with the paint equipment to be used, the speed of the production line, and factory finish requirements.

2. The job of paint equipment suppliers is to supply the necessary equipment to run a production paint line. Equipment suppliers must be thoroughly familiar with the paint materials, speed of the production line, and factory finish requirements.

3. The job of the car factory is to build and paint cars on a production line that is moving continuously. To do so requires expert painters and special paint application equipment, most of which is automated or automatic. Most production materials must dry or cure fast because of the speed of the production line. This requires a **high-bake** oven system. The primary objective of every production

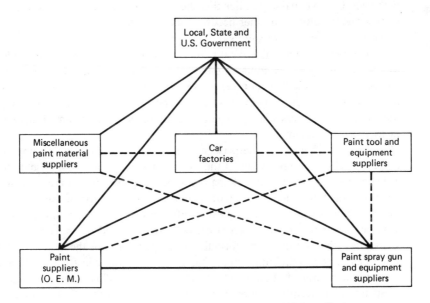

Figure 1-2 Car factory paint organizations (OEM suppliers).

plant is to **produce the best possible paint jobs.** To do so requires very close cooperation among factory painters, paint and equipment suppliers, and factory paint engineers. Paint and equipment suppliers furnishing materials to a production plant are known as **O.E.M. suppliers,** which means **original equipment manufacturers.**

Other essential items used at the factory to paint cars are:

1. Solvents, wiping towels, sandpaper, sanding blocks, masking tape, masking paper, and many other items furnished by miscellaneous paint material suppliers.
2. Power sanders and power polishers furnished by paint tool and equipment suppliers (Fig. 1-2).

The job of the city, state, and federal government is to see that factories that produce cars are doing so in accordance with federal, state, and local antipollution and health and safety regulations.

Businesses and Other Elements of the Refinish Trade

The automotive refinish trade businesses and organizations are named and numbered in Fig. 1-3 and are explained in the following pages.

Paint Suppliers (Fig. 1-3, item 1).   The purpose of refinish trade paint suppliers is to match original factory color standards and to make the refinish colors available all over the country. The paint suppliers also make available other refinish products that are needed for the repair of cars on the road. Every car factory has a thorough understanding with each O.E.M. paint supplier that the supplier make available to the trade all automotive repair colors and other necessary paint materials to do the job. This is effective at the start of any new model year.

Painters can determine what paint company supplies any specific color to any factory production plant by contacting the affected **factory zone office service manager** or a **paint supplier service representative.** Knowing this fact sometimes helps to achieve better color matches. However, knowing the O.E.M. supplier is not required, as all refinish paint suppliers who make colors available to the trade are obligated to match the factory color standards.

Because of our free-enterprise system, a number of additional paint companies also make available a complete line of their respective automotive colors and other necessary refinish products. Each paint company provides a **color chart** for each company car line every model year. Each color chart includes a complete list of refinish colors designed to match production colors. A question often asked is: "Are refinish colors exactly the same as production colors even when both are supplied by the same company?" The answer is: "Not quite." The formulation of pigments for the exact color match is the same, but there is a difference in the balance of the paint construction. Production colors are made to be **high-baked** to achieve the end result. This requires certain chemicals in the paint. Field refinish colors are made with slightly different ingredients so that they can air-dry.

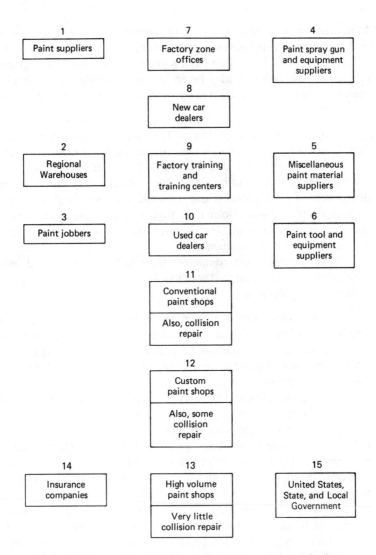

1	7	4
Paint suppliers	Factory zone offices	Paint spray gun and equipment suppliers

	8	
	New car dealers	

2	9	5
Regional Warehouses	Factory training and training centers	Miscellaneous paint material suppliers

3	10	6
Paint jobbers	Used car dealers	Paint tool and equipment suppliers

	11	
	Conventional paint shops	
	Also, collision repair	

	12	
	Custom paint shops	
	Also, some collision repair	

14	13	15
Insurance companies	High volume paint shops	United States, State, and Local Government
	Very little collision repair	

Figure 1-3 Automotive refinishing trade: businesses and organizations.

Other important refinish materials produced by each paint company in a number of paint systems are:

1. Primers
2. Primer–surfacers
3. Sealers
4. Solvents
5. Clear finishes

Structure of the Trade

Most large paint companies have a field service organization, usually called **field sales and service representatives,** located in key cities all over the country. The purpose of the representatives is to assist paint jobbers, paint shops, and painters to solve any specific paint problems that may be encountered. Service representatives are also expert painters. They can be contacted by obtaining their name and phone number from the local paint jobber.

Regional Warehouses (Fig. 1-3, item 2).   Most large refinish paint companies divide the country into regions and each region has a refinish warehouse. The purpose of a warehouse system is that they are well stocked with complete lines of refinishing products for fast distribution to all paint jobbers. Refinish warehouses are wholesale distributors of paint products and do not deal directly with the public. A painter may wish to obtain refinish information from a refinish paint warehouse if the local paint representative is not available. The local paint jobber can supply the name and phone number of the warehouse manager.

Some refinish paint companies are small and are located only within a limited regional area of the country. They, too, have sales and service representatives and paint jobbers serving the area.

Paint Jobbers (Fig. 1-3, item 3).   The purpose of the refinish paint jobber is to supply a complete line of refinish products to all paint shops in the automotive refinish trade. Refinish products can also be sold to vocational schools and colleges with professional paint instructors who are teaching the subject. Refinish products are not intended for sale to the general public.

Some paint jobbers carry only a single company's refinish paint line. Other jobbers, often located in remote areas, carry two or more different companies' paint products. In addition to paint products, jobbers often carry additional accessory paint materials such as sandpaper, masking tape, striping tape, and plastic filler. Some paint jobbers are authorized paint spray gun distributors. When a paint jobber is quite small, the owner may combine the business with automotive parts and accessories sales. Some paint jobbers have a paint delivery service and some do not. A delivery service promotes sales and pays for itself in the long run. Some paint jobbers are so large that they look like small paint factories. These jobbers handle so much business that they have automatic paint mixing equipment. Each paint jobber is a privately owned business.

Refinish colors are available from paint jobbers in two forms:

1. **Factory package colors** are ready for use and are available for a current model year and for one or more past model years, depending on the popularity of a given color.

2. **Past model colors** not stocked are formulated to be made up quickly on color-mixing machines upon request.

For paint jobber addresses and phone numbers in any area of the country, check the **Yellow Pages** index of the phone book under "Automobile Body Shop Equipment and Supplies." Each jobber is listed separately under the paint company name. **Yellow Pages** jobber listings vary from one city or suburban phone book to another. For further help to locate a particular **brand-name** paint jobber, ask the nearest car dealer, paint shop, or bump and paint shop.

Paint Spray Gun and Equipment Suppliers (Fig. 1-3, item 4). The purpose of automotive spray painting equipment suppliers is to supply the refinish trade with paint spray guns and other essential spray painting equipment that produce factory-quality results. Paint spray guns, the most important piece of equipment, are available through a number of paint jobbers and through a number of authorized spraying equipment jobbers all over the country. These jobbers have available, or can secure on request, all service parts necessary to service all spraying equipment, including spray guns.

Each equipment supplier makes available to the trade brochures and descriptive sales literature that cover the availability of all spray painting equipment and facilities. Leading paint equipment suppliers also have available to car dealers and independent paint shop owners, on request, a full line of service information and advice to set up, to fully equip, and to maintain any size of paint shop to do any planned volume of refinish business.

To get in touch with a paint equipment supplier, look in the *Yellow Pages* of the phone book under "Spraying Equipment." Two of the largest manufacturers of paint spraying equipment who supply most factories and paint shops are **Binks** and **De Vilbiss**. These companies have **authorized distributors** in all parts of the country. There are other paint spray gun manufacturers who produce high-quality equipment of equivalent status.

Miscellaneous Paint Material Suppliers (Fig. 1-3, item 5). Miscellaneous paint materials are needed to do high-quality paint repair work. Most miscellaneous items are essential tools of the trade and some are **shop cleanup** items. All miscellaneous paint materials are not necessarily supplied by a single store or company but by a number of stores, as follows:

1. Automotive paint jobbers
2. House paint jobbers
3. Department stores
4. Auto accessory stores
5. Hardware stores

Some examples of miscellaneous paint materials are:

1. Masking and striping tapes
2. Paint strainers
3. Sandpaper and sanding blocks
4. Cleaning solvents for paint and glass
5. Wheel covers (for masking)
6. Wiping towels (cloth and paper)
7. Car wash detergents

8. Water buckets, sponges, and chamois
9. Brooms, dust pans, and trash containers

Paint Tool and Equipment Suppliers (Fig. 1-3, item 6).   The purpose of paint tools and equipment is to speed up refinish operations and to make the job of refinishing easier for the painter. The following are classified as **power tools** in refinishing:

1. Power sanders
2. Power polishers
3. Power files
4. Drill motor and special accessory tools
5. Sandblasting unit

To locate stores handling power tools, check the *Yellow Pages* of the phone book under **"Power Tools"** or **"Tools—Electric and Pneumatic."**
The following are classified as **paint shop equipment:**

1. Paint shaker
2. Water hose
3. Masking machine
4. Blue-white fluorescent lights
5. Infrared heat lamps

To locate companies handling paint shop equipment, contact the nearest paint jobber or paint spray equipment supplier.

Factory Zone Offices (Fig. 1-3, item 7).   All the area of a country away from the car factories is known as the **field** to automotive sales and service personnel. Most car factories divide the country into regions and/or zones. Several zones make up a region. Each zone has an office located in a principal city called the **factory zone office.** The zone office is operated by a zone manager. The zone service manager oversees all service operations of a zone. The factory offers assistance to car dealers through factory-trained service representatives.
Each factory zone office plays an important role in the refinishing trade as follows:

1. Zone offices **guide the operation of dealerships.**
2. Zone offices **regulate the distribution of cars to dealers.**
3. Zones **monitor warranty accounts of dealers.**
4. Zones **offer service guidance to dealers.**
   a. Dealer painters must be **qualified painters.**
   b. Zone service managers have technical automotive refinishing help available to dealer painters whenever they need help.

New-Car Dealers (Fig. 1-3, item 8).   Next to the factory, the car dealers are the backbone of the automobile industry because every new car sold to the public passes through the hands of a dealer. All new cars must pass a thorough paint inspection. All car finishes must be repaired as required before cars are sold or delivered to the public. Thus, the painter is a key person in the success of a dealership. Prospective owners do not have to be paint experts to:

1. Notice a *poor* paint job.
2. Notice *off-color* repairs.
3. Notice *flaws* in a paint finish.

Dealers usually have a bump and paint shop that brings in a good share of insurance and cash collision repair business.

Factory Training and Training Centers (Fig. 1-3, item 9).   All car factories offer a certain amount of paint training to dealer and independent paint shop painters each new model year. Some car factories have training centers located in various cities throughout the country. Other factories confine their training to factory headquarter cities. One purpose of factory training is to train apprentice painters and to update experienced painters with the latest refinishing techniques and paint repair know-how.

Some car factories have mobile factory training units that are sent to the field to conduct special paint programs and other types of training programs periodically. Some car factories send experienced painter–teachers to various locations of the country to conduct special paint training programs, lasting from one day to one week. People attending these programs are usually painters who are being updated on the latest in refinishing techniques and products.

Additional programs are available at training centers that train dealer painter apprentices and collision repair apprentices as co-op students. They work at a dealership part time and go to school part time over a period of several months. This program provides new skilled technicians for expanding a dealer repair shop or for replacing persons who have retired.

Each major paint supplier conducts paint training programs each year, if not more often, to update paint jobbers on new refinish materials, procedures, and new sales techniques. Major paint equipment suppliers have training programs available to persons associated with the automotive refinish trade on proper use of the paint spray gun and on paint shop equipment. The program runs 1 week, or 5 full days. For further information regarding these programs, contact the nearest paint jobber or authorized paint equipment distributor.

Used-Car Dealers (Fig. 1-3, item 10).   Used-car dealers play a vital role in the refinish trade because, nationally, millions of cars pass through used-car dealers each year. Used-car dealers can be divided into two general categories:

1. Factory used-car dealers are connected with a new-car dealership. These dealers resell used cars they either buy or obtain as trade-ins on new cars.
2. Independent used-car dealers are not connected with a new-car dealership or factory. These dealers rely solely on the resale of used cars to stay in business.

Almost every car passing from one car owner to another needs paint repairs of one form or another. The painter plays a key role in the sale of used cars because making every used-car paint finish look like new is a routine part of the job of used-car appearance reconditioning.

Paint shops can be divided into many categories, depending on the type of painting done. The three most popular categories are:

1. **Conventional** paint shops
2. **Custom** paint shops
3. **High-volume, low-cost** paint shops

Conventional Paint Shops (Fig. 1-3, item 11).   Conventional paint shops are so called because:

1. They make up the greatest number of paint shops in the country.
2. They use refinish materials recommended by the factory.
3. They apply refinish material according to label directions as recommended by paint suppliers.
4. They work in close cooperation with insurance companies and charge for repair work on a mutually agreed on flat-rate basis.
5. Almost all metal repair shops are connected with a paint shop that fits the categories just listed and does repair work in accordance with factory recommendations.

Some paint shops specialize in both **custom** and **conventional** paint work and keep busy without the aid of a collision repair shop.

Custom Paint Shops (Fig. 1-3, item 12).   Custom paint shops are so called because:

1. Painters combine **artistic and refinish skills** that are the most advanced in the trade.
2. Custom painting requires more time than conventional forms of painting.
3. Custom painting involves the use of exotic color materials and systems not used on factory cars.
4. The charges for custom paint work are done on an individual job basis and usually are the highest in the refinish trade.

Some paint shops specialize in custom paint work only. Other custom paint shops are tied in with a conventional paint shop and with a collision repair shop.

High-Volume, Low-Cost Paint Shops (Fig. 1-3, item 13).   High-volume, low-cost paint shops are set up in a special manner, like a small assembly line, to do many paint jobs per day at a very low cost. They are set up as follows:

1. They have special paint made for them, which is done at very low cost and in only a limited set of colors.
2. They have production-line-type specialists to do surface preparation and masking.
3. Normally, they color-coat at a very fast production line speed.

NOTE: These shops have the capability, on special order, to do **conventional**-type paint work. They can also use the conventional method of pricing. Also, these shops specialize in paint work and generally are not tied in with a collision repair shop.

Insurance Companies (Fig. 1-3, item 14).   Insurance companies tie into the refinish trade in the following manner:

1. They make all driving on the roads possible. Without insurance most drivers could not afford to be on the road. That is why driving without insurance is unlawful.
2. Insurance companies play a key role in cooperation with the car factories in establishing flat-rate schedules for metal and paint repair work. These flat-rate schedules are called **flat-rate books** and are published by the car factories periodically.
3. Insurance companies compete with one another for insurance business. However, they work with one another in establishing groundwork for all metal and paint repairs.

Insurance companies pay for most of the collision repair work of the nation, which runs in the billions of dollars each year.

Federal, State, and Local Governments (Fig. 1-3, item 15).   Federal, state, and local governments play a key role in the refinishing trade as follows:

1. To operate, a paint shop must be properly licensed.
2. To operate, a paint shop must abide by a set of safety standards as established by the government, which:
   a. Protect the life of the painter.
   b. Protect the environment.
   c. Protect the life and property of people in the vicinity of the paint shop.

REVIEW QUESTIONS

1. List several important businesses that make up the automotive refinishing trade.
2. What is the center of the automotive refinishing trade?
3. List five major items a painter must know to become a qualified painter.

4. Name six responsibilities of a painter.
5. Name six responsibilities of a painter's helper.
6. What is the meaning of "O.E.M."?
7. Explain the purpose of the following businesses and organizations in the automotive refinishing trade:
    (a) Paint suppliers
    (b) Regional paint warehouses
    (c) Paint jobbers
    (d) Factory training and training centers
    (e) Conventional paint shops
    (f) Custom paint shops
    (g) Paint spray gun and equipment suppliers
    (h) Miscellaneous paint material and equipment suppliers
    (i) Insurance companies
    (j) Federal, state, and local governments

2

How Cars Are Painted at the Factory and in the Refinish Trade

The purpose of reviewing how cars are painted at the factory is to familiarize apprentices entering the automotive refinishing trade with factory paint systems and their characteristics. Painters should know how factory paint behaves when field repairs are made.

DESCRIPTION OF THE PRODUCTION LINE

A production line is a specially planned and engineered assembly line, moving continually at a particular speed, on which many assembly operations are performed for the purpose of building cars. Production-line methods of transporting car bodies are adapted to the work operations to be done. Sometimes car bodies go through production on **body assembly trucks,** and sometimes car bodies are switched to an **overhead conveyor line.** Production-line speeds vary from one car company to another. For passenger cars, production lines run as slowly as 40 per hour and as fast as 100 per hour. An average speed for an average-size car is between 60 and 70 per hour, depending on the factory. For truck production, an average speed is from 5 to 10 jobs per hour, depending on the truck company and the size of the truck. Truck lines move much more slowly because truck parts and equipment are much more involved and require more time for assembly.

FACTORY PAINTING

Factory automotive paint systems and products are the best available for painting cars at factories. As better systems are developed, they are added immediately. Factory paint systems are geared to the speed of the production line. Because of line speed, all materials are designed to be **high-baked** so that they can dry in time for car assembly. Production paint systems are not interchangeable with field repair systems. A production paint material requiring a high bake temperature would not work satisfactorily in the refinish trade because it is not designed to **air-dry** satisfactorily.

Paint Mixing Room

All paint materials to be sprayed on a production line are received and kept in large drums in a special room called the **paint mixing room.** Paint materials are mixed and prepared in drums at a specified **viscosity.** Viscosity is defined as the resistance of a paint material to flow. The heavier bodied a material, the slower it flows. The viscosity of a paint material is decreased as the amount of solvent in the material is increased. The viscosity of a paint material is measured by a **viscosity cup** and by how long it takes **(in seconds)** for a filled cup to empty through a hole at the bottom of the cup. How to check the viscosity of a paint material is discussed in Chapter 7. All paint materials are then pumped through paint system lines to assembly-line locations, where they are spray-painted. Once a drum of paint material is connected to factory paint lines and is pumped through the lines, paint materials are recirculated continually even when not in use at end of the shift. This prevents **settling** of essential paint ingredients.

Following are the stages through which a production line passes when going through a typical car factory paint department.

Metal Conditioning

As car bodies arrive for metal conditioning, two important operations are done initially:

1. Bodies are washed with a solvent to remove chalk marks, oil, and grease.
2. Body floors and all corners are then vacuum cleaned thoroughly to remove all dirt and metal-filing particles originating in the metal finishing department.

A metal conditioning booth is like a very long car wash booth, but it has no brushes. The booth is filled with many special spray nozzles located about every 3 feet in all directions on the floor, walls, and ceiling to surround each body. Nozzles are designed to produce a **full-jet** spray pattern, in which every square inch of space is filled with droplets of liquid chemicals or water. When all nozzles are turned on, they literally soak everything in the booth. Chemically treated and heated water is pumped through the nozzles under high pressure to saturate every car body. The stages of metal conditioning are as follows:

Stage 1: An acid cleaning of the body, followed by a clear water rinse.
Stage 2: The first **chemical treatment** (usually a **phosphate coating**) sprayed on the body. This is followed by a clear water rinse. When body metal is contacted by the chemical, the chemical coating builds instantaneously.

Stage 3: A second chemical treatment, also a phosphate coating, sprayed on the body. This is followed by a clear water rinse.

NOTE: The number and type of chemical treatments depend on the factory and the trade name of the metal conditioning system used.

At the conclusion of metal conditioning, the chemically treated bodies proceed through a heated oven to be dried.

Primer Application

After metal conditioning, the production line passes through the primer application department. Primer is applied to car bodies in two ways:

1. Some car factories are equipped with a **dip priming system.**
2. Other factories are equipped with **conventional spray priming systems.**

The **dip priming system** is made possible by the use of a special water-base primer. The dip system is made up of a long, large tank filled with water-base primer. The primer is electrically charged like a **negative.** A moving conveyor line runs overhead. Car bodies, hanging from the conveyor line, pass through the primer and are immersed completely or as required. The car bodies are electrically charged like a **positive.** As car bodies pass through the dip tank, they are primed automatically to the correct film thickness. The car bodies then proceed through a high-bake oven to dry.

The **conventional spray priming system** involves the use of pressure-feed spray equipment and lines. Several types of primer, and sometimes sealer, are generally used on passenger cars. This depends on the car factory.

1. Generally, a special **straight** primer is used in critical areas on outer surfaces of the body. Examples are:
   a. Body sides
   b. Window openings
   c. Door and rear compartment openings
2. Special primers are used on interior surfaces of car bodies.
3. Special primer–surfacer and sometimes a sealer are used on outer surfaces of car bodies.

Factory primer–surfacer application is done in two ways:

1. **Manual spraying is done by hand.** This system is used **to paint all hard-to-get-at areas.** They are:
   a. Body interiors
   b. Door openings

c. Hinge pillars

d. Rear compartment interiors

e. Rocker panel areas

f. Front end panels

g. Rear end panels

2. **Automatic spraying** is done by automatic equipment. As an **electric eye** is actuated by a car body, the automatic spray machine goes into operation.

   a. One machine is designed to spray the roof and rear deck areas. This machine sprays each time it makes a pass across a body. An interesting feature of this machine is that when spraying of the roof is completed, the machine drops down the necessary distance to spray the rear deck area. As each body is completed, the spray machine returns to its original height.

   b. A side spray machine is located on each side of the body. As an electric eye is actuated by a car body, each spray machine goes into operation. After the body passes the machines, the machines stop spraying.

When priming operations are completed, bodies pass through a **high-bake oven** to dry.

Wet Sand Operations

Bodies pass through the **wet sand** department for sanding of exterior body surfaces. All bodies are sanded to specifications. When sanding is completed, bodies pass through an oven to dry.

Color Application

The color coats on all production cars are applied by the **spray painting method,** which involves pressure equipment and paint lines. Color is applied in two or more applications, depending on the paint system. Acrylic lacquer and acrylic enamel are the most common paint systems used in painting production cars.

Spraying color coats is done in two ways:

1. **Manual spraying is done by hand.** This method is used **to paint hard-to-get-at areas.** They are:

   a. Body interiors

   b. Front and rear end panels

   c. Body door openings and door facings

   d. Rear compartment interiors

   e. Rocker panel areas

2. **Automatic spraying is done with special equipment.**

   a. A roof spray machine is used to spray the roof and rear deck areas similar to undercoat equipment.

b. Side spray machines are used to spray the sides of each body.

c. At older car factories, an attendant or painter must be present to switch color lines on automatic spray machines to match the color code on the body number plate. At the latest car factories, robotic spray machines are programmed to operate by themselves completely, which includes color changes.

Most car factories use the **wet-on-wet spray process** so that when all areas of a car body are painted, there is no **overspray.** The cars at this stage proceed through the oven system for drying.

Color Use by Manufacturers

The use of acrylic lacquers and acrylic enamels has become popularly accepted around the world. These two paint systems are used on almost all cars as follows:

1. All Ford, Chrysler, and American Motors plants use the acrylic enamal color system.

2. Some General Motors plants use acrylic lacquer and some use acrylic enamel. General Motors has always used enamels on vans, buses, and trucks.

3. *Most* imported car plants, including Canadian, use acrylic enamels. *Some* imported car plants, including Canadian, use acrylic lacquers.

REFINISH TRADE PAINTING

The purpose of reviewing generally how cars are painted in the refinish trade is to familiarize an apprentice with:

1. What is expected of the apprentice in the way of workmanship.

2. How to do field paint repairs.

Painters should know how and why paint repairs are made, and they should know the expected performance and durability of a field paint repair.

When a repair order is written up concerning the repair of a particular paint problem, it is the responsibility of the appraiser or painter making the estimate to determine the identity and cause of the problem (see Chapter 17). Accuracy in identifying the problem condition is very important before repairs are attempted.

Paint materials are ordered from the paint jobber as the repair order is written. Painters are encouraged to use the best recommended refinish products consistent with:

1. Factory recommendations

2. Age and general condition of car

3. Best known repair systems available

When the repair order is completed, usually the apprentice or painter's helper takes the car to the shop repair stall. Surface preparation usually involves the most labor in making paint repairs. Most if not all surface preparation is done in the shop work stall. Sandblasting and disc sanding are best done away from the work stall area. These operations are messy and require extra cleanup if done in a clean work area.

Surface Preparation

Surface preparation is an area where painters need the most help. These jobs are normally assigned to an apprentice or a painter's helper. This is the most difficult but the best way for apprentices to learn the trade. Surface preparation operations range in **degree of difficulty** from surfaces that are **very easy to prepare** to surfaces that are **difficult to prepare.** Surfaces that are **easy to prepare** are new cars that simply require color coating or compounding. Paint problems that require the most labor in surface preparation involve **rust repairs.** This is what an apprentice or painter's helper can expect a great deal of as he or she learns the trade. Rust repairs are among the most difficult to repair and to **guarantee.** However, by following proper repair fundamentals, all paint repairs, including rust repairs, can be guaranteed by a good painter for a reasonable period of time. This can be anywhere from one to three years, or more. These repairs can be done if an owner is advised of **extra parts and labor** that are required.

In general, refinish systems do a very good job of repairing cars, but they are not as durable as factory finishes. This is particularly true of the **factory high-bake primer** and/or **primer-surfacer. Factory primer should never be removed** unless necessary, as it is during metal repairs.

Color Application

The painter inspects the surface preparation and masking done by the apprentice. The painter prepares, applies, and blends the color to the car. Most color application operations are done with a **suction-feed production-type spray gun,** described in Chapter 3, in a special paint area with a good air exhaust system or in a paint spray booth, depending on the size of the repair and the type of paint used. **Enamel repairs require the most care and dirt-control measures.** Lacquer repairs dry fast and dirt is less of a concern, because they require compounding and polishing to complete the repairs. The apprentice can do compounding and polishing as he or she becomes qualified to do so.

PAINT SHOP SAFETY RULES

Compliance with sound safety rules is essential to the success and survival of a paint shop, because one bad accident could wipe out an entire business and possibly the lives of people working in the shop. All paint materials, especially lacquers, enamels, paint solvents, and cleaning solvents, are potential fire hazards. Paint fires burn violently and get out of control quickly. Vapors from evaporating solvents can quickly spread throughout an enclosed area and be ignited by sparks from electrical motors, hot lighting fixtures, lighted cigarettes, and welding torches. Before spray painting in any given locality, it is wise to check with local fire and city inspection authorities to become familiar with existing local, state, and federal safety regulations.

The federal government has established an industrial safety regulating department as a result of the **Occupational Safety and Health Act** (OSHA). OSHA regulations protect the health and safety of all people in industry, including painters. In doing so, the safety rules also protect the owner and the paint shop. Because of OSHA regulations, many safety devices that were **recommended before** are **now required.** It is better to be safe than sorry. Paint shops and painters are urged to incorporate the following paint safety rules in their everyday work operations.

Paint Storage

All flammable automotive paint materials that are used during a given day should be stored in metal cabinets with metal doors in the vicinity of paint spray operations. The doors should be marked clearly with **red paint** on a suitable background (preferably yellow):

FLAMMABLE MATERIALS
KEEP FIRE AND FLAME AWAY

The cabinet should be kept well away from welding outfits, heat lamps, power equipment, and all metal repair stalls.

Bulk storage of large volumes of paint and solvents should be in a separate building detached or cut off from the general work area by a firewall.

Ventilation

Provide a good ventilation system in the paint spray area to remove all paint spray fumes effectively during spray painting. Paint fumes are vaporized solvents and paint particles. Paint fumes can start fires and even explosions, and they are often toxic.

WARNING: When applying urethane finishes such as:

1. Polyurethane
2. Acrylic urethane
3. Acrylic enamel with urethane catalyst or hardener

always use an approved single or double organic vapor charcoal-type **respirator,** whether working in a paint spray booth or not. Approved respirators for urethane finishes are available through paint jobbers and authorized paint equipment distributors. When spraying in areas that are difficult to ventilate (such as the inside of large trucks), always use an oxygen supplied **hood or mask respirator.** These are available through authorized paint equipment distributors and paint jobbers.

Eye Protection

Compressed air dusting guns should be reduced to 30 psi (pounds per square inch) when used for cleaning purposes. Wear a face shield or tightly fitting safety goggles when using an air dusting gun.

Fire Protection

1. Display NO SMOKING and other caution signs in and around the paint mixing and spray areas. **Do not allow lit matches, cigarettes, or open flames in the paint spray area.**
2. Install an adequate supply of suitable portable **fire extinguishers** in all paint spraying areas. Check with local fire insurance officials or other fire authorities for advice.
3. **Avoid fires from spontaneous combustion** by disposing of soiled rags and paper at least daily. Use metal containers with good-fitting lids for rags, paper, and used paint cans.
4. Keep the spray area, including walls and floors, clean.
5. Before driving a car into or out of a paint spray booth, be sure that:
   a. The booth exhaust system has carried away all paint and overspray fumes.
   b. All containers in the booth with paint or solvents are covered securely.
6. When working near areas where spray painting is done:
   a. Check all electrically operated equipment regularly. Be sure that ground wires are intact to avoid a buildup of static electricity.
   b. When plugging electrical equipment into a socket, seal the socket completely with suitable rubber-backed (or equivalent) tape.

All injuries in a paint shop can be prevented. Accidents do not just **happen;** they are **caused.** It is up to each painter to become thoroughly safety minded **in** and **around** the paint shop. Following commonsense safety practices not only prevents injury, but it may save someone's life.

PAINT IDENTIFICATION

Body Number Plate

The purpose of a **body number plate** (this name is adopted for purposes of this book) is to familiarize automotive service personnel, like painters, with important car information that must be known to service a car according to factory specifications. The body number plate is known by the following names by American car factories:

1. a. **Body number plate:** General Motors Corporation (1984 and earlier models)
   b. **Service parts identification label** (1984 and later models)

2. **Vehicle certification label:** Ford Motor Company
3. **Body code plate:** Chrysler Corporation
4. **Vehicle code plate:** American Motors Corporation

Over the years, the refinish trade has generally adopted the general name **body number plate**. All refinish operations on a car are guided by the body number plate as follows:

1. The paint code specifies refinish paint materials for all **exterior paint repairs** needed on a car.
2. The trim code or interior color code specifies refinish paint materials for all **interior paint repairs** on a car.

These and all additional paint materials are available to the refinish trade by means of paint supplier color books explained in this section.

Location of the plate. Each car factory and each car model have a specific location where the body number plate is mounted. American car factories secure body number plates in approximate locations as shown in Fig. 2-1a and b. Imported car factories secure body number plates in approximate locations, as shown in Fig. 2-2a and b. The location of body number plates on American cars is as follows:

1. **General Motors Corporation:** On all cars built before 1984 and on "carryover" models built during and after 1984, the stamped metal **body number plate** is located on the upper horizontal or on the front vertical surface of the shroud on either side of the body in the areas shown in Fig. 2-1a. On past model Corvettes, the plate is located on the left body hinge pillar or on the instrument panel brace below the glove compartment. On **all new** body styles built during and after 1984, the clear plastic-coated paper **service parts identification label** is located as shown in Fig. 2-1b and c.
2. **Ford Motor Company:** The vehicle certification label is located on the left front door lock face panel or door pillar at the bottom, as shown in Fig. 2-1a.
3. **Chrysler Corporation:** The body code plate is located on the left front fender

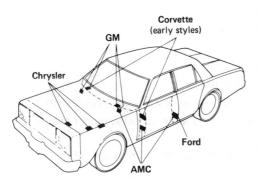

Figure 2-1(a) Location of body number plates on American cars. (Courtesy of the DuPont Company)

Body Type	Chevrolet	Pontiac	Oldsmobile	Buick	Cadillac
A	Celebrity	6000	Ciera	Century	
B & H	Impala Caprice	Parisienne	Delta 88	LeSabre	
C			Ninety-Eight	Electra	DeVille Fleetwood Limousine
D					
E			Toronado	Riviera	Eldorado
F	Camaro	Firebird			
G	Monte Carlo	Bonneville Grand Prix	Cutlass	Regal	
J	Cavalier	2000	Firenza	Skyhawk	Cimarron
K					Seville
M	Sprint				
N		Grand Am	Calais	Somerset Regal	
P		Fiero			
R	Spectrum				
S	Nova				
T	Chevette	1000			
X	Citation			Skylark	
Y	Corvette				

Figure 2-1(b)   General Motors body designations for 1984, 1985, and 1986. (Courtesy of General Motors Corporation)

side shield, wheelhousing, or the left side of the upper radiator support (Fig. 2-1a).

4. **American Motors Corporation:** The body identification plate is located on the left front door lock pillar facing at the bottom as shown. On Jeeps, the plate is located at the base of the left door on the body hinge pillar. (Figs. 2-1a and 2-6a and b).

Procedure for Inspecting the Plate for the Color Code

1. Locate the body number plate.
2. Inspect the plate under good lighting conditions.
   a. If necessary, use a flashlight, or
   b. Move the car into an adequately lit area.
3. Wipe and clean the plate to read the numbers.
4. Write down the code and WA numbers as they are seen (Figs. 2-3 to 2-6).
5. Check the make and model year of the car and turn to the proper chart in the color book.
6. Check the color code and WA number and the identity of the color. The color

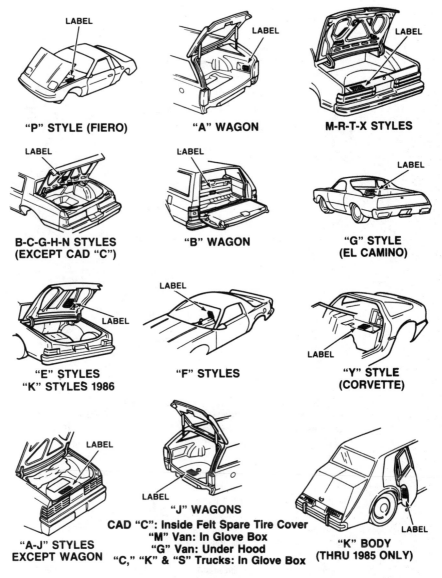

"P" STYLE (FIERO) "A" WAGON M-R-T-X STYLES

B-C-G-H-N STYLES (EXCEPT CAD "C") "B" WAGON "G" STYLE (EL CAMINO)

"E" STYLES "K" STYLES 1986 "F" STYLES "Y" STYLE (CORVETTE)

"A-J" STYLES EXCEPT WAGON

"J" WAGONS
CAD "C": Inside Felt Spare Tire Cover
"M" Van: In Glove Box
"G" Van: Under Hood
"C," "K" & "S" Trucks: In Glove Box

"K" BODY (THRU 1985 ONLY)

Figure 2-1(c) Location of service parts identification label on new 1984 and later General Motors cars. (Courtesy of General Motors Corporation)

code is correct when the color code and WA number of the car check with the color chart and the color chip matches the car.

NOTE: WA numbers and type of paint on the car are indicated on body number plate of 1984 and later new model General Motors cars.

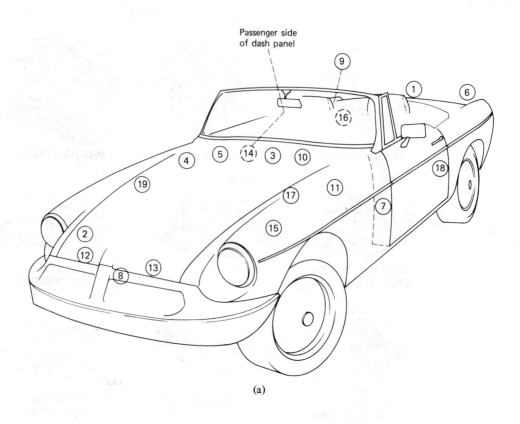

Passenger side
of dash panel

(a)

Alfa Romeo–1	Chrysler U.K.	Porsche–7
Aston Martin	(Hilman)–6	Renault–15–2
Audi–1	Honda–10	Rolls Royce
Austin–4–7–10–19	Jaguar	Rover
Bentley	Lamborghini	Saab–10
BMW–2	Lancia–7–18	Subaru
Capri–2	Land Rover	Chrysler France
Chevrolet LUV–5	Lotus	(Simca)–4
Citroen–3	Luv–5	Chrysler U.K.
Colt	Maserati	(Singer)–6–8
Cortina–4	Mazda–13	Chrysler U.K.
Courier (Ford)	Mercedes–7	(Sunbeam)–5–6
Chrysler U.K.	Mercedes Comm. Vehicle	Toyota–10
(Cricket)–3	MG	Triumph–10–11
Datsun–3–12	Opel–8	VW–8
Ferrari	Pantera (Ford Mtr.)	(tag behind spare tire)
Fiat–3	Peugeot–2	Volvo–5

(b)

Figure 2-2 (a) Location of body number plates on imported cars. Pictorial area designations by car factory. The location is approximate and will vary at times (N/C, no code is indicated.); (b) Area designations (indicated by number or name and location list). (Courtesy of the DuPont Company)

General Motors Paint and Trim Codes (Fig. 2-3a and b)

The paint and trim codes on General Motors cars are found on two types of body number plates:

    a. A **stamped metal** body number plate has been used on all GM cars until mid-1984 and on all carryover larger cars beyond 1984. (For the location of **metal** body number plates, see Fig. 2-1a.)

    b. A **printed white paper material with a plastic coating,** called the **Service Parts Identification Label,** is used on all **new** car lines since mid-1984. (For location of the **paper** body number plate, see Fig. 2-1b and c.)

1. **Paint code:** Fig. 2-3a

    a. On cars built before 1979 with a metal body number plate, the paint codes are stamped opposite plate letters **PNT,** which stands for **paint.** Paint codes are made up of two-digit numbers.

    b. On cars built between 1979 and 1984, the complete two-digit paint codes are located at the center of the plate and a new paint code for **accent color** has been added. To the right of the accent color is a letter designating the **type of paint on the car.** L stands for **acrylic lacquer** and E and W stand for **acrylic enamel.**

    c. If the complete car is painted with a single color, the two-digit paint code appears twice on the same line (Example: 24-24).

    d. If the car is painted with a two-tone paint combination, the **first paint code** (on the left side) stands for the **lower body color.** This is the area from the belt line down and includes the hood.

    e. The **second paint code** stands for the **upper body color.** This is the area above the belt line and includes the painted roof (e.g., 67–50).

    f. The **accent color** is a third predominant exterior color that GM uses to accentuate the individual appearance of a car. When used, accent colors appear in different locations (upper, center, or lower areas) on different makes and series of cars.

2. **Trim code:** The trim code is on the left side of the plate, on the same line as the paint code. Trim codes are usually made up of three or four digits which, in turn, may be made up of all numbers or a combination of numbers and letters. Example: 26E. The trim code indicates the color of interior trim and the type of trim in a car. Interior trim colors are available in two gloss levels to meet federal and factory specifications. This is covered in Chapter 15 and on paint supplier color charts.

3. **Paint codes** (Fig. 2-3b):

On **new body styles** built by GM during and after 1984, the body number plate is known as the **Service Parts Identification Label.** To obtain the proper color for repair purposes, the painter must be guided by three requirements:

    a. **WA number**

    b. **Color code**

    c. **Type of paint** on the car

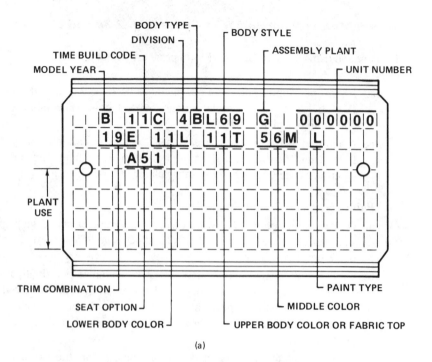

(a)

PAINT AND TRIM OPTIONS

THE FIRST TWO NUMBERS INDICATE THE BASIC COLOR, I.E., 19 = BLACK.
THE THIRD NUMBER OR LETTER INDICATES THE TYPE OR AREA COVERED.

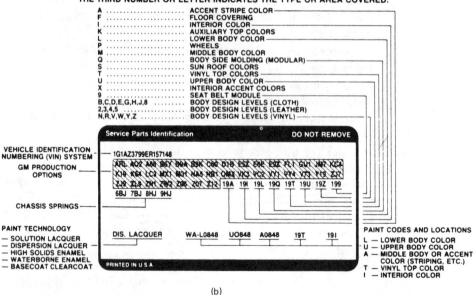

(b)

Figure 2-3 (a) Location of paint and trim codes on General Motors body number plate between 1979 and 1984 and later carryover models. (b) Location of paint and trim codes on General Motors service parts identification label (new 1984 and later-model cars). (Courtesy of General Motors Corporation)

To find the label, the painter must know the **model year** and **series make** of the car (Fig. 2-1b and c). Figure 2-1b displays the GM **body type** designations: **A, B, C** body, and so on. Figure 2-1c pinpoints the location of the lable on the various GM body styles. Once found, the label reads as illustrated in Fig. 2-3b and in the following:

a. **WA number:** Four-digit WA prefixed numbers are found at the bottom of each label. Each WA number is the official factory standard for each color. WA numbers are matched with color codes on paint supplier color cards. All paint suppliers are obligated to match each WA number with an approved color standard for repair purposes. Use of the correct WA number and color code is the key to successful color matching.

b. **Paint code** (Fig. 2-3b): The exterior paint code is determined by the letters **"L," "U," "A,"** and/or **"M,"** each of which is given with a WA number **at the bottom of the label**.

(1) **"L"** stands for the **lower body color.** The four-digit number is the official factory (WA) code for the lower body color. The paint code is found on the paint supplier color chart on the same line as the WA number. All paint codes are matched with WA numbers on the front or back of each paint supplier color chart for GM.

(2) **"U"** stands for the **upper body color.** The four-digit number is the WA number. The **color code is found on** the **paint supplier color chart on** the **same line as** the **WA number.**

(3) **"A"** or **"M"** stands for the **middle body** or **accent color.** This is the accent color, the striping color, etc. The **four-digit number** is the **WA number. The color code is found on** the **paint supplier color chart on** the **same line as** the **WA number.**

(4) **"T"** stands for the **vinyl top color** (if applicable). The **two-digit number** next to the "T" **is** the **color code** for the vinyl top color.

(5) **"I"** stands for the **interior color.** The **two-digit number** next to the "I" **is** the **color code** for the interior color.

c. **Type of paint on car:** (Fig. 2-3b) The type of paint on a car is is shown at the lower-left-hand corner of the label. General Motors uses one of five types of paint at each car factory. They are as follows:

Indication on label	Type of paint
(1) SOL LACQUER	= SOLUTION LACQUER
(2) DIS LACQUER	= DISPERSION LACQUER
(3) H.S. ENAMEL	= HIGH SOLIDS ENAMEL
(4) W or WB ENAMEL	= WATERBORNE ENAMEL
(5) BC/CC ENAMEL	= BASECOAT/CLEARCOAT ENAMEL

Each type of paint requires a specialized service repair procedure. Experienced painters are familiar with conventional acrylic lacquer and enamel repairs. However, repairing basecoat/clearcoat, and tri-coat finishes involves special surface preparation, special color materials, special precautions, special procedures, and special clear coatings. **Color materials from conventional and basecoat/clearcoat systems should never be intermixed.** For top quality, factory approved repairs, always follow label directions. These products and repairs are covered in detail in Chapters 9 through 16.

Ford Paint and Trim Codes

The paint and trim codes on Ford cars are stamped at the bottom of the vehicle certification label (Fig. 2-4a and b).

1. **Paint code:**
   a. On cars built before 1979, the paint code is stamped **after** the word "paint" at the lower area of the label (Fig. 2-4a).
   b. On cars built during 1979 and after, Ford paint codes were revised on the certification label, as shown in Fig. 2-4b. With this system, up to three exterior colors can be identified.
   c. Ford paint codes consist of:
      (1) A single number followed by a single letter. Example: 3P.
      (2) A double-digit number. Example: 75.
   d. If a complete car is painted with a single color, the paint code appears once. Example: 59.
   e. If a Ford car is painted with a two-tone paint combination, a two-digit paint code appears twice. The first paint code stands for the lower body color. The second paint code stands for the upper body color. Example: 45-9D.
2. **Trim code:** The Ford trim code is stamped on the label **after** the word **trim** on cars built before 1979 and **under** the word **trim** on cars built in 1979 and later. The trim code is made up of letters and numbers. There is no set pattern for Ford trim codes. They can change from one model year to the next. Ford trim codes are shown on paint supplier color charts.

Chrysler Paint, Trim, and Interior Color Codes

The exterior paint, trim, and interior color codes are stamped on the body code plate in the lower-left area of the plate (Fig. 2-5).

1. **Paint code:** Chrysler paint codes are located in rows 2 and 3 of the code plate, as shown in Fig. 2-5. Paint codes are made of a combination of letters and numbers.
   a. If the complete car is painted with a single color, the paint code is the same in rows 2 and 3.
   b. If a Chrysler product is painted with a two-tone paint combination, the paint code in row 2 stands for the **lower body color** (below the belt line). The paint code in row 3 stands for the **upper body color** (above the belt line).

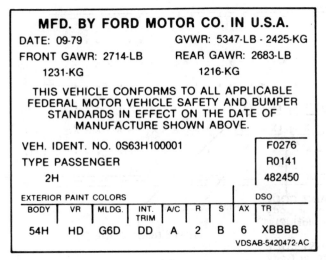

EXTERIOR PAINT COLORS							DSO	
BODY	VR	MLDG.	INT. TRIM	A/C	R	S	AX	TR
54H	HD	G6D	DD	A	2	B	6	XBBBB

VDSAB-5420472-AC

(a)

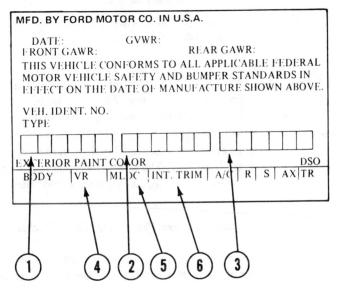

1. Exterior paint coding
2. Exterior paint coding
3. Exterior paint coding
4. Vinyl roof code
5. Color-keyed moulding code
6. Interior trim code

(b)

Figure 2-4 (a) Location of paint and trim codes on pre-1979 Ford certification label. (b) Location of paint and trim codes on latest Ford certification label. (Courtesy of Ford Motor Company)

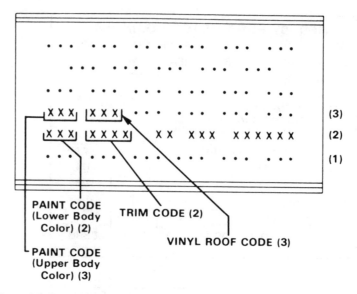

Figure 2-5 Location of paint and trim codes on Chrysler body code plate. (Courtesy of Chrysler Corporation)

2. **Trim code:** Chrysler trim codes are located in row 2 next to the lower body paint code as shown in Fig. 2-5. Chrysler trim codes are made up of a combination of letters and numbers and they can change from one model year to the next. Chrysler trim codes are shown on paint supplier color charts to help the painter.

3. **Interior color code:** Chrysler interior codes are located in row 2 at the right of the trim code. The codes are made up of letters and numbers and are shown on the back of each paint supplier's color charts for reference.

American Motors Paint and Trim Codes

The paint and trim codes on some American Motors cars are stamped at the lower left corner of the body identification plate (Fig. 2-6a, b, and c).

1. **Paint code:** The paint code is stamped on the bottom line of the identification plate after the word **"paint."** AMC paint codes are made up of numbers and letters.
   a. If the complete car is painted with a single color, the paint code appears just once. Example: G9.
   b. If an American Motors car is painted with a two-tone paint combination, the paint code appears twice. The first paint code stands for the **lower body color** (below the belt line). The second paint code stands for the **upper body color** (above the belt line). Example: 9A-9N.

2. **Trim code:** The trim code is stamped after **"trim,"** which is just above the paint code. There is no set pattern used by AMC for trim codes, and they usually vary

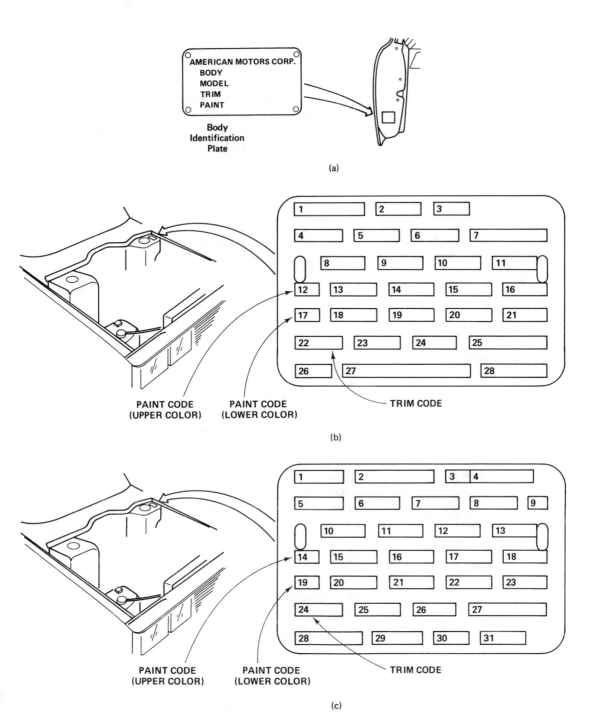

Figure 2-6 (a) Location of paint and trim codes on American Motors vehicle code plate (prior to August 1982 build). (b) Location of paint and trim codes on American Motors vehicle code plate (August 1982 through 1983). (c) Location of paint and trim codes on American Motors vehicle code plate (1984 and subsequent models). (Courtesy of American Motors Corporation)

Paint Identification

from one model year to the next. Trim codes are made up of numbers or a combination of numbers and letters. Examples: 78R14 and 75R2.

Whenever a painter cannot locate a body number plate, the painter is urged to call the nearest car dealer service manager or paint jobber for advice. If a body number plate is missing for some reason and the car is to be painted the same factory color, the local paint jobber can determine the color of paint for the car if the following information is known:

1. **Make and model year of car:** This can be determined from the car owner's car registration.
2. **Sample of paint required:** Bring the car or a small exterior or interior painted part of the car for which paint is required, such as a gas tank cover door or glove compartment door, to the jobber for analysis and color matching. With this information most jobbers can determine and match the required car color with factory-approved color formulation.

COLOR CHARTS (Fig. 2-7a and b)

A color chart is assembled for each car factory each model year. The color chart is the principal means by which a paint supplier communicates the ready availability of automotive refinish colors to the refinish trade. Each paint shop should have a book of color charts from each paint supplier and/or jobber in the area. Color charts should be kept in appropriate three-ring binders especially made for this purpose. Color books should cover all factory car line colors, including truck colors, for a given model year and for several years back. American and imported car color books should be kept separately for quick and easy reference. Color charts and binders are available through each paint supplier for paint shop use on request.

Exterior Colors (Fig. 2-8)

1. Each factory color code is listed in numerical order.
2. Next to each color code is a factory color control number. This number may be on the reverse side of the color chart.
3. The paint supplier color code is next to each factory color code.
4. A sample color chip next to the color code shows the painter what the color looks like.
5. At each color code is a car factory color usage designation. This indicates that a particular color belongs to the car line shown.
6. **Basecoat colors** are indicated by each paint supplier in a **special, bold way:** R-M

(a)

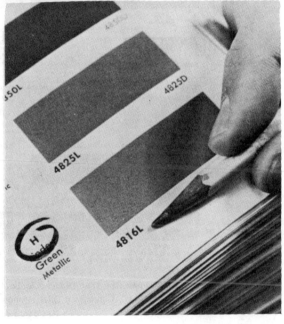

(b)

Figure 2-7 (a) Looking up the paint code in the paint supplier color chart book. (b) Matching the car factory paint code with the paint supplier color stock number. (Courtesy of the DuPont Company)

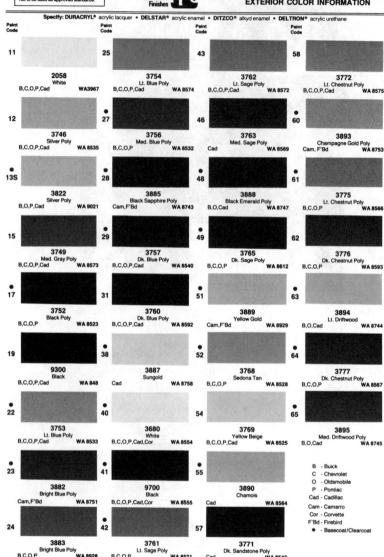

Figure 2-8 Sample page from Ditzler color book showing corporate exterior colors for General Motors cars. (Courtesy of Ditzler Automotive Finishes—PPG Industries, Inc.)

uses a **small black square topped by a small clear square;** DuPont uses bold letters, **B/C;** Ditzler uses a **bold black dot,** about **1/16** of an inch in diameter.

NOTE: Color chips reproduced on paper should not be used as a **color standard** to judge car factory standards. Color chips are provided to be used as a guide only to assist ordering proper colors.

Interior Colors

There is a big difference between interior and exterior colors, and the two should never be confused or interchanged. Interior colors are designed for car interiors. Each interior color is available in two **gloss** levels.

1. **Flat colors** are required in all driver-vision areas to prevent **glare** to drivers. This is a federal regulation. Most color charts list those parts that must be painted with a **flat** color. If necessary, refer to another paint supplier's color chart for this information.
2. **Semigloss colors** are usually recommended to paint all other interior trim parts.

Selection of the proper color and paint system for interior parts is covered in Chapter 15.

The trim code or interior color code is essential to ordering and painting of interior trim parts. Also, the trim code tells the following about a car interior:

1. Basic color of interior (this includes two-tone interiors)
2. Type and design of interiors:
   a. Cloth and vinyl
   b. All vinyl
   c. Leather

Color charts explain the availability of interior colors in two ways:

1. Some paint suppliers use **color chips** to aid identification and ordering of interior colors. These charts use less descriptive information and are easy to use.
2. Other paint suppliers do not use color chips to identify interior colors. They use a direct **trim code, color name,** and **stock number** system.

Additional refinish color systems are available through color charts for automotive refinishing as follows:

1. Striping colors
2. Vinyl roof colors
3. Painted vinyl roof molding colors
4. Luggage compartment interior colors

ORDERING COLORS FROM PAINT JOBBER

Exterior Colors

NOTE: Repair colors are available in two basic types. **Single-phase colors,** also called standard colors, have been used for many years. **Two-phase colors are** the

base-coat/clearcoat types used increasingly in recent years. Each system is entirely different. They are explained in detail in Chapter 9.

1. Refer to the proper color chart (model year and make of car).
   a. Check paint code of car with color chart and color chip.
   b. Check WA number of car with chart (if GM). The number may be on the reverse side of the chart.
   c. If GM car, determine type of paint on car from the service parts identification label. When color codes in steps "a" and "b" above match, the correct color is determined. If other than GM car, determine paint type by the color chart or by the sanding test (see Chapter 9). If problems are encountered, call the paint jobber.
2. Decide on the repair system to be used.
   a. Repair single-phase color systems with single-phase products. The paint jobber can help determine which system is best for the situation. See Table 9-1.
   b. If car is basecoat/clearcoat, or tri-coat finish, a two- or three-phase repair system should be used. See Table 9-1. The paint jobber can help determine which basecoat system is best for the situation.

   CAUTION: Paint systems in "a" and "b" above should never be interchanged.

3. Recheck all paint ordering facts with the paint jobber before ordering the paint.
   a. Make and model year of car
   b. Color codes (and WA numbers)
   c. Type of paint system and color stock numbers
   d. Amount of color and/or clear needed
   e. Amount and type of solvent, hardeners, and the like, needed

NOTE: It is easy to make a mistake when reading a body number plate. A mistake could mean that the wrong paint could be ordered. If the color is factory-packaged, this is not much of a problem. Factory-packaged paint could be exchanged without a loss. However, if the wrong paint color is ordered and **formulated** by the jobber (which means the jobber makes up paint with special equipment), the paint shop must pay for the loss.

Interior Colors

1. Refer to the proper color chart.
2. Locate the trim code, interior color code, or desired color chip on the color chart.
3. Determine if the color is to be:
   a. **Flat** color. (See flat color usage on the color chart. This is determined by the part to be painted.) Record the stock number.

b. **Semigloss** color. (All the other paintable parts on the interior are painted in this finish.) Record the stock number.

4. Determine the amount of paint needed.

5. Recheck and review the color ordering facts with the paint jobber before authorizing the paint order.

REVIEW QUESTIONS

1. Describe each of the following to explain how cars are painted in a car factory:
   (a) Production line
   (b) Paint mixing room
   (c) Metal conditioning
   (d) Manual spray painting
   (e) Automatic spray painting
   (f) "Dip" priming
   (g) Wet sanding primer-surfacer
   (h) Oven baking

2. Name the basic paint color system used by the following car factories:
   (a) American Motors
   (b) Chrysler
   (c) Ford Motor Company
   (d) General Motors

3. Explain where the body number plate is found on the following cars:
   (a) American Motors
   (b) Chrysler
   (c) Ford
   (d) General Motors (early and late model cars)

4. Explain where the paint code is found on the body number plate of the following car factories:
   (a) American Motors
   (b) Chrysler
   (c) Ford
   (d) General Motors

5. Explain specifically where the trim code is found on the body number plate of the following car factories:
   (a) American Motors
   (b) Chrysler
   (c) Ford
   (d) General Motors

6. How is the type of paint identified on a 1979 model and later GM body number plate?

7. Explain how to tie in the paint code (and WA number) with the paint supplier stock number and where these stock numbers are displayed for the painter.

8. Explain how to tie in the trim code or interior color code with the paint supplier stock number and where these stock numbers are displayed for the painter.
9. At what gloss level are interior trim colors available for the following?
   (a) Driver's vision-area trim parts
   (b) Side wall and seat trim parts
10. Explain how to order car exterior color from the paint jobber.
11. Explain how to order car interior color from the paint jobber.
12. Describe three paint shop safety rules for fire prevention.

3

Paint Spray Guns and Paint Cups

INTRODUCTION

The paint spray gun is considered the heart of the paint spray operation and is the painter's most important tool. A painter should clean up the spray gun after every use. Also, the painter should lubricate the spray gun after every major paint job and spray gun cleanup. A painter should have a complete understanding of how a spray gun works. The apprentice painter learns how to understand a spray gun by carefully taking all the parts off the gun body, by studying the purpose and construction of each part, and by putting the spray gun back together.

Spraying techniques involve using the spray gun in all types of paint spray applications. Basic to good spraying techniques are proper grip; good arm, hand, and finger control; good eyes; and good judgment. The painter must know how to handle a wide range of spray application techniques, such as complete car painting, panel painting, and spot repairing. The painter should master parallel, arcing, and feathering strokes. The painter must be able to spray all types of surfaces: large, small, high, low, curved, flat, or whatever the case may be. The best way to learn spraying techniques is by proper practice under the guidance of an experienced instructor or painter.

PAINT SPRAY GUNS: DESCRIPTION AND OPERATION

A spray gun may be compared to a degree with a paint brush. The paint brush is a very important tool for a house painter. First, the painter gets the house, the paint, and the brush "ready" to paint. Then the painter uses the brush to apply liquid paint to the house surface and the paint flows out to form a smooth, uniform coating before it dries.

The **automotive paint spray gun** is a precision tool that atomizes sprayable liquid paint materials with compressed air and applies the materials to the surface to be painted. To **atomize** means to break up a liquid paint material into small particles. Air and liquid paint materials enter the gun through separate passages (Fig. 3-3) and are ejected and mixed at the air cap in a controlled pattern (Fig. 3-6). When sprayed on a surface, the paint particles, made up of paint material and solvents, stick to the surface and flow together to form a smooth, uniform coating.

Types of Spray Guns

The spray guns used most popularly in the automotive refinish trade are known as **production-type** guns and are available in two types: **suction-** and **pressure-feed.** The suction-feed spray gun is the most popular.

Suction-feed Spray Gun (Fig. 3-1). The **suction-feed** spray gun is easily identified by the fluid tip, **which extends slightly beyond the air cap.** This type of spray gun is operated by a stream of compressed air that passes by the fluid tip to create a partial vacuum. This vacuum causes atmospheric pressure to force paint material from an attached container through the spray head of the gun. The suction-feed spray gun is usually limited to quart-size or smaller containers. Suction-feed spray guns are used most popularly in paint repair shops because many color changes can be made quickly and small amounts of materials are generally used. Unless otherwise stated, all references to spray guns in this book refer to the suction-feed type.

Pressure-feed Spray Gun (Fig. 3-2). On a **pressure-feed** spray gun, the fluid tip generally is **flush** with the air cap. The fluid tip and air cap on pressure-feed guns are not designed to create a vacuum. Paint material is forced to the gun by compressed air pressure (usually 8 to 11 psi) acting on the material in the cup or tank. A pressure-feed system is used when large amounts of the same material are being used, when fast application is required, or when the material is too heavy for the suction-feed gun.

Parts of the Spray Gun

Two of the largest paint equipment suppliers are Binks and DeVilbiss. Both companies have branches in all principal cities of the country. Both companies can be reached

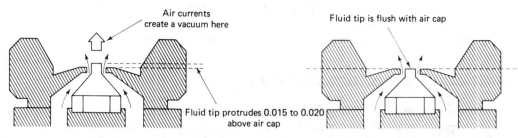

Figure 3-1 Suction-feed spray gun. (Courtesy of the DeVilbiss Company)

Figure 3-2 Pressure-feed spray gun. (Courtesy of the DeVilbiss Company)

Paint Spray Guns and Paint Cups   Chap. 3

through the **Yellow Pages** of the telephone book. A number of other paint equipment suppliers also produce high-quality equipment, but space limits coverage of them all.

Figure 3-3 shows a cutaway view of a Binks Model 18 spray gun. Figure 3-4 shows a Model JGA spray gun by DeVilbiss. While the spray guns shown are very popular in the refinishing trade, both equipment suppliers have other models of spray guns available. It will be noted that in some cases each equipment supplier has a different name for some spray gun parts that function in the same way. Other parts of the spray gun have the same names. The painter should know how to obtain each company's service parts in case repairs are required.

An apprentice can obtain a **general** understanding of a spray gun by studying the spray gun illustrations (Figs. 3-3 and 3-4) and the text on the spray gun parts. However,

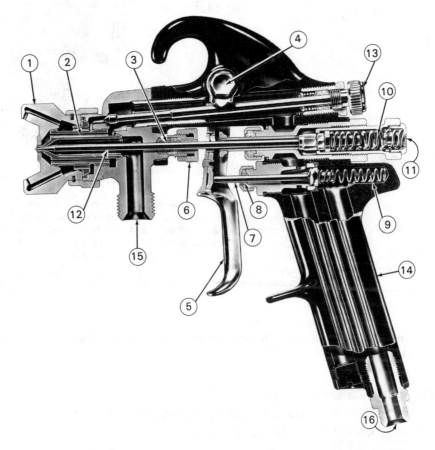

Figure 3-3 Cross section of new Binks Model 18 spray gun. 1, Air nozzle; 2, fluid nozzle; 3, fluid valve packing; 4, trigger bearing stud; 5, trigger; 6, fluid packing nut; 7, air valve; 8, air valve packing; 9, air valve spring; 10, fluid control spring; 11, fluid control knob; 12, fluid needle; 13, pattern control valve; 14, gun body (or handle); 15, fluid inlet; 16, air inlet. Items 3, 4, 8, 10, 11, and 13 should be lubricated as described under "Spray Gun Lubrication." For lubrication of spray gun components, see Chapter 4, Fig. 4-21. (Courtesy of Binks Manufacturing Company)

Paint Spray Guns: Description and Operation

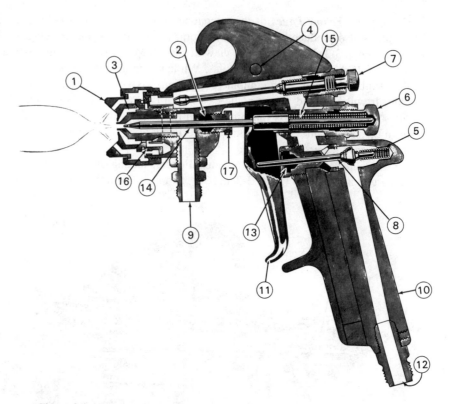

Figure 3-4 Cross section of DeVilbiss Model JGA spray gun. 1, Air cap; 2, fluid needle packing; 3, fluid tip; 4, trigger bearing stud; 5, air valve spring; 6, fluid feed valve; 7, spreader control valve; 8, air valve; 9, fluid inlet; 10, gun body (or handle); 11, trigger; 12, air inlet; 13, air valve packing (leather); 14, fluid needle; 15, fluid needle spring; 16, baffle; 17, fluid needle packing nut. Items 2, 4, 6, 7, 13, and 15 should be lubricated as described under "Spray Gun Lubrication." For lubrication of spray gun components, see Chapter 4, Fig. 4-21. (Courtesy of the DeVilbiss Company)

an apprentice can gain a more complete understanding of how a spray gun works as follows:

1. Disassemble a spray gun.
2. Study the design, construction, and purpose of each part.
3. Reassemble and use the spray gun.

CAUTION: When available, use **special** company-supplied spray gun wrenches for spray gun disassembly and assembly. Otherwise, use a properly fitting wrench on each part to be removed. Avoid **stripping** attaching parts. Use a vise **with care** to hold the gun body when removing and installing the fluid tip.

In a classroom situation, several students can be assigned to one gun. It is beneficial to disassemble at least one spray gun for an entire class. While original spray gun gaskets could be reused perhaps one time, it is best to have on hand and to use new gaskets. The situation is similar to installing spark plugs on a car. Damaged gaskets and parts should be replaced. For the availability of spray gun parts and gaskets, contact the equipment supplier.

The name, purpose, and description of each spray gun part is as follows.

Air Nozzle (Binks, Fig. 3-3, Item 1); Air Cap (DeVilbiss, Fig. 3-4, Item 1). The purpose of the air cap is to break up a solid stream of liquid paint into a spray fan made up of finely atomized paint particles and to direct the spray fan toward the surface to be painted. The spray fan is formed by equal and opposing forces of air coming from the horn holes (and **containment** and **auxiliary** holes, if present) of the air cap (Figs. 3-5 and 3-6). The containment and auxiliary holes aid in better atomization. In the event one horn hole is plugged, the spray pattern is thrown off balance, with most of the sprayed material being directed toward the side affected. All holes in air caps must be kept clean at all times, not only after painting operations but during spraying operations. Air caps do their best work when used with matching fluid nozzles and fluid needles, as shown in Table 3-1. Air caps with a greater number of holes require a greater volume of air for proper operation. Air caps are available with 3, 5, 7, 9, 11, and more holes. The number of holes is always an *odd* number because of the single center hole (Fig. 3-5, item 1).

Fluid Nozzle (Binks, Fig. 3-3, Item 2); Fluid Tip (DeVilbiss, Fig. 3-4, Item 3). The purpose of the fluid tip, working with the fluid needle, is to create a round, controlled stream of paint at the fluid tip when the trigger is operated. Also, the fluid tip forms a seat for the fluid needle to shut off the stream of paint when the trigger is released. Fluid tips and needles are available in a variety of sizes and are made to fit each other in matched sets (Table 3-1).

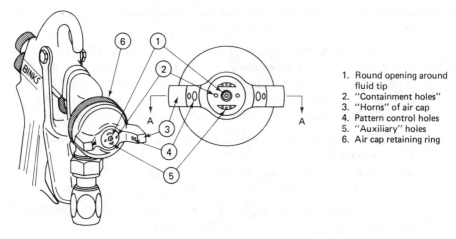

1. Round opening around fluid tip
2. "Containment holes"
3. "Horns" of air cap
4. Pattern control holes
5. "Auxiliary" holes
6. Air cap retaining ring

Figure 3-5 Air cap construction. (Courtesy of Binks Manufacturing Company)

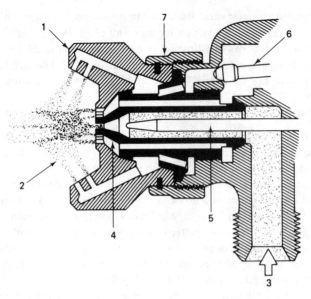

1. Air nozzle
2. Atomization air
3. Material flow
4. Fluid nozzle
5. Fluid needle
6. Spray pattern control stem
7. Air nozzle retaining ring

Figure 3-6 Atomization air and material flow. (Courtesy of Binks Manufacturing Company)

Fluid Needle (Binks, Fig. 3-3, Item 12; DeVilbiss, Fig. 3-4, Item 14). The fluid needle is designed to limit and control the amount of fluid leaving the fluid tip. The fluid needle is controlled by the trigger. The fluid needle is fully adjustable by means of the fluid control knob. This is one of the primary adjustments on the spray gun. Each fluid needle is designed to match a specific fluid tip (Table 3-1).

Fluid Needle Packing Nut (DeVilbiss, Fig. 3-4, Item 17); Fluid Packing Nut (Binks, Fig. 3-3, Item 6). The purpose of the packing nut is to tighten the packing on the fluid needle to prevent leakage at this point. To adjust the packing more tightly, turn the packing nut clockwise with the fingers.

Fluid Needle Packing (DeVilbiss, Fig. 3-4, Item 2); Fluid Valve Packing (Binks, Fig. 3-3, Item 3). The purpose of the fluid needle packing is to seal the fluid needle at this point during spray painting operations. The packing should be lubricated as described in the section "Spray Gun Lubrication," Chapter 4. The packing must be tight against the fluid needle while allowing the needle to operate freely.

Fluid Control Spring (Binks, Fig. 3-3, Item 10); Fluid Needle Spring (DeVilbiss, Fig. 3-4, Item 15). The fluid control spring is designed to shut off the material flow when the trigger is released. The spring should be lubricated periodically as described in "Spray Gun Lubrication," Chapter 4.

Fluid Feed Valve (DeVilbiss, Fig. 3-4, Item 6); Fluid Control Knob (Binks, Fig. 3-3, Item 11). The purpose of the fluid feed valve is to control the amount of fluid leaving the fluid tip when the trigger is operated. When the knob is turned all the way **in (clockwise), no fluid** can leave the fluid tip. When the fluid feed valve is turned all the way **out, counterclockwise** until one thread shows, the fluid valve is **wide open.** This is considered the most important adjustment on the spray gun. Between fully open and almost closed is a full range of adjustments that the painter is called on to use in the course of all types of refinish work.

Spreader Control Valve (DeVilbiss, Fig. 3-4, Item 7); Pattern Control Valve (Binks, Fig. 3-3, Item 13). The purpose of the spreader control valve is to control the amount of air going through the horn holes of the air cap. The amount of air going through the horn holes determines and controls the width of the spray fan. When air is cut off completely from the horn holes, the spray forms a small round pattern (Fig. 3-7a). This adjustment is done by turning the spreader control valve all the way **in,** clockwise. For spot repairs and solvent blending, a midrange setting of the valve is used (Fig. 3-7b). This is a medium-size fan. For full panel painting and complete refinishing, a full spray fan is used. To open the spreader control valve fully, turn the valve counterclockwise all the way. This adjustment produces a spray fan 10 to 12 inches wide (Fig. 3-7c). Next to the fluid feed, this is the most important adjustment on the spray gun.

Trigger (Binks, Fig. 3-3, Item 5; DeVilbiss, Fig. 3-4, Item 11). The purpose of the trigger is to actuate the air valve and the fluid feed valve. The trigger is designed to fit two fingers and the handle is designed for the other two fingers (Fig. 4-7). Initial operation of the trigger allows the spray gun to work as an air gun only. Further operation of the trigger causes contact with and movement of the fluid needle. Movement of the needle from the fluid tip seat causes the gun to spray paint.

Trigger Bearing Stud and Screw (Binks, Fig. 3-3, Item 4; DeVilbiss, Fig. 3-4, Item 4). The stud and screw retain the trigger to the gun body and allow the trigger to pivot at this point. The bearing stud should be lubricated as described in "Spray Gun Lubrication," Chapter 4.

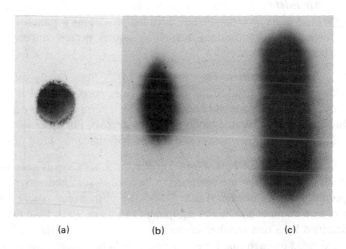

(a)   (b)   (c)

Figure 3-7 Normal spray patterns. (a) Small. (b) Medium. (c) Full size. (Courtesy of Binks Manufacturing Company)

Air Valve (Binks, Fig. 3-3, Item 7; DeVilbiss, Fig. 3-4, Item 8). The purpose of the air valve is to control the flow of compressed air through the spray gun air passages when the trigger is pulled. Initial operation of the air valve allows only a small amount of air to pass through the gun. Further operation of the valve opens the fluid needle at the fluid tip, and this causes paint to be sprayed.

Air Valve Packing (Binks, Fig. 3-3, Item 8; DeVilbiss, Fig. 3-4, Item 13). The purpose of the air valve packing is to seal the valve stem at this location. Packings are commonly made of leather. The packing should be lubricated as covered in ''Spray Gun Lubrication,'' Chapter 4. To improve the seal, simply tighten the packing nut with the fingers.

Air Valve Spring (Binks, Fig. 3-3, Item 9; DeVilbiss, Fig. 3-4, Item 5). The air valve spring causes the air valve to close when the trigger is released. This shuts down the operation of the spray gun.

Gun Body (Binks, Fig. 3-3, Item 14; DeVilbiss, Fig. 3-4, Item 10). Most gun bodies are made of a hard, tough aluminum alloy. As such, they are balanced, easy to handle, and very durable. The gun body is the principal unit of the spray gun to which all other parts attach. The handle of the gun has a raised flange that fits the fingers to help support the gun as it is being used. Properly cared for, gun bodies can last a lifetime.

Fluid Inlet (Binks, Fig. 3-3, Item 15; DeVilbiss, Fig. 3-4, Item 9). The fluid inlet at the front of the gun is designed for attachment of the paint cup on suction-feed guns. On pressure-feed guns, the fluid inlet is designed for attachment of a pressure cup or pressure-feed hose. The fluid inlet guides paint material from the container, through the material passages, and through the fluid tip.

CAUTION: All fluid passages and connections must be absolutely airtight or the spray operation will be faulty. The thread on the fluid inlet is usually $\frac{3}{8}$-inch NPS.

Air Inlet (Binks, Fig. 3-3, Item 16; DeVilbiss, Fig. 3-4, Item 12). The air inlet at the base of the gun handle has threaded provisions for an air-line adapter. The size of the threads in the handle are $\frac{1}{4}$-inch NPS. A quick-detach connector or threaded connector attaches to this adapter.

Baffle (DeVilbiss, Fig. 3-4, Item 16). Some spray guns are equipped with a baffle at the spray head of the gun. The chief purpose of a baffle is to direct a uniform amount of air to the air cap horn holes, which helps to achieve a balanced spray pattern. On some spray guns, the baffle is a separate part. On other spray guns, the baffle principle of equal air distribution is designed into the spray head of the gun.

Chart of Fluid Tips, Fluid Needles, and Air Caps (Table 3-1). Fluid tips, fluid needles, and air caps are designed to be used in matched sets. Each fluid tip requires a specific diameter needle. Table 3-1 shows correct equipment combinations for spray guns as recommended by the equipment suppliers. Each fluid tip, needle, and air cap is identified by a part number stamped on it. These parts should be used in matched sets as indicated on each line for each company. When purchasing parts for spray guns made by other equipment suppliers, follow the same principles of parts procurement.

TABLE 3-1 CORRECT EQUIPMENT COMBINATIONS FOR SPRAY GUNS: AUTOMOTIVE LACQUER AND ENAMEL REFINISHING.

Binks equipment					DeVilbiss equipment				
Spray gun	Fluid nozzle	Fluid needle	Air nozzle	Inside diameter of fluid nozzle	Spray gun	Fluid tip	Fluid needle	Air cap	Inside diameter of fluid tip
Standard production spray guns: Suction feed									
7	36	36	36SD	0.070	MBC-510	AV601EX	496DEX	36	0.070
18	66	65	66SD	0.070	JGA-502	AV601EX	496DEX	36	0.070
62	66	365	66SD	0.070	MBC-510	AV601EX	496DEX	30	0.070
69	66	565	66SH	0.070	JGA-502	AV601EX	496DEX	30	0.070
					MBC-510	AV601EX	496DEX	43	0.070
					JGA-502	AV601EX	496DEX	43	0.070
Standard production spray guns: Pressure feed									
7	33	33	33PR	0.040	MBC and JGA	601FX	a	765	0.0425
18	63B	63A	66PE	0.046	MBC and JGA	601FX	a	74	0.0425
62	63B	363A	66PE	0.046	MBC and JGA	601FX	a	704	0.0425
69	63C	563A	63PE	0.052	MBC and JGA	601FX	a	705	0.0425
					MBC and JGA	601FX	a	54	0.0425
Small spray guns: Suction feed									
15	78	78	78S	0.052	EGA-502	608E	406E	395E	0.070
26	78	78	78SD	0.040					
Small spray guns: Pressure feed									
15	78	78	78P	0.040	EGA-502	608F	406F	390F	0.041

[a]Use MBC-444 or JGA-402 FX.

Principles of Suction-feed Spray Gun Operation (Fig. 3-8)

Initial operation of the trigger opens the air valve but does not move the fluid needle. This allows compressed air to travel past the air valve, past the fluid control bypass, through the gun air passages, and out of the center opening of the air cap. At this stage the spray gun operates only as an air gun.

As the trigger is operated beyond the initial movement, it opens the fluid needle and opens the air valve more. The compressed air, traveling out of the center opening of the air cap and past the extended fluid tip, creates a **partial vacuum** at the fluid tip. A **vacuum** may be defined as the partial or complete absence of air. **Atmospheric pressure** (see the Glossary of Terms at the end of the book) **pushing on the fluid in the cup through the vent hole forces the fluid through the fluid passages of the gun and out of the fluid tip. The ejected fluid and compressed air mix to form a spray pattern.**

The air cap functions as follows. **The air cap horn holes are equal to and opposite each other. The counteracting forces of air coming out of the horn holes create a flat but wide spray pattern** (Fig. 3-6). **As the volume of air going through the horn holes increases, the spray fan becomes wider.** The size of the spray pattern

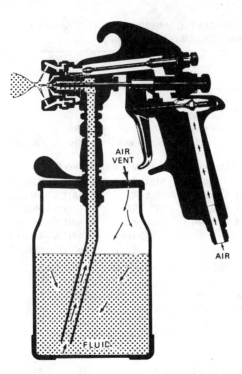

Figure 3-8 Principles of spray gun operation. (Courtesy of the DeVilbiss Company)

is controlled by the spreader control valve, which controls the amount of air passing through the air cap. A variety of spray patterns is available from a spray gun. The three most popular **ranges** of spray patterns used in automotive refinishing are:

1. **Small spray pattern** (Fig. 3-7a)
2. **Medium spray pattern** (Fig. 3-7b)
3. **Full spray pattern** (Fig. 3-7c); see "Spray Gun Adjustments," Chapter 4

The amount of fluid passing through the gun is controlled by the fluid feed valve. The range is from just barely open to full open. The air cap is adjustable to provide **vertical** and **horizontal** spray fans. The vertical spray fan is the most popular among painters.

FLUID CONTAINERS: GENERAL DESCRIPTION

Fluid containers are made of metal, plastic, or glass. They are available in many sizes and in two basic types: suction- and pressure-feed. Very small suction-feed paint cups, 1- and 2-ounce capacity, are used in custom paint work with an **air brush.** Next in size, small spray guns and cups, such as the DeVilbiss Model EGA and Binks Models 15 and

26, are used for spot repairs and for gaining access to small areas where painting cannot be done with the full-size standard spray gun. The 1-quart paint cup is the most popular in the suction-feed system. Pressure-type containers range in size from 1 quart to several gallons. The most popular are the 2-quart remote cup and the several-gallon tank-type containers. These are used in large paint shops that do high-volume paint work (Fig. 3-11).

Suction-feed Cups (Fig. 3-9)

Conventional Suction-feed Cup. The conventional suction-feed cup is a small vented container ranging in size from several-ounce capacity to 1 quart. The vent hole must be clear to allow atmospheric pressure to force the fluid through the spray gun. The proper installed position of a suction cup cover is with the vent hole at the **rear** of the cup. This minimizes the possibility of fluid drippage at the vent hole during paint spray operations on a horizontal surface.

The fluid tube, when properly positioned on the cup cover assembly, **should point forward** in the direction that the spray gun faces. Cup covers are equipped with a gasket to create a **fluid-tight seal between the cup and cover** during paint spray operations on a horizontal surface. Several types of gaskets are available: plastic, leather, and rubber. Each painter learns through experience which works best for him or her.

The popular 1-quart suction feed paint cups are designed for quick attachment to and detachment from a spray gun. DeVilbiss features a 180° or half-turn swivel clamp that secures and tightens a paint cup to a cup cover. To install a DeVilbiss cup, position the cup to cover assembly, engage the cup lock pins into cover lock hooks fully, and rotate the locking clamp half a turn clockwise firmly, and tighten. To remove the cup, hold the cup firmly and rotate the locking clamp counterclockwise. Never assume that a cup is locked securely to a cup cover before painting. Always check the locked position of the clamps to assure that they are fully engaged.

Binks features a revolving screw clamp that secures a cup cover to a cup. To install a Binks cup, position the cup to cover assembly, engage the cup lock pins and cover lock hooks fully, and turn the screw clamp firmly clockwise and tighten. To remove the cup, hold the cup firmly, and rotate the screw clamp counterclockwise to disengage the cover.

Figure 3-9 Conventional suction-feed cup. (Courtesy of the DeVilbiss Company)

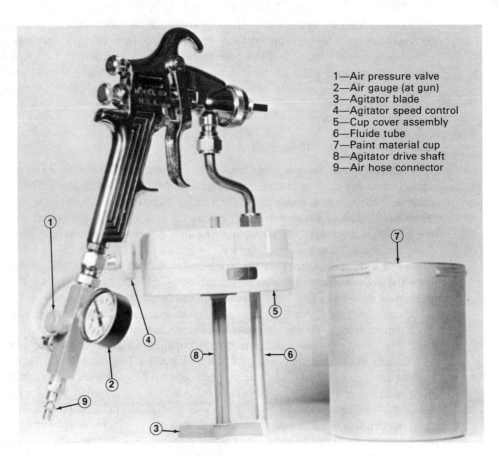

1—Air pressure valve
2—Air gauge (at gun)
3—Agitator blade
4—Agitator speed control
5—Cup cover assembly
6—Fluide tube
7—Paint material cup
8—Agitator drive shaft
9—Air hose connector

Figure 3-10 Agitator-type suction-feed cup. 1, Air pressure control valve; 2, air gauge (at gun); 3, agitator blade; 4, agitator speed control valve; 5, cup cover assembly; 6, fluid tube; 7, paint material cup; 8, agitator drive shaft; 9, air hose connector. (Courtesy of J. L. Terrels & Son, Inc.)

Agitator-type Suction-feed Cup (Fig. 3-10).   A number of **agitator-type cups** are available to the refinish trade. One of the best agitator cups is supplied by J. L. Terrels, Inc., of 111 S. Bolmar Street, West Chester, Pa. 19380. "**The Cup,**" as it is called, is available through a number of independent tool and equipment suppliers all over the country. Terrels can advise any painter where "**The Cup**" can be secured in any area of the country. "**The Cup**" has adapter provisions for attachment to any large suction-feed spray gun. **A special design features an adjustable, air-driven agitator that thoroughly mixes any reduced paint material into a homogeneous mixture for ease of application.** In the event that a painter encounters a fast-settling material, such as highly reduced metallic lacquer, the agitator cup prevents the problem of settling. "**The Cup" produces a uniform application of all metallic colors at the touch of the trigger.**

The features of the agitator cup are:

1. Can be attached to any large suction feed spray gun
2. Complete control of agitation at all times
3. Dripless
4. Air-pressure control valve and air gauge at gun assure proper air pressure while spraying
5. Available in 32-ounce (1-quart) and 40-ounce cups

The benefits of the agitator cup are:

1. Eliminates streaks in any finish
2. Helps in color matching
3. Great for spot repair and overall finishing
4. Makes application of **Metalflake** and other metallic finishes as easy to apply as solid colors
5. Highly recommended for custom painters

Pressure-feed Cups

A pressure-feed cup is a material container usually 1 or 2 quarts in size. One-quart pressure cups almost always attach directly to the spray gun. When larger containers are used, the containers are separated from the gun by hoses because of the heavy weight involved. On pressure equipment, the material is forced from the container to the gun by compressed air. Pressure-feed cups are used for application of fluids too heavy for suction-feed application.

Pressure-feed Remote Cup (Fig. 3-11). The remote cup involves the use of a 2-quart pressure-feed cup with regulator-type provisions. One regulator and gauge control the pressure on the fluid in the cup. A separate regulator controls the air pressure to the gun. As the term "remote" indicates, the cup is separated from the spray gun by means of two hoses. One hose is for fluid and the second hose is an air hose. In this spray system, the spray gun can be handled very easily because it is very light. The remote cup method of spraying makes possible the highest precision and fastest paint application with excellent quality control. All the things that make up the best spray patterns can be set correctly. They are:

1. Large, full spray pattern
2. Controlled fluid pressure and fluid flow
3. Excellent atomization

The remote cup method of painting provides the following features:

1. Improved gun handling because the cup can be held by the other hand

Figure 3-11 Remote pressure cup (2 quart). (Courtesy of the DeVilbiss Company)

2. Better and faster application of all finishes
3. Method of spraying is similar to production method
4. Easy cleaning considering the system used

Pressure-feed Attached Cup (Fig. 3-12).   The pressure-feed attached cup is available in two ways: one is with **regulator** provisions, and the other is without. On regulator pressure cups (Fig. 3-12), one regulator (A) controls pressure on material in the cup; a gauge (B) indicates this pressure; a valve (C) releases pressure from the cup and prevents excessive pressure buildup; and an air-adjusting valve (D) controls atomization air pressure through gun. These cups are ideal for spraying vinyl top and trim adhesives.

Nonregulator-type pressure cups have no pressure-controlling devices. Pressure on the material is the same as the atomization air pressure. This cup is generally used with small air compressing units. On some pressure cups, the air line pressure in the cup is relieved by a **bleeder valve** on the cup cover. Nonregulator pressure cups are not used to any great extent in the refinish trade.

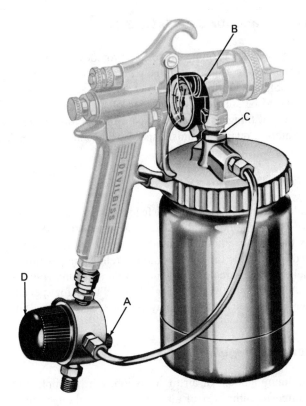

Figure 3-12 Regulator pressure cup (1 quart). (Courtesy of the DeVilbiss Company)

FACTORS AFFECTING THE SPRAY PAINTING PROCESS

Before starting to practice spray painting techniques, the apprentice should become familiarized with **things that affect the spray painting process,** as described in the following. The painter should know **why** things happen as they do in refinishing, **"how"** to adapt to the environment to do quality work, and **"when"** special adjustments are required on equipment.

The Right Gun for the Job

Before a painter even starts to do a job, the proper spray gun must be on hand. The painter decides whether to use a pressure- or a suction-feed system. This is determined by the equipment on hand at the paint shop and by the size of the job to be done. Small and standard-size spray guns are available. A small spray gun is most practical for small paint jobs where access cannot be gained with a standard-size gun. A standard production-type spray gun provides the fastest rate of application and is used for large surfaces and complete paint jobs.

The Right Fluid Tip, Needle, and Air Cap (Table 3-1)

To help the painter select a proper spray gun, Table 3-1 provides a chart of correct equipment combinations. When buying a spray gun, the painter should be guided by the chart or by the equipment supplier. The fluid tip and needle size are governed by the type of spray gun, the material to be sprayed, and the rate of fluid flow required. The air cap size is governed by several things: the compressed air supply available, size of area to be painted, type of material, quality of finish, speed of finishing, and method of fluid feed.

Spreader Control and Fluid Feed Valves

A properly operating spreader control valve and fluid feed valve are essential to high-quality spray painting. The spreader control valve determines the size of the spray fan and the fluid feed supplies the proper amount of fluid for every spray pattern. Three basic spray patterns are used most of the time in automotive refinishing. A full-size fan (Fig. 3-7c) is used for panel and large-area painting. A medium-size fan (Fig. 3-7b) is used for spot repair work. A small spray pattern (Fig. 3-7a) is used for special repair systems. To achieve proper adjustment of these spray patterns, see "Spray Gun Adjustments," Chapter 4.

Air Supply, Air Filter, and Air Regulator

Every air cap requires a minimum amount of air to do its job. Air, as applied to automotive refinishing, is measured in cubic feet of air per minute. Although paint shops have an ample supply of air, this becomes a problem when a painter must supply a compressor for personal use. The large production-type (suction-feed) spray gun, such as DeVilbiss Model JGA (with No. 30 air cap) or Binks Model 69 (with 66SH air nozzle), requires 11 to 12 cubic feet of air per minute for proper and continuous operation. Compressed air for refinishing should be free of moisture and clean. Also, an air regulator is required to follow paint application standards.

Ventilation and Lighting

A good ventilation system and proper lighting are musts in any good paint shop. Spray fumes, made up of paint particles and solvents, must be carried away continually and fast enough to make good-quality refinishing possible. A poor ventilating system causes poor-quality workmanship and is dangerous to the lungs and health of the painter. Applying paint without **seeing** precisely what is happening is like working with a **blindfold;** paint is missing in some areas and is overapplied in others. A painter should be able to see and to check on every "pass" of color application.

Temperature and Humidity

Temperature and humidity have an important effect on the quality of newly applied automotive finishes. These are discussed in greater detail in Chapters 7 and 10. A painter should understand how all applied finishes and solvents behave in **hot, average,** and **cold temperature** and **humidity conditions.**

Use of Respirators

A respirator is a face mask or hood consisting of a filtering device to protect the painter's lungs against contaminants during spray painting. A healthy painter produces the best results. Coming up with safe and approved equipment is not the easiest thing. Many respirators on the market designed for specific areas of work **are inadequate for spray painting.** When spray painting **polyurethane finishes and enamel finishes containing isocyanate catalysts, the painter should use a respirator recommended for this purpose.** A painter who does not use a respirator or who uses a nonconforming respirator is risking his or her health. Selection and use of a respirator is entirely the painter's responsibility. The best recommendation is to use a respirator, approved by a major respirator supplier, which is claimed to meet NIOSH or OSHA minimum requirements. See "Respirators," Chapter 5.

REVIEW QUESTIONS

1. Explain how a suction-feed spray gun is identified by looking at the fluid tip and air cap.
2. Explain how a pressure-feed spray gun is identified by looking at the fluid tip and air cap.
3. Explain how an air cap works on a paint spray gun to make a spray fan.
4. Explain how a spreader control valve works to make a large spray fan and a small spray fan.
5. Explain how the fluid tip and fluid needle work to make a large spray fan and a small spray fan.
6. Explain how the fluid control valve works to control the amount of fluid passing through a gun.
7. Describe three popular sizes of spray fans for spray painting.
8. Explain the operation of the trigger on a paint spray gun:
   a. Initial movement
   b. Full movement
9. Explain how paint is caused to pass through a suction-feed spray gun (see "Principles of Suction-feed Spray Gun Operation").
10. Explain how an agitator-type suction-feed paint cup works to mix paint.
11. Explain how a pressure-feed remote cup works to spray paint.

4

Spraying Techniques

INTRODUCTION

It is possible, unfortunately, when spray painting, to do a number of things wrong and still produce a salable paint job. By salable is meant "one that gets out the door and the driver takes it home." One might say: "Then why worry about proper techniques?" The reasons are that when doing poor workmanship the painter's reputation and costs are at stake. When poor techniques are used, the painter invariably uses up a lot more time and material on each job, which translates into more money and a lot more energy. This means that fewer jobs are done and the ones that are finished are poor. Poor workmanship leads to a high rejection rate of paint jobs because of poor finish, off-color, peeling, premature rust, or some other paint failure. A car owner does not have to be a paint expert to detect a poor paint job.

Proper techniques are easy to develop. Practicing the right way to do refinishing will end up becoming the painter's habit and he or she will be on the right road to success. Just as bad spray techniques are learned, proper spray techniques can be learned just as easily. All the painter has to do is let the proper techniques become good habits. **Always remember:** No matter how precise or expensive a spray gun may be, its value is practically nil if it is used improperly.

Automotive refinishing is made up of two parts:

1. **Theory**
2. **Skill development**

Theory is understanding the "why" behind every refinishing step, tool, product,

58

and procedure. Theory includes "why" paint finishes are good and "why" some paint finishes fail. Theory includes "what" causes a good spray pattern, "how" paint application is controlled by the painter, and the "things" that produce the best-quality results. Theory is learned by reading, by study, by discussion, and by asking questions of the proper people when any doubt exists in a student's or painter's mind.

Skill development is achieved primarily by practicing manual exercises, "doing things by hand," as outlined in this chapter. Spraying techniques are learned by practicing how to handle the spray gun under all spray painting conditions. Spraying techniques become mastered when the painter or apprentice can do them by habit. This is doing an operation with minimum thought. A person must learn both theory and skill development to become a qualified painter.

It is up to each person to practice the spraying techniques repeatedly, as required, with all types of paint materials and paint systems (lacquers and enamels) and under all types of painting conditions to completely master the spraying techniques. Skill operations are also involved in other phases of refinishing such as **featheredging, final sanding before color application**, and **masking.**

Chapter 3 covered the basic construction and principles of spray gun operation. This chapter discusses how to use and take care of the spray gun.

SPRAY GUN ADJUSTMENTS

Spray guns have a number of basic adjustments with which the painter must be thoroughly familiar. Before applying paint to a car, the painter decides on the type of spray gun adjustments that the job requires. The following spray gun adjustments and spray pattern checks are the most popular among the best painters.

Air Cap Adjustments

Air caps are the simplest of spray gun adjustments. They are adjustable to create two popular spray fans:

1. The **perpendicular spray fan** is straight up and down.
   a. This fan is achieved when air cap horns are parallel to the floor (Fig. 3-5).
   b. This adjustment is the most used by painters because it is the easiest to use.
2. The **horizontal spray fan** is flat and parallel to the floor.
   a. This fan is achieved when air cap horns are perpendicular to the floor (Fig. 3-6).
   b. This fan is used on occasion when cross-coating is done.

To **adjust air cap:**

1. Loosen the air cap retaining ring one-half to one turn counterclockwise.
2. Locate and **hold** the air cap horns in the precise position desired.
3. Tighten the air cap retaining ring.

Spray Gun Adjustments

The three most popular spray gun adjustments and their uses are:

1. **Full-open adjustment**
   a. For complete paint jobs
   b. For full panel and large-area painting
2. **Spot-repair adjustment**
   a. For spot repairs
   b. For solvent blending
3. **Dry-spray adjustment**
   a. For special repairs during refinishing
   b. For the fast material buildup system

Full-open Spray Gun Adjustment

1. Prepare the spray gun for adjustment as follows:
   a. Fill the cup with paint material and secure the cup to the gun (Chapters 7 and 10).
   b. Attach the spray gun to the air line.
   c. Adjust the air-line pressure (see "Air Hose" and "Pressure Drop," Chapter 5):
      (1) 35 psi (at gun) for lacquer reduced 150%
      (2) 60 psi (at gun) for enamel reduced 25% to 33%
2. Position the air cap on the gun for the **horizontal** spray pattern and tighten the air cap.
3. Open the spreader control valve, counterclockwise, to the full-open position (Fig. 4-1).
4. Open the fluid feed valve, counterclockwise, to the full-open position. This is when one thread on the fluid valve is visible (Fig. 4-2).
5. While holding the gun one hand span from the surface (Fig. 4-8), apply a **flooding**

Figure 4-1 Adjusting spreader control valve. (Courtesy of the DuPont Company)

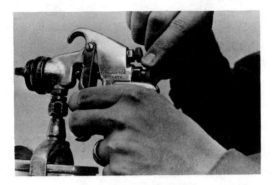

Figure 4-2 Adjusting fluid feed valve.
(Courtesy of the DuPont Company)

test pattern at one spot on a suitably masked vertical wall. Apply material for **3 to 4 full seconds** to purposely **flood** the spray pattern.

6. Check the flooded spray pattern for the **length** of paint runs:
Condition A: A **split pattern** (Fig. 4-3) is present when outer paint runs are longer than center paint runs.
Remedy 1: (a) Reduce the spreader control valve a **fraction** of a turn clockwise. (b) Repeat the flooding test pattern and check the results.

Remedy 2: (a) Raise the air pressure a nominal 5 psi at the gun. (b) Repeat the flooding test pattern and check the results. (c) If necessary, repeat remedy 1 and 2 until paint runs are of approximately equal length.

NOTE: The objective of this test is to achieve paint runs of equal or almost equal length while the fluid feed is **wide open** (Fig. 4-5).

Condition B: A **heavy-center pattern** (Fig. 4-4) is present when the center paint runs are longer than the outer paint runs.

Remedy 1: (a) Turn the fluid feed valve, clockwise, one-half turn or a fraction of

Figure 4-3 Flooding test showing split pattern.

Figure 4-4 Flooding test showing heavy-center pattern.

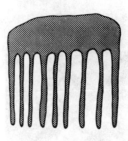

Figure 4-5 Flooding test showing balanced pattern.

a half. (b) Repeat the flooding test pattern and check the results. (c) Repeat steps a and b until paint runs are of approximately equal length (Fig. 4-5).

Remedy 2: (a) Open the spreader control valve, counterclockwise, half a turn or a fraction of a half each time. (b) Repeat the flooding test pattern and check the results. (c) Repeat steps a and b until the paint runs are of approximately equal length (Fig. 4-5).

Spot-repair Spray Gun Adjustment

Spray gun adjustments for spot repairs are most often in the midrange or half-open settings. The size of the spray fan is determined by the size of the spot repair to be done. Spot-repair spray fans vary in size from **just barely open** to **three-fourths of full open.** The smaller the spot-repair fan, the greater is the saving in material and labor.

1. On the spreader control valve (Fig. 4-1), determine the number of half-turns from fully closed to fully open settings. Make a note of it. The reason for the **half-turns** is that the control valves could be turned only a half-turn at a time with one grip. Set the valve at the midpoint range.
2. On the fluid feed valve (Fig. 4-2), determine the number of half-turns from fully closed to fully open settings. Set the valve at the midpoint range.
3. Apply a flooding test pattern at one spot on a suitably masked vertical wall to create material runs. See step 5 of "Full-open Spray Gun Adjustment."
4. Check the flooded spray pattern to analyze material runs. Achieve **equal** paint runs (Fig. 4-5) with the least movement of controls as follows:

   Condition A: In a **heavy-center pattern** the runs at center are much longer than at outer ends (Fig. 4-4).

   Remedy: (a) Cut down on the amount of fluid feed by turning the valve clockwise one-fourth of a turn at a time. (b) Reapply the flooding test pattern and check the fluid runs. (c) Repeat steps a and b until the pattern is balanced (Fig. 4-5).

Condition B: In a **split pattern** the runs at outer ends are longer than at center (Fig. 4-3).

Remedy: (a) Increase the amount of fluid feed by turning the control valve counterclockwise one-fourth of a turn at a time. (b) Repeat the flooding test pattern and check the results. (c) Repeat steps a and b until the pattern is balanced (Fig. 4-5).

Dry-spray Adjustment

The term "dry spray" means exactly what it says, to apply paint material very dry. The painter should be able to wipe the dry-sprayed surface with a cloth, such as a tack rag, immediately after dry-spray paint application to remove any settled dirt or rough and loose overspray. This method of material application is covered here and in Chapter 10. Only the adjustment procedure is covered at this time.

1. Close the fluid feed valve and the spreader control valve completely.
2. Open the spreader control valve one-eighth to one-fourth of a turn.
3. Open the fluid feed valve one-fourth to one-half turn.
4. Apply a fine dry spray to one spot, 2 to 3 inches in diameter, with the following technique:
   a. Using a fully pulled trigger, apply material with continually moving circular stroke.
   b. Keep 4 to 6 inches from the surface.
   c. The air-line pressure should be the same as for applying conventional material.
   d. Every 5 to 10 seconds, stop application and observe progress as follows:
      (1) View the surface for smoothness.
      (2) Tack-wipe with a special cloth to assure smoothness.
   e. Continue application until the desired coverage is achieved.

Precautions

1. If the material is going on too dry, increase the fluid feed one-eighth of a turn at a time. Recheck application.
2. If the material is going on too wet (material is "sticky" or "glossy"):
   a. Increase the distance of the spray gun from the surface (move back 1 to 2 inches).
   b. Cut down the fluid feed one-eighth of a turn at a time and recheck application.
   c. The painter must be able to tack-wipe the surface at any time during application to remove entrapped dirt or rough surface.

The amount of dry spraying is determined by the paint system and by the problem condition.

ATOMIZING AIR PRESSURE

Atomization is the breaking up of a stream of paint by counteracting streams of air forming tiny, round, uniform particles of paint, which are applied on the surface being sprayed (Fig. 4-6). On suction-feed air caps, the horn holes are angled forward more than on pressure air caps to give the fluid forward direction. While this is happening, about 30% of lacquer thinner in reduction is ''gassed off'' or vaporized and never reaches the surface. While lesser amounts of reducers are vaporized during enamel application, the same principle holds true. Solvents not vaporized go along with the solids and serve to flow out the applied paint according to design.

Vaporization is the changing of a liquid to a gas that passes into the air. The objective of the painter is to get maximum atomization of paint with least vaporization of solvents. Under normal conditions (70° to 80°F), a generally acceptable range for spraying acrylic lacquers is between 35 and 40 psi (at the gun). For acrylic lacquers reduced 150%, 35 psi (at the gun) is a good atomizing air pressure. For acrylic lacquers reduced 125%, 40 psi (at the gun) seems best. Acrylic enamels and other enamels are designed for application between 55 and 60 psi (at the gun). A good average for enamels is 60 psi. The best thing for any painter to do is to follow paint supplier recommendations for best results. Pressures lower than those recommended result in poor finishes due to

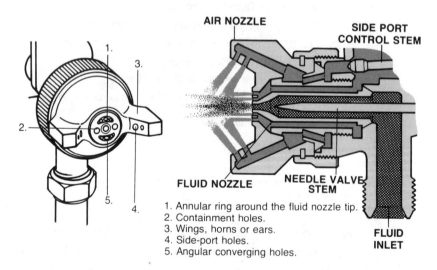

1. Annular ring around the fluid nozzle tip.
2. Containment holes.
3. Wings, horns or ears.
4. Side-port holes.
5. Angular converging holes.

Figure 4-6 Atomization air and material flow. (Courtesy of Binks Manufacturing Company)

spatter-type incomplete atomization. Pressures in excess of those recommended result in excessive vaporization and number of paint finish problems.

Determining the Proper Atomizing Air Pressure without an Air Gauge

When in doubt about what atomizing air pressure to use, follow this simple rule:

1. Achieve the balanced spray pattern as outlined in "Spray Gun Adjustments." Use 40 psi for lacquers and 50 psi for enamels.
2. Then set the air pressure at the regulator purposely low, such as 20 psi. Use black lacquer.
3. With the spray gun in one hand, pull the trigger to make a spray fan. With the other hand, make an excessively fast pass **across the spray fan** with a rolled up sheet of $8\frac{1}{2}$ by 11 or larger white paper. The hand may be covered with a glove. Keep the **length** of the paper aligned with the **length** of the spray fan. Initial fast passes spread the spray pattern into paint particles of noticeably different sizes. This means that pressure is low.
4. Increase pressure a little at a time (about 5 psi) and make another fast pass at each pressure increase. Also, use a new sheet of paper each time. Inspect paint particles closely; if necessary, use a magnifying glass. At a given pressure, the paint particles will appear very uniform in size and will stay that way even though air pressure is increased. The lowest air pressure that produces a uniformity of paint particles is the correct atomizing air pressure.
5. Increasing the air pressure beyond the correct atomizing pressure reveals that the paint particles will not decrease in size. This proves that higher-than-required pressures are not necessary.

SPRAY PAINTING STROKE

Watching a veteran painter at work applying a color coat to a car is a magnificent sight for the apprentice, or anyone for that matter, to behold. The spray painting strokes seem so effortless and smooth and the finish goes on like a magic mirror. One does not only see a painter at work, one sees an artist with pride.

In analyzing the spray painting stroke, imagine the stroke being performed, like a sports event on television, with slow-motion replays and stop-action shots. The first action to be analyzed is the grip as the spray gun nears the target area.

The Grip

Most painters use the conventional grip shown in Fig. 4-7. In this grip the spray gun is supported by the lower two fingers, the hand, and the thumb as shown. The first two fingers are used for triggering. Some painters use an alternative grip in which the gun is

Figure 4-7 The conventional grip.
(Courtesy of the DuPont Company)

supported by only the small finger at the bottom, the index finger (or forefinger), the hand, and the thumb. The middle two fingers are used for triggering. Selecting a grip is a matter of "feel" to the painter, which quickly becomes a habit.

Position of the Gun to the Surface

The spray gun should be held perpendicular to the surface, or as close to perpendicular as possible. Tilting the gun excessively results in flooding the surface with one side of the spray pattern and starving the opposite side. As in an unbalanced spray pattern, this can result in a streaky finish. For this reason, pressure equipment is best for painting roofs, hoods, and rear deck areas.

When using suction-feed equipment on large flat surfaces, it is suggested that an apprentice use a **"diaper"** made of cloth or paper toweling wrapped around the cup lid to catch any paint dripping. Apply suitable cloth or paper toweling around the cup cover and secure it with masking tape until spray application on horizontal surfaces is completed. Improvements in plastic cup lid gaskets and antidripping devices minimize the dripping problem on suction-feed cups.

Distance of the Gun from the Surface (Fig. 4-8)

The suction-feed gun is made to do its best work on automotive finishes normally at a spraying distance of 6 to 8 inches from the surface. Holding the gun too close results in flooding the surface, which can cause runs, mottling, color change in metallics, and other problems. Holding the gun more than 8 inches away can result in excessive dry spray, overspray, a color change in metallics, and poor flowout. Any of these conditions may require rework. A pressure-feed gun should be held from 8 to 12 inches from the surface.

Speed

The speed with which a paint spraying stroke is made is vitally important to the end result. If the gun is moved too fast, the surface is starved, resulting in poor flowout,

Figure 4-8 Distance of gun from surface. (Courtesy of the DuPont Company)

rough surface, and insufficient material. If the gun is moved too slowly, the material is piled on and may sag. There is a proper speed for every spray pattern and fluid feed. The best speed is a steady deliberate pass that leaves a full, wet coat just short of running. In actual practice, the painter must be able to use several speeds to meet changing conditions and equipment.

Pressure equipment, because of the pressurized material feed, requires faster speeds. Whatever the equipment used, the painter must be able to vary the speed and be able to apply thin-wet coats, medium-wet coats, and full-wet coats.

Triggering

The trigger controls the action of the spray gun and the painter should use the trigger during each stroke. The farther the trigger is drawn back, the greater is the flow of material. During conventional strokes, the trigger should be pulled back completely, not partially. To avoid excessive buildup of material at the end of each stroke, the trigger should be released. The correct procedure for triggering is:

1. First, begin the (arm movement) stroke; then pull the trigger as the gun lines up with the starting work edge. This can be:
   a. Two inches before the starting work edge, or
   b. In the middle of a vertical banding stroke.
2. Release the trigger as the stroke lines up with the finishing work edge. This can be:
   a. Two inches past the finishing edge, or
   b. In the middle of a vertical banding stroke.

To the expert painter, the art of triggering becomes automatic. The triggering action is performed with no concentrated thought. Thus, triggering is the heart of the spray painting technique. The objective of the painter is to hit the edge of the work and to maintain full coverage with minimum overspray.

Proper triggering makes possible uniform coverage of the surface, minimum waste of material, and a reduction of overspray. Also, proper triggering cuts down muscle fatigue because a muscle that alternately flexes and relaxes does not get as tired as one that is flexed all the time.

Feathering

Feathering is a type of control a painter uses during spot-repair and color-blending operations. **Feathering** means to apply a spray material starting with very little material at the start of a stroke (fluid feed barely open) to a gradually thickening material (fluid feed opens gradually with trigger pull) at end of stroke. At this point, the trigger is released suddenly. The correct procedure for feathering is as follows:

1. Start spray gun motion smoothly and start pulling the trigger gradually as the gun approaches the target area and apply color at the correct wetness. Then release trigger suddenly but smoothly. Spray gun motion continues. This is considered spraying ''from the outside in.''
2. Start spray gun motion smoothly and pull the trigger fully over the target area; begin releasing the trigger as the spray gun nears the blend area. For smoothness of operation, spray gun motion continues. This is considered spraying ''from the inside out.''

Arcing

Arcing is not recommended when spraying full panels as shown in Fig. 4-10. But arcing is used in spot repairs and blending. Arcing is used to good advantage because the painter can control the arcing and feathering at the same time. The best painters have excellent control of and great confidence in a combination of good arcing and feathering techniques. Arcing can be done by pivoting the gun at the wrist or by using an arm movement pivoting at the elbow. To maintain uniformity of distance and gun position, the painter's arm and wrist must be conveniently flexible.

Stroke Movement (Fig. 4-9)

The conventional spray painting stroke is made by moving the gun parallel to the surface while maintaining the correct gun distance and perpendicular position. This is an easier thing to say than to do. To maintain a parallel and perpendicular position of the spray gun to the surface, the painter must make a special effort at the beginning and end of each stroke to change the arm and wrist position as the painter remains still. As shown in Fig. 4-9, the spray gun is the important thing as it travels back and forth in spray painting. **The painter's job is to adapt to the spray gun movement.**

Arcing (Fig. 4-10) is a common fault among apprentices and beginners when conventional spraying techniques are required on full panels. Arcing in this case causes

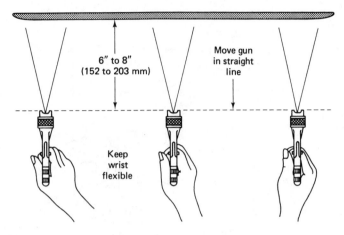

Figure 4-9 Keep gun parallel and perpendicular to surface. (Courtesy of the DeVilbiss Company)

an uneven application of paint at the beginning and end of each pass as shown. Also, this poor technique causes excessive overspray and dry spray at the outer ends.

Spraying a Panel with a Single Coat

When spraying panels on cars, the most popular technique is to spray left to right and right to left alternately, as shown in Fig. 4-11a and b. While the trigger starts and stops fluid flow at the end of each stroke, the spray gun continues moving for positioning into the next stroke. In this manner the movements are smooth and coordinated.

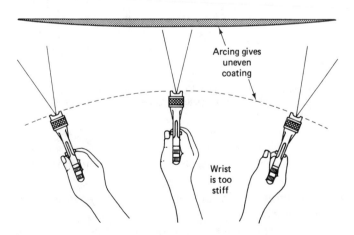

Figure 4-10 Arcing the spray gun. (Courtesy of the DeVilbiss Company)

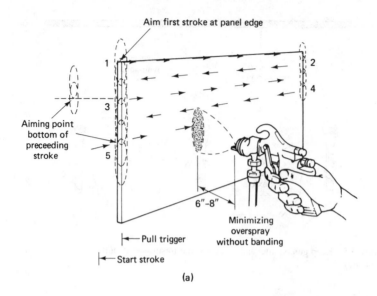

Aim first stroke at panel edge

Aiming point
bottom of
preceeding
stroke

6"–8"

Minimizing
overspray
without banding

Pull trigger

Start stroke

(a)

(b)

Figure 4-11 Panel spraying technique (single coat). (a) Directions for application. (Courtesy of Binks Manufacturing Company); (b) What the technique looks like. (Courtesy of the DuPont Company)

1. In the first stroke, the center of the spray pattern is aimed at the top edge of the panel.
2. On all other strokes, the center of the spray fan is aimed at the bottom of each previous pass.
3. The top and bottom edges are sprayed twice for proper coverage.

4. Actually, triggering takes place 1 to 2 inches before and after each panel edge to be sure of complete and uniform panel coverage.

5. The 50% overlap described in this procedure and in Fig. 4-11 is known as a **single coat** in the refinish trade.

Banding

To reduce overspray in a shop, many painters use a **banding** technique, as shown in Fig. 4-12. The narrow vertical stroke at each end of the panel is made with a small spray fan about 4 inches wide as shown. Banding assures complete coverage of a panel and reduces the waste of paint that results from trying to spray right up to the vertical edge with the usual horizontal strokes. When using the banding technique, start and stop triggering action on the sprayed band, preferably at the center.

Spraying a Panel with a Double Coat

A **double coat** is one single coat followed immediately by a second single coat. A double coat most often applies to the application of fast-drying paint systems such as lacquers. Sometimes paint suppliers recommend that the second coat be sprayed in the opposite direction to the first coat, one horizontal and one vertical. Enamel system products are most always applied in single coats with a waiting period between coats.

The painter who tries to cover an object by using many strokes in all directions is known as a "fanner." This is actually a waste of time, materials, and energy.

The painter should study and determine in advance a way of spraying every paint job with a definite plan of strokes and panel sequence. In this manner, all paint jobs are easier to do, missing panels or areas is avoided, and the results are always better.

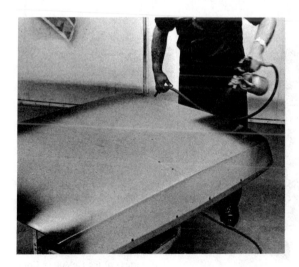

Figure 4-12 Banding technique.
(Courtesy of the DuPont Company)

TYPES OF SURFACES TO BE SPRAYED

Spraying a Long Panel (Fig. 4-13)

A long panel can be sprayed with vertical strokes, but most painters have better control with natural horizontal strokes. Spray a long panel in short sections, 18 to 36 inches long, with similar triggering and motions as used on a small panel. Banding or vertical strokes are not necessary at other than edge areas. However, use about a 4-inch overlap for each coat. When applying succeeding coats, it is wise to change the location of the overlap area to prevent excessive color buildup.

Spraying Edges and Corners

When spraying panel edges and corners, aim the center of the spray pattern at the edge so that 50% of the spray is deposited on each side of the corner (Fig. 4-14). In these

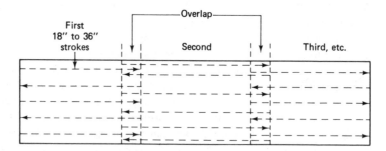

Figure 4-13 Spraying long work. Long panels are sprayed in sections of convenient length. Each section overlaps the previous section about 4 inches.

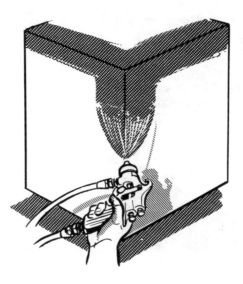

Figure 4-14 Spraying edges and corners. (Courtesy of the DeVilbiss Company)

cases, **hold the gun an inch or two closer than the normal distance.** One stroke along each corner coats the edges and bands the face of the panel on each side at the same time.

Spraying Slender Work (Fig. 4-15)

When spraying long, narrow, slender parts, or parts of cars, it is best to make the spray pattern fit the job. Many painters are lazy and do not like to disturb their gun adjustments. But when a painter gets to know the gun as well as the back of his or her hand, it is only a matter of a few seconds to adjust a gun. It is not wise to use a wide horizontal pattern on a slender, vertical pillar. A smaller horizontal pattern or a large vertical spray fan gives complete coverage without excessive overspray.

Spraying Large Horizontal Surfaces

When spraying a large flat surface such as a roof, hood, or the rear deck of a car, always start at the near edge and work to the center. Then, working on the opposite side, continue spraying from the center to the near edge. This process results in a fully wet sprayed panel while minimizing overspray and dry spray.

When a suction-feed gun is used on a job that requires the gun to be tilted, care must be exercised not to drip on the surface. This can be prevented by taking necessary precautions in advance, which are:

1. Do not overfill the cup.
2. Avoid sudden or jerky motions.
3. Be sure the air vent on the cup is to the rear.
4. Be sure the fluid tube is to the front.
5. Be sure the cup gasket is fluid-tight.
6. It is suggested that apprentices use a **diaper** made of cloth or paper toweling wrapped around the cup lid to catch any dripping paint. Apply suitable cloth or paper toweling around the cup cover and secure it with masking tape until spray application on the horizontal surface is completed.

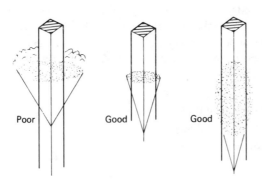

Poor   Good   Good

Figure 4-15 Spraying slender work. (Courtesy of the DeVilbiss Company)

Types of Surfaces to be Sprayed

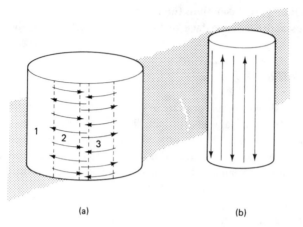

(a)

(b)

Figure 4-16 Spraying curved surfaces. (Courtesy of the DeVilbiss Company)

DeVilbiss has available a plastic diaphragm and gasket that can be used on their standard suction-feed cups. The gasket and diaphragm make standard paint cups drip-free when they are used properly. There are also other brands of spray cup covers available on the market that are designed to be 100% drip-free.

Spraying Curved Surfaces (Fig. 4-16)

When spraying a large-diameter curved surface, keep the gun at the proper distance by following the curves of the surface (Fig. 4-16a). When spraying slender curved surfaces of a smaller diameter, it is best to spray with the length of the part (Fig. 4-16b).

SPRAY TECHNIQUES FOR DIFFERENT PURPOSES

Spot-repair Technique

Spot repairs involve applying color (including undercoats, if necessary) to a spot area within a panel or at a panel edge. Repairs can vary from very small to quite large. A number of special techniques are available to the painter. These are covered in detail in Chapter 13. At this time, the spot-repair technique is described in a general manner. To become expert in spot repairing, the painter must first become familiarized with the following:

1. Color-coating systems and materials
2. Color application procedures and techniques
3. Knowledge of paint solvent behavior
4. Spot-repair techniques

The spot-repair technique includes the following:

1. Spreader control to suit the size of the repair, generally in the midrange.
2. Fluid feed to suit the size of the spray pattern.
3. Air pressure to suit the repair procedure.
4. Color reduction according to label directions.
5. Mist-coat solvent: straight solvent or a blend, as required.
6. Achieve color match and blend, as required.
7. Apply a mist coat for blend or gloss, as required.
8. Final compounding and polishing, as required.
9. Application of striping, as required.
10. Use of "clears" on special finishes, as required.

Mist-coat Technique (See Exercise 9, page 96)

Mist coating involves applying a high-volume solvent to a finish after color has been applied. Generally, two types of mist coating are used in the refinish trade.

1. On acrylic lacquers, mist coating serves to blend newly applied repair color with the original color. The system is used mainly at edges and blend areas.
2. On newly applied acrylic and alkyd enamels, mist coating is sometimes applied when necessary, as a final operation to produce matching gloss. The system is also used in blending spot repairs.

Mist-coating technique is as follows:

1. For spot repairs using acrylic lacquers:
   a. Adjust the spray fan to suit the size of the repair.
   b. Adjust the fluid feed to suit the size of the fan.
   c. Set the air pressure at 15 to 30 psi.
   d. Distance of gun: 4 to 6 inches.
   e. Application technique:
      (1) Use immediately after each color application.
      (2) Use feathering and arcing strokes at edges and blend areas.
      (3) Achieve a wet coat in the blend area in several passes, not in one pass.
      (4) **Do not apply a mist coat on freshly applied lacquer color if metallic colors are used.**
2. For enamel systems, mist coating can be done two ways:
   a. For spot repair of enamel color with enamel color:
      (1) Use midrange spray gun adjustments.
      (2) Use 15 to 30 psi.
      (3) Apply a mist coat to repair color and blend areas, as required.

b. For producing a final gloss when necessary on enamels:
   (1) Adjust the spray gun for a full fan.
   (2) Use 20 to 30 psi.
   (3) Apply a full wet mist coat to the complete painted surface.

Fog-coating Technique (See Exercise 8, page 95)

The fog-coating technique is used primarily when applying metallic colors and when problem conditions such as streaking or mottling are encountered. This technique can be used when applying lacquers or enamels, but it is most generally used when applying enamels. The system makes use of colors reduced according to label directions. The fog-coating technique is applied as follows:

1. **Spray gun adjustments:** full open
2. **Distance:** This is very important; hold the spray gun 12 to 18 inches from the surface.
3. **Stroke**
   a. Pull the trigger from 75% to full open and keep it pulled.
   b. Use continuously swirling, circular strokes to achieve uniformity of metallic application and uniformity of appearance.
   c. Move gradually to an adjacent area as desired appearance in step b is achieved.

Dry-spray Color Application Technique (See Exercise 10)

The dry-spray technique is another technique that can be used to good advantage by a painter because color and/or undercoats can be applied to a surface in repair situations with a minimum of overspray. This speeds up the repair process.

1. Open the spreader control valve one-eighth to one-fourth of a turn.
2. Open the fluid feed valve one-fourth to one-half of a turn.
3. Apply a fine dry spray to one spot, 2 to 3 inches in diameter, with the following technique:
   a. Using a fully pulled trigger, apply material with a continually moving circular stroke.
   b. Keep at 4 to 6 inches from the surface.
   c. The air-line pressure should be the same as for applying conventional material.
   d. Every 5 to 10 seconds, stop application and observe progress as follows:
      (1) Examine the surface for smoothness.
      (2) Wipe with a tack rag to assure smoothness.
   e. Continue application until the desired coverage is achieved.

Precautions

1. If material is going on too dry, increase the fluid feed one-eighth of a turn at a time. Recheck application.
2. If material is going on too wet, the material becomes sticky:
   a. Increase the distance of the spray gun to the surface; move back 1 to 2 inches.
   b. Cut down the fluid feed one-eighth of a turn at a time, and recheck application.
3. The painter must be able to tack-wipe the surface at any time during application to remove entrapped dirt or rough surface.

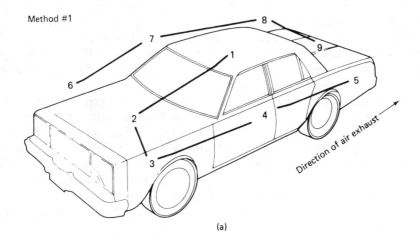

(a)

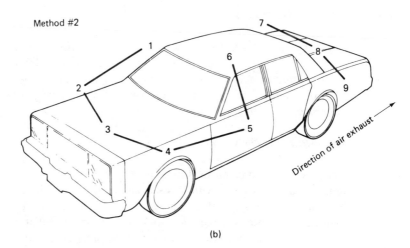

(b)

Figure 4-17 Two methods for complete refinishing.

The amount of dry spraying is determined by the paint system and by the problem condition. This is discussed in Chapter 13.

Complete Refinishing Techniques

Painters should decide before starting how each paint job will be done. This is as important for single-panel jobs as it is for complete paint jobs. Figure 4-17 shows two methods for doing an **overall** or **complete** paint job. There is no one plan that is best for all situations. The two plans shown are simply typical plans as recommended by R-M Automotive Products, BASF Inmont Corp., and are shown in their *Refinisher's Guide.*

The most critical parts of a car that are judged most easily when a paint job is completed and evaluated are the hood, the roof, and the rear deck areas. These parts reflect the most daylight and are easily seen by everyone. One of the greatest, if not the greatest, problems facing the painter in refinishing is dirt control. For this reason, many painters like to paint the hood area first, the roof second, and the rear deck third before painting the sides, front, and rear of a car.

In complete paint job refinishing, it is important to plan ahead and to secure the paint materials for painting hidden parts of the car, such as door jambs (door facings: front, bottom, and rear), body lock and hinge pillar facings, rocker panels, exterior plastic parts, valance panels, wheels, and striping colors. When necessary, colors for these parts should be ordered when orders are placed for exterior colors and solvents.

Normally, when a complete refinish is done in a different color from the original, the hidden parts, such as door jambs, and lock pillar facings, are best done with a lacquer system even when the exterior is to be acrylic enamel or urethane enamel. Lacquers dry much more quickly.

SPRAY GUN MAINTENANCE

The spray gun is the painter's most important tool. It should be cleaned thoroughly after each use. Every painter appears to clean a spray gun in a different manner. Also, not all painters lubricate spray guns as they should be lubricated. Neglect and carelessness cause most of a spray gun's problems. Proper care of a spray gun takes very little time and effort and it is well worth it.

Cleaning the Air Cap

The air cap should be cleaned by removing it from the gun, soaking it in clean solvent, brush cleaning all holes with solvent, and then keeping it clean. Some painters like to blow the air cap dry with compressed air after cleaning. This is a good idea. Other painters like to keep their air caps soaking in clean solvent at the bottom of their cleaned paint cups. This, too, is a good idea. If cleaning small holes in the air cap becomes necessary, do it in a recommended manner: (1) soak the air cap in lacquer thinner; (2) clean out holes with soft items such as round-type toothpicks or suitable plastic bristles;

finish by brush cleaning holes and blowing out the complete air cap with compressed air. Then test the air cap for proper spray fan. Resoaking and recleaning may be necessary. If a problem with the air cap persists, contact the equipment supplier for factory help. They can fix it if the air cap is not damaged.

Cleaning a Suction-feed Gun and Cup

Clean a suction-feed gun and cup as follows. Loosen the cup from the gun and, while the fluid tube is still in the cup, unscrew the air cap (two or three turns). Hold a folded cloth over the air cap and pull the trigger (Fig. 4-18). Air, diverted into fluid passages, forces material back into the container. Empty the cup of paint material and clean up the cup and the cup cover with solvent and a suitable brush and then with a clean rag soaked with solvent. Then fill the cup about one-third full with clean solvent and spray solvent through the gun to clean out the fluid passages. The painter can usually see when the fluid passages are clean. Wipe off the gun with a solvent-soaked rag. The quality of cleanup is proportional to the attention and detail of a painter's good housekeeping habits.

Cleaning a Pressure-feed System
(Tank or 2-Quart Cup Type) (Figs. 4-19 and 4-20)

In a pressure-feed system, the fluid is fed to the spray gun under pressure usually from a separate container through a hose. The pressure-feed system is very speedy because

Figure 4-18 Cleaning suction-feed gun. (Courtesy of the DeVilbiss Company)

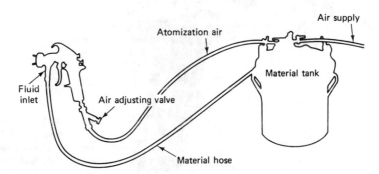

Figure 4-19 Typical pressure-feed hookup (tank type). (Courtesy of the DeVilbiss Company)

Figure 4-20 Remote pressure cup (2 quart). (Courtesy of the DeVilbiss Company)

the spray gun responds immediately when the trigger is pulled. The material hose and the container have paint material in them and they are under pressure. This is where the cleanup begins.

Procedure

1. Turn the air pressure regulating adjusting screw on the fluid container counterclockwise to cut off air pressure to the container.
2. Release pressure from the container by means of the relief valve or safety valve.

Figure 4-21 Spray gun lubrication. A, oil trigger bearing stud; B, oil fluid needle and packing; C, oil air valve stem and packing; D, fluid control screw threads; E, spreader control screw threads; F and G, springs. (Courtesy of Binks Manufacturing Company)

3. Loosen the spray gun air cap three turns.

4. Hold a folded cloth over the air cap and pull the trigger to force paint fluid from the hose back into the container.

5. Clean out the material container as required and partially fill it with solvent.

6. Reassemble the fluid container; turn on all air pressure controls and run the solvent through the fluid hose by pulling the trigger to clean out the hose.

7. Dry the fluid hose by running compressed air through it for 10 to 15 seconds.

8. Clean up the spray gun and air cap.

9. Clean out the container and reassemble it for future use.

Spray Gun Lubrication (Fig. 4-21)

Parts of the spray gun that require lubrication with a drop of light machine oil at the end of each day the spray gun has been used are indicated by letters A through E as follows:

Location	Description
A	Oil trigger bearing stud
B	Oil fluid needle and packing (apply oil to needle)
C	Oil air valve stem and packing (apply oil to stem)
D	Fluid control screw threads (apply oil to threads)
E	Spreader control screw threads (apply oil to threads)

If the spray gun is used every day, apply a light grease to springs, items F and G, twice per year. Disassembly of the fluid needle spring and air valve spring is necessary to perform this operation. If the spray gun is used two or three times per week, apply light grease to the springs once per year.

SPRAY GUN TROUBLES AND REMEDIES

If a problem is encountered in a spray gun, the spray gun should be checked out and repaired before it is used for any spray painting work. The most common spray gun problems and remedies for the problems are outlined for easy reference in the following charts.

Sometimes a spray gun appears to be working properly at the beginning of painting operations. Then, during cup refilling operations or after break periods, the spray pattern becomes faulty. The spray pattern should always be checked and corrected as soon as a faulty spray pattern is detected. To check a spray pattern quickly, apply a spray fan on a properly masked off wall. Apply material for only 1 or 2 seconds from a normal spraying distance, 6 to 8 inches from the wall, and check the results. Small-, medium-, and full-size patterns are illustrated in Fig. 3-7. These are normal spray patterns. For proper adjustment of normal spray patterns, see "Spray Gun Adjustments." The cause and correction of defective spray patterns are covered in the following charts.

Leakage

Problem 1: Fluid Leakage from the Fluid Needle Packing Nut (Figs. 3-3 and 3-4)

Cause of problem	Remedy
Loose packing nut	Tighten packing nut
Worn packing	Replace packing
Dry fluid needle packing	Soak packing with oil; then tighten packing nut

Problem 2: Air Leakage from the Front of the Gun (Fig. 4-22)

Location	Cause of problem	Remedy
A	Foreign matter on valve or seat	Clean
B	Worn or damaged valve or seat	Repair or replace damaged parts
C	Broken air valve spring	Replace spring
D	Sticking valve stem due to lack of lubrication	Lubricate with light oil
E	Bent valve stem	Repair or replace damaged stem
F	Packing nut too tight	Loosen nut and apply oil to packing
G	Gasket damaged or omitted	Secure proper gasket and install as required

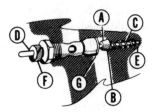

Figure 4-22 Air leakage problems. (Courtesy of the DeVilbiss Company)

Problem 3: Fluid Leakage from the Front of the Gun (Fig. 4-23)

Location	Cause of problem	Remedy
A	Fluid needle not seating due to damaged tip or needle	Repair or replace damaged tip or needle
B	Lumps or dirt lodged in fluid tip	Remove fluid tip and clean as required
C	Packing nut too tight	Loosen packing nut
D	Broken fluid needle spring	Replace broken spring
E	Wrong-size needle	Replace needle

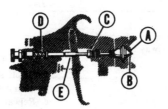

Figure 4-23 Fluid leakage problems. (Courtesy of the DeVilbiss Company)

Jerky Spray; Defective Spray Patterns

Problem 4: Jerky or Fluttering Spray (Fig. 4-24)

Location	Cause of problem	Remedy
	Suction and pressure feed	
A	Lack of sufficient material in container	Refill container
B	Tipping container at excessive angle	Add fluid to container to keep fluid tube buried
C	Blocked fluid passageway	Detach fluid feed at gun body and clean fluid passageway
D	Loose or cracked fluid tube in cup or tank	Tighten all fluid tube connections, or replace cracked fluid tube
E	Loose fluid tip or damaged tip seat	Tighten fluid tip, or replace damaged tip
	Suction feed only	
F	Too heavy a material for suction feed	Switch to pressure-feed system
G	Clogged air vent in cup lid	Open vent hole with nail or suitable wire
H	Loose, dirty, or damaged coupling nut or cup lid	Clean and retighten coupling nut and/or cup lid; replace damaged parts as required
I	Dry packing, or loose fluid needle packing nut	Lubricate packing with oil and/or tighten fluid needle packing

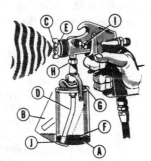

Figure 4-24 Jerky or fluttering spray. (Courtesy of the DeVilbiss Company)

Problem 5: Heavy-center Pattern. Figure 4-25 shows what a **heavy-center pattern** looks like when the pattern is sprayed vertically in normal spray position. Figure 4-26 shows how to identify a heavy-center pattern when applying the flooding test as explained in ''Spray Gun Adjustments.'' In Fig. 4-26, the spray pattern is flooded purposely in a horizontal position.

Spray Gun Troubles and Remedies   **83**

Cause of problem	Remedy

1. Too much fluid for size of spray fan	1A
	  a. Close fluid control valve a little at a time
	  b. Apply flooding test pattern (see "Spray Gun Adjustments" and Fig. 4-26)
	  c. Repeat steps a and b until spray pattern is balanced (Fig. 4-29)
	1B
	  a. Open spreader control valve a little at a time
	  b. Apply flooding test pattern (see "Spray Gun Adjustments" and Fig. 4-26)
	  c. Repeat steps a and b until spray pattern is balanced (Fig. 4-29)

2. With pressure feed, too much fluid for air cap to handle	2. Change to proper-size air cap (see Table 3-1)
3. With pressure feed, air cap atomization air pressure too low	3. Increase air cap atomization air pressure
4. Too large a nozzle for material used	4. Change to proper-size nozzle; or check equipment supplier (see Table 3-1)

Figure 4-25 Heavy-center pattern (applied vertically). (Courtesy of the DeVilbiss Company)

Figure 4-26 Flooding test: heavy-center pattern (applied horizontally).

Problem 6: Split Pattern. Figure 4-27 shows what a split pattern looks like when the pattern is sprayed vertically in normal spray position. Figure 4-28 shows how to identify a split pattern when applying the flooding test as explained in "Spray Gun Adjustments." In Fig. 4-28 the spray pattern is flooded purposely in a horizontal position.

Cause of problem	Remedy

1. Too low a setting of fluid adjustment for size of fan	1. a. Open fluid control valve a little at a time
	  b. Apply flooding test pattern (see "Spray Gun Adjustments" and Fig. 4-28)
	  c. Repeat steps a and b until spray pattern is balanced (Fig. 4-29)

2. With pressure feed, too high an atomization pressure and insufficient fluid feed	2. Increase fluid feed pressure slightly, and decrease atomization pressure slightly until balanced spray pattern is achieved (Fig. 4-29)
3. Too small a nozzle for material used	3. Use larger nozzle as required; or check equipment supplier (see Table 3-1)

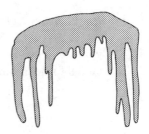

Figure 4-27 Split pattern (applied vertically). (Courtesy of the DeVilbiss Company)

Figure 4-28 Flooding test: split pattern (applied horizontally).

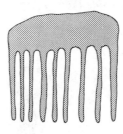

Figure 4-29 Flooding test: balanced pattern (applied horizontally).

Problem 7: Top-heavy Pattern (Fig. 4-30). This is caused by:

1. Horn holes partially plugged
2. Obstruction on top of fluid tip
3. Dirt on air cap seat or fluid tip seat

Figure 4-30 Top-heavy pattern (applied vertically). (Courtesy of the DeVilbiss Company)

Problem 8: Heavy-bottom Pattern (Fig. 4-31). This is caused by:

1. Horn holes partially plugged
2. Obstruction on bottom side of fluid tip
3. Dirt on air cap seat or fluid tip seat

Figure 4-31 Heavy-bottom pattern (applied vertically). (Courtesy of the DeVilbiss Company)

Problem 9: Heavy-right-side Pattern (Fig. 4-32). This is caused by:

1. Right-side horn holes partially plugged
2. Dirt on right side of fluid tip

Figure 4-32 Heavy-right-side pattern (applied vertically). (Courtesy of the DeVilbiss Company)

Problem 10: Heavy-left-side Pattern (Fig. 4-33). This is caused by:

1. Left-side horn holes partially clogged
2. Dirt on left side of fluid tip

Figure 4-33 Heavy-left-side pattern (applied vertically). (Courtesy of the DeVilbiss Company)

Remedies for Problems 7 to 10 (Fig. 4-34)

1. Determine if the obstruction is on the air cap or the fluid tip. This is done by making a test spray pattern, then rotating the air cap one-half turn, and spraying another pattern. If the defect is inverted, obstruction is on the air cap. If not inverted, it is on the fluid tip. Clean the air cap as required.
2. Check for a fine burr on the edge of the fluid tip; remove the burr with No. 600 wet or dry sandpaper. Check for dried paint on the fluid tip; remove by washing.

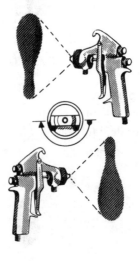

Figure 4-34 Inverting the air cap (one half-turn) and spray testing. (Courtesy of the DeVilbiss Company)

SPRAY GUN EXERCISES

To practice the spray gun exercises described in this section, several basic items are needed, such as a spray painting practice location, spray painting equipment, and miscellaneous materials as follows:

1. A properly ventilated and lighted spray painting work area, which should include an adequate air supply, hose, air filter, and air regulator. While a fully equipped and approved paint spray booth is best for this purpose, an adequate paint shop spray area with the basic equipment mentioned would serve the purpose.

2. A large production-type suction-feed spray gun, such as a Binks Model 62, DeVilbiss Model P-JGA 502, or equivalent.

3. A training aid on which to do the spray gun exercises. This can be a properly masked-off wall in a spray booth, a paint spray stand (Fig. 4-35); or a stable chart stand on which is mounted a 26 by 30 inch (approximately) section of sheet metal (18 or 20 gauge) or a $\frac{3}{8}$- or $\frac{1}{2}$-inch section of plywood. By ''stable'' is meant that the stand will not turn or move when spray painting operations are performed on it.

4. An adequate supply of paint material (lacquer or enamel) and solvent. Recom-

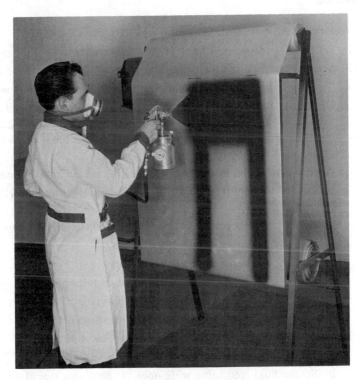

Figure 4-35 Paint spray stand with crank handle at bottom. (Courtesy of General Motors Corporation)

mendation: Use black or dark acrylic lacquer color reduced with medium-grade lacquer thinner. As an option, use plain tap water on a beige wrapping paper.

5. An ample supply of old newspapers or wrapping paper.

6. A roll of $\frac{1}{2}$- or $\frac{3}{4}$-inch masking tape.

7. Paint cleanup materials consisting of medium-grade lacquer thinner, a short-bristled brush, a small metal pan (4 by 4 by 8 inches) for cleanup solvent, and clean wiping towels (cloth or paper). A small glass or cup comes in handy for cleaning the air cap.

8. It is recommended that the spray gun be equipped with quick attach and detach connectors (Fig. 3-10). This aid makes possible quick attachment and detachment of air lines at the gun.

9. Special trash container for paper.

10. Special 5- to 10-gallon container with a small spout (and funnel) for throwaway solvents and liquid paint materials.

Exercise 1: Spray Gun Adjustments

The instructor will explain and demonstrate each spray gun adjustment as outlined in the following. Each student will perform and practice the operations under instructor guidance.

1. Prepare the paint material for practice (Chapters 7 and 10).

2. Set the air pressure at 40 psi (at gun) for lacquer; 50 psi for enamel.

3. Secure newspaper on the paint stand with masking tape at the corners only.

4. Turn ''in'' spreader control and fluid feed valves on spray gun.

5. **Determine and record the number of half-turns** for each valve from fully closed to fully open position. Reason for half-turns: determine how much of each valve could be gripped and turned conveniently at one time. Open both valves to fully open.

6. Apply **vertical** and **horizontal** test patterns on a practice stand (Fig. 4-36):
   a. Do this by adjusting the air cap for each test pattern (see ''Spray Gun Adjustments'').
   b. Apply each test pattern on the spray stand for only 1 second (Fig. 4-36).

7. Purposely create a **split pattern** (Fig. 4-37):
   a. Set the spreader control valve wide open.
   b. Set the fluid feed valve at **half** or **less** of full open.
   c. Apply a **horizontal** flooding test pattern (see ''Spray Gun Adjustments'').
   d. Analyze and compare **split pattern** paint runs.

8. Purposely create a **heavy-center** pattern (Fig. 4-38):
   a. Set the spreader control valve at half or less of full open.
   b. Set the fluid feed valve **wide open**. (''See'' one thread on the valve.)

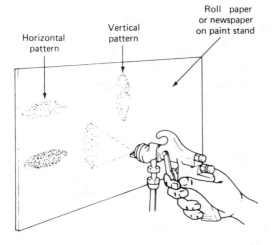

Figure 4-36 Horizontal and vertical test patterns.

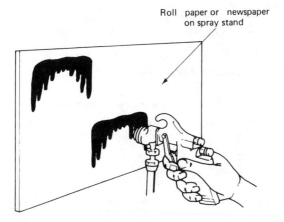

Figure 4-37 Creating a split pattern.

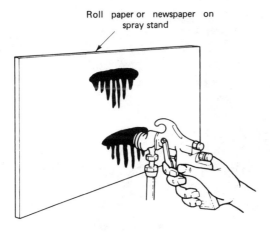

Figure 4-38 Creating a heavy-center pattern.

c. Apply a horizontal flooding test pattern.

d. Analyze and compare heavy-center paint runs.

9. Create a **balanced** pattern (Fig. 4-39):

a. Set the spreader control and fluid feed valves wide open. Set the air pressure at 40 psi (at gun) for lacquer and at 50 psi for enamel.

b. Apply a flooding test pattern.

c. Analyze and compare paint runs.

To achieve equal paint runs as in Fig. 4-39:

a. If necessary, reduce the spreader valve a fraction of a turn, such as one-eighth of a turn.

b. Repeat the flooding test pattern and check the results.

c. If necessary, increase or decrease the air pressure about 5 psi.

d. Increase or decrease the fluid feed a fraction of a turn.

e. Repeat the flooding test pattern and check the results.

The objective of this test is to achieve paint runs of equal or almost equal length while the fluid feed valve is as wide open as is practicable.

Exercise 2: Achieving the Correct Atomizing Air Pressure

For this exercise, the paint should be **black** and the $8\frac{1}{2}$ by 11 inch sheets of paper should be white. To see atomized paint particles clearly, they must be spread out. A spray fan can be spread for analysis two ways.

Method 1

1. Roll up a sheet of $8\frac{1}{2}$ by 11 inch white paper lengthwise to about a $1\frac{1}{4}$- or $1\frac{1}{2}$-inch diameter. Maintain the rolled position of the paper with a short section of tape.

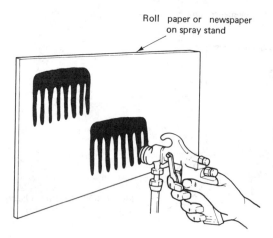

Roll paper or newspaper on spray stand

Figure 4-39 Creating a balanced pattern.

2. Hold the spray gun in one hand with the trigger pulled.
3. Aligning the rolled paper in the same direction with the width of the spray pattern, pass the rolled paper across the path of the spray pattern very quickly.
4. Unroll the paper and inspect the atomized paint particles.

Method 2

1. Secure a sheet of $8\frac{1}{2}$ by 11 inch white paper on the paint stand with a short section of masking tape at each corner.
2. Make a fast pass with the spray gun across the paper while the trigger is pulled.

Procedure (for a Classroom Situation)

1. The person making the atomization test sets up the paper and the spray gun. A second person operates the air regulator at the wall.
2. Start the first test at 20 psi at the air regulator while air is passing through gun.
   a. Increase the air pressure about 5 psi at a time for each test.
   b. Go up to 60 or 70 psi.
3. Make a spray test at each air pressure setting.
   The person making the test and the class determine the lowest air pressure that results in correct atomization. Use of a magnifying glass is helpful.

Exercise 3: Spraying a Rectangular Panel

The purpose of this exercise is to practice the technique of spraying a rectangular panel (Fig. 4-40). The instructor will explain and demonstrate the techniques on the paint practice stand. Each student will be given an opportunity to practice the techniques on the paint stand under the guidance of the instructor. Each student should practice the technique, repeatedly, until all elements of the technique are being performed properly.

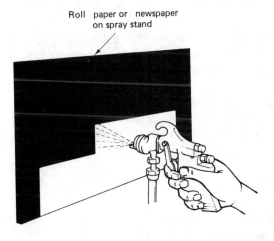

Roll paper or newspaper on spray stand

Figure 4-40 Spraying a rectangular panel (single coat). (Courtesy of Binks Manufacturing Company)

1. Prepare the paint material for practice (Chapters 7 and 10).
2. Secure newspaper on the paint stand with masking tape at the corners.
3. Adjust the spray gun and apply vertical banding passes at the left and right edges of the paper. Bands should be about 4 inches wide.
4. Adjust the spray gun for a full-open spray gun adjustment. While observing proper gun positioning and stroking techniques, apply horizontal passes with 50% overlap for complete coverage of the panel.
5. Start and stop paint application **on** the vertical banding passes. Avoid overspray. Obtain complete coverage.
6. Paint the entire panel with continuous motions without stopping.
7. Strive for uniform and wet application of color. Also, strive for accuracy in hitting the target (banding) with proper triggering and smoothness of stroke movement.
8. Some apprentices may be helped at the beginning by going through all the spray gun motions without pulling the trigger. Particularly, allow the wrist to bend at the end of each stroke to maintain the perpendicular position of the gun to the surface. **Avoid arcing when painting complete panels.**
9. **Helpful hints for the apprentice:** When applying full spray painting strokes, check the following fundamentals of the stroke very closely to see that they are being done properly.
    a. Spray gun grip (Fig. 4-7): Be sure that it is comfortable and fully controlled.
    b. Distance of the gun from the surface (Fig. 4-8): Follow the contour of the surface. Always maintain the **same** distance from the surface.
    c. Position of the gun to the surface (Fig. 4-9): Keep as perpendicular as possible.
    d. Speed of gun travel: Be guided by the sight of visual application. Never spray when the application cannot be seen; this is like spraying with a blindfold on the eyes.
    e. Stroke movement (Fig. 4-11): Be smooth and relaxed. Use continuous motions at the beginning and end of each stroke.
    f. Triggering: Keep the initial air always **on;** be smooth and accurate; trigger at target areas only.
    g. Avoid arcing on full panels (Fig. 4-10): The painter must make an extra effort at the beginning and end of each stroke to bend the wrist to adapt the arm to the perpendicular position of the gun to the surface.

When learning spray painting, concentrated thought must be given to each fundamental. As practice continues and the stroke becomes more of a habit, less thought is given to each fundamental. This gives the painter the opportunity to watch for the most important items, which are:

1. Wetness of application
2. Desired overlap
3. Target areas where triggering takes place
4. Review of complete panel paint application

Exercise 4: Spraying a Long Panel in Sections (Fig. 4-41)

The purpose of this exercise is to practice the technique of painting a long panel, such as a quarter panel or the side of a van while practicing correct overlap. Long panels should be painted in sections with each section overlapping a previously painted section about 4 inches.

1. Prepare paint material for practice (Chapters 7 and 10).
2. Secure newspaper on paint stand as required.
3. Make two vertical banding passes on spray stand (Figs. 4-41 and 4-35).
4. Adjust spray gun for full-open spray fan.
5. Observing correct gun positioning and stroking technique, apply color to right half of paint stand between center and right banding pass, and from top to bottom of paper (Fig. 4-41).
6. Fill in left half of space in conventional manner, being sure that passes overlap about 4 inches at center. When painting a car, the overlap location of each succeeding coat should be changed to a different location to prevent excessive color buildup.
7. Strive to use smooth, free-flowing motions throughout the exercise.
8. Also strive for uniformity and wetness of application while observing correct spraying technique.

Exercise 5: Triggering Practice (The Big ''X''; Fig. 4-42)

The purpose of this exercise is to practice triggering while the spray gun is in motion according to the following procedure.

1. Prepare the paint material for practice (Chapters 7 and 10).
2. Position fresh roll paper or secure newspaper on the paint stand with masking tape.
3. With a banding stroke, make a large ''X'' on the spray stand from the upper-left corner to the lower-right corner, and from the upper-right corner to lower-left corner.

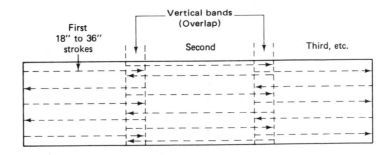

Figure 4-41 Spraying a long panel.

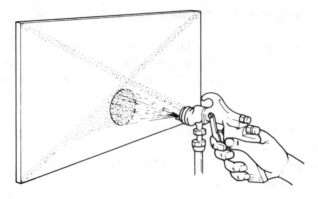

Figure 4-42 Triggering practice: fill in "X."

4. Adjust the spray gun for spot-repair or **midrange adjustment.** Using only horizontal strokes and starting at the top or bottom, fill in the top section of the "X" **without crossing the lines.** Use 50% overlap. Keep the arm and spray gun moving continually until the complete triangle is filled. Use a good spraying technique. Practice until arm motions are smooth and free flowing. Achieve full coverage.
5. Fill in the bottom section without crossing the lines.
6. Fill in each side triangle without crossing the lines.
7. Strive for accuracy, uniformity, and wetness of application. When done, the "X" **should not be readily visible.**

Exercise 6: Overlap Practice (Fig. 4-43) The Big "O"

The purpose of this exercise is to practice overlapping in a way that is unique and at the same time gives the sprayer an opportunity to develop eye-to-muscle directional control. For this exercise, adjust the spray gun for the smallest spray pattern by **turning the**

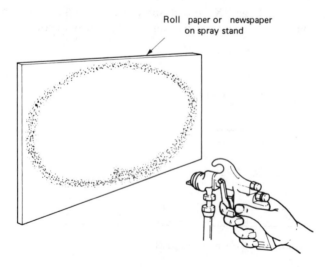

Roll paper or newspaper on spray stand

Figure 4-43 Overlap practice: fill in "O" with banding spray pattern.

spreader control valve off completely and **by opening the fluid feed valve for a small balanced pattern.**

1. Prepare the paint material for practice (Chapters 7 and 10).
2. Secure newspaper on the paint stand with masking tape.
3. With a banding-type pass, make as large a circle as possible on the paint stand.
4. Fill in the circle **with one continuous spiral pass.** Spray from the outside in or from the inside out. Maintain overlap at 50%. Avoid streaks or sags by moving at the proper speed.
5. Strive for accuracy, uniformity of coverage, and wetness of application. **When done, the circle and all overlapping passes should not be readily visible.**

Exercise 7: Overlap and Triggering Practice (Fig. 4-44)

The purpose of this exercise is to practice overlapping and triggering with a left-to-right and right-to-left conventional spraying technique. Use the full-size spray pattern in this exercise.

1. Prepare the paint material for practice (Chapters 7 and 10).
2. Secure newspaper on the paint stand with masking tape.
3. With a banding-type pass, make as large a circle as possible on the paint stand.
4. Adjust the spray gun for a full-size spray pattern.
5. Using mostly horizontal strokes with 50% overlap, fill in the circle. Avoid crossing the lines.
6. Strive for accuracy, uniformity of coverage, and wetness of application. **When done, the circle and all overlapping passes should not be readily visible.**

Exercise 8: Fog-coating Technique

The purpose of this exercise is to get a feeling for fog coating because it is quite different from conventional spraying. This technique is used as a repair system by painters when

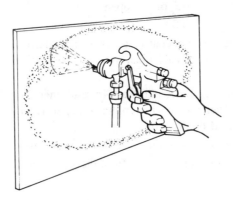

Figure 4-44 Overlap and triggering practice: fill in "O."

applying metallic-type colors. As the term "fog" indicates, the material is applied from a greater distance in a fog-type fashion rather than in a wet-spray fashion.

1. Prepare the paint material for practice. Use a high metallic color if available.
2. Secure newspaper on the paint stand with masking tape.
3. Adjust the spray gun for a full-size spray pattern.
4. Apply a full, wet single coat of color on the practice stand.
5. Apply a fog coat over the color coat as follows:
    a. Use the same spray gun adjustments as in step 4.
    b. Hold the spray gun 12 to 18 inches from the surface. This is important. **Check the distance with a ruler before spraying.**
    c. Pull the trigger from 75% to full open; keep the trigger pulled but keep the gun moving in a circular fashion.
    d. While maintaining a 12- to 18-inch distance, use continuously swirling, circular strokes to achieve uniformity of color application and appearance. Use six to eight swirls over a given area.
    e. Move gradually to an adjacent area as the desired, uniform appearance in metallic finish is achieved. Normally, it is necessary to follow the fog coating with a mist coating. This is described in the next exercise.

Exercise 9: Mist-coating Technique

The purpose of this exercise is to get a feeling for applying mist-coat materials. A mist coat is an application of mostly solvent material to rewet a freshly applied color coat. Mist-coat material is prepared by mixing from 5% to 10% color or clear resin with the balance solvent. Sometimes a straight solvent is used. When sprayed, the material looks and acts like a heavy mist. Mist coating should be used only when recommended by the paint supplier or as recommended in this book.

1. Prepare the spray gun with mist-coat material as described previously. Recommendation: Use 95% solvent and 5% color or clear resin.
2. Adjust the spray gun in midrange settings (see "Spray Gun Adjustments"):
    a. Set the fan and fluid at 50% of full open.
    b. Reduce the air pressure to 30 psi or less at the gun.
3. Apply a full, wet coat of mist-coat material over Exercise 8. Use 50% overlap; apply the material wet, but avoid runs. When lacquer solvents are used, evaporation is fast.
4. Using $\frac{1}{2}$- or $\frac{3}{4}$-inch masking tape, **make a 6-inch-diameter circle** (approximately) on the paint stand. Then, with tape, **make a larger (18-inch-diameter) circle** (approximately) **around the first one.**
5. Apply mist-coat material between the two circles as follows:
    a. Control all stroking toward or away from the small circle.

b. **Practice feathering and arcing control. Avoid getting the small circle wet.** The objective of the exercise is to get the area between the two circles uniformly wet. This technique is used in spot repairing.

Exercise 10: Dry-spray Application Technique (Fig. 4-45)

The purpose of this exercise is to practice application of dry-sprayed material. The dry-spray technique is another special system for doing spot-repair work. Dry-spray application of material can be used to repair undercoats, color coats, and freshly applied finishes. The dry-spray technique requires mist coating or color coating as a final operation.

1. Prepare the paint material for practice (Chapter 10).
2. Secure newspaper on the paint stand with masking tape.
3. Adjust the spray gun as follows:
    a. Open the fluid feed valve one-fourth to one-half turn.
    b. Open the spreader control valve one-eighth to one-fourth turn.
    c. Adjust air at 35 psi at the gun.
4. Apply a fine dry spray to one spot, 3 to 4 inches in diameter, with the following technique:
    a. Using a fully pulled trigger, apply material with a continuously moving, circular stroke.
    b. Keep at 4 to 6 inches from the surface.
    c. Stop application every 5 to 10 seconds and check the surface smoothness. This is done by **tack wiping.**
    d. Continue application until the desired coverage is achieved.

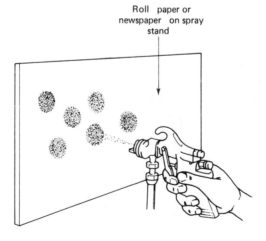

Roll paper or
newspaper on spray
stand

Figure 4-45 Dry-spray application technique.

Precautions

1. If the material is going on too dry, increase the fluid feed slightly.
2. If the material is going on too wet, the material becomes sticky.
   a. Increase the distance of the spray gun from the surface; or
   b. Cut down the fluid feed a fraction of a turn at a time and recheck application.

Exercise 11: Spot-repair Techniques (Fig. 4-46)

The purpose of this exercise is to practice basic spray techniques used in spot-repairing automotive finishes with standard acrylic lacquers. Spot-repair techniques require special gun adjustments, triggering, and gun movement. Also, the techniques require greater color control by the painter. All automotive colors are spot-repairable. It is up to each painter to learn how each color behaves and what is required to achieve good color matches.

1. Prepare the paint material for practice:
   a. Set up one gun with color. Mark the cup "Color."
   b. Set up a second gun with mist-coat material.
2. Secure newspaper on the paint stand with masking tape.
3. Adjust both spray guns in midrange for spot repairing (see "Spray Gun Adjustments").
4. Using a pencil, draw about a 6-inch-diameter circle on the paint stand. Then draw five additional circles, 1 to 2 inches larger, around the small one. Keep the distance between the circles 1 to 2 inches.
5. Practice feathering and arcing techniques at the beginning and end of each stroke. Proceed to make the spot repair as follows:
   a. Using 20 psi (at the gun), apply the first color coat to fill in the area within the 6-inch circle. Apply a mist coat to the edges and allow to flash.

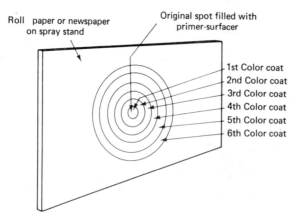

Roll paper or newspaper on spray stand

Original spot filled with primer-surfacer

1st Color coat
2nd Color coat
3rd Color coat
4th Color coat
5th Color coat
6th Color coat

Figure 4-46 Spot-repair technique; acrylic lacquer repair system. (Courtesy of the DuPont Company)

b. Raise the air pressure 5 psi for each additional coat. Apply four to six additional coats to the repair area. Extend each coat to the next line beyond the previous coat. Mist-coat the edges of each applied color coat, allowing each to flash.

NOTE: Raising the air pressure a nominal 5 psi from a lower pressure for each additional color coat is one technique used by many painters when color matching metallic colors. This holds down the amount of overspray. Never exceed 40 psi with acrylic lacquers unless it is necessary to do so. To become more familiar with spot repairing, see Chapters 9, 13, and 14.

REVIEW QUESTIONS

1. Spray painting is made up of theory and skill development. Explain each.
2. Explain how to make and test the full-open spray gun adjustment on a suction-feed spray gun.
3. Explain how to make and test a spot-repair or midrange spray gun adjustment on a suction-feed spray gun.
4. Explain how to make and test a dry-spray adjustment on a suction-feed spray gun.
5. Explain atomization of paint materials during spray painting.
6. Describe how a painter can determine the proper atomizing air pressure without an air gauge.
7. Describe the proper form of each of the components of the spray painting stroke:
    (a) Grip
    (b) Position of gun to surface
    (c) Distance of gun from surface
    (d) Speed of stroke
    (e) Triggering
    (f) Feathering of paint application
8. Describe each of the following spray techniques:
    (a) Parallel stroke movement
    (b) Arcing stroke movement
9. Describe the conventional single coat of spray paint application.
10. Describe how to apply a single coat of paint on a complete panel:
    (a) Starting stroke(s)
    (b) Continuing midsection stroke(s)
    (c) Finishing stroke(s)
11. What is the conventional double coat?
12. What is the technique for spraying edges and corners?
13. What is the banding technique?
14. What is the technique for spraying long, narrow, slender parts?

15. What is the technique for spraying large horizontal surfaces such as the roof, hood, and rear deck of a car?

16. What precautions can a painter take to prevent drippage on large horizontal surfaces?

17. Explain the spot-repair technique.

18. Explain the mist-coating technique:
    (a) For spot repairs
    (b) For full-panel repairs

19. Explain the fog-coating technique.

20. Explain the dry-spray color application technique.

21. Explain by major panel areas and sides of a car a system for painting a complete car.

Spray Gun Cleanup and Maintenance

1. Explain how to clean up an air cap after painting.

2. Explain how to clean a suction-feed spray gun and cup after painting.

3. Explain how to clean a pressure-feed spray outfit after painting.

4. Explain how to lubricate a spray gun as follows:
    (a) What lubricant should be used?
    (b) List the items to be lubricated.
    (c) How often should spray gun parts be lubricated?
    (d) What lubricant is used on spray gun springs? How often should they be lubricated?

Spray Gun Troubles and Remedies

1. What causes fluid leakage at the fluid needle packing nut? (three causes)

2. What causes air leakage from the front of the gun? (seven causes)

3. What causes fluid leakage from the front of the gun? (five causes)

4. List several causes of jerky or fluttering spray.

5. What causes a heavy-center pattern?

6. What causes a split pattern?

7. What causes a top-heavy pattern?

8. What causes a heavy-bottom pattern?

9. What causes a heavy-right-side pattern?

10. What causes a heavy-left-side pattern?

5

Spray-Painting Equipment and Facilities

INTRODUCTION

Automotive refinishing can be divided into three areas (Fig. 5-1):

1. Paint equipment
2. Paint materials
3. The painter

This chapter deals with the general description of paint equipment and the role equipment

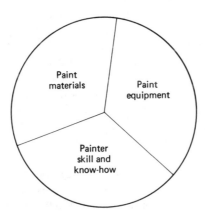

Figure 5-1 Three parts of automotive refinishing.

plays in the overall refinish picture. How to use each piece of equipment is covered in applicable chapters of the book.

ROLE OF OSHA AND NIOSH

In 1970, Congress passed the **Occupational Safety and Health Act**. The purpose of the act is "to assure as far as possible every working man and woman in the nation safe and healthful working conditions and to preserve our human resources." To administer the act, the Labor Department's Occupational Safety and Health Administration (OSHA) issues standards and rules, called **regulations**, for safe and/or healthful working conditions, tools, equipment, facilities, and processes, and conducts inspections to assure they are followed.

In the automotive refinish trade, OSHA regulations protect the health and safety of the painter and protect the investment of the owner. OSHA does not test, approve, or certify products or devices in industry. OSHA establishes safety and health regulations and enforces them. OSHA encourages states to develop plans for their own safety and health programs. OSHA grants states up to 50% of the cost of operating an OSHA-approved plan that "is at least as effective as" OSHA's program. The act and the standards issued by OSHA apply to every employer with one or more employees.

Under the act, employers have the general duty of providing both conditions of employment and a place of employment free from recognized hazards to safety and health and the specific duty of complying with OSHA standards. Employees must comply with standards and with job safety and health rules and regulations that apply to their own conduct.

Prior to 1970, the federal government had established the **National Institute for Occupational Safety and Health**, or NIOSH. This agency now serves in cooperation with OSHA. NIOSH has many responsibilities. The two most important responsibilities that affect the refinishing trade are:

1. NIOSH makes recommendations for particular safety regulations.
2. NIOSH has the responsibility of **testing** and **certifying** the safety of tools and equipment designed and built for industry. Tools and equipment certified by NIOSH are so marked, and approval limitations are stated on each box or container.

Paint shop owners are urged to cooperate with both OSHA and NIOSH. To do business, a body and paint shop must be licensed each year by the city and state. To become licensed, each shop must be inspected. Compliance with local, state, and federal regulations is observed very closely by authorities when licenses are renewed each year.

RESPIRATORS

Proper respiratory protection for painters is extremely important. All automotive painters, apprentices, and painter's helpers are urged to use **only approved respirators** when spray painting. Respirators cost very little compared to the protection they give a painter's lungs. Many refinish material chemicals, particularly the isocyanate vapors of ure-thane finishes, can cause lung irritation and allergic respiratory reactions. NIOSH is the official approving agency for automotive refinishing respirators. However, respirator suppliers can stamp respirators as **approved** when respirators meet NIOSH minimum requirements.

Painters should be instructed in the following:

1. How to select the proper respirator.
2. How to fit and test a respirator before starting to paint.
3. The health hazards involved.
4. How to clean and sanitize the respirator.
5. How to store the respirator for the next use.

Three types of respirators are needed by the painter to do all-around automotive refinishing:

1. General spray painting respirator **(NIOSH spec. number TC-23C)**
2. Air-supplied mask or hood respirator **(NIOSH spec. number TC-19C)**
3. Dust respirator **(NIOSH spec. number TC-21C)**

General Spray Painting Respirator (for All Factory-approved Paint Systems)

The general spray painting respirator is a chemical and mechanical filter respirator designed to protect the painter against atomized paint particles, dirt, and toxic vapors when spray painting conventional paint finishes such as universal undercoats, acrylic lacquers, and conventional enamels. These respirators are available through leading paint suppliers, equipment suppliers, and paint jobbers.

When spray painting materials carry a "Hazardous Warning" label, as is true of urethanes and urethane-catalyzed finishes, use a vapor/particulate respirator that the equipment supplier recommends as effective for isocyanate vapors and mists. This respirator should never be used to spray in an enclosed area such as inside a truck, where there is no air movement. For best results, follow the manufacturer's fitting and usage instructions.

Components of respirators are serviced by jobbers selling them. Painters should make it a habit to wash their face masks periodically with a germicidal solution or soap and water. Respirators should be kept in a clean, dry, protected place ready for the next use. Cartridges should be replaced when the painter begins to smell or taste any paint materials coming through them.

One good test for cartridges is as follows: Smell household ammonia through respirator. If smell does not come through, cartridge is good. If smell comes through, replace the cartridge.

WARNING: Always read a label of this type carefully and slowly, or have someone read it for you.

The following typical warning label appears on many automotive refinishing products when they contain isocyanate chemicals:

WARNING! VAPOR AND SPRAY MIST HARMFUL. MAY CAUSE LUNG IRRITATION AND ALLERGIC RESPIRATORY REACTION. MAY IRRITATE SKIN AND EYES. COMBUSTIBLE.

Gives off harmful vapor of solvents and isocyanates (a hazardous material). DO NOT USE IF YOU HAVE CHRONIC (LONG-TERM) LUNG OR BREATHING PROBLEMS, OR IF YOU HAVE EVER HAD A REACTION TO ISOCYANATES. USE ONLY WITH ADEQUATE VENTILATION. WHERE OVER-SPRAY IS PRESENT, A POSITIVE PRESSURE AIR-SUPPLIED RESPIRATOR (TC19C NIOSH/MESA) IS RECOMMENDED. IF NOT AVAILABLE, USE A VAPOR/PARTICULATE RESPIRATOR THAT RESPIRATOR SUPPLIER RECOMMENDS AS EFFECTIVE FOR ISOCYANATE VAPORS AND MISTS (SUCH AS 3M COMPANY'S SPRAY PAINT RESPIRATOR No. 6984 OR No. 6986.) Follow directions for respirator use. Wear the respirator for the whole time of spraying and until all vapors and mists are gone.

Avoid breathing of vapor or spray mist. Avoid contact with eyes and skin. Keep away from heat and open flame. Keep closures tight and upright to prevent leakage. Keep container closed when not in use. In case of spillage, absorb and then dispose of in accordance with local applicable regulations.

FIRST AID: If affected by inhalation of vapor or spray mist, remove to fresh air. If breathing difficulty persists or occurs later, consult a physician and have label information available. In case of eye contact, flush immediately with plenty of water for 15 minutes: CALL A PHYSICIAN. In case of skin contact, wash thoroughly with soap and water.

KEEP OUT OF THE REACH OF CHILDREN.

General spray painting respirators are available in two forms:

1. **A mask with replaceable cartridges** (Fig. 5-2): These respirators are available through leading paint equipment suppliers, such as Binks and DeVilbiss, and through leading paint jobbers. **Prefilters** are available for cartridge-type respirators. Prefilters fit over cartridges; they trap dust and dirt and allow cartridges to last longer.

2. **One-piece mask with unitized construction** (Fig. 5-3): A new, lightweight spray paint respirator made by the 3M Company is sold under part numbers 6984 and 6986. This is a chemical and mechanical filter-type respirator that protects the painter against paint particles, dirt, and toxic vapors when spray painting. The respirator is constructed in one piece and has no replaceable parts. The respirator is designed to be effective for 5 days of use. After this time, the respirator must be discarded.

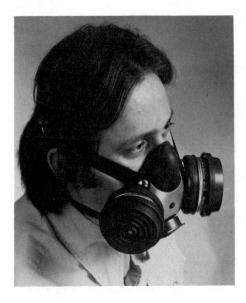

Figure 5-2 General spray painting respirator: dual-cartridge type. (Courtesy of Binks Manufacturing Company)

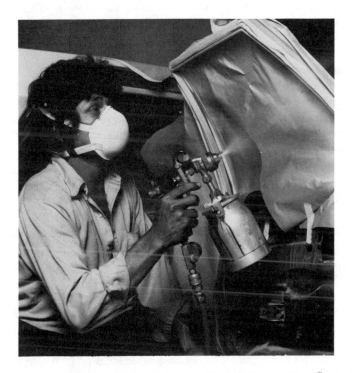

Figure 5-3 General spray painting respirator: unitized, throw-away type. (Courtesy of the 3M Company)

Air-supplied Mask or Hood Respirator

Air-supplied mask or hood respirators, as approved by NIOSH spec. number TC-19C, are suitable for spray painting urethane paint finishes and other paint finishes even when spraying in confined areas with poor air circulation, when the painter would be forced to breathe high concentrations of toxic vapors, chemicals, and overspray.

Air-supplied mask or hood respirators are approved by NIOSH as a **"package"** consisting of several components. Violation of any single component by painters or paint shop owners violates the complete NIOSH approval. The components of approval are:

1. **Mask** or **hood respirators** must meet NIOSH approval.
2. The **hose** must meet NIOSH approval.
3. The **air filter** must meet NIOSH approval.
4. The **air regulator** must meet NIOSH approval.
5. The **air gauge** must meet NIOSH requirements.
6. A **single air line** to supply the respirator *and* the spray gun **cannot be used**. The spray gun and the respirator must each have their own separate air lines.
7. If an oil-lubricated, piston-type compressor is used to supply air to the air-supplied respirator, overheating may produce **carbon monoxide**. To guard against this, routine and continuous testing for carbon monoxide is required by adding a **constant monitoring analyzer** in the air line for breathing. Also, a **high-temperature alarm** must be installed on the compressor.

Mask and hood respirators are described as follows:

1. The air-supplied half-mask unit is used where eye protection is not required (Fig. 5-4). An air-supplied mask respirator covers only the face and offers breathing protection against hazardous vapors and chemicals.
2. The air-supplied hood respirator covers the entire head and is required to protect the painter's lungs, eyes, and face from toxic chemicals, paint vapors, and dust. The air-supplied hood respirator requires the use of the same air-supplying components that are used with the half-mask respirator.

Binks' air-supplied mask (and hood) respirator package, as approved, is made up of the following components:

1. **Mask respirator** (Model 40-160) (Fig. 5-4): The chin cup and soft rolled edge provide a good seal to the face with high resistance to facial oils. Double headbands and floating-yoke suspension distribute seal pressure uniformly around the face-piece rim. The half-mask respirator is to be used only in atmospheres not immediately dangerous to life or health. Minimum air supply requirements are 4 cubic feet per minute (cfm) of breathable air at pressures under 40 psi.
2. **Air-supply hose:** One or more sections of approved supply hose must be used with air-mask or air-hood respirator to maintain approval. The necessary amount of hose must be ordered by the user.

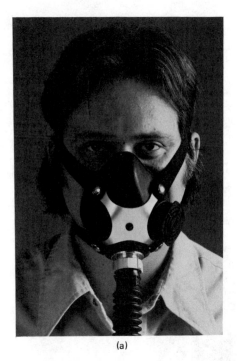

(a)   (b)

Figure 5-4 (a) Air-supplied mask respirator (face shot). (b) Air-supplied mask respirator (complete unit). (Courtesy of Binks Manufacturing Company)

    a. 40-154 air hose, 25 feet long with fittings and adapter

    b. 40-155 air hose, 50 feet long with fittings and adapter

    c. 40-152 adapter, $\frac{3}{4}$ inch male $\times$ $\frac{1}{4}$ inch female.

3. **Oil and water coalescer (air filter)** (Model 86-964) (Fig. 5-5): The coalescer removes oil particles, water droplets, and dirt particles as small as 0.6 micron, thus filtering the air for breathing purposes. **The coalescer is not designed to remove carbon monoxide.**

4. **Oilless air compressor** (Model 34-1051) (Fig. 5-6): An oilless compressor of this type is required to supply air for mask- or hood-type respirators.

5. **Air regulator:** An air regulator is required on the air line supplying air to the mask or hood. The air must be regulated at and below 40 psi, as required. A number of regulators are available to meet the needs of the package for approval. Check with the equipment supplier.

In the event that an air-supplied hood respirator is required, the following Binks hood respirators are available and have been approved by NIOSH:

1. Model 40-170, neck-length hood respirator

2. Model 40-175, waist-length hood respirator

Respirators   **107**

Figure 5-5 Oil and water coalescer (air filter) for hood or mask respirator. (Courtesy of Binks Manufacturing Company)

Figure 5-6 Oilless air compressor for hood or mask respirator. (Courtesy of Binks Manufacturing Company)

The full face, head, and neck are protected during spray painting. Each unit has a built-in hard hat. Each respirator requires 6 cfm minimum breathable air supply.

   WARNING: These respirators are for respiratory protection only in atmospheres not immediately dangerous to life or health and from which the wearer can escape without the aid of the respirator.

   All component parts, including pull-off cover lenses, are available through Binks paint jobbers and branch warehouses. For best results, follow the manufacturer's maintenance instructions. Wash and clean the hood with soap and water or with a germicidal solution as often as required. When not in use, store in a clean, dry location.

   NOTE: Other paint equipment suppliers, like Survivair (see Fig. 5-7), have

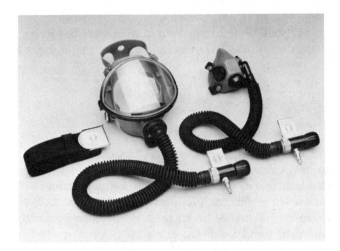

Figure 5-7 Survivair full and half-mask style of air-supplied respirators. (Courtesy of Survivair, U.S.D. Corp.)

NIOSH-approved air-supplied respirators available. Check with the local equipment distributor, paint supplier, or paint jobber for availability.

Dust Respirator (Fig. 5-8)

Dust respirators are mechanical-type respirators designed with filters that remove dust and solid particles from the air a painter breathes. Dust respirators cover the nose and mouth. Most dust respirators are of the throw-away variety: after they become saturated with dust or dirt, they are discarded. Dust respirators are used mostly in the paint shop when dry-sanding paint and plastic fillers, particularly with power equipment. Dust respirators should be used whenever a very dusty situation is encountered.

WARNING: Simple face masks or loosely fitting respirators should not be used. For best results, use dust respirators that have been approved by NIOSH, the Bureau of Mines, or MESA. They fit snugly.

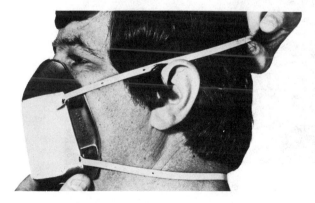

Figure 5-8 Dust respirator. (Courtesy of Binks Manufacturing Company)

Respirators

Respirators should be stored in a clean box. Cleaning by light brushing, tapping on a hard surface to free dirt, and vacuuming can make dust respirators last longer. When heavily clogged with plastic dust such as fiberglass residue, it is better to discard the respirator.

DUSTING GUN (Fig. 5-9)

A dusting gun is a small air gun that attaches directly to an air-line hose by means of a quick attach and detach connector. A dusting gun is a very popular tool in a body and paint shop because it is used to clean up cars with compressed air before painting.

Before OSHA came into existence, full line pressures were often used to clean cars. These pressures often exceeded 100 psi. At times, painters or helpers accidently blew dirt or foreign matter into their own or someone else's eyes, which resulted in serious problems. Good eyesight is one of the most important possessions a painter has.

OSHA Regulation Regarding Dusting Guns

"Compressed air shall not be used for cleaning purposes except where reduced to less than 30 psi, and then only with effective chip guarding and personal protective equipment."

To meet this OSHA regulation:

1. Paint equipment suppliers have specially designed dusting guns available that develop less than 30 psi at the nozzle even when high air pressure is used.
2. Also, **conversion nozzles**, which meet the same OSHA requirements, are available

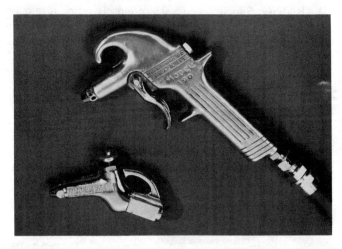

Figure 5-9 Dusting guns (Binks Models 190 and 152). (Courtesy of Binks Manufacturing Company)

from equipment suppliers to adapt *older* dusting guns having $\frac{5}{16}$ inch by 24 NFS or $\frac{7}{16}$ inch by 20 NFS thread for screw-in tips.

To meet the second portion of the OSHA regulation, the painter must observe the following safety rules:

1. Before dusting, the painter should wear suitable eye protection (such as a face shield or goggles).
2. No other person may be close to the person with the dusting gun unless he or she is wearing suitable eye protection.

AIR COMPRESSOR

For air-operated equipment to function, it is necessary to have a certain amount of con-tinuously supplied air available at a required pressure. The equipment that performs this operation is commonly known as the **air compressor**. Compressed air is **atmospheric air** (the air we breath) that has been compressed and then forced mechanically into a storage container. Then, with special controls, the air is released to do a specific type of work.

The most important specification of a compressor is the volume of air that the compressor delivers, measured in cubic feet of air per minute (cfm). Unfortunately, many people think that pressure is the most important factor. Without adequate air vol-ume, air pressure drops fast and air equipment cannot function. The greater the volume of air available, the more air-driven equipment that can be used. A rule of thumb for calculating the cfm is: a 1-horsepower electric motor will produce at least 4 cfm at 100 psi of free air. Once a compressor is selected according to the air requirements, the next requirement is adequate current and voltage to operate the electric motor. If in doubt as to the adequacy of the electrical power available, check with the electric company.

Atmosphere consists of approximately 80% nitrogen and 20% oxygen. Air has weight and, at sea level, this weight is known as **atmospheric pressure**. At sea level, this pressure is 14.7 psi. This means that the air pressure exerted on every square inch of the earth's surface at sea level is 14.7 psi. This pressure is also exerted in all directions at sea level. Therefore, air entering the compressor intake is at a pressure of 14.7 psi.

Types of Compressors

Compressors can be divided into many categories. Two of the most popular types are the piston and diaphragm types.

Piston-type Compressors. This type is available as stationary units, which are anchored in place, and as portable units, which are on wheels and can be moved to the job. A piston-type compressor develops pressure through the action of a reciprocating piston much like that of an automobile engine. Air enters the compressor through an intake valve on the **downstroke** (Fig. 5-10a). The air is compressed and expelled through an exhaust valve on the **upstroke** (Fig. 5-10b) to an air tank or an air line.

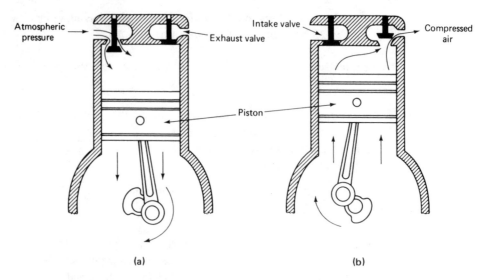

Figure 5-10 Piston-type air compressor (single stage). (a) Downstroke: intake. (b) Upstroke: compression. (Courtesy of Binks Manufacturing Company)

When air is drawn from the atmosphere and compressed to a given pressure in a single stroke, the compressor is classified as a single-stage unit (Fig. 5-11). **The efficiency of single-stage units is good up to 100 psi but poor over 100 psi.**

When air is drawn from the atmosphere and first compressed to an intermediate pressure (approximately 40 psi), then passed through an intercooler to a high-pressure cylinder for recompression, the air compressor is a two-stage unit. The high-pressure cylinder is approximately one-half the diameter of the low-pressure cylinder (Fig. 5-12). **Two-stage air compressors are used when air pressure is required in excess of 100 psi but less than 200 psi.**

Figure 5-11 Single-stage compressor. (Courtesy of the DeVilbiss Company)

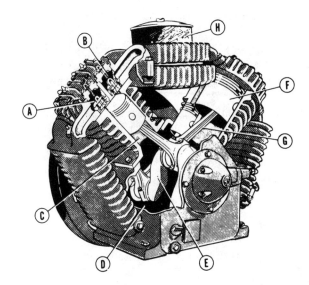

Figure 5-12 Two-stage compressor. A, intake valve assembly; B, exhaust valve assembly; C, cylinder; D, crankcase; E, crankshaft; F, piston; G, connecting rod assembly; H, air intake filter. (Courtesy of the DeVilbiss Company)

Diaphragm-type Compressors. These are usually small and portable, and are designed for low-air-volume use. The diaphragm compressor develops pressure through the reciprocating (pushing and pulling) action of a flexible diaphragm. An electric motor causes the pushing and pulling action on the diaphragm. On the **downstroke** action, a valve opens to fill the chamber above the diaphragm with air (Fig. 5-13b). On the **upstroke**, the valve closes and air is pushed out of the compressor by the diaphragm (Fig. 5-13a).

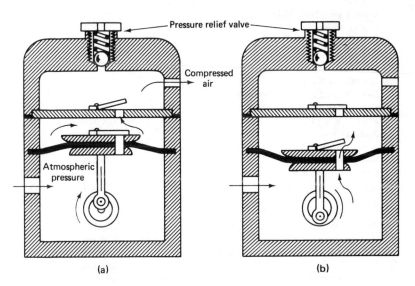

Figure 5-13 Diaphragm-type air compressor. (a) Upstroke: compression. (b) Downstroke: intake. (Courtesy of Binks Manufacturing Company)

How to Select the Right Compressor

It is very important that the compressor selected be of the correct type and size for the total work to be done. Tables 5-1 and 5-2 have been compiled to assist in making the proper choice. Following are additional suggestions to help determine choice:

1. List all air-operated tools and equipment expected to be run by the compressor with the average free air consumption (see Table 5-1 for tool and equipment capacities).
2. Total all figures of free air consumption.
3. For intermittent service, refer to Table 5-2, column A.
4. For constant use of most tools, refer to Table 5-2, column B.

TABLE 5-1 OPERATING AIR CONSUMPTION AND AIR REQUIREMENTS

Device	Air pressure range (psi)	Average free air consumption
Air filter cleaner	70–100	3.0
Air hammer	70–100	16.5
Body polisher	70–100	2.0
Body sander	70–100	5.0
Brake tester	70–100	3.5
Carbon remover	70–100	3.0
Car rocker	120–150	5.75
Car washer	70–100	8.5
Dusting gun (blow gun)	70–100	2.5
Engine cleaner	70–100	5.0
Fender hammer	70–100	8.75
Grease gun (high pressure)	120–150	3.0
Hoist (one ton)	70–100	1.0
Hydraulic lift[a]	145–175	5.25
Paint spray gun (large, production type)	70–100	8.5
Paint spray gun (small, touch-up type)	70–100	2.25
Pneumatic garage door	120–150	2.0
Radiator tester	70–100	1.0
Rim stripper	120–150	6.0
Spark plug cleaner	70–100	5.0
Spark plug tester	70–100	0.5
Spray gun (undercoating)	70–100	19.0
Spring oiler	70–100	3.75
Tire changer	120–150	1.0
Tire inflation line	120–150	1.5
Tire spreader	120–150	1.0
Transmission and differential flusher	70–100	3.0
Vacuum cleaner	120–150	6.5

[a] For 8000-lb capacity. Add 0.65 cfm for each additional 1000-lb capacity. Courtesy of the DeVilbiss Company.

TABLE 5-2 COMPRESSOR CAPACITY

Compressor pressure per square inch		(A) Average service station or garage use: free air consumption of total equipment[a] (cfm)	(B) Continuous operation: free air consumption of total equipment[b] (cfm)	Compressor[c] (hp)
Cut in	Cut out			
80	100	Up to 6.6	Up to 1.9	$\frac{1}{2}$
		6.7–10.5	2.0–3.0	$\frac{3}{4}$
		10.6–13.6	3.1–3.9	1
		13.7–20.3	4.0–5.8	$1\frac{1}{2}$
		20.4–26.6	5.9–7.6	2
		30.5–46.2	8.8–13.2	3
100	125	46.3–60.0	13.3–20.0	5
		60.1–73.0	20.1–29.2	$7\frac{1}{2}$
		73.1–100.0	29.3–40.0	10
		100.1–125.0	40.1–50.0	15
120	150	Up to 3.8	Up to 1.1	$\frac{1}{2}$
		3.9–7.3	1.2–2.1	$\frac{3}{4}$
		7.4–10.1	2.2–2.9	1
		10.2–15.0	3.0–4.3	$1\frac{1}{2}$
		15.1–20.00	4.4–5.7	2
140	175	Up to 11.9	Up to 3.4	1
		12.0–18.5	3.5–5.3	$1\frac{1}{2}$
		18.6–24.2	5.4–6.9	2
		24.3–36.4	7.0–10.4	3
		36.5–51.0	10.5–17.0	5
		51.1–66.0	17.1–26.4	$7\frac{1}{2}$
		66.1–88.2	26.5–35.3	10
		88.3–120.0	35.4–48.0	15

Courtesy of the DeVilbiss Company

[a]These figures are not to be regarded as the capacity of the compressor in free air output, but instead, are the combined free air consumption of all the tools in the shop, as well as tools anticipated for future added equipment. A factor has been introduced to take into account intermittent operation of tools likely to be in use simultaneously in the average shop or service station.

[b]These figures are to be employed when the nature of the device is such that normal operation requires a continuous supply of compressed air. Therefore, no factor for intermittent operation has been used, and the figures given represent the compressor capacity in free air output.

[c]Do not use a compressor of less than 1½ hp if the pneumatic equipment includes a lift of 8000-lb capacity.

5. Within this range, locate the total air consumption of all tools.

6. Follow the line across to the recommended compressor horsepower for the air volume required.

Keeping compressors operating as cool as possible is very important to compressor efficiency. Selecting the right size of compressor to run intermittently throughout the day will achieve this.

OSHA Regulation Regarding Air Compressors

"Where running compressor belts are exposed, and within 42 inches of the floor, the belts shall be fully enclosed by appropriate belt guards."

Totally enclosed belt guards are furnished on all new Binks and DeVilbiss air compressors. Guards are also available to convert most older-model compressors to meet new safety specifications.

Installation (Fig. 5-14)

Compressors should be installed as follows:

1. Install the compressor in a cool, clean area with plenty of access for maintenance.
2. If floor mounted, be sure the compressor is level, with all four feet resting firmly on a solid floor or foundation.

Automatic Pressure Switch

An automatic pressure switch is an air-operated electric switch for starting and stopping electric motors at predetermined minimum and maximum pressures. Switches with various cut-in and cut-out pressures are available for different requirements. They are used

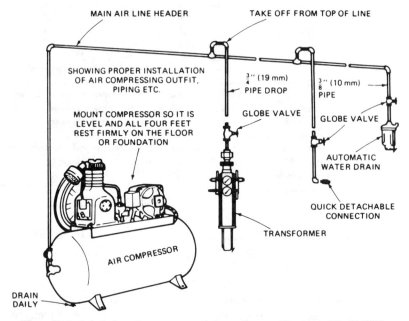

Figure 5-14 Installation of compressor and air transformer. (Courtesy of the DeVilbiss Company)

when it is convenient and economical to start and stop the motor. Any outfit that runs intermittently and less than 60% of the time is best controlled with a pressure switch.

Maintenance

A compressor crankcase should be filled with a good grade of oil to the proper level, SAE No. 10 for ordinary conditions and SAE 20 for temperatures above 100°F. The oil should be changed every 2 to 3 months and the level should be checked every week. The bearings on the electric motor should be oiled weekly unless they are life-lubricated bearings.

The belt should be checked for proper tension and alignment so that the proper power transmission is achieved. All dust should be blown away from the cooling fins, including the intercooler and aftercooler. The air intake strainer should be cleaned once a week. The safety valve handle on the tank should be lifted at least once a week to check if it is functioning properly. The flywheel should be checked for tightness on the crankshaft. The tank should be drained of moisture every day, especially in high-humidity areas (Fig. 5-14).

A compressor, if properly cared for, will last a long time. But if trouble develops, consult the manufacturer's manual supplied to the purchaser.

COMPRESSED AIR CLEANER AND REGULATOR (TRANSFORMER)

To do top-quality paint repair work, painters need a supply of compressed air that is clean and regulated. That is the purpose of an air cleaner and regulating device. De-Vilbiss calls their device that does these operations an **air transformer;** Binks calls their device an **extractor/regulator.**

There are many types of this equipment on the market. It is up to the management of each paint shop to become properly equipped. If heavy amounts of moisture and/or oil are passed through the lines to the spray gun during spray painting, the result is trouble for the painter or a poor-quality final paint finish. This problem is covered in Chapter 17. For purposes of this book, the author refers to the device as an air transformer.

Installation (Fig. 5-14)

The best location for an air transformer in a spray booth is at the side or at the center of the spray booth. Figure 5-14 shows how a typical transformer is installed. Transformers are usually hooked up off the main line at least 25 feet from the compressor. Notice that the takeoff line for the transformer goes up first; then the line is routed down to the transformer. The purpose of this design is to control any water that may be in the main line. From the point of transformer takeoff, the main line slopes downward toward the compressor. Also, from the transformer takeoff, the main line slopes downward to the rear. The reason for this is to control water in the line. Water should be drained at the transformer, at the rear drain, and at the compressor periodically. When highly humid air is compressed for long periods of time, a good amount of water collects in the lines as a result of condensation. If not removed, this water could be squirted right out of the air line. This is no way to do paint work.

The air transformer should be bolted securely to the spray booth wall or similar sturdy object near the painter for convenience in reading the gauges and operating the valves. Use piping of sufficient size for the volume of air passed and the length of pipe used (see Table 5-3). The pipes must always be of the recommended size or larger. Otherwise, excessive pressure drop will occur.

TABLE 5-3 MINIMUM PIPE SIZE RECOMMENDATIONS

Compressing outfit		Main air line	
Size (hp)	Capacity (cfm)	Length (ft)	Size (in.)
$1\frac{1}{2}$ and 2	6–9	Over 50	$\frac{3}{4}$
3 and 5	12–20	Up to 200	$\frac{3}{4}$
		Over 200	1
5–10	20–40	Up to 100	$\frac{3}{4}$
		Over 100 to 200	1
		Over 200	$1\frac{1}{4}$
10–15	40–60	Up to 100	1
		Over 100 to 200	$1\frac{1}{4}$
		Over 200	$1\frac{1}{2}$

Courtesy of the DeVilbiss Company.

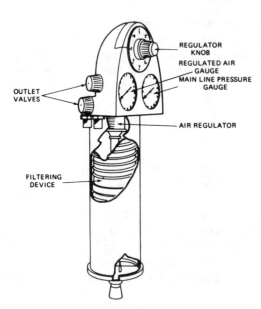

REGULATOR KNOB
REGULATED AIR GAUGE
MAIN LINE PRESSURE GAUGE
OUTLET VALVES
AIR REGULATOR
FILTERING DEVICE

Figure 5-15 Description of air transformer. (Courtesy of the DeVilbiss Company)

Functions (Fig. 5-15)

A typical good transformer does the following things for the painter:

1. Condensers and filters remove water, dirt, and oil.
2. The regulator knob operates regulated air line.
3. The regulated air gauge tells the painter the setting for proper air pressure.
4. The main line air gauge tells the painter the amount of pressure in the main air line.
5. Regulated air outlets are provided for attaching the spray gun hose.
6. Main line air outlets are provided for operating the air tools.
7. The drain valve allows the painter to drain the transformer.

HOSE CONSTRUCTION (Fig. 5-16)

Two basic types of hoses are used in the automotive refinishing trade: **air hose** and **fluid hose**. Hoses are made up of four basic components, depending on design. Three of the components shown in Fig. 5-16 are vulcanized together, then connections are added. Typical hose construction is as follows:

1. **Tube:** This is the inner part of the hose and is carefully selected to resist solvent action (fluid hoses), pressure, and temperature.
2. **Carcass:** This section is made up of one or more layers of strong (high-tensile-strength) fabric braid that is bonded to the tube and jacket. The carcass must provide satisfactory high work pressures and maximum flexibility.
3. **Jacket:** This is the protective outer cover of the hose. It is chosen to resist damage from abrasion and water, contact with oils and chemicals, and general exposure.

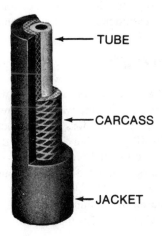

← TUBE

← CARCASS

← JACKET

Figure 5-16 Typical refinishing hose construction. (Courtesy of Binks Manufacturing Company)

Air Hose

Air hoses are made up as follows:

1. **Tube:** nitrile rubber (Buna-N)
2. **Carcass:** high-tensile-strength rayon braid reinforcement
3. **Jacket:** neoprene or natural rubber, smooth, red
4. *Connections:* reusable; plated brass

Air hoses are used in suction- and pressure-feed paint systems. Air hoses are designed to be resistant to internal and external oil contamination. The most commonly used air hose for a large spray gun is $\frac{5}{16}$ inch in diameter. The most popular length of air hose used in refinishing is between 25 and 50 feet. Hoses over 50 feet long are not recommended for suction-feed spray painting. Hoses for air brush painting are usually $\frac{1}{4}$ inch in inside diameter and 12 feet or less in length. These hoses are usually covered with black/orange or black/yellow braid.

Fluid Hose

Fluid hoses are solvent-resistant for acrylic lacquers, enamels, water-base paints, and a wide variety of liquid chemicals. They can be used as air and water lines. Fluid hoses are made up as follows:

1. **Tube:** nylon
2. **Carcass:** high-tensile-strength rayon braid reinforcement
3. **Jacket:** neoprene rubber, smooth, black
4. **Connections:** reusable; plated brass

Fluid hoses are used primarily with pressure-feed paint systems. Pressure hoses are used in many lengths, depending on need. The 2-quart pressure remote cup uses a short length of hose. Pressure hoses 25 to 50 feet in length are common in high-volume paint shops. The most commonly used pressure hoses are $\frac{3}{8}$ and $\frac{5}{16}$ inch in inside diameter.

Pressure Drop (Fig. 5-17)

Pressure drop is the loss of air pressure in the hose between the air transformer and the spray gun. The regulated air gauge on the wall may show 46 psi at the transformer but, because there is a 6-pound air pressure loss in a 25-foot hose, the actual delivered air pressure at the spray gun is 40 psi. Table 5-4 shows the amount of pressure drop for varying lengths of hose. The estimated pressures shown in Table 5-4 already have the correct amount of pressure drop subtracted for the various lengths of hose. This is a help to the painter.

    Pressure drops are caused by friction between the flowing air and the walls of the hose, constricted fittings, and the passages the air travels through. The smaller the inside

Figure 5-17 Checking drop of air pressure between air regulator and spray gun (see Table 5-4). (Courtesy of the DuPont Company)

TABLE 5-4 ESTIMATED AIR PRESSURES AT THE GUN

Hose diameter (in.)	Pressure reading at the transformer (lb)	Pressure at the gun for various hose lengths[a] (ft)					
		5	10	15	20	25	50
$\frac{5}{16}$-Inch hose	30	29	$28\frac{1}{2}$	28	$27\frac{1}{2}$	27	23
	40	38	37	37	37	36	32
	50	47	48	46	46	45	40
	60	57	56	55	55	54	49
	70	66	65	64	63	63	57
	80	75	74	73	72	71	66
	90	84	83	82	81	80	74
$\frac{1}{4}$-Inch hose	30	26	24	23	22	21	9
	40	34	32	31	29	27	16
	50	43	40	38	36	34	22
	60	51	48	46	43	41	29
	70	59	56	53	51	48	36
	80	68	64	61	58	55	43
	90	76	71	68	65	61	51

Courtesy of the Du Pont Company.
[a]Snap hose connectors will further reduce the pressure that reaches the gun by 1 lb. Pressures given are approximate and only apply to new hoses.

Hose Construction

diameter of a hose and the longer the hose, the greater is the pressure drop. The painter must understand the following about pressure drop:

1. That pressure drop exists.
2. That is has an effect on the quality of paint repair work.
3. How to determine correct atomization air pressure at the gun.

Table 5-4 shows how pressure drops for $\frac{1}{4}$- and $\frac{5}{16}$-inch hoses of varying lengths. As illustrated in Fig. 5-17, the difference between the regulated air pressure at the source and at the gun is determined by the size and the length of the air hose.

Hose Care and Maintenance

1. The hose should never be subjected to any form of abuse, and it should always receive reasonable care.
2. The hose should never be dragged over sharp objects, tools, car parts, or abrasive surfaces.
3. Care should be taken never to inflict severe ''end pull,'' for which the hose and coupling were not designed.
4. The hose should always be used at or below its working pressure. Changes in pressure should be made gradually without subjecting the hose to excessive surge pressures.
5. The hose should never be kinked severely, purposely or accidentally.
6. The hose should never be run over by a car or heavy equipment.
7. If the hose is accidentally smeared with body fillers, paint materials, or grease, it should be cleaned up as soon as practicable.
8. At the end of each day, the hose should be rolled up in a 2- or 3-foot loop and hung on a designated hose hanger.

OSHA Regulation Regarding Pressure Hoses

''All pressure hose and couplings shall be inspected at regular intervals appropriate to this service. The hose and couplings shall be tested with the hose extended, and using the in-service maximum operating pressures. Any hose showing material deteriorations, signs of leakage, or weakness in its carcass or at the couplings, shall be withdrawn from service and repaired or discarded.'' Air and fluid hoses are classified as ''pressure hoses.''

SPRAY BOOTHS

The spray booths of leading paint equipment suppliers are engineered and installed to conform to the safety regulations of OSHA and NFPA (National Fire Protection Association) and to local code requirements. After installation, compliance with all requirements becomes the responsibility of the spray booth owner.

Turning out a paint job that meets the top standards of the trade is not always easy in spite of a good painter, a good spray gun, and the best paint materials available. The right kind of paint spray booth is often the difference between a second-rate paint job and the gleaming paint finish that car owners have come to expect.

There is no question that a very common problem in automotive refinishing is control of dirt in paint. There is no better solution to the problem than to do paint work in a top-quality spray booth.

The purpose of a paint spray booth is:

1. To provide the best available conditions for top-quality spray painting.
2. To provide maximum safety to the painter and paint shop.
3. To protect the painter's health by removing atomized paint particles and solvent fumes.
4. To guard against fire hazards.
5. To prevent dust and dirt from entering the booth.

Two additional bonuses an owner has with a spray booth are:

1. **Lower insurance rates:** Some states even provide a tax advantage to paint shops using a spray booth for painting.
2. **Better community relations:** Proper filtration of exhausted air minimizes air pollution in the neighborhood.

Two types of spray booths are available in the refinish trade: a dry type and a waterwash type.

1. **Dry-type spray booth:** A dry-type spray booth is a power-ventilated booth built to help spray painting by filtering all exhaust air by means of dry-type filters before exhausting the air outside the building through an exhaust system. This type of booth is the most popular in the refinish trade.
2. **Waterwash-type spray booth:** A waterwash spray booth is equipped with a water-washing system designed to minimize dust or residue entering exhaust ducts and to permit the recovery of atomized paint particles. The waterwash spray booth reduces fire hazards and is most popular in car factories and in high-volume parts painting shops. Waterwash spray booths are more costly to operate and require more space.

Before OSHA (Fig. 5-18)

Before OSHA came into being, a typical dry-type spray booth was equipped and built with the following features:

1. **Disposable paint arrestor filters:** The exhaust air from the spray booth passes through these filters. As it passes through, overspray from painting is trapped as

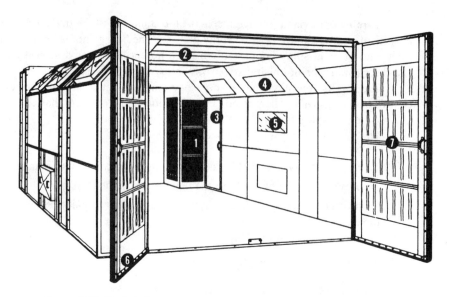

Figure 5-18 Typical dry-type paint spray booth (before OSHA was established). (Courtesy of the DeVilbiss Company)

it leaves the booth to keep the exhaust fan and stack free of paint buildup. Filters are designed for easy removal and installation.

2. **Prefabricated panels for easy, simple assembly:** All major spray booth panels have prepunched holes for quick, easy assembly. All hardware and caulking compound are used for a dust-tight seal of all panel joints:

3. **Access door:** Provides convenient access to booth without opening large doors.

4. **Effective lighting:** With top light fixtures positioned at 45° and the horizontal lights at knee level, light is concentrated where it is most needed. This system provides better lighting for vans and large, medium, and small cars.

5. **Observation window:** A window at the side provides a means of work supervision or observation from outside the booth.

6. **Filter-type entrance doors:** The doors have rubber, leakproof, wipertype seals at the bottom and center junctions. Each door has a stop and a heavy-duty latch for positive closing.

7. **Intake filters:** Filters are centered on the doors. When operating, the exhaust air becomes concentrated over the form of the car for more efficient overspray removal. Special filters are a self-sealing type with soft, pliable, plastic fibers coated with a special adhesive for efficient dust trapping.

After OSHA (Fig. 5-19)

Since OSHA came into being, spray booths have been and are being built for compliance with the following construction features added as mandatory safety regulations (see Fig. 5-19 for items 1 to 10):

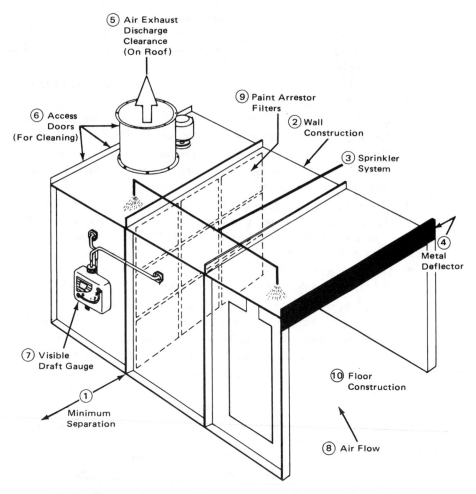

Figure 5-19 Dry-type paint spray booth, including OSHA mandatory requirements. (Compiled by Binks Manufacturing Company)

1. **Minimum separation:** "There shall be **no open flame or spark-producing equipment** in any spraying area nor **within 20 feet thereof,** unless separated by a partition."

2. **Construction:** "**Spray booths** shall be substantially constructed of **steel not thinner than No. 18 U.S. gauge,** securely and rigidly supported, or of concrete or masonry construction."

3. **Fire protection:** "**Space within the spray booth** on the **downstream and upstream** sides of filters **shall be protected with approved automatic sprinklers.**"

4. **Frontal area:** "Each spray booth having a frontal area larger than 9 square feet **shall have a metal deflector or curtain not less than $2\frac{1}{2}$ inches deep** installed at the upper outer edge of the booth over the opening."

5. **Discharge clearance:** "Unless the spray booth exhaust duct terminal is from a

waterwash spray booth, the terminal discharge point shall be not less than 6 feet from any combustible exterior wall or roof nor discharge in the direction of any combustible construction or unprotected opening in any noncombustible exterior wall within 25 feet.''

6. **Access doors:** "When necessary to facilitate cleaning, exhaust ducts shall be provided with an ample number of access doors.''

7. **Air velocity:** "Visible draft gauges or audible alarm or pressure-activated devices shall be installed to indicate or insure that the required air velocity is maintained.''

8. **Air flow:** "The average air velocity over the open face of the booth (or booth cross section during spraying operations) shall be **not less than 100 linear feet per minute** as indicated on visible draft gauge.''

9. **Arrestor (filter) bank:** "All discarded filter pads and filter rolls shall be immediately removed to a safe, well-detached location or placed in a water-filled metal container and disposed of at the close of the day's operation unless maintained completely in water.''

10. **Floor surface:** "The floor surface of a spray booth and operator's working area, if combustible, shall be covered with noncombustible material.''

11. **Electrical wiring:** "All electrical wiring and equipment shall conform to OSHA regulations, which, in turn, are in agreement with the National Electrical Code.''

12. **Air replacement:** "Clean fresh air . . . shall be supplied to a spray booth or room in quantities equal to the volume of air exhausted through the spray booth.''

13. **Heating make-up air:** "Means for heating make-up air to any spray booth . . . shall be provided in all places where the outdoor temperature may be expected to remain below 55°F for appreciable periods of time . . . .''

14. **Air replacement alternative:** "As an alternative to an air replacement system complying with the preceding section, general heating of the building . . . may be employed provided that all occupied parts of the building are maintained at not less than 65°F when the exhaust system is in operation. . . .''

15. **Cleaning:** Spray booths shall be so installed that all portions are readily accessible for cleaning. A clear space of not less than 3 feet on all sides shall be kept free from storage or combustible construction.''

16. **Portable lamps:** "Portable electric lamps shall not be used in any spraying area during spraying operations.''

Operation of Exhaust-type Filters

Filter booths provide a mechanical means of filtering air by passing it through a dry-type filter. This filter also serves as a means of distributing the air flow uniformly through a spray booth. As the filter removes the solids, it gradually builds up a restriction to the flow of air, requiring replacement of the affected filter(s). An air pressure differential gauge (manometer, Fig. 5-19, item 7) is used as the filter arrestor bank to indicate when filters should be replaced.

A manometer is installed as follows:

1. As shown in Fig. 5-19, one tube is installed on the intake side of the arrestor bank.
2. A second tube is installed on the exhaust side of the arrestor bank.
3. The manometer is installed outside the spray booth as shown in Fig. 5-19. The pilot tubes indicate a pressure differential (drop) across the arrestor bank. When a new filter has been installed, a reading should be taken and noted. Filters require replacement when a 0.25-inch increase is indicated on the manometer.

Some states require that a pressure differential switch be installed to cut off the air to the spray guns in the spray booth whenever the air velocity drops below a certain point. The pressure drop is generally measured in inches of rise in a column of water.

Replacement of Paint Arrestor-type Filters (Courtesy of Binks Manufacturing Company)

Paint arrestor filters are made of a fire-retardant-treated paper. They are formed into a honeycomb configuration. The filtering action is accomplished by the rapid back-and-forth movement of air as it passes through the filter. A centrifugal force throws the solids against the treated paper, where they stick. As a filter loads up with paint particles, the air movement through the spray booth diminishes. A $\frac{1}{2}$-inch (total) rise in a column of water on a Binks manometer indicates that the filters require replacement.

Two paper filters are placed in each filter frame at the back of the spray booth. The number of frames in any spray booth is determined by the size of the filter bank. The two most common sizes of filters used are 1 by 20 by 20 inches and 1 by 20 by 25 inches. They are held in place by a press-fitted wire grid. Additional sizes are available on request.

When replacing filters, the outer, dirty filter that traps most of the paint is removed and disposed of in the manner prescribed. The inner filter is also removed but is not discarded. A new filter is then placed in the filter frame and the old inner filter is placed "over" the new filter. Using this procedure cuts down on filter replacement costs.

Why Air Replacement? (Courtesy of the DeVilbiss Company)

Depending on the size of the paint spray booth and specific federal and local code requirements, an automotive spray booth will generally exhaust from 9000 to 12,000 cubic feet of air per minute. There is no practical way of reusing the same air since it is filled with volatile fumes and must be exhausted. OSHA regulations state that the air expelled from a spray booth must be replaced. Furthermore, the replacement air must be heated whenever the outside temperature remains below 55°F for appreciable periods of time and the general building heating system is not capable of maintaining 65°F in all parts of the building area whenever the booth exhaust is in operation.

Primary Solution (Fig. 5-20). The ideal solution to the problem is an air replace-

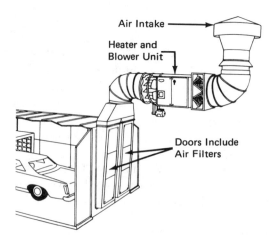

Air Intake

Heater and
Blower Unit

Doors Include
Air Filters

Figure 5-20 Paint spray booth air replacement unit. (Courtesy of the DeVilbiss Company)

ment unit that takes in fresh air from the outside, filters it, and, if necessary, heats and dries the air. The replacement air is then delivered either into the spray booth or into the general shop area. The unit operates only when the spray booth fan is on and heats the air only when required.

Alternative Solution. If the heating plant for the entire shop is large enough to replenish the heat loss within the shop area when the booth exhaust fan is operating, the paint shop owner may or may not want to select an air replacement package assembly. However, if the owner chooses the alternate solution, care should be taken to provide a means for having adequate air enter the building without strong drafts.

Suggestions for Updating Spray Booths

1. With regard to sprinklers, it is suggested that federal and local authorities as well as fire insurance underwriters be contacted to determine the fire protection system needed for compliance.
2. When a spray booth electrical wiring system needs updating to OSHA regulations, it is best to have the electrical wiring inspected and updated by a licensed electrician who is familiar with the National Electrical Code.
3. In cases where the floor of the spray booth is combustible, the easiest way to comply with this OSHA regulation is to install sheet metal or other suitable, noncombustible material to the spray booth floor.

Spray Booth Maintenance

1. Sweep the spray booth floor before the start of any paint job. Also, wet down the spray booth floor to minimize the dust problem.
2. Keep the spray booth free from haphazard storage of boxes, junk, miscellaneous parts, water buckets, trash cans, brooms, and dust pans.

3. Change the spray booth intake and exhaust filters periodically as required.

4. Check and repair all door seals to ensure that they provide good dust seals for the booth.

5. Clean the glass panels over the lamps periodically for better illumination.

6. Wash down the spray booth walls periodically to remove excess dust accumulation.

DRYING EQUIPMENT

Drying equipment is very important to the success of a paint shop. After cars are painted, the next objective is to help speed the drying of the paint finishes. The success of any paint shop is determined by the type and amount of drying equipment on hand. Basically, three types of drying are used in the refinishing trade.

1. *Air drying:* Temperature range from 60° to 100°F. In this process cars are usually left where they are painted until they are dry enough to be moved. All refinish materials are designed to air-dry in a reasonable period of time.

2. *Force drying:* Temperature range from 100° to 180°F. Infrared drying equipment is best suited for the refinish trade. Force drying reduces drying time from 1 day to 30 or 45 minutes. Infrared drying equipment provides ideal drying conditions for the paint repair trade. Infrared drying equipment is available in various sizes to fit any equipment need:

   a. Very small, one or two bulb units on an adjustable stand are ideal for small spot repairs.

   b. Medium-size units with four bulbs on portable and adjustable stands are ideal for panel repairs.

   c. Multibanked units (24, 36, or more bulbs) are ideal for a complete side of a car (Fig. 5-21).

   d. Traveling units (Fig. 5-22) that travel automatically back and forth on tracks are adjustable for small and large cars and for vans. Traveling heat units are designed to do 4 to 8 cars per 8-hour shift provided that the shop has the space for the complete installation.

3. **Oven baking:** Temperature range: 200°F and higher. Baking, in the true sense of the word, is not too common in the refinish trade. However, equipment for gas-fired ovens is available. Gas-fired ovens are highly restricted in most localities of the country. Usually, these ovens are limited to 140°F approximately.

   Baking complete cars at 200°F and higher is not too practicable in the refinish trade because:

   a. The gasoline in cars can cause fires and/or explosion.

   b. Plastic parts will melt and deform.

   c. The ''safety plate'' windshield glass used in American cars is very apt to break at these temperatures.

Figure 5-21 Multibanked infrared force-dry unit. (Courtesy of the DeVilbiss Company)

Figure 5-22 U-shaped infrared traveling unit. (Courtesy of the DeVilbiss Company)

True oven baking is designed for factory use before final assembly where there is no danger of fire or parts damage.

One might ask: What is an infrared heat unit, and how does it work? The answer is as follows:

1. Infrared heat lamps radiate or transfer energy in the form of heat waves which travel in a straight line.
2. The heat waves are invisible to the human eye.
3. The heat waves go from the lamp right through the paint finish and contact the metal or plastic substrate.
4. The substrate becomes hotter as it absorbs greater amounts of infrared heat waves.
5. The hot substrate drives the solvents from the paint finish and lacquers. At this point the paint is essentially dry (but hot). In enamels, after initial solvent evaporation, a further chemical change takes place (polymerization) and the enamel dries and hardens. In urethane finishes, there is less solvent evaporation, the chemical change takes place faster than in enamels, and the paint dries and is hot.
6. Thus, under infrared lamps, paint dries from the inside out, or from the substrate to the outer paint surface.

For best results in using infrared heat units, follow the manufacturer's directions and maintenance instructions. Every modernly equipped shop has a drying area where force drying is done.

Use of an infrared heat lamp involves a certain number of safety precautions. One of these precautions is that the area should be properly ventilated. A spray booth could be used for drying purposes if it is not needed at the time for spray painting.

Painters should know what specific temperatures work best for each specific paint job. A painter can determine how hot any given paint surface gets when positioning a heat lamp at the surface by employing the following procedure:

1. Secure a **candy-type** thermometer from a kitchenware store, department store, or instrument equipment firm.
2. Remove the thermometer from the container and secure it to a dry section of the car paint finish with a piece of masking tape.
3. Position the heat lamp 18 to 20 inches from the car panel with the heat lamp parallel to the car panel. The thermometer should be centered under the heat lamp.
4. Turn on the heat lamp and let it heat the surface for 7 to 10 minutes.
5. Check the temperature on the thermometer, which should be resting flush against the car panel. The heat lamp should never allow the thermometer to hit or go over 180°F. If the temperature goes over 180°F, move the heat lamp away from the panel the required distance and recheck the temperature. A good safety factor is 150° to 170°F. It is much better to know the proper distance rather than to guess at it.

OSHA Regulations Regarding Drying (General)

1. "Freshly spray articles only in spaces provided with adequate ventilation to prevent the formation of explosive vapors. In the event adequate and reliable ventilation is not provided, such drying spaces shall be considered a spraying area."
2. "Automobile refinishing spray booths or enclosures, otherwise installed and maintained in full conformity with this section, may alternately be used for drying with portable electric drying apparatus when conforming with the following:
   a. "Interior (especially floors) of spray enclosures shall be kept free of overspray deposits."
   b. "During spray operations, the drying apparatus and electrical connections . . . shall not be located within spray enclosure nor in any other location, where spray residues may be deposited thereon."
   c. "The spraying apparatus, the drying apparatus, and the ventilating system of the spray enclosure shall be equipped with suitable interlocks so arranged that:
      (1) "The spraying apparatus cannot be operated while the drying apparatus is inside the spray enclosure."
      (2) "The spray enclosure will be purged of spray vapors for a period of not less than 3 minutes before the drying apparatus can be energized."
      (3) "The ventilating system will maintain a safe atmosphere within the enclosure during the drying process and the drying apparatus will automatically shut off in the event of failure of the ventilating system."

OSHA Regulations Regarding Drying (Infrared)

1. "All electrical wiring and equipment of the drying apparatus shall conform with the applicable sections of Subpart S of this Part (National Electrical Code). Only equipment of a type approved for Class I, Division 2 hazardous locations shall be located within 18 inches of floor level. All metallic parts of the drying apparatus shall be properly electrically bonded and grounded."
2. "The drying apparatus shall contain a prominently located, permanently attached warning sign indicating that ventilation should be maintained during the drying period and that spraying should not be conducted in the vicinity that spray will deposit on apparatus."

REVIEW QUESTIONS

1. What is the purpose of OSHA?
2. What is the purpose of NIOSH?
3. In what five areas should all painters be instructed regarding respirators?
4. Name three types of respirators needed by a painter to do all-around automotive refinishing.

5. Describe the general spray painting respirator.

6. Describe an air-supplied mask or hood respirator.

7. At what maximum air pressure do NIOSH-approved dusting guns operate?

8. What is compressed air?

9. What are two of the most popular types of air compressor?

10. When are two-stage air compressors required?

11. What is an automatic pressure switch?

12. How often should a compressor be drained of moisture collection?

13. What is the purpose of an air cleaner and an air regulator?

14. What is the inside diameter of the commonly used air hose for spray painting?

15. What is the typical average length of hose in a paint shop?
    (a) Minimum
    (b) Maximum

16. What is pressure drop?

17. At what pressure should the painter set the air regulator (on wall) to be assured that the spray gun at the end of the hose has the correct air pressure setting?

18. What is the meaning of **psi**?

19. What is the purpose of a paint spray booth?

20. What two additional bonuses does a paint shop owner have when using a paint spray booth?

21. What is a commonsense procedure for replacing arrestor-type exhaust filters in a paint spray booth?

22. What is an air replacement package assembly for a paint spray booth, and how does it work?

23. What is the procedure for cleaning up and preparing a paint spray booth before spraying enamel paint jobs?

24. What is the highest temperature that could be used safely on cars when force drying in a paint shop?

25. Since OSHA came into being, describe several paint spray booth construction features and safety regulations that must be incorporated or observed.

6

Surface Preparation

INTRODUCTION

Automotive refinishing, like any type of high-quality paint work, requires that a surface be properly prepared before repair painting or finishing can be done. Surface preparation consists of many forms and types of repairs, ranging from simple cleaning and/or compounding of a surface to complete removal and rebuilding of a paint finish. Paint repairs range from small brush touch-up and small spot repairs to large panel repairs and complete refinishing. In this range lie many thousands of paint repair categories. Most of these categories are summarized and presented in Chapter 17.

Considering the refinishing materials and repair methods available, for every **paint condition,** that is, every automotive paint problem, there is a specific way that each problem surface should be prepared before high-quality painting can be done. For example, take the case of a rust spot on a panel. All rust must be removed completely, and the metal must be conditioned properly if a paint repair is to be guaranteeable. Every paint repair should be done with the intent that it is guaranteed consistent with the price paid for the work.

CAR WASHING

After a repair order is written up and before the car is brought into the paint shop for repairs, the first operation, generally, is a car wash. Every paint shop should have a car wash stall equipped with the following minimum equipment:

1. Cement or equivalent floor with adequate water drainage.
2. Adequate lighting and water supply.
3. Suitably long hose with "squeeze-handle" nozzle, which shuts off the water when the handle is released. These are available in hardware and department stores.
4. Water buckets, suitable sponges, a chamois, car wash detergent, window cleaning solvent, cloth towels, and paper towels.
5. Air line, air hose, dusting gun, safety goggles and/or face shield, rubber boots, and waterproof apron.

The price of a car wash should be included in the cost of the paint job. The inside and outside of the car should be cleaned as required. Having an owner take home a car with a high-quality paint finish that is clean outside and inside builds good customer relations.

Procedure: Indoors

1. Remove the floor mats (wash these separately, rinse, and hang up to dry). Empty and reinstall ashtrays and litter bag or bucket. Vacuum the floors, seats, and trim, as required.
2. Close all the windows tightly and close the doors.
3. Soak or wet down the entire car before starting the washing operation. This reduces the possibility of scratching the car finish.
4. Prepare the car wash detergent (according to label directions) or prepare a bucket of water with half a cup of laundry soap. Using a suitable soft sponge, wash the car in 2 by 2 foot sections progressively around the car in the following sequence:
   a. Roof and windshield
   b. Hood
   c. Front end grille, headlamps, parking lamps, and bumper
   d. One side of car, including side glass
   e. Rear deck, including back window, rear lid, tail lamps, and rear bumper
   f. Opposite side of car, including side glass
   g. Wheels
   Wheels are always done last to minimize scratching the car finish.
5. Rinse the car thoroughly, following the sequence of step 4. Work water back and forth to distribute the water equally in each area (steps 4a through 4g) until no soap suds or bubbles are evident.
6. With safety goggles or face shield in place, use compressed air and blow off the car in the same sequence as in rinsing. Use a handy clean towel to wipe off any splatters.

   NOTE: If compressed air is not available, use a chamois to wipe off the car as follows:
   a. Soak the chamois in clear water until it is saturated.

b. Then fold the chamois in half several times and wring out the chamois thoroughly with one continuous effort. The chamois is wrung out when a continuous run of water changes to droplets.

c. Unfold the chamois and fold it in half several times until it is a suitable wiping pad.

d. With the pad, wipe off all remaining water from the car surface working a 2 by 2 foot area at a time and following the sequence of step 4.

CAUTION: Never wipe a car surface with a chamois right after wiping the wheels or wheel openings, as severe scratching could result. Soak and rinse the chamois in clean clear water to remove all sand and dirt before wiping the car.

7. Wash each car window, first outside and then inside, with a water-dampened cloth and an application of ammoniated window solvent. Wipe each window dry with a clean cloth.

8. Wash the hinge and lock pillars of the door and body, and wash the rocker panel on each side of the car with a sponge soaked and rinsed in soapy water. Use care not to contact the door lock and/or lock pillar striker to prevent smearing with dirty oil or grease. If necessary, follow this operation by wiping all pillars and similar surfaces with a sponge soaked and rung out in clear water.

Procedure: Outdoors

CAUTION: Never wash a car on a hot day in the direct rays of the sun if the temperature is over 85°F. This is especially true between 10 A.M. and 3 P.M., when the sun is the hottest. Allowing soapy water to evaporate from an acrylic lacquer or an acrylic enamel in a bright sun on a very hot day could stain the paint finish. See "Water Spotting" in Chapter 17.

If washing is necessary under the conditions noted previously, wash and rinse one panel at a time as follows:

1. Use a hose without a nozzle and a controlled flow of water.

2. Soak the panel to be washed with plain water.

3. Wash the panel with soapy water, restricting water as much as possible to the panel being washed.

4. Rinse the panel immediately with clear water.

5. Wipe the panel and all wet surfaces on the sunny side of the car with a chamois to remove the water before it evaporates in the sun. A helper may be needed for this operation.

MATERIALS NEEDED FOR SURFACE PREPARATION

Paint Finish Cleaning Solvent (Table 6-1)

The purpose of a paint finish cleaning solvent is to dissolve and remove road oils, road tars, grease, pollution contaminants, wax and silicon polishes, rubbing compound oils, and fingerprints. If not removed, these contaminants could affect the adhesion or appearance of the repair finish. All cleaning solvents are not compatible with all finishes. Follow factory recommendations.

Procedure for General Cleaning

1. Using a clean white cloth, apply paint finish cleaning solvent freely to the painted surface work area and adjacent surfaces.
2. Clean the surface up to 2 square feet at a time with as much pressure as is required. Overlap the previously cleaned surface by 2 to 4 inches.
3. For maximum results, wipe the surface dry with clean white cloths while the surface is still wet. Change cloths frequently when doing large areas or a complete car.

Procedure for Removing Silicones

1. Using a clean white cloth, apply cleaning solvent freely to the painted surface, wash as required, and wipe dry with a clean white cloth.
2. Apply cleaning solvent to the surface freely with a clean white cloth and sand surface thoroughly with No. 500, No. 600 or Ultra Fine sandpaper.
3. Reclean surface with solvent and then wipe dry with a clean white cloth. **Caution:** Do not rewipe the surface with **used** or **contaminated** cloths.

CAUTION: Never clean the surface of a plastic-filled repair with paint finish cleaning solvent. Plastic fillers absorb and retain solvents, which later results in blistering.

Cleaning solvents should always be used before and after sanding operations.

TABLE 6-1 PAINT FINISH CLEANING SOLVENTS (BY TRADE NAME)

Paint supplier	Trade name	Stock number
DuPont	Prep-Sol	3919-S
	Prep-Sol II	3929-S
Rinshed-Mason	Pre-Kleano	900
Ditzler	Acryli-Clean	DX-330
Sherwin-Williams	Sher-Wil-Clean	R7K156
Martin-Senour	Kleans-Easy	6383
	Fin-L-Wash	6387

CAUTION: Before using a cleaning solvent on acrylic finishes, read the label instructions. Some cleaning solvents are not safe for use on all acrylic finishes. Be sure that the label instructions say specifically: "Designed for safe use on acrylic finishes." The solvents listed in Table 6-1 are the best available for acrylic finishes. Cleaning solvents that are incompatible with acrylic finishes should be so labeled.

General Maintenance Cleaning Solvent

To save money, every shop should have a plentiful supply of mineral spirits, sometimes called oleum spirits, which is much like kerosene. Mineral spirits makes an excellent maintenance and cleanup solvent around the shop. It is an excellent solvent for removing tar, grease, smeared motor oil, and smeared anticorrosion compounds from all car surfaces. It serves as a good hand-washing solvent for mechanics. This solvent should not be used for cleaning a car surface just before painting as it leaves an oily film after evaporation or wipe-off. If used before the painting operation, the surface must be cleaned with a paint finish cleaning solvent, discussed earlier.

Mineral spirits can be used as the lubricant in oil sanding. This is discussed in Chapter 11.

The best way to use a paint finish cleaning solvent is right out of a 1-gallon container.

Metal Conditioner (Table 6-2)

Metal conditioners for refinishing are available in a two-part system:

Part I: The purpose of part I is to clean the metal of any oil, dirt, grease, fingerprints, casual corrosion, and other foreign contaminants through a process known as acid cleaning and chemical etching.

Part II: The purpose of part II is to impart a heavy chemical coating on the surface, which promotes finish adhesion and durability.

TABLE 6-2 METAL CONDITIONERS (BY PAINT SUPPLIER IDENTITY NUMBER)

Use	DuPont	Ditzler	Rinshed-Mason	Sherwin-Williams	Martin-Senour
For steel					
Part I: acid cleaner	5717-S	DX-579	801	W4K-263	6879
Part II: phosphate coating	224-S	DX-520		W4K-289	
For galvanized steel					
Part I: acid cleaner	5717-S	DX-579	801	W4K-263	6877
Part II: phosphate coating	227-S	DX-520	802		
For aluminum					
Part I: acid cleaner	225-S	DX-533	801	W4K-263	6879
Part II: phosphate coating	226-S	DX-503			

Painters encounter three types of metal when doing paint repair work:

1. **Steel:** Most exterior car panels are made of steel. (**Note:** Most front end panels are plastic.)
2. **Galvanized steel:** Most car rocker panels have been made of galvanized steel since the early 1960s.
3. **Aluminum:** Use of aluminum is increasingly being made for car panels to reduce overall weight. Early major uses were in hoods and rear compartment lids.

To determine if metal is aluminum or steel, use a magnet as follows:

1. If metal panel shows a magnetic pull toward a magnet, the metal is steel.
2. If panel shows no magnetic pull, the panel is aluminum or plastic.

NOTE: This test does not include Corvette and other cars that are made mostly of plastic exterior panels.

The two-part metal conditioning system provides the best-known methods of conditioning metal in the refinish trade. The methods closely resemble the metal treating process used in car factories. The metal conditioning, priming, and color coating must be used together properly to provide the designed paint finish durability.

Metal conditioners are acids and are made available in bottled, concentrated form. In this form, the metal conditioner is inactive. Therefore, reduction with water according to the manufacturer's directions is necessary.

Procedure for Use (Table 6-2)

Part I: Clean bare metal with prescribed metal conditioner by reducing and applying the conditioner as described on the label directions.

Part II: Treat bare metal with the second metal conditioner according to the label directions. An important part of the application is the time factor. Allow the proper amount of time for the chemical reaction to take place. Then wash the bare metal area and adjacent surfaces with a cloth and water and wipe dry. Simple application and immediate wipe-off does not do the job.

Shop Towels

In the general operation of a paint shop, three types of towels are most popular (check with paint jobber for best type available):

1. Shop towels are about 12 by 12 inches square and can be rented from a local towel supplier. The supplier picks up, launders, and delivers towels on a weekly or other arranged basis for a nominal charge. Shop towels are available in a given color, which helps to locate and control them. Clean towels should always be kept in a definite location. A special container should be provided for soiled shop towels.

2. Disposable white cheesecloth and miscellaneous white rags are available by the pound from special towel suppliers. These rags are ideal for any general purpose, after which they can be thrown away.

3. Disposable paper towels of industrial weight are very popular in paint shops for equipment and general cleanup operations. These towels are available in many forms; the most popular are 12 by 12 inch folded sheets or 12-inch rolls. These towels are available through paint jobbers.

Tack Rags

Tack rags, also called tack cloths, are made of cheesecloth treated with a nondrying, nonsmearing, sticky varnish. They are about 12 by 12 inches in size and are available through paint jobbers. When folded, tack rags are about $4\frac{1}{2}$ by $8\frac{1}{2}$ inches in size and are convenient for hand use. Tack rags safely remove loose dirt, dust, sanding particles, and overspray from metal, plastic, or painted surfaces prior to painting. Use of an air gun in conjunction with a tack rag is an efficient and fast way of tack-wiping and cleaning a surface prior to painting. Avoid too much pressure on a fresh tack rag. This may leave an imprint of varnish on the surface.

Squeegees (Fig. 6-1)

Squeegees are made of flexible rubber and are available through paint jobbers in several sizes. The most popular size is 2 by 3 inches and is used primarily to remove slush and to check the progress of wet sanding. The $2\frac{3}{4}$ by $4\frac{1}{4}$ inch size is used popularly to apply

Figure 6-1 Small and large squeegees. (Courtesy of the 3M Company)

plastic fillers and glazing putty. However, these two squeegees are interchangeable. Also, both squeegees can be used as small sanding blocks by wrapping cut sections of wet or dry sandpaper around them.

Sanding Blocks (Fig. 6-2a and b)

The purpose of a sanding block is to spread the cutting action of sandpaper uniformly over the surface of the sanding block. This automatically eliminates highlights in work surfaces caused by finger pressure. Sanding blocks are available through paint jobbers. A sanding block is made of pliable rubber, which holds sandpaper securely during wet or dry sanding operations. The standard sheet of sandpaper is 9 by 11 inches. A sanding block can accommodate four sections of $2\frac{3}{4}$ by 9 inch strips from a single sheet of sandpaper. More than four strips of sandpaper could be used at one time.

Sponge Pads (Fig. 6-3a and b)

Small sponge rubber pads, about the size of rubber squeegees, and conventional sanding blocks are available through jobbers. Equivalent sponge pads could be made up by painters from larger sponge pads. Sponge pads used with a threefold wrap of wet or dry sandpaper provide excellent support and flexibility to make hand sanding easy. A sponge sanding pad helps spread the sanding effort uniformly on concave and convex surfaces while sanding. Avoid cut-throughs at creaselines and edges by avoiding them and/or by sanding with due care.

Sandpaper

> **WARNING:** Always think safety. **Safety,** like a work skill, improves with practice until it becomes a strong automatic **habit.** To make safety become an unconscious habit takes a certain amount of conscious, deliberate practice.

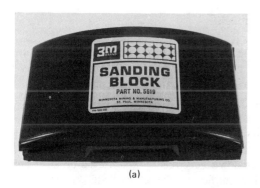

(a)

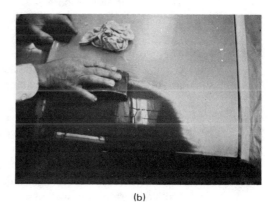

(b)

Figure 6-2 (a) Sanding block (Courtesy of the 3M Company); (b) Block sanding technique. (Courtesy of Ditzler Automotive Finishes, PPG Industries, Inc.)

(a)

(b)

Figure 6-3 (a) Sponge sanding pad (Courtesy of the 3M Company); (b) Sanding concave surfaces with sandpaper backed with a sponge pad. (Courtesy of the DuPont Company)

Before using power sanding equipment (and in some cases when dry sanding by hand):

1. Wear an approved dust respirator.
2. Wear an approved face shield or properly fitted safety goggles.

The purpose of sandpaper is to do required sanding operations on a surface before paint repairs can be made, such as:

1. To remove early stages of rust
2. To remove paint
3. To featheredge
4. To sand undercoats
5. To make surfaces smooth
6. To make a smooth surface coarse or rough

The two most popular abrasives in the refinish trade are silicon carbide and aluminum oxide. The abrasive does the actual cutting or sanding operation. Table 6-3 is a summary of abrasives used in the automotive refinishing and metal repair trades.

1. **Silicon carbide** is the sharpest abrasive known, it is black in color, and it does the best job of sanding automotive finishes. Most sandpaper used to do fine sanding of car finishes is made with silicon carbide abrasive. Although silicon carbide lasts very well on paint finishes, it breaks down very readily when used on steel and other hard metals. Silicon carbide is identified by the letters "SiC" or the name "silicon carbide" is spelled out in full on the back side of the sandpaper. The grit identification number is also shown. The most popular grit usage of silicon carbide is in the range between No. 220 and No. 1500 grit (see Table 6-3).

TABLE 6-3 COMMONLY USED ABRASIVES IN U.S. AUTOMOTIVE REFINISHING AND METAL REPAIR TRADES

General category	Sheet sandpaper: silicon carbide (closed coat)	Sheet sandpaper: aluminum oxide (closed coat)	5 to 8 inch sandpaper discs: aluminum oxide (open coat)	Portable sander discs: aluminum oxide open coat	closed coat
		Paint repair abrasives			
[a]Micro Fine	1500				
[b]Micro Fine	1200				
[c]Ultra Fine	—				
Fine	600	600			
	500	500			
Medium	400	400	400		
	360	360			
Coarse	320	320	320		
	280	280			
	240	240	240		
	220	220	220		
		Metal and plastic repair abrasives			
Fine	180	180	180		
	150	150	150		
	120	120	120		120
Medium	100	100	100		100
	80	80	80D		80
Coarse	60	60	60D	Fine	60
	50	50			50
	40	40	40D	Medium	
	36	36	36D	36	36
	30	30		Coarse	
Extra	24	24		24	24
coarse	16	16		16	16

[a]Micro Fine 1500 is used for removal of minor imperfections, like dirt, etc., in BC/CC finishes. 1500 sanding followed by light compounding produces the best scratch-free "Show Car" finish.

[b]Micro Fine 1200 is used to level orange peel and to remove minor imperfections in BC/CC finishes.

[c]Ultra Fine is used for leveling orange peel in standard acrylic lacquer topcoats. Also reduces compounding time.

2. **Aluminum oxide** is the best abrasive for metal repair because it is the hardest and most durable abrasive known. All discs for portable power sanders are made with aluminum oxide abrasive. Normally, aluminum oxide is reddish brown in color and that is how discs appear in metal repair. However, to assist in paint removal, open-coat discs are treated with a white chemical and appear white in color. Aluminum oxide abrasives are identified with the letters "AlO" or the name "alu-

Materials Needed for Surface Preparation

minum oxide'' is written out in full on the reverse side. For the grit sizes available, see Table 6-3.

Comparison of sandpaper as Used in U.S. and Europe (Table 6-4)

The grit size of U.S.-produced sandpapers is indicated by a numbering system established by the American National Standards Institute (ANSI) for the Coated Abrasives Manufacturers Institute (CAMI). The U.S. refinishing trade generally uses CAMI grit sizes ranging from 16 to 600 on most standard acrylic lacquer and enamel finishes. However, with the advent of basecoat/clearcoat finishes, an ultra fine, 1200, and 1500 grit sandpaper has been developed.

European manufacturers use a different grading system, one established by the Federation of European Producers of Abrasives (FEPA) and designated with the prefix ''P'' followed by a number. As in the U.S. CAMI grading system, the higher the number, the finer the grit.

From about CAMI 220 on down, the U.S. and European grit grades are nearly identical and interchangeable. But in finer grades the differences can be dramatic. See Table 6-4.

CAMI 240, for example, is equivalent to FEPA P280 paper, and CAMI 320 is a bit finer than FEPA P400. CAMI 400 grit paper is just a touch coarser than FEPA P800. Note that CAMI 600 is a little bit finer than FEPA P1200.

If you use imported sandpaper in your shop, consult the chart in Table 6-4 to make sure you are using the proper grit for the job at hand.

Closed Coat. Closed coat abrasives are designed so that all possible space on the sanding surface is covered with the maximum amount of abrasive. Abrasives are applied and bonded to sandpaper backing by an electrostatic process that enables the sharpest cutting edges of the abrasives to be exposed.

Open Coat. The term ''open coat'' means that the grit particles on a backing are spaced a short distance from each other, causing an open space between the grit particles. This is done by means of a screen. Additionally, the open surface and the abrasive particles are covered with a chemical treatment called zinc stearate, which is white. The chemical prevents things from sticking to it. This combination of construction makes possible the sanding of paint finishes for long periods of time without paint loading up on the disc or sandpaper.

Waterproof Sandpaper. Waterproof sandpaper, available in 9 by 11 inch sheets, is the most popular abrasive in the refinish trade. This sandpaper can be used wet with water or mineral spirits and dry for sanding old finishes, fine featheredging, and surface sanding. Waterproof sandpaper cuts fast and stays flexible. The term ''wet'' or ''dry'' means that the sandpaper can be used for wet or dry sanding.

Dry-type Sandpaper. This terminology is given to the sandpaper because it is

TABLE 6-4 COMPARISON OF U.S. AND EUROPEAN
SANDPAPER GRIT GRADES

U.S. CAMI grade	European "P" grade
Micro Fine 1500	Not available
Micro Fine 1200	Not available
Ultra Fine	Not available
600	P1200
500	P1000
400	P800
	P600
360	
320	P500
	P400
280	P360
	P320
240	P280
	P240
220	P220
180	P180
150	P150
120	P120
100	P100
80	P80
60	P60
50	P50
40	P40
36	P36
30	P30
24	P24
20	P20
16	P16
	P12
12	

Courtesy of The DuPont and 3M Companies

always used dry. To promote durability and to prevent loading, dry-type sandpaper is made with three features:

1. Aluminum oxide abrasive remains durable
2. Use of open-coat design
3. Nonloading chemical treatment (zinc stearate)

THE ART OF SANDING

Sanding operations range from sanding the color coat only to removal of the complete paint finish. How fast and efficient sanding operations are depends on the painter's ability to select the proper abrasive in the proper form to fit the needs of the repair job at hand. This is best learned through experience. Sanding is divided into two general categories: **hand** and **power sanding.** For greatest efficiency in hand and power sanding, sanding is done in two or more stages. Coarse abrasives speed up sanding in the early stages and fine abrasives finish the work.

Sanding and the Sander's Health

Sometimes a person needs to be hit over the head to gain his or her attention to the fact that safety is meant for the person's own good. Wherever there is considerable dry sanding taking place, the air in the area is filled with particles of pollutants. The pollutants are inhaled by people in the area unless they are protected with a dust respirator. Wearing a respirator is a commonsense way of protecting one's lungs. Most types of pollutants (steel, certain dusts, plastics, etc.) are inhaled into the lungs and stay there. In time, they contribute to emphysema or something similar. It sounds like a sales talk and it involves another product to buy. The question is: How valuable is a person's health? What would a person give to be able to breathe and live normally?

HAND SANDING

1. Select the proper grade of sandpaper for the work to be done (Table 6-3).
2. Cut down sandpaper to the suitable size according to one of three popular methods as follows:
   a. Reducing sheet sandpaper to "thirds" (for small-area work) (Fig. 6-4):
      (1) Mark sandpaper at two cut locations, each $3\frac{2}{3}$ inches wide.
      (2) Cut or tear paper into three equal section or strips.
      (3) Fold each strip into a threefold wrap, one third each wrap. This forms a small sanding pad of three sandpaper thicknesses. As each sanding surface is used up, the pad is turned over or repositioned to a new sanding surface. This is getting the most out of a piece of sandpaper.

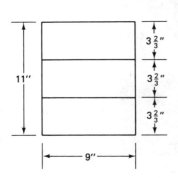

Figure 6-4 Reducing sheet sandpaper to thirds.

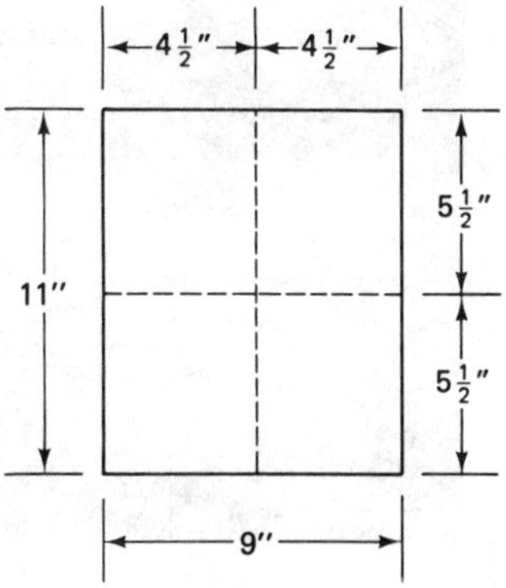

Figure 6-5 Reducing sheet sandpaper to quarters.

b. Reducing sheet sandpaper to "quarters" (for large area work) (Fig. 6-5):
  (1) Fold sandpaper sheet exactly in half and press the creaseline firmly. Carefully tear or cut the sandpaper in half.
  (2) Fold and crease each half of the sandpaper and tear or cut along the creaseline into quarters. Many paint shops reduce sandpaper to quarters. This is a matter of painter preference.

c. Reducing sheet sandpaper for standard sanding block (Fig. 6-6):
  (1) Mark the 11-inch dimension of sandpaper at $2\frac{3}{4}$-inch intervals.
  (2) Draw a line or form a crease at each interval for cutting or for tearing.
  (3) Cut or tear sandpaper into four equal strips each 9 inches long.
  (4) Align and install four sandpaper strips on a sanding block. Sanding blocks are equipped with various devices to retain sandpaper securely.

How to Hold and Use Sandpaper

Grip. Grip is important to sandpaper control. Three basic grips are most popular among painters:

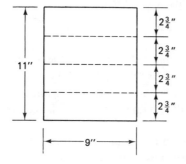

Figure 6-6 Reducing sheet sandpaper for standard sanding block.

Figure 6-7 How to hold and use sandpaper. (Courtesy of Ditzler Automotive Finishes, PPG Industries, Inc.)

1. The most natural grip is holding the sandpaper between the thumb and the hand as the hand is laid flat on the surface (Fig. 6-7).
2. An optional grip is holding the sandpaper between the little finger and the third finger as the hand is laid flat on the surface.
3. Many painters like to combine both grips, holding the sandpaper by the thumb and little finger.

Position of Sanding Hand on Surface

1. The position that is the most comfortable is the best.
2. A straight fore-and-aft finger position is best for large panels (Fig. 6-7).
3. The hand must adapt to the special conditions of surface construction.

Pressure on Sanding Hand (Varies by Needs of Sanding Job)

1. Keep pressure on sandpaper to a minimum.
2. Do not press hard.
3. Use about the same effort as used in washing a car.
4. Let the weight of the entire hand and sandpaper do the sanding.
5. Distribute weight uniformly over the entire hand.
6. Use just enough "feel" and hand pressure to do the job. At times, a little extra pressure is needed. This is a variable.

Finger Sanding Technique

1. Raising the palm of the hand slightly shifts the weight of the hand to the fingers. At times, this is where most sanding or cutting action needs to be done.
2. Raising the hand still more and stiffening the fingers shifts the weight to the fingertips. At times, sanding with the fingertips is required.

All three techniques of sanding are required from time to time. It depends on what the surface requires. This is known as "sanding control."

Circle Sanding Technique. Circle sanding with the fingers means moving the sandpaper in a circular fashion over a small area. This technique results in a faster sanding action with good-quality results if certain cautions are observed. What the sander actually does is to simulate an orbital sander.

CAUTION: Circle sanding by hand should never be done on a large panel with large circular motions 10 or more inches in diameter. Circle sanding should never be done with a sanding block.

Cross-cutting Technique. The best sanding strokes for large-area sanding are in a straight line. This form of sanding blends best with adjacent surfaces. The best leveling action is achieved when a sander changes directions frequently while sanding. A change of direction causes a cross-cutting action that levels any surface much more quickly. If cross-sanding at a 90° angle cannot be done because panel construction does not allow it, even a 30° or 45° direction change is very helpful.

Wet-sanding Technique (with or without Sanding Block) (Fig. 6-8a, b, and c)

1. Secure the proper sandpaper, a bucket of clean water, a suitable hand sponge, and a squeegee.
2. Soak the sponge and sandpaper and wet the surface to be sanded.
3. Position a wet (but not-too-soaked) sponge above the area being sanded.
4. Check your grip on the sandpaper, lay the sandpaper flat on the panel, align the fingers in the direction of sanding, or at a 45-degree angle to the direction, depending on the surface contours. Then start sanding. If sanding a large area, work an area no larger than 1 square foot at a time. Do not bear down on the sandpaper. Use light pressure and allow the sandpaper to do the work. This is the correct way to sand.
5. Feed water to the surface being sanded by squeezing the sponge as sanding progresses.
6. Stop periodically and check the progress of the sanding as follows:
    a. Squeegee water from the area being sanded. The surface must be free of water for inspection.
    b. View the sanded area from a gunsight angle in the presence of good lighting to check the surface condition. Check for a surface orange-peel condition. Adequate light must be reflected from the surface for an orange-peel condition to be seen by the sander.

NOTE: For better water control in an area with no floor drain, spread several thicknesses of used newspaper on the floor below the wet sanding area. At the conclusion of sanding and car cleanup, simply roll up the wet newspapers and place them in a trash container.

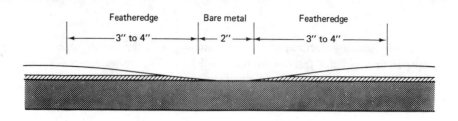

Legend:

☐ Original color (About 2.5 mils)

▨ Original undercoat (About 1.00 mil)

▩ Metal

(a)

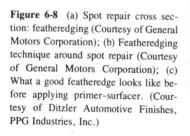

(b)

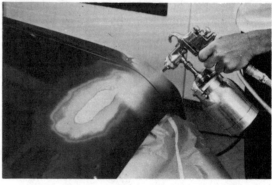

(c)

Figure 6-8 (a) Spot repair cross section: featheredging (Courtesy of General Motors Corporation); (b) Featheredging technique around spot repair (Courtesy of General Motors Corporation); (c) What a good featheredge looks like before applying primer–surfacer. (Courtesy of Ditzler Automotive Finishes, PPG Industries, Inc.)

Selection of a Backup Agent

Before sanding starts, the sander has the option to select the most efficient method of sanding. In addition to selecting the proper sandpaper, it is important to use a suitable backup block or pad as required. Any of the following can be used to back up the sandpaper. These can be used for any form of sanding.

1. Use of conventional sanding block: Best for large flat areas.
2. Use of squeegee as small sanding block: Works good with threefold wrap of sandpaper.
3. Use of suitable sponge pad: Excellent for sanding concave areas or surfaces; many types of pad are available.
4. Painter's "homemade" sanding block: This can be anything suitable. Examples: Thick felt pad like a school blackboard eraser; small rectangular wooden block; small section of wooden paint paddle.

Dry-sanding Technique

Dry sanding is the backbone of most surface preparation in automotive paint repair. More sanding is required in surface preparation than in any other phase of paint repair. The sanding must be fast. The most efficient speed sanding is done with two or more abrasive grit sizes (see Tables 6-5 and 6-6).

No single repair procedure or recommended grit sequence works the same in all repair situations. It is up to each sander and painter to determine his or her repair sequence and procedure based on individual know-how and ability.

TABLE 6-5 SANDING PLASTIC FILLERS: TWO-STEP METHODS

Operation	Abrasive	Method	Standing methods
Step 1: rough sanding; plastic filler	36D or 40D	I	Orbital and straight-line air files and hand file boards
	36D or 40D	II	Random orbit and jitterbug-type sanders
	36D or 40D	III	8-inch disc with 3M pad No. 5600 on a slow 1500- to 3000-rpm polisher
Step 2: finish sanding; plastic filler	80D	I	Orbital and straight-line air files and hand file boards
	80D	II	Random orbit and jitterbug-type sanders
	80D	III	8-inch disc with 3M pad No. 5600 on a slow 1500- to 3000-rpm polisher

Courtesy of the 3M Company.

Hand Sanding

TABLE 6-6 TWO-STEP SYSTEMS FOR FINE FEATHEREDGING OF PAINT

Type of sanding	Acrylic lacquers		Acrylic enamel and all enamels	
	Start	Finish	Start	Finish
Hand	320	400	220	360
Power	220	320	180	280

1. Select the proper abrasive. Open-coat aluminum oxide sandpaper is best for dry sanding (see Table 6-3).
2. Have the air gun available.
3. Wear a NIOSH-approved dust respirator when dry sanding.
4. Cut or tear sandpaper to a suitable size and fold or fit sandpaper to a sanding block as required.
5. Sand small spots 50% to 75% with coarse sandpaper and finish with finer sandpaper (see Table 6-5). Use of a sanding block is optional.
6. Use a suitable sanding block or backup pad for large-area sanding. Use coarse sandpaper for sanding the first 50% to 75% and finish sanding with finer paper.

CAUTION: When sanding plastic filler material adjacent to a good paint finish that will be saved and blended into later, protect this paint finish with masking tape until all coarse-sanding operations are completed. Avoid contacting masking tape.

7. The objective of coarse sanding is to quickly remove problem conditions such as rust and to quickly reduce the heavy buildup of plastic filler to final metal finishing dimensions.
8. Check the metal finish condition of the plastic filler by checking repair through a cotton glove or a shop towel.

NOTE: An inspector can detect surface irregularities (high and low spots) in plastic repair by using a cotton glove or shop towel and by running the hand lengthwise with the fingers across the repair. Irregularities can thus be detected by "feel." Anything that can be felt will look very obvious when it is painted.

9. Finish sanding plastic filler by hand with No. 180 or 220 sandpaper until the surface condition is acceptable. **Note:** If sandpaper tends to load with plastic, it can be cleaned up with an air gun or pointed tool.
10. Clean up sanding residue from the car and floor by sweeping the floor and blowing off the car.
11. If too much plastic is removed in the sanding operation or if air pockets are opened up, a repair plastic glazing coat must be added. Repeat step 9.

Scuff Sanding Technique

The term **"scuff"** means to make rough. The term **"scuff sand"** means to make a smooth surface rough by sanding. Scuff sanding is required on factory acrylic enamel and on other nonsoluble enamel surfaces that are to be repainted. Scuff sanding is required to make repair paint stick to the surface. There are additional reasons why scuff sanding is required.

Scuff sanding could mean to remove dirt nibs and dirt particles off nonsanding sealers and primers. In this case, sanding makes the surface smoother. Scuff sanding is done as follows:

1. Select the proper grit sandpaper. For sanding automotive finishes, scuff sanding with a medium- to coarse-grit paper such as No. 400, 360, 320, or 220 is best. Open- or closed-coat abrasives are satisfactory, as scuff sanding does not involve too much sanding.
2. Cut the sandpaper to size for use by itself or on a sanding block.
3. Dry-sand in a conventional, straight-line fashion to remove the desired amount of gloss or to impart the desired amount of dullness.
4. Check the sandpaper frequently for full cutting power. If the sandpaper loads with paint, clean the sandpaper with a stiff whiskbroom, steel brush, or compressed air. If the sandpaper does not clean up readily, change to a new section of sandpaper.

Featheredging Technique (Fig. 6-8a, b and c)

Featheredging, as the word implies, means to taper the thickness of a paint film at the broken edges from full paint film thickness gradually to a fine feather point (Fig. 6-8a). When a break occurs in a paint film, tapering the edge in a very fine fashion is necessary to make flawless paint repairs. As shown in Fig. 6-8a, a properly made featheredge extends several inches from the bare metal area to the top of the paint film. There are many ways to featheredge paint. Each painter develops special sanding techniques based on the type of paint and the painter's experience. Following is a suggested procedure.

1. Select the proper sandpaper (see Table 6-5). A finer sandpaper grit is used when sanding by hand. However, whether sanding by hand or with power, the two-sandpaper system is fastest and provides the best-quality results.
2. If the repair area is small, 6 to 8 inches in diameter, use a squeegee as a sanding block. Otherwise, use a large sanding block (Fig. 6-8b).
3. Apply water and sand from the outside in or from the inside out. On a small area, circle sanding speeds the operation. On a large area, use straight-line sanding motions. Soak the sandpaper frequently. Soak the sponge and half wring out occasionally.
4. After a featheredge is formed at the center (bare metal area), concentrate the sanding effort at the perimeter to extend the edge of the sanding area 1 to 2 inches from bare metal in all directions. Use plenty of water and continue the cross-cutting action with the sandpaper by changing directions frequently.

Hand Sanding   **153**

5. Change to fine grit sandpaper and continue sanding to remove all initial sand scratches, and extend the featheredge 2 to 3 inches from bare metal in all directions (Fig. 6-8b).

6. Change the water in the sanding area frequently by rinsing the sponge and sandpaper as sanding continues to completion.

NOTE: Sanding is finished when the featheredge extends several inches from bare metal in all directions (Fig. 6-8c). A featheredge checks out as ideal when checking the area with extended fingers and hand reveals that there is no marked or noticeable depression in the sanded area.

POWER SANDERS AND POWER FILES

The big advantage of power sanders and files is that they can do sanding work much faster and much more easily than it can be done by hand. Power tools for surface preparation are available in several forms through paint jobbers. These power tools are made by a number of paint tool and equipment suppliers. Each tool is designed to do a given specific job. Abrasives (sandpaper) for power sanders and power files are available through paint jobbers (see Table 6-5). These abrasives are made available to the refinish trade through a number of miscellaneous paint material suppliers like the 3M Company. The most popular power tools for surface preparation are:

1. Orbital and straight-line air files
2. Random orbit-type sanders
3. Jitterbug-type sanders
4. Eight-inch disc with a part No. 5600 (3M Company) type of pad on a slow-speed polisher (1500 to 3000 rpm)
5. Variable-speed drill motors with 3-, 4-, or 5-inch sanding pad attachment

Rectangular-shaped sandpaper is secured to power files and jitterbug sanders by built-in retainers or by adhesive. Sandpaper discs are secured to sander pads by adhesive. Some discs are available with pressure-sensitive adhesive for easy-on, easy-off application.

Sanding Disc Adhesive

Special disc adhesives are available for securing and removing sanding discs quickly and efficiently, such as Feathering Disc Adhesive by 3M. This adhesive is designed to allow removal of used discs without paper delamination. Tackiness is maintained to allow several discs to be replaced before recoating with adhesive. Follow the label instructions.

1. Apply 5 or 6 drops of adhesive to the pad, spacing the drops equally around the pad. Recap the tube and keep in a special handy place.

2. Hold the disc to the pad and rotate the disc to spread the adhesive uniformly between the two surfaces.

3. Remove the disc and allow the surfaces to air-dry about 5 seconds.

4. Carefully position the disc to the pad, being sure that all disc edges line up with the pad and press into place.

Small Power Sander Operating Technique

1. Be sure to wear safety goggles and a dust respirator.

2. With a cotton work glove on one hand, check the surface to be sanded by passing the hand lightly over the surface. This helps the sander to determine how sanding will be done. If sanding plastic filler, see Table 6-5.

3. Holding the sander firmly, turn on the switch and position the sander at a 5° to 10° angle to the work surface.

4. Position the left upper quarter of the disc to the surface when moving to the right in a straight line across the work (Fig. 6-9).

5. Position the right upper quarter of the disc to the surface and move to the left in a straight line across the work (Fig. 6-10). Steps 4 and 5 are the proper way to sand high-crown surfaces safely. They also apply to sanding low-crown and flat sur-

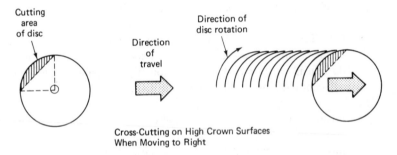

Cross-Cutting on High Crown Surfaces
When Moving to Right

Figure 6-9 Disc sander marks: left upper quarter.

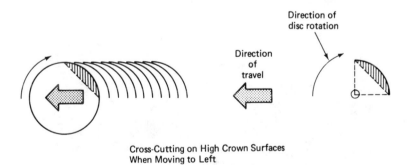

Cross-Cutting on High Crown Surfaces
When Moving to Left

Figure 6-10 Disc sander marks: right upper quarter.

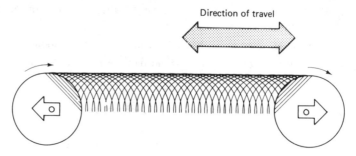

Figure 6-11   Disc sander marks: cross-cutting action (paint removal method for high-crown surfaces).

faces. Steps 4 and 5 cause a cross-cutting action (Fig. 6-11) on high-crown surfaces without cutting across the high crown. This produces a maximum leveling of surface. When using jitterbugs and power files to level high-crown surfaces, move and sand in the direction of the panel. **Do not cut across the high crown of the panel.** Check and clean the abrasive periodically to assure that it is cutting properly. If the abrasive becomes clogged with plastic filler permaturely, clean the abrasive with a pointed tool, steel wire brush, or air gun. The plastic filler must be cured sufficiently before it can be sanded satisfactorily.

CAUTION: Do not allow coarse abrasive to cut 90 degrees across a high-crown surface. This causes very deep sand scratches that are difficult to remove. Also, do not allow coarse abrasive to touch good paint on adjacent surfaces. Protect adjacent paint as required with masking.

6. Position the top center area of the disc (Fig. 6-12) to the surface by rotating the bottom away from the surface slightly. This is a buffing action. While maintaining this position, move the sander disc up and down, across the entire work surface. Overlap each pass by 50% to 60%. This creates an additional and final leveling action.

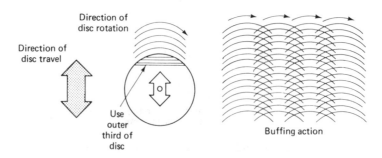

Figure 6-12   Disc sander marks: buffing action (for high- and low-crown surfaces).

7. Check for high spots by passing a gloved hand over the repair surface. Repeat sanding operations until about three-fourths of the sanding is completed.

8. On all sanders, change the sandpaper to a finer grit for finishing the plastic filler (see Table 6-5).

9. Repeat the basic sanding operations over the entire surface, starting with cross cutting and finishing with buffing until the surface is acceptably smooth.

10. Clean up the car and floor area as required.

Disc Sanding

Disc sanding is the fastest way of removing paint from a steel surface. However, the method is not too popular for paint removal because of the many cautions that must be exercised and because of the potential problems that disc sanding can cause. Basically, the disc sander belongs in the metal repair shop as an essential tool. Other tools (e.g., the Stikit 8-inch disc and disc pad by 3M) and other equivalent pads work very well on low-rpm polishers. They are safer to use and present fewer problems on the modern automobile when paint removal only is required.

Safety rules

1. Wear tight-fitting safety goggles and a face shield.

2. Wear an approved respirator for dust conditions.

3. Disc sanding can be hazardous if not done safely. Disc sanding should be done only by a person who is qualified to do it properly. When misused or used incorrectly, disc sanding can be very dangerous.

4. Wear protective clothing, including safety shoes, long sleeves, rubber soles, protective gloves with wrist protection, and no loose-fitting clothing that could get caught in the sander, such as long neckties.

5. Never disc-sand aluminum or plastic panels with coarse abrasives. Aluminum and plastic use is ever-increasing. Check the entire panel with a magnet. If panel does not react to magnet, **do not disc-sand the panel.**

6. Never disc-sand across a high crown of steel or any panel.

7. Never disc-sand across any panel edges or sharp crease lines.

8. Never disc-sand at or over exterior body moldings, into corners, into crevices, or over drip moldings.

9. Never disc-sand deep concave areas with a full pad behind the disc.

10. Never disc-sand over solder- or plastic-filled body joints or over plastic-filled repair areas.

11. Always start a disc sander off the job and stop it on the job.

12. Before connecting the disc sander to the power supply, make sure that it is grounded properly and that it is in its correct position (sanding disc facing up), with the operating switch in the "off" position.

13. Before operating the disc sander, make sure that the disc is installed properly.

When changing a disc, make sure that the lead is pulled out from the power supply. This will prevent accidental starting of the sander while discs are being changed.

14. When not in use, lay the sander on the floor. This prevents accidental dropping and damaging of the sander.

15. When using the disc sander near sharp panel edges, loose clips and bolts, lap-joint construction, and badly rusted out panels, exercise great care not to touch these items to prevent the sander from being caught and torn, which could cause serious injury to someone.

Installing a Backing Pad and Disc on a Portable Sander. The procedure for installing a backing pad and disc on a portable sander is as follows. Normally, backing pads should be the same size as a sanding disc. Backing pads should be smaller than a disc when a "special-cut" five-sided disc is used for concave areas.

1. Position the backing pad to the sander spindle B (Fig. 6-13). Turn the pad clockwise to install while keeping the spindle lock button, A, depressed. This keeps the spindle from turning. Turn the pad all the way down manually and tighten securely.

2. Position the sanding disc B (Fig. 6-14) on the backing pad A.

3. Position the clamp nut C on the spindle with the flange up and start turning the clamp nut one or two turns clockwise with the fingers.

4. While holding the backing pad with one hand, grasp and turn the disc clockwise several turns until the disc clamp nut is firmly tight. A special wrench (Fig. 6-15) is available as an accessory. The wrench can be used to loosen and to tighten the clamp nut.

What the Technician Must Know before Operating a Disc Sander. The follow-

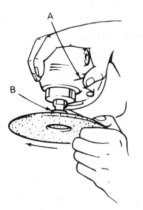

Figure 6-13 Disc sander backing pad attachment. (Courtesy of Black & Decker Mfg. Co. Ltd.)

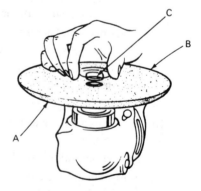

Figure 6-14 Sanding disc attachment. (Courtesy of Black & Decker Mfg. Co. Ltd.)

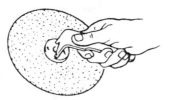

Figure 6-15 Tightening sanding disc clamp nut. (Courtesy of Black & Decker Mfg. Co. Ltd.)

ing procedure guides a person in the proper use of a disc sander. Before using a disc sander on a car, the operator should become familiar with:

1. How to change a disc
2. How to hold a disc sander
3. How to properly position the sanding disc to the surface for the various cross-cutting and buffing operations required; there are just a few techniques that must be learned

A person can become proficient in the use of a disc sander only one way: by practicing proper techniques on a practice panel repeatedly in the presence of an experienced metal or paint repair person until he or she masters the techniques. These techniques are not that difficult to learn. These panels could be junk panels that have been removed from cars and are to be scrapped.

Disc sanding in metal and paint repair is divided into two categories: cross-cutting and buffing.

1. To remove paint and to do general metal finishing, special cross-cutting action is used with an **open-coat** disc (No. 36 grit preferred at the start on steel panels).
2. To do final cleanup and final sanding operations, buffing action is required to remove the sand scratches caused by the previous cross-cutting action. Buffing is done with a No. 50, No. 60, or No. 80 grit **closed-coat** disc.

Used properly a disc sander can do a great deal of work very fast. Used improperly, a disc sander can cause a great deal of damage and considerable uncalled-for repair work. To become qualified with a disc sander, the apprentice must learn:

1. How to do cross-cutting on high- and low-crown surfaces. There is a difference.
2. How to do buffing on high- and low-crown surfaces. Buffing operations make metal smooth for painting.
3. How to prevent doing damage to panels and adjacent parts.
4. How to disc-sand safely.

Disc Sander Operating Technique

1. As a protective measure, tape all gap spacings, panel edges, and creaselines according to the following. Use $\frac{3}{4}$-inch masking tape so that all panel edges and

Power Sanders and Power Files **159**

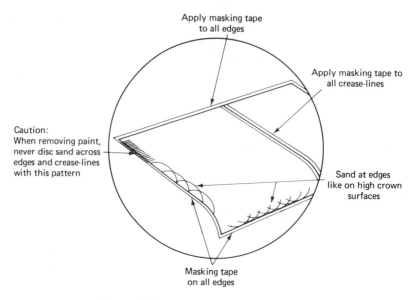

Apply masking tape
to all edges

Apply masking tape to
all crease-lines

Caution:
When removing paint,
never disc sand across
edges and crease-lines
with this pattern

Sand at edges
like on high crown
surfaces

Masking tape
on all edges

Figure 6-16 Discing technique at panel edges.

creaselines are protected with a $\frac{1}{4}$-inch-wide minimum of tape (Fig. 6-16). **Do not touch the tape with abrasive when disc sanding.** Remove paint from these areas after disc sanding with a smaller power sander or by hand, as required. Protect the following with masking tape:

a. Roof edges (front, rear, and sides)

b. All gap spacings around doors, hood, rear lid, or tail gate

c. All moldings not removed from the car

d. All handles, nameplates, and insignias

e. All special tapes and decals to be saved

f. All rocker panels (these panels are galvanized steel)

2. Check all panels to be sanded with a magnet. **All panels that do not react with magnetic pull** are to be marked with a large ''X'' with tape, or equivalent means, and **are not to be disc-sanded**. If only a small area does not react, mark off the area with masking tape and keep off this area with the disc sander. Chances are that it is plastic-filled.

3. Be sure that goggles and face shield are in place.

4. Wear an approved dust respirator. Be sure that it fits snugly to the face.

5. Have plenty of room to operate.

6. Grip the sander firmly with both hands (Fig. 6-17) and turn on the switch.

7. Position and maintain the disc sander at the work surface so that the disc and disc pad are inclined 5 to 10 degrees to the work surface at all times (Fig. 6-17). The left hand should be on the side handle below the disc and the right hand should be

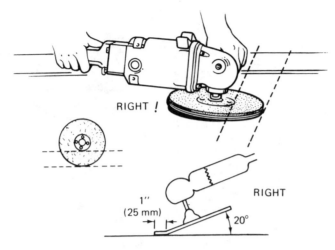

RIGHT !

RIGHT

1″
(25 mm)

20°

Figure 6-17 Disc sander grip and correct position to surface. (Courtesy of Black & Decker Mfg. Co. Ltd.)

on the main handle. Do not position the disc to the surface, as shown in Figs. 6-18 and 6-19.

8. Position the left upper quarter of the disc to the surface with a slight tilt of the disc (Fig. 6-9) when moving to the right in a straight line across the work surface a convenient distance of 12 to 14 inches. Disc-cutting marks should match those of Fig. 6-9.

9. Rock the disc slightly to the right so that the right upper quarter of the disc contacts the surface. Maintain this position when moving to the left in a straight line across the work surface. Disc-cutting marks should match those of Fig. 6-10. These disc

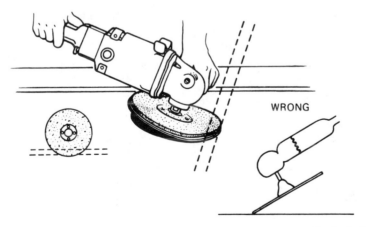

WRONG

Figure 6-18 Excessive tilt of disc sander. (Courtesy of Black & Decker Mfg. Co. Ltd.)

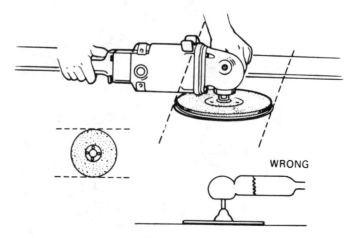

Figure 6-19 Insufficient tilt of disc sander. (Courtesy of Black & Decker Mfg. Co. Ltd.)

marks should overlap the step 8 disc marks by 100%. When disc-cutting marks of step 9 overlap disc-cutting marks of step 8 by 100%, the result should look like Fig. 6-11. This is cross-cutting action, which is safe on high-crown surfaces (such as curved fenders). It is important that the disc travels in the same direction as the flat or low-crown surface of the panel. Cross-cutting is always done with the coarser disc.

CAUTION: Do not allow coarse abrasive to cut 90 degrees across high-crown surfaces. This causes very deep sand scratches that are difficult to remove.

10. Change to No. 50, 60, or 80 grit disc. Position the top center area of the disc to the surface by rotating the bottom away from the surface slightly (Figs. 6-12, 6-20, and 6-21). This is buffing action. While maintaining this position, move the sander

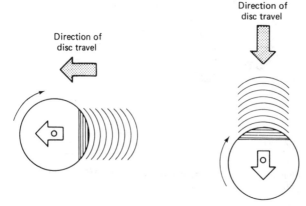

Figure 6-20 Disc sander marks: cross cutting action (for low-crown surfaces).

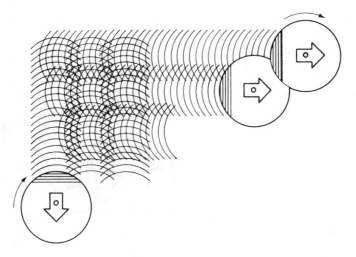

Figure 6-21 Disc sander marks: crosscutting action for low-crown surfaces.

disc up and down across the entire work surface. Overlap each pass 50% to 60%. Buffing removes the sand scratches from a No. 36 grit disc and prepares a surface for paint. On low-crown or flat surfaces, buffing or cross-cutting could also be done with the left portion of the disc, with the right portion of the disc, or with the lower portion of the disc, whichever suits the buffing or sanding conditions best.

Disc-sanding Paint from Concave Surfaces. To remove paint from concave surfaces with a disc sander, a special flexible disc is required. Flexible discs can be made from conventional discs as follows:

1. Use a No. 36 grit disc for paint removal and a No. 50 or 60 grit disc for final buffing.
2. On the back side of each disc, draw as large a five-sided figure as possible. This is like drawing a five-pointed star and connecting the star points with straight lines. Keep the sides of the star-shaped figure as equal as possible, but the sides need not be exact (Fig. 6-22a and b).
3. Using a special disc cutting tool (Fig. 6-22b), tin snips, or an equivalent cutting tool, cut a five-sided disc from a 9-inch disc.
4. Install the No. 36 grit five-sided disc and **4-inch backup pad** on the disc sander. The use of a small backup pad behind a large disc allows the disc to flex in an unsupported area to make uniform sanding possible on concave surfaces. Tighten the disc clamp nut securely.

Use a flexible star-shaped disc at concave surfaces as follows:

1. Position the disc at an angle to the surface as shown in Fig. 6-18 and apply a slight pressure to the disc so that it can flex properly.

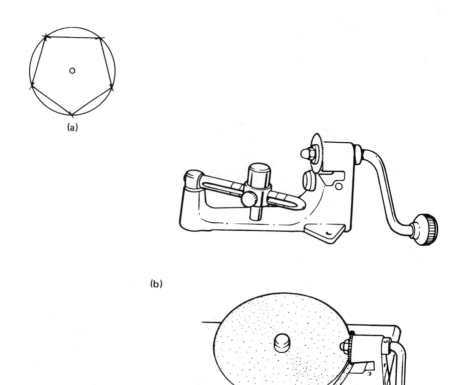

Figure 6-22 (a) Star-shaped disc. (b) Disc trimming tool. (Courtesy of Black & Decker Mfg. Co. Ltd.)

2. Turn on the sander and use cross-cut action to remove the paint:
   a. Use the left upper quarter of the disc when moving to the right (Fig. 6-9).
   b. Use the right upper quarter of the disc when moving to the left (Fig. 6-10).
   c. Overlap these strokes 100%.
3. Use only enough pressure and the proper angle on the disc so that it does the job.
4. Use convenient, short overlapping strokes to remove paint.
5. Stay away from all edges and corners with the star-shaped disc to prevent damaging the tips of the disc.
6. After removing the paint, change the disc on the sander to a five-sided closed-coat No. 50 or 60 grit disc for buffing.
7. Using the top center of the disc for buffing action (Fig. 6-12), apply up and down buffing strokes to the entire sanded area to remove No. 36 grit sand scratches.
8. Overlap each buffing pass about 50% to 60%, as required.

TABLE 6-7 ACRYLIC LACQUER REMOVING SOLVENT (BY PAINT SUPPLIER)

Paint supplier	Product name	Product identity
DuPont	Acrylic removing solvent	3907-S
Rinshed-Mason	Featheredger	830
Sherwin-Williams	Lacquer remover	R7K210
Martin-Senour	Lacquer remover	6805

ACRYLIC LACQUER REMOVING SOLVENT (Table 6-7)

The purpose of acrylic lacquer removing solvent is to assist the painter in removing an acrylic lacquer finish from a spot area quickly. This time- and sandpaper-saving solvent often comes in handy. The removing solvent is designed for use on acrylic lacquers and has no effect on factory enamels. For best results, follow the label directions.

Procedure for Use

1. Form a small, hard ball with a clean, throwaway type of cloth or shop towel.
2. Saturate the cloth ball with removing solvent, restricting the solvent to the cloth.
3. Hold the saturated cloth ball against the repair spot on the paint for about 5 seconds. Then rub the solvent in a circular motion on the affected spot for several more seconds. If necessary, reapply solvent to the cloth and repeat the washing operation. The painter will notice the undercoat showing through the color.
4. When sufficient color has been removed, allow the repair spot to air-dry about 1 minute. The spot dries while the painter prepares a second or more spots.
5. Using No. 400 or 500 sandpaper and water, sand the repair spot as required to complete featheredging.

PAINT REMOVERS

There are many types of paint removers on the market. Two types of paint removers are popular in the refinish trade.

1. Paint removers designed primarily to remove lacquer-type products, such as:
   a. Acrylic lacquer colors (factory and refinish trade colors)
   b. Lacquer-base undercoats (refinish trade type) (Table 6-8)

NOTE: This type of paint remover does not affect factory high-bake undercoats. This is good because factory undercoats should never be removed unless absolutely necessary.

2. Paint removers designed to remove all types of finishes down to the bare metal.

TABLE 6-8 PAINT REMOVERS FOR REMOVAL OF ACRYLIC LACQUER COLOR ONLY

Paint supplier	Product name	Product identity
Ditzler	Acrylic color remover	DX-525
DuPont	Paint remover	5662-S
Rinshed-Mason	Acrylic top coat stripper	817

Note: These removers do not remove enamel color or undercoats.

TABLE 6-9 PAINT REMOVERS FOR REMOVAL OF COMPLETE FINISH (ACRYLIC, URETHANE, AND ALKYD ENAMELS)

Paint supplier	Product name	Product identity
Ditzler	Aircraft remover (extra strength)	DX-586
Rinshed-Mason	All finish topcoat stripper	815
Sherwin-Williams	Water rinsable stripper	V3K-168
	Paint remover additive	V3K-773
Martin-Senour	Paint blitz	6801
	Paint remover additive	6803

These include enamel and urethane color and undercoats (Table 6-9). There are many other paint removers available that do an equally good job.

General Description

Paint removers are known as "cold strippers" because they are designed for use in average temperature conditions. Paint removers are made up of special strong chemicals that attack and dissolve paint finishes according to design. These chemicals work in conjunction with a special wax as follows:

1. Label directions advise applying paint remover at a very heavy thickness, as heavy as can be applied on a vertical surface.
2. At this thickness, wax floats to the surface to act as a seal or screen. This keeps the active chemical ingredients in contact with the paint, and active chemicals enter the paint film.
3. The chemicals attack, soften, and dissolve the paint film. This action takes place within several minutes, as explained in the label directions.
4. When dissolved, the paint film can be scraped off the surface with a squeegee or a suitable scraper.

Removal of stripped paint from a car involves handling a very gummy, slippery, and heavy-bodied material. The material flows like extra-heavy molasses. If controlled as outlined, stripping paint can be a very neat and rewarding experience. However, lack of preparation and poor control of dissolved paint material usually results in a very messy operation. Negligence in allowing dissolved paint and excess paint remover to run into gap spacings, the engine compartment, and the rear compartment gutter causes much extra, uncalled-for work. Also, stripped paint does not clean up too readily from any type of floor. Good planning and proper preparation control the stripped paint and keep it off the floor. Good planning is essential to neat, fast workmanship. Haste usually causes waste. It is best to proceed in a planned and well-organized manner. Have all tools and equipment on hand well in advance of their need. Plan stripping paint from each major area individually. Control of stripped paint is the major problem.

Never strip a car under a bright sun when the temperature is over 90°F and the car temperature is over 150°F. Allow the car to cool off to a normal temperature range, 72° to 80°F.

Safety Precautions

1. Use paint removers only with adequate ventilation.
2. Avoid prolonged or repeated breathing of vapor and contact with skin or eyes.
3. Contact with skin may cause irritation. If skin is contacted accidentally by remover, wash off immediately with clear water.
4. Contact with flame or hot surfaces may produce toxic vapors.
5. Contains methylene chloride, propylene dichloride, alcohols, and ammonia.
6. If swallowed, call a physician immediately.
7. Keep the container closed when not in use.
8. Keep out of the reach of children.
9. If splashed in the eyes, immediately flush with clear water for at least 15 minutes. Get medical attention.

Not all paint removers are alike. They appear alike in name only. To know specifically what a paint remover will do, the painter must know by experience, or the painter should ask the paint jobber. Normally, a product will do the job promised by a paint jobber. All paint remover companies back up their products as stated on the label or in company sales literature.

As a rule, paint removers can stain the finish on anodized aluminum parts and on many plastic parts. Necessary precautions must be taken to prevent contact with these parts. Care must be exercised to prevent paint remover from getting trapped at body side moldings, nameplates, and in door and deck lid gap spacings. This is accomplished through proper masking. Even a diluted paint remover can run down over a fresh paint finish and stain the finish.

Necessary precautions should be taken to keep removed paint off the floor. This makes cleanup difficult. Catch removed paint on protective paper of sufficient size and strength to allow easy control and disposal. For best results when using paint remover, follow the label directions.

Techniques for Using Paint Remover

There are a number of paint removers available in the refinish trade. Before stripping the color off a car, the painter must know in advance if the complete paint finish is to be removed or if only the color coat is to be removed. This determines the **type of paint remover** to be used (see Tables 6-8 and 6-9).

There are a number of ways to strip color (and undercoats) off any car. The following technique is generally popular among a great number of painters.

1. Mask the floor as required. Double masking is recommended as follows:
   a. Apply a first layer of masking to protect the floor.
   b. Apply a second layer of masking so that it can catch removed paint and is prepared for immediate removal without disturbing the first masking.
2. Have all necessary tools and equipment on hand.
3. Mask the car as required. Each area of the car to be stripped requires specialized masking and should be stripped individually.
4. Use rubber gloves and safety goggles.
5. Fill a smaller container, such as a 1-quart container, from 1 gallon of paint remover. Using a 4-inch (or suitable) paintbrush and a smaller container, apply a generous coating of paint remover on the finish to be stripped. Spread the remover quickly with minimum brushing.

   CAUTION: Do not rebrush any area. Simply spread the remover in a very heavy coating as directed and leave it alone.

6. Allow the paint remover to work on the paint finish a sufficient amount of time, according to the label directions. Usually, this ranges from 7 to 10 minutes. Do one area at a time.
7. Remove loosened paint with a squeegee or plastic scraper as follows:
   a. From horizontal surfaces. Either of two methods can be used to remove paint from surfaces such as the roof, rear deck, and hood.
      (1) Method 1 involves using a dust pan and squeegee. Collect paint from a 1- to 2-square foot area at a time, squeegee onto a dust pan, and remove. Wash the dust pan in a thinner bath quickly each time.
      (2) Method 2 involves making troughs out of masking paper or newspaper (about 3 inches deep, 3 inches wide, for the length of the area) and securing the trough to the long, straight side of the car with masking tape. The paper should be folded several times for strength, and the trough should be bridged at intervals with tape. Squeegee paint from a large area adjacent to the trough into the trough and carefully remove. Removing the trough is best done with the assistance of a helper.
      (3) Removed paint is best disposed of by placing paint on several sheets of newspaper, wrapping the newspaper, and placing it in a trash barrel or container.

b. From vertical surfaces. When removing paint from vertical surfaces such as all sides of the car, it is best to take advantage of gravity and let the loosened paint fall straight down as follows:

(1) Position necessary masking on the floor below the area being stripped.

(2) Starting at the top, apply paint remover to the sides of the car slowly by carefully pouring from a paper cup and by spreading uniformly with a large, 4-inch paintbrush. Work by brushing in an upward direction only. Keep brushing to a minimum.

(3) It may be necessary to apply two coats, one immediately after another, to obtain a generous film.

(4) Catch the paint remover run off with a section of cardboard or equivalent, and reapply it to a higher area.

(5) Remove paint from the car with a squeegee or scraper after waiting the necessary time and by allowing loosened paint to fall straight down.

8. In the case of excess paint film due to a car being repainted one or more times, it is usually necessary to reapply a second coating of paint remover. This takes extra work and material, and a painter should catch this item when he or she makes the estimate.

9. After the color has been removed, wash the panel surface with a medium-grade thinner. Wash the surface thoroughly and remove the thinner while still wet. Do only a small area at a time, 2 by 2 feet, and overlap as required.

10. Remove the masking. Remove the balance of color hidden by masking as required. On enamel cars, it is best to remove the balance of color by sanding with No. 60 or 80 grit sandpaper. On lacquer cars, it is best to remove the balance of the color with lacquer removing solvent.

11. Clean the entire surface from which color was removed with paint finish cleaning solvent to remove any traces of wax.

SANDBLASTING

Sandblasting has become increasingly popular in the automotive refinishing trade as the fastest and most efficient method of removing rust and other contaminants from metal surfaces. Also, sandblasting can remove rust from localized areas that are inaccessible with conventional sanding methods. A number of companies, including the major department stores, have reasonably priced sandblasting units available to the trade. To determine why sandblasting is required to remove rust, see Chapter 18. Sandblasting units are available in suction- and pressure-feed types and should have the following components:

1. Container or tank for sand
2. Screen to filter sand, and a funnel if the opening in the tank is small
3. Airtight cover (to keep the unit dry in storage)

4. Hose and air-line fittings
5. Sandblasting gun with air control trigger

Sandblasting originated as a method of engraving and cutting glass and other hard materials by the violent force of particles of sand driven by an air blast. In auto-body surface preparation for paint, this force is particularly useful to remove rust very quickly from spot or hard-to-get-at areas.

Because of the nature of sandblasting and the cost of facilities and equipment, such as special dirt control equipment and air conditioning, only firms specializing in sand-blasting can make the operation practicable indoors on a year-round basis.

The best way for a paint shop to do sandblasting from a safety standpoint is to do the operation out-of-doors or in a paint spray booth. In warm climates, sandblasting can be done on a year-round basis out-of-doors. In cold climates, sandblasting is done best indoors.

If the operator expects to recover much of the sand used, it is best to do the work on a cement or hard floor where the sand could be swept up. When reused, the sand should be properly filtered.

Sand for the Sandblasting Unit

Many types of sand are commercially available for sandblasting. A silica sand or No. 5 blasting sand is best suited for sandblasting to remove rust from automotive surfaces. Not all sand is suited for sandblasting to remove rust. Some sands have round spheres and are used for engine polishing operations. This type of sand is not suited for rust removal. A reasonable and good-quality silica sand is play sand and beach sand, available through local lumber and building supply companies. This sand is very sharp and does a good job of rust removal. Reputable sand supply companies post the following warning label on containers for sandblasting sand. Warnings are surrounded by a solid black line.

> **WARNING: This product contains free silica. Suggest posting work areas where product is used, handled, or stored, warning employees that repeated inhalation of respirable silica dust for extended periods of time may cause delayed lung injury. Follow present OSHA Safety and Health Standards or as hereafter amended.**

How the Sandblasting Unit Works (Fig. 6-23)

Most low-cost sandblasting units operate on a suction-feed principle similar to that of a paint spray gun.

1. As the trigger is pulled, air passes through the air hose and sandblasting gun.
2. As air passes the sand feed junction at a high rate of speed, the air creates a strong suction at the sand feed hose.

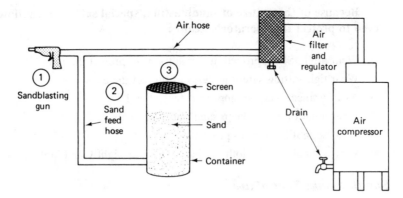

Figure 6-23 Sandblasting outfit.

3. Atmospheric pressure and gravity cause the sand to go down in the tank continually as the gun is operating.

4. Sand is drawn through the sand feed hose to the gun by a strong suction in the hose.

5. As the sand mixes with compressed air in the gun, it becomes violently turbulated. The amount of turbulence is proportional to the air pressure setting. Fifty to seventy-five psi is a good working range for the removal of average rust conditions.

6. As violently turbulated sand and air from the gun strike the surface, the repeated high cutting force of the sand cuts away the surface condition in front of it. This is sandblasting.

Safety Precautions

Since sandblasting has exceptional cutting qualities, the following precautions must be taken if sandblasting is done near any items listed. Mask and/or protect items as required with suitably strong materials such as heavy cloth-backed tape, plastic, or metal.

1. All glass
2. All plastic parts
3. All chrome parts
4. All adjacent paint to be saved
5. Front grille parts
6. All aluminum parts
7. Vinyl top and all soft trim parts
8. Where practicable, remove parts for protection
9. Before working in door or window openings exposing the interior of the car, cover all interior trim and hardware parts with suitable cloth or plastic covers as required.

Because of the nature of sandblasting, special safety precautions must be observed to protect the operator's health:

1. Wear a NIOSH-approved dust respirator to protect the lungs.
2. Wear tight-fitting safety goggles to protect the eyes.
3. As insurance, wear an approved face shield.
4. Wear a hat or cap to keep sand out of the hair.
5. Wear suitable gloves to protect the hands.
6. Wear suitable work clothing that buttons up tightly and high at the neck.

Sandblasting Technique

WARNING: Only a person who is qualified in the use of a sandblast unit, or a person who has been properly instructed, should be allowed to operate the unit.

1. Check the compressor and transformer to assure that the air is moisture-free.
2. The air line should be $\frac{5}{16}$ inch or larger, as used in spray painting. Never use a $\frac{1}{4}$-inch air line for body repair.
3. Clean and dry out the sand container with compressed air.
4. Blow out the sandblasting air hose with clean, dry air.
5. Fill the container with **clean, dry, and screened** sand according to the manufacturer's instructions.
6. Adjust all controls to proper pressure at the blasting area.
7. Analyze the area to be sandblasted before starting.
8. Be sure that safety equipment is in place.
9. Always aim the gun at an angle to deflect the blowing air stream away from the operator.
10. Use a small, continuously circular and overlapping stroke, about $\frac{1}{2}$ to 1 inch in diameter. Work a small area at a time to get the feel of the gun; then progress accordingly.
11. Work only as fast as the sandblaster will allow.
12. When removing rust, use a little extra time on each spot to sandblast the metal to its normal steel gray appearance.
13. Clean up the interior and exterior of the car and the work area, as required.
14. Clean up and put away equipment. Always keep the sandblast unit and sand in a sealed plastic (trash) bag to keep it dry.
15. For proper maintenance, follow the manufacturer's recommendations.

How to Remove Small, Severe, Localized Rust

On occasion, small, severe, localized rust spots are encountered that are not removable with conventional hand or power sanding. Chapter 18 deals with repair of these rust conditions with the best method, sandblasting, before paint repairs. In the event that sandblasting is not available immediately for a small condition of this type, the rust can be removed with a special, small cutting tool according to the following procedure.

Procedure

1. Wear safety glasses.
2. Install a special cutting tip in a $\frac{1}{4}$-inch drill motor.
3. Using very light pressure as required, cut away rust from each corrosive pit by positioning the cutting tool into the pit and by rotating the drill motor. Use small, circular, overlapping strokes to remove the balance of the rust deposits from the spot area. Some spots are removed in a few seconds. Other spots, if deep and large, require more time.
4. Fill the spot with two-part epoxy-type plastic or the plastic recommended in Chapter 18. As an alternate method, solder-fill the spots to prevent recurrence of the rust.

Small, steel cutting tools with a $\frac{1}{8}$-inch-diameter shank are available through hardware stores. These tools are about $1\frac{1}{2}$ inches long and have variously shaped cutting tips. The best cutting tool for removal of corrosive pits has a tapered point or a teardrop design. See Fig. 18-2 for the cross section of a corrosive pit.

Use of Tinning to Guarantee Rust Repairs in a Spot Area

If a rust condition recurs in the same spot after repairs are made, this is evidence that the rust was not removed completely when repairs were made. The problem can be remedied and guaranteed not to recur by removing the rust and by tinning the affected spot according to the following procedure. When tinning, use 50/50 acid core solder, or 30/70 body solder and tinning acid. These solders are selected because they require less heat to do the job. Rust cannot take place on a surface that has been properly tinned. Also, tinning cannot be done on a surface that is rusted. Tinning and rusting are incompatible.

Procedure

1. Wear the required safety equipment.
2. Remove all traces of rust:
   a. By sandblasting, or
   b. By use of a special pointed cutting tool. Remove the rust completely from every corrosive pit (see Chapter 18).

   CAUTION: Preheat a large panel area surrounding the affected spot uniformly as required before tinning is done in a spot area. Careless use of heat on a large panel can cause severe distortion and ruin the appearance of the panel. If necessary, have an experienced metal repair technician perform the tinning operation.

3. Heat metal to the required temperature. Apply acid if necessary. Apply solder to

the metal and note the initial melting of the solder. Heat the adjacent metal and spread the solder with a suitable clean cloth, as required. Wipe across the heated, tinned spot several times to assure that tinning is 100% continuous with no breaks in the surface.

4. Allow the repaired surface to cool at room temperature. **Do not quench.**

MASKING

The manner in which a job is masked often spells the difference between a top-quality and a poor-quality paint job. Careful masking provides clean paint edges and prevents a ragged appearance at glass, sealing strips, exterior moldings, grille parts, and so on. Careful and precision masking is the mark of a true craftsperson. How to mask a car in the best possible way is largely a matter of understanding fundamentals, of using good judgment, and practice.

Before any portion of a car is masked, every part on the car and every surface involved should be washed and cleaned as required. Mask the car under good lighting conditions for a close inspection of the masking job. Masking, like painting, should not be done in temperatures below 50°F.

Masking Materials

Masking materials are designed for fast and efficient application, protection, and removal from surfaces of a car that are not painted. Masking materials such as tape and paper are specially made for masking. Many other items, such as newspapers, wrapping paper, and plastic covers, can also be used for masking, but only in a limited way, as described in this chapter. Professional shops use approved masking paper because of its superior masking qualities.

Masking Tape

Masking tape is available in several forms for automotive refinishing. The two most popular are general-purpose masking tape, which is available from a number of suppliers through paint jobbers, and Fine-Line masking tape supplied by the 3M Company, also available through paint jobbers.

General-purpose Masking Tape. General-purpose masking tape is designed especially for the professional painter. Every feature is perfectly balanced to give maximum masking results. Masking tape is designed to resist breaking, lifting, adhesive transfer, splitting, shrinking, and curling away under normal- and high-temperature conditions. Good-quality masking tape conforms to the surface, hugs curves, goes on quickly and easily, sticks at a touch, and stays put. Masking tape has a good shelf life. This means that if a given tape is not used for a year, or even longer, it is still as good as it was when new. The qualifications are that the tape not be subjected to excessively high or low temperatures for too long a period of time. Also, masking tape must be water-resistant so that it is not affected after getting wet from wet sanding. Masking tape is available in 60-yard rolls in the following inch sizes: $\frac{1}{8}$, $\frac{1}{4}$, $\frac{3}{8}$, $\frac{1}{2}$, $\frac{3}{4}$, $\frac{7}{8}$, 1, $1\frac{1}{2}$, $1\frac{3}{4}$, 2, and 3. The $\frac{1}{4}$- and $\frac{3}{4}$-inch masking tapes are the most popular in refinishing.

Fine-Line Masking Tape (Fig. 6-24). Fine-Line masking tape is a 3M product that is especially suited to custom painting as well as to general automotive refinishing. This tape has a special processed film backing that allows taping over freshly painted acrylic lacquer or enamel surfaces sooner with less chance of imprint damage. The backing for this tape is polypropylene plastic, which provides flexibility for curves and has excellent resistance to solvent penetration. Fine-Line tape provides the finest color separation line possible for several-color striping, for two-toning, and for custom painting. Fine-Line masking tape is excellent for lettering. This tape is not designed for outdoor application. Fine-Line masking tape is available in 60-yard rolls in the following inch sizes through local paint jobbers: $\frac{1}{16}$, $\frac{1}{8}$, $\frac{3}{16}$, $\frac{1}{4}$, $\frac{3}{8}$, $\frac{1}{2}$, and $\frac{3}{4}$.

Masking Paper

Masking paper is strong, flexible, and pliable. It is formulated to resist penetration of solvents, lacquers, and enamels. It is especially designed to protect against overspray on every paint job. Masking paper is able to withstand water from wet sanding. Masking paper is available in 1000-foot rolls in a number of widths. The most popular widths are 15, 12, and 6 inches. The 15-inch width is popular for windows and windshields. Masking paper is also available in 18-, 24-, 30-, and 36-inch widths.

Other types of paper that are used for masking are newspaper and various weights of store wrapping paper. Newspapers are satisfactory for masking glass and chrome parts.

CAUTION: Newspaper should never be used flush against lacquer colors when

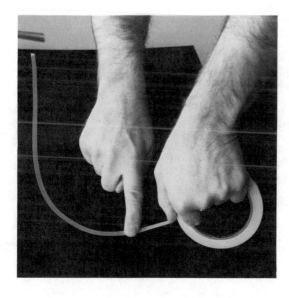

Figure 6-24 Using Fine-Line masking tape by 3M. (Courtesy of the 3M Company)

Masking

color matching. Solvents can dissolve newspaper ink and carry it into colors being protected.

Masking Covers

Masking covers for wheels are available commercially through paint jobbers and specialty equipment firms. Covers can also be made by a painter who is ingenious. Using wheel covers is the fastest way of masking wheels. Wheel covers are usually made of a heavy cloth or heavy vinyl. Wheel covers have a spring steel wire insert ($\frac{1}{8}$ to $\frac{1}{4}$ inch in diameter) in the shape of an arc sewn at the upper area, which aids cover control and handling. Large pliable plastic covers are also available to painters. These covers are suitable for throwing over a vinyl top or hood quickly to protect against overspray. These covers are available through paint equipment suppliers, who can be reached through paint jobbers.

General-purpose Masking Units

Masking units, sometimes called **"apron tapers"** or **"handy maskers,"** are available through paint jobbers. Masking units provide instant aprons of pretaped paper for masking. These units apply masking tape to the paper as the required amount of masking paper is unrolled. A cutting edge is provided on the masking unit to cut the paper at the desired length. The units are very efficient because they cut down masking time. Some units are designed for mounting on a bench or table (Fig. 6-25), and the more popular units are mounted on casters or wheels and are portable (Fig. 6-26). They can be brought to the car and are a time saver.

Figure 6-25 Bench-type masking unit. (Courtesy of the 3M Company)

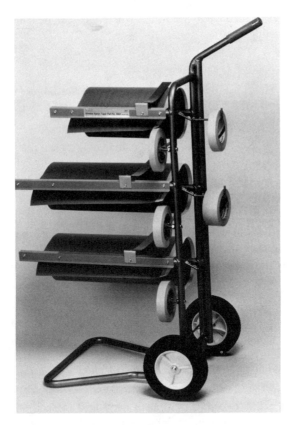

Figure 6-26 Portable-type masking unit. (Courtesy of the 3M Company)

Special Masking Tools

Most painters find the following special tools handy when installing and removing masking tape:

1. A 1-inch paintbrush with bristles shortened to $\frac{1}{2}$ inch. This is done easily by cutting the bristles off with scissors. The tool helps the painter to install masking tape on surfaces that cannot be reached with fingers, such as behind curved moldings and tight corners.
2. A small scraping stick can be made from a wooden clothespin. Split a clothespin in half to make two sticks. Sand the end of each stick to the desired shape. This tool also helps to position masking tape in tight corners and helps to scrape away dirt and sealers that cannot be removed with normal washing without scratching the paint.
3. A small can opener with a screwdriver-shaped tip and slightly curved at the end can help considerably to remove masking as follows. File the end of the tip to be knife-sharp. The tool is used to aid loosening dried, hard-to-remove tape. Simply

scrape and lift the edges of the tape to a position where they can be handled. This tool saves the painter's fingernails.

Masking Technique

How to Hold Tape.   Pick up a roll of masking tape with the fingers inside and the thumb outside the tape roll, and with the adhesive side of the tape away from the painter (when unrolled). This is the conventional way of holding tape.

How to Unroll Tape (Fig. 6-27).   With the opposite hand, loosen the tape edge, grip the tape, and unroll a several-inch length by pulling the tape while allowing the tape roll to pivot on the fingers. Notice how the tape unrolls naturally while pulling on the free end of the tape.

How to Snap-tear Tape (Off Job) (Fig. 6-28a).   Snap-tear tape off the roll by pressing on the tape edge of the roll with the thumbnail while pulling the tape quickly in the opposite direction. On the car, the thumbnail does best as a cutting agent (Fig. 6-28b). This is the usual way of tearing tape at a precise location when applying masking tape on a car.

How to Precision-tear Tape.   Prior to applying a pretaped apron of masking on a car, tear several short sections of tape quickly from the roll and stick them to the back side of the hand as follows:

1. Hold the tape roll in the last two fingers and thumb of one hand.
2. Unroll about $2\frac{1}{2}$ inches of tape with the opposite hand.
3. Position the ends of the first two fingers of each hand next to each other on the adhesive side of the tape and place the thumbs on the tape behind the fingers.

Figure 6-27 How to hold and unroll masking tape. (Courtesy of the 3M Company)

(a)

(b)

Figure 6-28 (a) How to snap-tear masking tape (off job). (b) How to snap-tear masking tape (on job). (Courtesy of the 3M Company)

4. While squeezing the fingers against the thumb, twist the fingers quickly in opposite directions to snap-tear the tape about 1 inch long. The nickname given to a short piece of tape is **"tack tape."** Short pieces of tack tape hold large sections of pretaped aprons to a car in spot locations opposite long sections of tape. So the word **"tack"** means to hold masking in a spot location.

When applying taped aprons to a car, the prepared painter has a series of short sections of tape ready so that when the apron is installed, the tape tacks are ready for use. Properly prepared tack taping is a time saver.

Tips on Masking

1. Apply masking to the part to be protected but avoid contacting the surface to be painted with the tape. Contacting or overlapping the surface to be painted is a poor practice that leads to edge lifting of finish when the tape is removed. Positioning and securing tape properly the first time is a matter of painter judgment and practice. To be sure that the tape goes on properly, **look at each detail** as the work progresses. **A safe distance to maintain between the tape edge and the paint surface is $\frac{1}{32}$ inch.**

2. Masking tape is designed with a certain amount of stretch. Make use of this characteristic by pulling on the tape edge as tape is applied at the corners and on curved surfaces.

3. **When overlapping tape over tape,** the edges at the painted surface should be **flush** for a straight, uniform line. When overlapping **paper over paper,** start installation at the bottom to create a shingling effect. This prevents the possible seepage of paint materials toward the protected parts.

4. Tape could be removed as soon as the paint is no longer sticky or tacky. This is determined by rubbing the back of a finger on a lower rear corner of a paint job.

   CAUTION: Never allow masking tape to contact fresh painted surfaces when removing the tape on the same day a car is painted. Masking tape will take fresh paint right off the surface.

5. Remove the tape by pulling in the opposite direction and on the same side of any curved edges.

6. On freshly painted and on lacquer surfaces when contact between the paper and the surface cannot be avoided, use two or three thicknesses of masking paper. Also, remove this masking as soon as painting is completed.

7. Care should be exercised never to oversoak a single layer of masking paper if the surface underneath will be affected by solvent bleed-through.

8. Use proper-width tape for each masking job. Using too wide a tape where a narrower tape will do is a waste of money.

9. Always unroll a length of tape that can be positioned and secured most easily. Observe the installation carefully. If any tape installation is noted to be faulty, stop and make the correction immediately.

   CAUTION: Never use newspaper to mask lacquer-painted surfaces when adjacent surfaces are being painted with a lacquer repair system. Newspaper ink is dissolved by lacquer solvents and fumes, and the ink can cause serious staining problems. Use of newspaper should be limited to nonpainted surfaces such as headlamps, bumpers, and wheels. These surfaces could be cleaned up readily with a solvent after painting is finished.

10. Before masking door and other weatherstrips of foam rubber construction that are covered with a skin of sheet rubber, apply a clear acrylic lacquer to the weatherstrip with a brush as follows:

   a. Clean the weatherstrip with paint **finish cleaning solvent** (see Table 6-1), as required.

   b. Reduce clear acrylic lacquer to brushing consistency with medium thinner. Reduction up to 150% is satisfactory. Apply clear lacquer with suitable brush.

   c. Allow to dry thoroughly (1 hour, minimum).

   CAUTION: Always disconnect the battery when working on door jambs unless dome (or courtesy) lights are not affected by open doors.

11. For best results, remove tape as follows:

   a. Remove tape at temperatures above 60°F.

   b. Pull off tape at a 90° angle to the surface.

   c. Remove tape with a slow to medium pace without tearing.

Molding Masking

How to Mask a Molding with a Curved Edge (Fig. 6-29a and b)

1. Using $\frac{3}{4}$-inch masking tape, position the tape along the edge of the molding so that the tape protrudes beyond the molding edge sufficiently to cover the molding when the tape is slicked down (Fig. 6-29b).

2. Unroll the tape with one hand while positioning the tape with the other hand.

3. Using a short-bristled brush or other suitable tool, lay the tape down flush to the molding at edges unreachable with fingers.

4. When masking corners, it is sometimes easier to mask with a fresh end of tape. Position the tape to the molding curved edge while pulling on the tape with one hand and conforming the tape to the molding with the other hand. Make the tape stretch to fit the corner.

5. Follow this procedure to tape the complete perimeter of the molding and apply filler tape on the molding as required.

How to Mask a Molding with a Flush Edge (Fig. 6-30a and b)

1. Using proper-width tape, apply tape to the molding around the complete perimeter of the molding. Position the tape to the side of the molding so that the tape is $\frac{1}{32}$ inch from the paint surface.

2. Lay the tape, applied in step 1, flush to the molding and apply filler tape as required. **Note:** Use of a small special tool may be required to lay the tape flush to the molding or nameplate. A short-bristled paintbrush or small stick is very helpful.

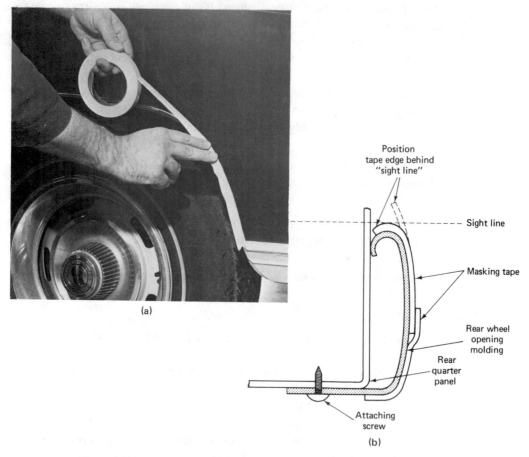

Figure 6-29 (a) How to mask molding with curved edge (Courtesy of the 3M Company); (b) Masking molding with curved edge (cross section).

Perimeter Masking (Fig. 6-31)

Perimeter masking is used around the outside edge of a large area that is to be masked. Once this masking is completed, the masking operation is simplified. Perimeter masking is used on the following areas and parts: windshields, back windows, vinyl tops, two-tone colors, wood-grain transfers, sun roofs, side windows, wide decals, front end and rear end flexible plastic parts, wheels, door jambs, front grille work, door handles, and accent colors.

Filler Masking (Fig. 6-31)

Filler masking is done in conjunction with perimeter masking. As the term indicates, filler masking completes the masking within a given perimeter. All filler masking, if

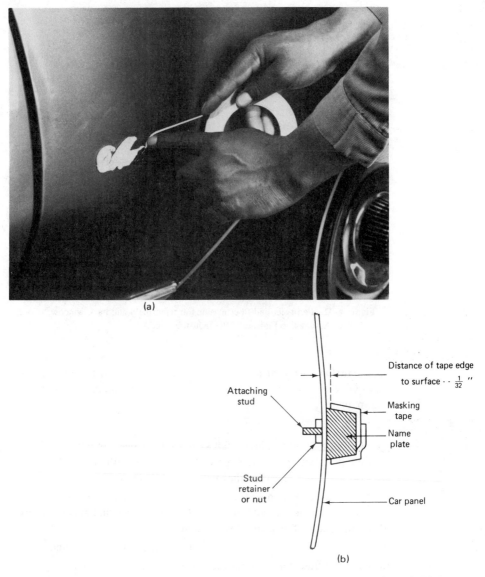

Figure 6-30 (a) How to mask molding with flush edge (Courtesy of the 3M Company); (b) Masking molding with flush edge (cross section).

made up of sections, must be sealed by taping all joints completely. There should be no leakage of paint spray fumes and paint materials through filler masking.

One can see why apron tapers are so important to a paint shop. While detail masking is always important and requires the most time, filler masking covers the greatest amount of square foot area quickly.

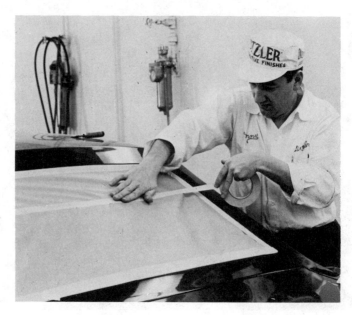

Figure 6-31 Perimeter and filler masking at windshield and back window. (Courtesy of Ditzler Automotive Finishes, PPG Industries, Inc.)

Filler masking without an apron Taper. Automatic masking equipment is not always available to the painter. In these situations, painters do filler masking in the following manner:

1. Lay a large section of paper on a clean, flat surface such as a hood or bench.
2. Apply tape, starting at one edge of the paper, lengthwise so that half of the tape goes on the paper and the other half goes on the hood or bench.
3. Do about 12 or 18 inches in length at a time and slick the tape down on the paper and surface. Tear the tape at the end of the paper and raise the taped apron by lifting the end of the secured paper and tape.
4. Prepare three or four tape tacks and put on the back of the hand.
5. Install taped filler masking on the car and tack tape in place.

The preceding operations apply to masking large sections of paper. The same operations apply to preparing a small apron, or follows:

1. Tear paper to a suitable size. Lay on a flat surface.
2. Apply tape at one straight edge of the apron. Tear the tape at the paper edge.
3. Apply masking to the car as required.

Masking Parts of the Car

Windshield (and/or Back Window) (Fig. 6-31)

1. Apply masking tape to the perimeter of windshield moldings as required. If glass is retained by a rubber channel, clean the channel as required with paint finish cleaning solvent. Then apply perimeter masking to the rubber channel.
2. Apply filler masking as required. Apply masking across the bottom first, then mask the sides and finish across the top.
3. Apply masking to all exposed joints to make a unitized, sealed mask.
4. Make a special "window" in the masking on the driver's side if the car is to be moved to the spray area after masking.

Side Windows (Fig. 6-32a and b).   Side windows require precision masking of components around the perimeter of the opening. Closed-style (sedan) windows are masked individually. On most hard-top styles (without pillar), windows can be filler-masked as a unit. Hard-top styles require special attention to perimeter masking around the window openings because of the window and sealing strip design.

1. Apply masking to the perimeter of side windows as required.
   a. On sedan styles (Fig. 6-32a), use care to mask the glass run channels properly.
   b. On hard-top styles (Fig. 6-32b), apply perimeter masking as required to sealing strips, weatherstrips, and retainers around the opening. Complete detail masking on the body and door lock pillars before closing the door and before filler masking.
2. Apply filler masking to the side windows as required. Seal all overlapping joints with tape.
3. If the car must be driven or moved from the surface preparation area to the spray painting area, special masking attention must be given to the driver's door.
   a. Mask the driver's door (including the door window and sealing strips) to allow the door to be opened and closed without disturbing the masking.
   b. Make a special opening in the windshield masking so that it can be closed after the car is moved.

Door Handles (Fig. 6-33).   A similar masking procedure can be used on protruding (push button) and flush-type (pull-out) door handles. Also, the perimeter and filler masking can be done in reverse.

1. Use $\frac{1}{4}$-inch tape around the base perimeter of the handle at the paint surface. Maintain the proper distance, $\frac{1}{32}$ inch. Keep the tape off rubber or plastic gaskets at the base of the handle.
2. Use $\frac{3}{4}$-inch tape. Apply filler tape lengthwise to the handle. Apply $\frac{3}{4}$-inch tape flush around the push button and check its operation on the left door only. Double-mask

Masking   **185**

(a)

(b)

Figure 6-32 (a) Masking side windows (sedan styles). (b) Masking side windows (hard-top styles). (Courtesy of the 3M Company)

the pull-out handle and check its operation on the left door only. "Double" means tape **under** and **over** the pull-out section on the left door only. This allows operation of the handle after masking.

Lock Cylinders

1. Use $\frac{1}{4}$-inch tape around the base perimeter of the cylinder.
2. Apply filler tape as required.

Aerials (Fig. 6-34).   Two methods are available for masking aerials. In both methods, the base is masked with $\frac{1}{4}$- or $\frac{3}{4}$-inch perimeter masking tape.

Figure 6-33   Masking flush-type door handle. (Courtesy of R-M Automotive Products, BASF Inmont Corp.)

Figure 6-34   Masking aerials. (Courtesy of the 3M Company)

Method 1: Make a long sleeve (envelope) of the proper length by rolling up a long section of paper, sealing it with tape, and slipping it over the aerial. Seal the envelope to the base masking with tape.

Method 2: Apply two sections of sufficiently wide tape (usually $\frac{3}{4}$ inch) lengthwise to the aerial, one on each side, and press them together. This is the most popular method. Seal both strips of masking at the base.

Wheels (Fig. 6-35)

1. Using $\frac{3}{8}$- or $\frac{1}{2}$-inch tape, apply masking to the tire completely around the perimeter of the wheel. Keep the tape within $\frac{1}{16}$ or $\frac{1}{8}$ inch of the wheel behind the edge of the wheel rim.

Figure 6-35 Masking wheels. (Courtesy of the 3M Company)

2. Using sections of pretaped aprons (6 inches wide), complete filler masking of the tire for wheel painting as shown in Fig. 6-35.

Front Ends, Grilles, and Bumpers (Fig. 6-36).   On most cars, front ends, grilles, and bumpers can be masked with a combination of perimeter and filler masking as shown in Fig. 6-36. Gather up the loose edges of the masking along the bottom of the bumper, tape together, and secure at the bottom of the bumper.

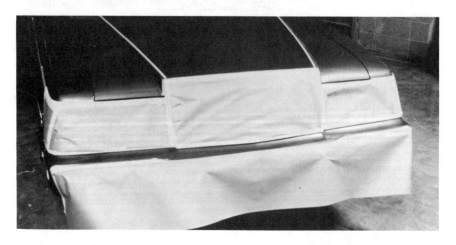

Figure 6-36   Masking front ends, grilles, and bumpers. (Courtesy of the 3M Company)

Masking the Car for Painting Exterior Flexible Plastic Parts (See Fig. 16-2)

When used, flexible plastic parts are located between the front and/or rear bumper and the car. These parts are usually named **"filler panels"** because they fill the space between the bumpers and the car. These parts are made of flexible plastic and are designed to flex when the bumpers are pushed in, such as during incidental contact upon parking the car. These parts are painted with a special paint system that must flex with the panels when the parts are bent or flexed in normal or cold weather without cracking. This paint system is covered in Chapter 16. Masking the car to paint these parts is done as follows:

1. Mask the front and/or rear bumpers as follows:
   a. Mask around the perimeter of the bumpers next to the filler panels only. This is across the edges of the bumper nearest the car only.
   b. Then filler-mask the balance of the bumper as shown in Fig. 6-36.
2. Mask off the car front and/or rear end. First, perimeter-mask the adjacent parts; then apply filler masking to the necessary height (12 or more inches).

Crease-Line or Reverse Masking

Various methods of crease-line masking have been used in the refinish trade since crease-lines became popular in the 1960s. Crease-line masking consists of using natural panel crease-lines, where present, for masking purposes to minimize paint repair areas. Crease-lines must run all the way across a panel for this type of masking to be most effective. Use of crease-lines for sectional panel repairs reduces the volume of refinish paint material used, and it cuts down paint labor because a smaller area is painted.

The 3M Company has available a masking tape called **"Feather Edge"** tape, part number 06355. The tape allows the painter to do faster and better quality work along panel crease-lines with less effort. As shown in Fig. 6-37, simply unroll and apply Feather Edge tape along panel crease-lines as needed. Complete masking the adjacent panels and proceed with color application. Feather Edge Tape provides the painter with the following benefits:

1. Faster masking means more jobs can be done quickly.
2. Ready-for-use means precision masking immediately.
3. The strong tape holds its shape firmly until job is done.
4. Saves paint, saves time, and does a professional job.

IMPORTANT: Change the position of masking tape at crease-lines just slightly outwardly after each coating application to aid in feathering the material at blend areas. For this reason, do the masking at crease-lines last, just before each new coating application. Properly done, perfectly feathered edges are achieved.

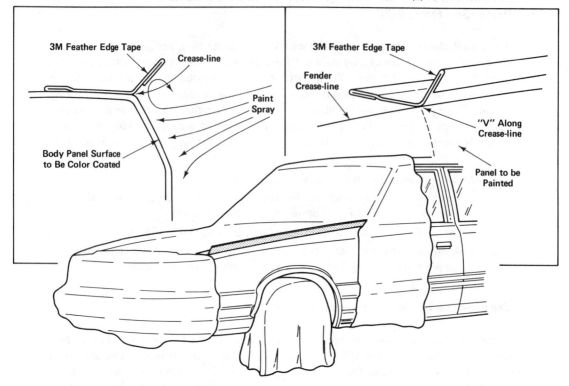

Figure 6-37 Masking along panel crease-line with 3M Feather Edge Tape. (Courtesy of the 3M Company)

Procedure for Reverse Masking along Crease-lines. An alternate method of masking along panel crease-lines, but more time consuming, is the reverse masking procedure, also a 3M development. Reverse masking is described in Fig. 6-38.

1. Using a 6-inch or wider premasked apron of masking paper, position the centerline of exposed tape attached to masking paper along the center of the crease-line (Fig. 6-38a) and slick down the tape for the length of the crease-line as required on the surface to be protected. Use one or more sections of premasked paper as needed.
2. Reverse the position of the masking paper over the crease-line by raising the paper onto the panel to be protected and secure the paper to the panel as shown (Fig. 6-38b).

Masking Door Jambs (Fig. 6-39)

The term **door jambs** means all the facing panels **around the doors,** such as the door hinge pillar, lock pillar, bottom, and upper frame. Door jambs include all facing panels **on the body** around the doors, such as the body hinge pillar, lock pillar, rocker panel

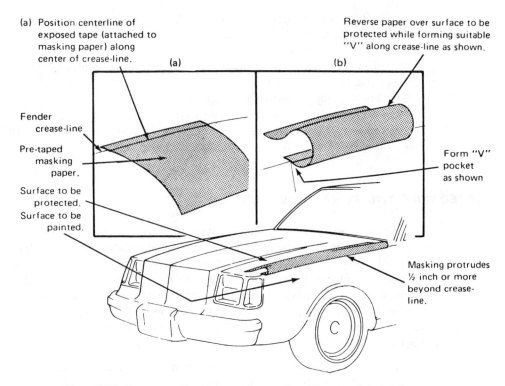

(a) Position centerline of exposed tape (attached to masking paper) along center of crease-line.

Reverse paper over surface to be protected while forming suitable "V" along crease-line as shown.

(a)   (b)

Fender crease-line

Pre-taped masking paper.

Surface to be protected.
Surface to be painted.

Form "V" pocket as shown

Masking protrudes ½ inch or more beyond crease-line.

Figure 6-38 Reverse masking along panel crease-line. (Courtesy of the 3M Company)

Figure 6-39 Masking door jambs. (Courtesy of the 3M Company)

(bottom), and side roof rail (upper). When door jambs are to be painted, it is necessary to mask off all adjacent weatherstrips, door lock and striker components, body number plates, and all trim components.

Door jambs are masked best by first detail-perimeter-masking adjacent parts and then completing the job with a 6-inch or wider pretaped apron similar to that shown in Fig. 6-39. For masking weatherstrips, see item 10 of "Tips on Masking."

Door jambs are best spray-painted with acrylic lacquer because of the paint's quick-dry characteristics, even on enamel paint jobs. On complete paint jobs, door jambs are always painted before the exterior paint finish is applied.

DETERMINE THE SURFACE CONDITION

Before starting work on a car, always examine the surface carefully. The best paint in the world will not provide the durability and appearance expected of it if applied over an improperly prepared surface. Analyze the original paint finish to determine the nature of a particular problem, if any, and to determine the type and extent of surface preparation required. Chapter 17 covers description and remedies for common paint problems. By calling on his or her personal experience and good judgment, the painter should determine if the surface to be refinished is in good condition, in poor condition, or in a combination of these conditions.

Surface in Good Condition.   A surface in good condition is one that consists primarily of surface problems such as off-color, excessive orange peel, and localized rust conditions due to chipped edges, stone bruises, and so on. A surface in good condition can be repaired by the spot-repair method or by correction of the color coat only, as the paint, where not damaged, is basically sound.

Surface in Poor Condition.   A surface in poor condition is one that has problems that affect the entire thickness of the paint film, color, and undercoats over large areas of the panels in several locations of the car. This is particularly evident when such conditions as excessively deep scratching, rust under paint, and lifting and peeling are encountered. Normally, a finish in poor condition must be removed down to the bare metal for satisfactory refinishing.

Aids for Thorough Paint Analysis (for Checking Spot Areas on a Car)

Any one or combination of the following aids will assist the painter in analyzing a paint finish to determine if the finish is in good or in poor condition.

1. Adequate light is most important to a good inspection.
2. Wash the car for a better visual inspection.
3. Solvent-clean the finish to remove any deposits not removed by a soap and water wash.

4. Use a magnifying glass to observe suspected "crazing" or paint cracking conditions more closely.

5. Compound the finish to determine the gloss restoration and depth penetration of the particular condition.

6. Sand the finish as required to determine the depth penetration of the particular condition.

7. Use a fine-pointed tool to examine blisters and peeling paint more closely.

The life of a paint finish and the appearance of that finish depend directly on the condition of the surface over which the paint is applied. A thoroughly clean and level surface for paint to grip is essential. All dirt, oil, grease, wax, silicone, moisture, and rust must be removed. Any of these contaminants can affect the durability and appearance of the final finish.

Surface preparation, including the application of undercoats, involves all steps necessary to get good adhesion. Experienced painters know that refinish color coats are not designed with special surface-filling qualities. A finished paint job is no smoother than the surface over which color coats are applied.

Preparing a Surface in Good Condition

A paint surface in good condition is easy to prepare for repainting. Use of the following steps ensures proper surface preparation for topcoats regardless of type, acrylic lacquer, or enamel.

1. Wash the surface to remove dirt and road film. Use a *small* amount of detergent for better results. Be sure to rinse the car thoroughly with clean water.

2. After washing, clean the surface with paint finish cleaning solvent (see Table 6-1) to ensure removal of all wax, grease, oil, silicone, and other contaminants. **Using plenty of clean, white cloths, clean only small areas at a time and wipe dry while still wet.**

3. Water-sand surface with No. 360 grit sandpaper or finer to:
   a. Reduce final total film thickness
   b. Remove case-hardened film surface
   c. Smooth out surface
   d. Remove surface problem conditions

   Use sanding block and proper sanding technique. If acrylic lacquer is to be used over acrylic lacquer, finish sanding with No. 400 sandpaper if a light color is to be used. Finish sanding with No. 500 sandpaper if a dark color is to be used.

4. If sanding through the entire paint finish, such as when removing rust, featheredge broken paint edges as required. The fingertips should feel no break or ridge between the metal and the paint.

5. To remove sanding residue, wash the entire area, including bare metal, with a solvent-type cleaner if small or with water if large. Allow the area to dry thor-

oughly. Blow off surfaces and crevices with compressed air. Force drying with infrared equipment is helpful.

6. Mask off the car as required.

Preparing a Surface in Poor Condition

Anything that is lasting or successful is always built on a strong foundation, and paint is no exception. A paint surface in poor condition always needs the most preparation work. If the required preparation work is disregarded, the final paint finish will soon fail in appearance and durability. The penalty is loss of future business or the cost of re-painting.

A paint finish in **poor condition** usually **must be removed to the depth of the original undercoat or down to the metal.** If the paint failure is confined to the color coat, only the color coat should be removed. **Original factory-baked primer should not be removed unless a failure is clearly evident.**

The following steps are necessary to prepare a surface in poor condition:

1. If the area to be painted is crossed or edged by a molding, nameplate, or emblem, remove the parts. Moldings hinder proper repairs by trapping water, dirt, and paint removers. Save parts in a special place.
2. Remove old finish as required. This can be done by any one or a combination of the following:
   a. Hand sanding (see "Hand Sanding")
   b. Disc sanding or power sanding (see applicable sections under "Power Sanders and Power Files")
   c. Paint remover (see "Paint Removers")
   d. Sandblasting (see "Sandblasting")
3. **On bare metal, perform any cleanup sanding operations,** manual or power, as required. **Remove all rust** and other surface blemishes.
4. If paint remover was used and most of the original undercoat is still on the job, wash the panel with (medium) lacquer thinner and wipe dry.
5. If the replacement part is primed with a black factory primer, first dry-sand the panel lightly and carefully with No. 500 sandpaper. Avoid cut-throughs. Then clean the part with paint finish cleaning solvent. Next, apply the required sealer for paint system to be used.
6. Brush clean and blow out all crevices and moldings.
7. Mask off the car as required.

REVIEW QUESTIONS

1. Explain the purpose and procedure for using paint finish cleaning solvent.
2. What is the procedure for removing silicones?

3. Metal conditioners should be used in two parts. What is the purpose of each part, and what is the correct use of each? (Include reduction of conditioner.)
   (a) On steel surfaces
   (b) On galvanized surfaces
   (c) On aluminum surfaces
4. What is a quick, simple way to determine if the base, which is painted, is steel?
5. What is the purpose and correct use of a tack rag?
6. What is the purpose and correct use of a squeegee?
7. What is the purpose of a sanding block?
8. What is the purpose of sandpaper? (Give four uses.)
9. What are the two most popular abrasives in the refinishing trade, and for what is each best suited?
10. What does "open coat" mean, and for what purpose is it used?
11. What does "closed coat" mean, and for what purpose is it used?
12. What is the safety rule for eyes when using a disc sander?
13. Explain the purpose of type C and type D discs as used with a portable sander.
14. Why is most sanding done in two stages: a coarse followed by a fine sanding?
15. Explain how to reduce sheet sandpaper into "thirds" for hand sanding small areas (this includes folding).
16. Explain the block sanding technique.
17. Explain the hand sanding technique (without sanding block).
18. Explain the finger sanding technique.
19. Explain the circle sanding technique.
20. Explain the cross-cutting technique.
21. Explain wet-sanding technique by hand (with and without a sanding block).
22. Explain the dry-sanding technique by hand.
23. Explain the scuff-sanding technique.
24. Explain the featheredging technique.
25. Explain how to use sanding disc adhesive.
26. Explain the small power sander operating technique.
27. Explain how to install a backing pad and disc on a large portable disc sander.
28. Explain the operating technique for a large portable disc sander:
    (a) Include safety rules.
    (b) Include protection of edges.
29. What is the purpose and correct use of acrylic lacquer removing solvent?
30. What are the two primary types of paint removers on the market? Describe the purpose and correct use of each.
31. Explain how to protect a floor when using paint remover.
32. Explain how to keep paint remover from gap spacings.
33. What safety equipment and clothing should the painter use when sandblasting to remove rust?

34. Explain how sand is caused to go from the sand container through the gun during sandblasting.

35. What type of sand is best suited for sandblasting to remove rust?

36. What is the best place to do sandblasting in the paint shop during cold weather?

37. Explain how to remove rust from a small, severe corrosive pit if a sandblast unit is not available.

38. Explain how to repair a rust condition that has recurred on the same spot after repairs were made previously.

39. Explain why tinning as a rust-repair operation guarantees rust prevention.

40. What type of respirator is best suited for sandblasting?

41. What is the purpose of masking?

42. Name or describe two types of masking tape.

43. List several qualities of a good masking tape.

44. List several qualities of a good masking paper.

45. What two widths of masking tape are most popular in the refinishing trade?

46. What special tools assist the painter in applying and/or removing masking tape?

47. Explain how to hold and unroll masking tape.

48. Explain the technique for snap-tearing masking tape.

49. What is a good safe distance to maintain between the tape edge and the paint surface?

50. How soon after painting can masking tape be removed?

51. When removing masking tape from curved edges, on what side and in what direction is emphasis placed when pulling the tape?

52. What precautions can be taken with masking paper to prevent bleed-through on adjacent lacquer surfaces when applying very slow-drying lacquers?

53. How could a painter prevent masking tape from pulling the rubber skin off foam rubber door weatherstrips when removing masking tape?

54. What is perimeter masking?

55. What is filler masking?

56. How is filler masking done most quickly when there is no apron taper or masking machine on hand?

57. Explain how to mask a complete windshield or back window.

58. Explain how to mask the complete side windows of a car.

59. Explain how to mask the complete door outside handle.

60. Explain how to mask the complete outside vertical aerial.

61. Explain how to mask a tire as required for spray painting the wheel.

62. Why must exterior flexible plastic parts be masked off when repainting the exterior car color?

63. Why must the car exterior color be masked off when repainting the exterior flexible plastic parts?

64. What is crease-line masking, and how is it done?

7

Automotive Refinishing

Solvents

PURPOSE OF SOLVENTS

The purpose of solvents in automotive refinishing is as follows:

1. To reduce paint materials to a lower viscosity for application.
2. To make spray painting possible by:
   a. Vaporizing up to one-third of the solvent in a paint cup before paint reaches the surface (Fig. 7-1).
   b. Carrying the paint finish to the surface through proper atomization.
   c. Flowing out the paint finish smoothly and evenly on the surface.
   d. Helping the paint film dry (Fig. 7-2):
      (1) Enamels dry by (a) Polymerization and oxidation mostly (a chemical change that is speeded up if a catalyst is used), and (b) Evaporation of some solvent.
      (2) Lacquers dry only by evaporation of solvent.
3. To aid in blending lacquer and enamel spot repairs.
4. To clean up equipment and painter when painting is done.

Automotive paint solvents are classified into two categories:

1. In enamel systems, the solvent is known as **"reducer."**
2. In lacquer systems, the solvent is known as **"thinner."**

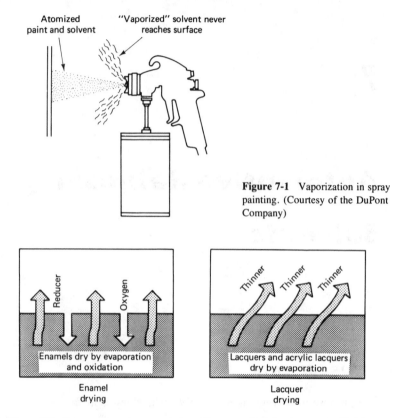

Figure 7-1 Vaporization in spray painting. (Courtesy of the DuPont Company)

Figure 7-2 Evaporation and spray painting. (Courtesy of Ditzler Automotive Finishes, PPG Industries, Inc.)

COMPONENT PARTS OF SOLVENTS

Automotive paint solvents (reducers and thinners) are made of mixtures or blends of different types of solvents. Although the principle of making solvents is similar, the ingredients that go into reducers are entirely different from the ingredients that are used for thinners. Therefore, the two materials are never meant to be and never should be used interchangeably.

Basically, thinners and reducers are made of three different types of solvents:

1. True solvent
2. Latent solvent
3. Diluent

True Solvent. A true solvent is a liquid capable of dissolving something, that is, causing it to pass into solution. For instance, water is a solvent for sugar but gasoline is not. The main job of solvent is to dissolve the resin portion of a paint system and cause it to go into solution.

Latent Solvent.   A latent solvent is a liquid that when used alone is not a good solvent, but when added to a good solvent makes the resultant blend of equal performance to the original good solvent. Good solvents are usually higher-priced than latent solvents. Thus, through blending, paint suppliers are able to mix good solvents and latent solvents to achieve the excellent results of a good solvent while keeping the price of the thinner and reducer competitive.

Diluent.   A diluent is a liquid that makes more liquid of the material to which it is added. In other words, it thins or dilutes. Some diluents in lacquer thinners also serve as resin solvents.

HOW SOLVENTS ARE MADE

The chemists of a reputable paint company or chemical firm build paint solvents for the automobile factories and refinishing trade as surely and precisely as a contractor builds a building. In producing good-quality solvents for the factory and field, the chemist balances one solvent against another for the ultimate, desired action. One combination of solvent and latent solvent produce flow-out. The addition of another solvent produces blush resistance. Another combination produces better solvency, and so on. The right combination of solvent types in the proper proportions results in a thinner or reducer that is right for the job. All steps in the manufacture of quality thinners and reducers are carefully watched and controlled by the paint supplier laboratory and quality control people in order to give the painter in factories and in the field the right solvent for the job.

TYPES OF SOLVENTS REQUIRED

Experience has proved that no one solvent will meet every refinishing requirement. To do quality refinishing on a year-round basis, a paint shop should be supplied with four different types of solvent for each paint system used.

Slow-drying Solvent (65°F and up) (Table 7-1).   A slow-drying solvent is designed for the application of acrylic colors in average and higher shop temperatures, 65°F and up. This solvent produces a high gloss because it possesses excellent flow-out characteristics. In metallics, it produces standard color shades. The flash-time evaporation rate for slow lacquer thinner ranges from $3\frac{1}{2}$ to 5 minutes when applied wet (with an eye dropper) on a red oxide primer-surfaced panel at about 75°F with no exhaust system operating. For slow enamel reducer, the flash time is slightly longer. This is how dry time is determined.

TABLE 7-1 THINNERS AND REDUCERS: EVAPORATION RATE AND RECOMMENDED USE

	Rinshed-Mason	Ditzler	DuPont	Martin-Senour	Sherwin-Williams
ACRYLIC LACQUER THINNERS					
Fast (50° to 65°F)	PNT-48	DTL-151	3613S	3088	R7K205
Medium-fast (60° to 70°F)	PNT-62	DTL-16	3608S	2092	R7K214
Medium (65° to 80°F)	PNT-88	DTL-876	3661S	3099	R7K248
Slow (65° to 80°F)		DTL-135	3602S	3095	R7K203
Extra-slow (70°F and up)	PNT-90	DTL-105	3696S	3094	R7K6231
Retarder (mix with above) to prevent blushing)	883	DTX-1140	3979S	8840	R7K251
ACRYLIC ENAMEL REDUCERS					
Fast (50° to 70°F)	MS-5	DTR-601	8034S	8834	R7K227
Medium (70° to 90°F)	MS-6	DTR-602	8022S	8831	R7K211
Slow (85°F and up)	MS-7	DTR-604	8093S	8832	R7K212
Retarder/hot weather	MS-8	DTR-607	8096S	8833	R7K244
(100°F and up)	883		8100S	8840	R7K6251
Special	BC-25[a]				
ACRYLIC URETHANE REDUCERS					
Fast (50° to 70° F)		DTU-501		8431	R7K6200
				8432	R7K6202
Medium (65° to 85°F)		DTU-504		8433	R7K6204
		DT-170[b]			
		DT-870[b]			
Slow (80°F and up)		DT-185[b]		8434	R7K6206
		DT-885[b]			
Retarder (mix with above)		DTU-505		8455	R7K6208
POLYURETHANE REDUCERS					
Fast (60° to 80°F)	MR-16	DTU-800	8575S	8834	R7K227
Medium (65° to 85°F)	MR-17	DTU-801	8585S	8831	R7K211
Slow (80° to 95°F)	MR-18	DTU-803	8595S	8832	R7K212
Retarder (95°F and	883	DTU-805		8833	R7K244
above)				8840	R7K6251

[a]Special reducer for Miracryl-2- basecoat colors only.

[b]For Deltron basecoat colors only.

Note: Although not shown in this table, alkyd enamel reducers are still available through your paint jobbers.

Uses

1. For applying acrylic colors in average shop temperatures.
2. For mist-coating blend areas of spot repairs when a slow evaporation rate is needed.
3. For mist coating in its pure form over an entire spot or panel repair (within 10 to 20 minutes **after** thorough flash-off) to achieve additional gloss and/or darkening of metallic colors.

4. For reduction in a modified conventional system, which involves a blend with retarder and the use of less solvent by volume to produce darker color shades in metallics.

5. For mist coating, by blending with retarder and adding 5% to 20% clear acrylic, to produce darker shades in a given metallic color. Use after thorough flash-off, but within 20 to 30 minutes after color application.

6. Slow-drying solvent can be speeded up by blending with a faster solvent. A 50–50 blend of slow and medium solvents makes an excellent mist-coat solvent for blending in average shop temperatures (65° to 85°F).

Medium-drying Solvent (65°F and up) (Table 7-1). A medium-drying solvent is designed for primer–surfacer application in average shop temperature conditions, 65°F and up. This thinner produces good flow-out of primer-surfacer and dries more quickly than the slow, high-gloss solvent. The average flash-time evaporation rate for medium thinner is about 2 minutes when applied wet (with an eye dropper) on a red oxide primer-surfaced panel at about 72°F with no exhaust system operating. Flash time for medium reducers is slightly longer.

Medium thinner slows down in evaporation rate as the temperature drops. To obtain equal wetting action and flow-out of primer–surfacer in 60° to 65°F temperature, a medium-fast solvent can be developed. This is a blend of about 50% fast solvent and 50% medium solvent. Medium-fast solvent evaporates in about 1 minute.

Uses

1. For application of primer–surfacer (65° to 85°F)
2. For solid colors (60° to 70°F)
3. For mist coating (60° to 70°F)
4. For speeding up slow solvent
5. For slowing down fast solvent

Medium-fast Solvent

1. For primer–surfacer (60° to 65°F)
2. For solid colors (60° to 65°F)
3. For mist coating (60° to 65°F)

Application of primer–surfacer with too fast a solvent for the temperature results in a very porous undercoat, which could result in poor hold-out, rough surface, excessive shrinkage, and less gloss.

Fast-drying Solvent (below 60°F) (Table 7-1). A very fast drying solvent is necessary for the repair of original acrylic lacquers, which could craze if top-coated with slower solvents in average shop temperatures (65° to 85°F). **Fast thinners** evaporate so quickly in average temperatures that they do not penetrate aged acrylic lacquers. They are classified as nonpenetrating. The flash-time evaporation rate for fast thinners ranges from 15 to 20 seconds when applied wet with an eye dropper on a red oxide primer-surfaced panel at about 72°F with no exhaust system operating. The flash time for **fast reducers** is slightly longer.

Uses

1. To prevent crazing in average temperature (65° to 85°F), use in a conventional manner and first apply two or three color coats somewhat on the dry side. Then top-coat as required.
2. For spot or panel repairs, if metallic lacquer is involved and the color shade is too light, use initial color coats as a sealer by applying them dry and mist-coating lightly. Allow to dry and scuff-sand if necessary. Then use slower thinner as required and color-coat to match.
3. May be used for primer–surfacer application in temperatures below 60°F.
4. Many paint shops feel they save money by using fast-drying thinner slowed down with retarder for color application. Although this system of painting has its advantages, it often leads to comebacks, particularly in metallic color matching.
5. The use of fast-drying thinner for primer–surfacer application in temperatures over 70°F results in a very porous, spongy undercoat. This leads to a number of problems, such as poor holdout, rough surface, and excessive shrinkage.
6. Fast-drying thinner may be used to speed the evaporation rate of the slower thinners when the need arises.

Retarder (Very Slow Drying; for Hot Weather Use) (Table 7-1).   Retarder is not a true thinner. It is a pure form of a single ingredient. Cellosolve acetate is an example. It is added to reduced material or to another solvent when a slower drying time is desired. This is one solvent that could be used effectively in both acrylic lacquer and acrylic enamel paint systems. Retarder prevents blushing because it has an inherent affinity for water. As condensation of water takes place on the surface of freshly applied acrylic paint with retarder, the retarder absorbs the water and keeps it from mixing with the paint ingredients, which would cause a kick-out or a blushing condition. The flash-time evaporation rate of retarder is about 30 minutes when applied on a red oxide undercoated panel at about 72°F with no exhaust system operating.

Uses of Retarder

1. Prevents blushing (see Chapter 17)
2. Makes possible color application in hot, humid weather
3. Provides better flow-out by lengthening the evaporation time
4. Enriches the solvent action when added to a slow solvent
5. Enriches a slow solvent for mist coating in spot repairs, to eliminate overspray, to provide more flow-out, and to create more gloss.

Temperature can affect the final smoothness of the finish in terms of flow-out, gloss, orange peel, and other properties that depend on drying of the finish. Temperature and humidity problems are most easily overcome by the proper selection of solvents.

The ideal spraying temperature range is between 68° and 75°F. All paint suppliers usually recommend this temperature range for spray painting. Repair of acrylic finishes should not be done in temperatures below 60°F.

When paint supplier recommendations are made in label directions, they are made for "average" temperature and humidity conditions: 68° to 75°F temperature and 50% to 80% humidity. There is no set formula or method for determining the "ideal solvent mixture" that works perfectly on all colors in all temperatures and all humidity conditions. Each painter must use his or her good judgment and knowledge of solvent behavior and selection in all temperature and humidity conditions. The painter must be able to select and to adjust solvents to meet the needs of the job being painted. A painter must be able to assemble the right combination of solvents to do high-quality work in all types of weather conditions. A painter must be able to:

1. Use the fastest evaporation solvents on cold days.
2. Use the slowest evaporation solvents, including retarder, in extra hot and humid weather.
3. Use a combination of solvents between the above two extremes.

The proper solvent is a key tool in successful refinishing. It is up to the painter to determine and use the solvent combination that is proper for any spray painting application. Sometimes a painter does not realize the full importance of temperature and humidity on the refinish process. Much of the time a painter is busy thinking about getting done the jobs he or she is working on; ordering color and supplies for the next job; and while he or she is doing these, a color-matching problem crops up. The higher the temperature, the faster the solvents evaporate between the spray gun and the work surface. When solvents evaporate too fast, this has a marked effect on the painting results, particularly when color-matching metallic colors. This is the same as dry spraying or not getting enough solvent on the part being painted for proper flow-out.

The painter is able to control spraying techniques, which are important to the final results of a paint job. The essential items a painter can control when painting are:

1. Thinner selection and reduction
2. Proper spray gun adjustments
3. Distance of gun from surface
4. Speed of spraying
5. Overlap
6. Air pressure at gun

Three things a painter cannot control are temperature, humidity, and ventilation. The rate of evaporation on a hot summer day (90° to 110°F) can be approximately 50% faster than it is on an average day of 72°F. But what the painter can do is to select the proper solvent that does a high-quality job under the circumstances. The chart of variables (Table 7-2) was assembled as a result of many years of experience matching metallic-type colors. Table 7-2 charts three shop variables: temperature, humidity, and ventilation and the effect these variables have on metallic colors. Although the painter

TABLE 7-2 VARIABLES AFFECTING COLOR OF METALLICS.

VARIABLE	TO MAKE COLOR LIGHTER	TO MAKE COLOR DARKER
SHOP CONDITIONS:		
a. Temperature	Increase	Decrease
b. Humidity	Decrease	Increase
c. Ventilation	Increase	Decrease
SPRAY EQUIPMENT & ADJUSTMENTS:		
a. Fluid Tip	Use Smaller Size	Use Larger Size
b. Air Cap	Use Air Cap with Greater Number of Openings	Use Air Cap with Lesser Number of Openings
c. Fluid Adjustment Valve	Reduce Volume of Material Flow	Increase Volume of Material Flow
d. Spreader Adjustment Valve	Increase Fan Width	Decrease Fan Width
e. Air Pressure (at Gun)	Increase Air Pressure	Decrease Air Pressure
THINNER USAGE:		
a. Type of Thinner	Use Faster Evaporating Thinner	Use Slower Evaporating Thinner
b. Reduction of Color	Increase Volume of Thinner	Decrease Volume of Thinner
c. Use of Retarder	(Do Not Use Retarder)	Add Proportional Amount of Retarder to Thinner
SPRAYING TECHNIQUES:		
a. Gun Distance	Increase Distance	Decrease Distance
b. Gun Speed	Increase Speed	Decrease Speed
c. Flash Time Between Coats	Allow More Flash Time	Allow Less Flash Time
d. Mist Coat	(Will Not Lighten Color)	The Wetter the Mist Coat the Darker the Color

cannot control these variables, he or she must learn how to adapt to the variables and still do required paint work. A **variable** in refinishing means that, as a variable changes, corresponding changes also take place in the final shade of metallic colors, as shown in Table 7-2. Ventilation is included as an uncontrollable variable because generally the painter is not responsible for providing shop ventilation. This is a responsibility of the paint shop. Not all paint shops have 100% foolproof ventilation.

Factories usually have a large paint mixing room (Fig. 7-3) where paint materials

Figure 7-3 Paint mixing department in car factory. (Courtesy of Ditzler Automotive Finishes, PPG Industries, Inc.)

Figure 7-4 Ford paint viscosity cup with thermometer and stop watch. (Courtesy of Ditzler Automotive Finishes, PPG Industries, Inc.)

are reduced before being sent to the department where painting is done. Paint is kept agitated continuously, 24 hours per day, until all of it is used up. A special person has the responsibility of checking and controlling the viscosity of all paint materials continually to keep up with changing temperature conditions. In this manner the paint is always correctly prepared. Figure 7-4 shows a Ford-type viscosity cup as used at many car factory test labs. Note the use of a thermometer to check the temperature of the paint. In factory paint mixing rooms, the thermometer is immersed in the paint being tested.

PAINT VISCOSITY CUP (Fig. 7-5)

Too many painters fail to be concerned with the spraying viscosity of paint materials. Over- or underreduction of paint results in a number of problems, such as mismatches with metallics, runs or sags, excessive orange peel, and generally poor paint repairability. The best ways to check the viscosity of a reduced paint material is with a viscosity cup.

Temperature influences viscosity directly. Body shop thermometers are available to the trade through a number of sources. Figure 7-6 is an example of a thermometer that paint suppliers have available on occasion. Primarily designed for body shop use, the $-40°$ to $120°F$ thermometer features a solvent scale for automotive paint reduction, as well as an exact percentage humidity scale.

If cold paint is brought into an average temperature room, cold paint will be thicker and more viscous. Simply adding solvent to make it sprayable is not always the best thing to do. It is best to allow paint to reach workable or average room temperature.

Paint Viscosity Cup   **205**

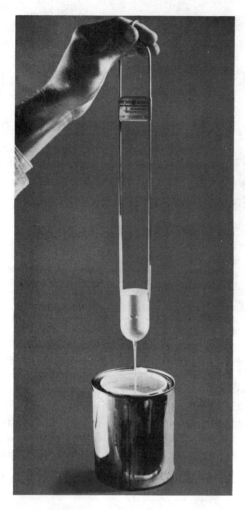

Figure 7-5 Zahn No. 2 paint viscosity cup. (Courtesy of General Electric Company)

However, if paint must be applied in cool temperatures, below 70°F, the viscosity should still read within the time limits indicated in Table 7-3. Viscosity is adjusted as required by adding solvent or unreduced paint to the reduction.

Directions for Using a Viscosity Cup (Zahn No. 2 or Equivalent)

1. Dip the cup into reduced paint until it is full and have a stopwatch ready.
2. Remove the cup and as the bottom of the cup clears the surface of the paint, start timing the flow of paint from the small hole in the bottom of the cup (Fig. 7-5). (Use of a stopwatch is preferred for this step.)
3. Stop the timer when a continuous stream of paint "breaks." Check the time in seconds against Table 7-3 for type of material and make adjustments as required.

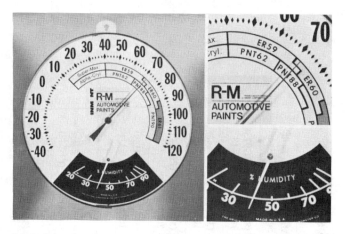

Figure 7-6 Paint shop thermometer (R-M type shown). (Courtesy of R-M Automotive Products, BASF Inmont Corp.)

Availability of a Viscosity Cup

The Zahn No. 2 paint viscosity cup is available to the trade through a number of paint and equipment jobbers and through a number of General Electric distributors around the country. For more specific availability information, contact Robert Dalferro, Instrument Products Operation, General Electric Company, 40 Federal Street, West Lynn, Mass. 01910. Mr. Dalferro will advise painters on the price and a list of Zahn cup distributors nationally.

PERCENTAGE OF REDUCTION AND MIXING RATIO

No matter how much experience a painter has, it is always wise to read the label directions before using a paint material. As the old saying goes: "If a person cannot read the label directions, he or she should get someone to read the directions out loud." Products go through changes on a continual basis. Reading the labels before they get messed up is one good way to keep up with the product.

When label directions make a statement such as "Reduce 125%" or "33%," the **percentage figure** always applies to the **solvent system.** Table 7-4 is a reduction ratio guide. It explains the mixing ratio for each common reduction percentage figure from $12\frac{1}{2}\%$ to 300%. Also included is an expansion of the mixing ratio that simplifies each reduction into parts by volume of each material used. Painters can usually tell how much mixed paint they need by the size of the paint repair.

How to Reduce Paint in a Paint Cup (Fig. 7-7)

1. Prepare the paint paddle as follows and position in the paint cup:
   a. Apply masking tape on the paint paddle as shown.

TABLE 7-3 VISCOSITY CUP READINGS FOR AUTOMOTIVE REFINISH TRADE USAGE: ZAHN NO. 2 CUP (FIG. 7-5) (TIMING IS IN SECONDS)

UNDERCOAT SYSTEMS	Rinshed-Mason	Ditzler	DuPont	Martin-Senour	Sherwin-Williams
Primer	(834) 16	(DP40/401) 21	(615/616S)	(8827) 16–18	(E2G973) 16–18
Primer-surfacer	(831, 832) 21	(DZ-3) 19–21	(131S) 23–24	(3254) 16–18	(P2A43) 16–18
Primer-surfacer (option)		(K200/201) 25	(181S) 23–24	(5100) 20–21	(P6H 49)
Sealer	(GP-75) 21	(DL-1970) RFU	(1984S) RFU	(5105) 18–20	(E6H59)
Sealer (option)	(PS-19)27	(DAS-1980) RFU	(1985S) RFU		
Sealer for repair of OEM BC/CC with acrylic lacquer	(811)RFU	(DSX-1900) RFU	(222S) RFU	(3061) RFU	(P1C48) RFU
Sealer for repair of acrylic lacquer with acrylic lacquer	(PS-19) 27	(DL-1947) RFU	(1984S) RFU	(3060) RFU	(P1A38) RFU
Sealer option for acrylic lacquer repair with acrylic lacquer	(870) RFU	(DL-1970) RFU	(1985S) RFU	(3060) RFU	(P1A38) RFU
Primer-sealer under acrylic enamel	(PS-21) RFU	(DL-1980) RFU	(1984S) RFU	(8823)	(E2A52)
Barrier Coat (over cracked finishes, etc.)	(806) RFU	—	—	—	—

COLOR COAT SYSTEMS

Acrylic lacquer (standard type)	17–20	19–21	18–22	20–22	20–22
Acrylic lacquer (BC/CC type)	17		18–22		
Clear acrylic lacquer for standard and BC/CC types	16–18	19–21	18–22	20–22	20–22
Clear urethane for BC/CC lacquer			18–22	(3073)	(T1C276)
Acrylic enamel (standard type)	19	21–23	18–22	20–22	20–22
Urethane or acrylic enamel (BC/CC type)	M'cryl-2 16	Deltron	Centari	Acr.Enam.	Acr.Enam.
Clear acrylic urethane for enamel BC colors			18–22	(8853)	(V2V398)
Acrylic urethane colors		20–22		18–22	
Polyurethane enamel colors	18–20	21–23	18–22	24–27	24–27

NOTE: Above material is reduced per label instructions and is ready for spray application. RFU items are packaged ready for use and require no reduction.

209

TABLE 7-4 REDUCTION RATIO GUIDE

Percentage of reduction	Mixing ratio	Paint material	Solvent material
$12\frac{1}{2}$	8:1 =	8 parts	1 part
25	4:1 =	4 parts	1 part
33	3:1 =	3 parts	1 part
50	2:1 =	2 parts	1 part
75	4:3 =	4 parts	3 parts
100	1:1 =	1 part	1 part
125	4:5 =	4 parts	5 parts
150	2:3 =	2 parts	3 parts
175	4:7 =	4 parts	7 parts
200	1:2 =	1 part	2 parts
225	4:9 =	4 parts	9 parts
250	4:10 =	4 parts	10 parts
275	4:11 =	4 parts	11 parts
300	1:3 =	1 part	3 parts

b. Determine the total number of units for reduction: paint and solvent. Equally space unit marks on the paddle, such as $\frac{3}{4}$ inch apart, or other suitable measurement, as shown. Use a ruler for uniform measurements. Also, use a sharp pencil or fine pen for markings.

c. Add the **agitated** paint up to the paint line on the ruled paddle. Keep the paddle in the vertical position.

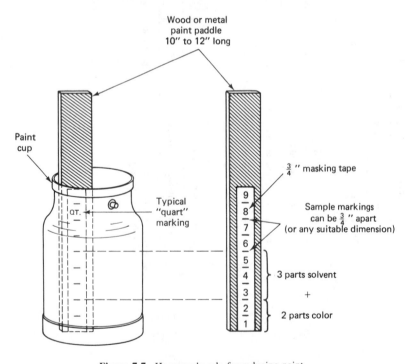

Figure 7-7 Homemade rule for reducing paint.

Automotive Refinishing Solvents   *Chap. 7*

d. Add solvent to the solvent line on the ruled paddle. Pour solvent from a square can as shown in Fig. 7-8.
2. Mix the reduction thoroughly and strain into the spray gun cup.

Conventional Reduction (for Standard Color Shades)

Reduction is the process of preparing "package viscosity" color (the way color comes in a can) for spray painting by adding and mixing the proper amount of recommended solvent. The term **"conventional reduction"** means reducing color according to label directions. This method is designed to produce **standard color shades** for all colors.

Modified-conventional Reduction (for Darker Shades of Metallics)

The term **modified-conventional** means modifying or changing the label directions to produce a darker shade of metallic color. Also, what the painter would gain is to apply more color with fewer coats. Experience has proved that the shade of a metallic color is darkened by using less volume of solvent than called for by the label directions. This requires slowing down the reduction by adding "retarder" to the regular solvent recommended. **Retarder should make up 5% to 10% of the total solvent used** for normal temperature conditions.

In extremely hot weather conditions, painters may have to use 100% retarder. Not all retarders have the same composition. Some retarders are nearly all pure cellosolve acetate. Other retarders have been "cut" (diluted) with other solvents. A painter can tell the difference with the evaporation test. A good retarder should require at least 30 minutes to evaporate, as explained in the section on "Retarder."

Figure 7-8 Pouring solvent from square container. (Courtesy of the DuPont Company)

Q: What is a good rule to follow when purchasing solvents?

A: In selecting a thinner or reducer, always use the solvent recommended by the paint manufacturer of the color or undercoat being used. There should be no exception to this rule.

Q: Why isn't a thinner or reducer all pure solvent?

A: Better solvents are made from blends of solvents. If a thinner were all pure solvent, sprayed material on a vertical wall would "sag" because there would be insufficient vaporization of solvent. The sprayed material on the wall would be almost the same viscosity as the paint material in the cup. Paint material at reduced cup viscosity just cannot be applied on a vertical surface. This is where the chemists determine the viscosity needed to allow paint to come up through the fluid tube and to get rid of excess fluid through vaporization before the paint material builds up on the surface without running. Even with properly reduced materials, if a spray gun is held too close to the surface, such as 1 to 2 inches, the material runs. Why? Because there is insufficient vaporization of solvent.

Q: What is vaporization?

A: Vaporization is changing solvent in a container into vapors or gases during spray painting (Fig. 7-1). Vaporized solvents never reach the surface being painted. The vaporization loss factor of solvent is planned when reduction is determined.

Q: What is a good way to tell a good solvent from a poor one?

A: Reduce the paint according to volume proportions as indicated on label directions, stir it thoroughly, and pour it on a flat section of window glass. Hold the glass at a 45° angle and let paint run down the glass. Ridges, uneven flow, poor flowout, and dulling of the film denote a poor solvent. A good solvent provides uniform flow, a very smooth surface, and a high gloss.

Q: What happens when a painter uses the wrong company's solvent?

A: When a painter uses improper solvents in a paint material, no one will back up the painter when things go wrong. The painter must assume full responsibility. Each paint supplier has its own (patented) formulations for each product. Solvents are designed to dissolve specific products. When solvents are used to dissolve other company's products, even though they serve a similar purpose, the products are most likely to be *not 100% compatible*. This leads to problems, which, in turn, leads to poor results or paint failures.

Q: Should leftover thinned material be poured back into the original container?

A: No, for two reasons. First, additional solvent in any can of paint promotes extra-hard settling of the paint ingredients. Second, it changes the standard method of reducing paint for the next paint job. Some colors of overreduced paint, if left to stand on the shelf for long periods of time, will change in color. It is better to put leftover paint in another container and mark it "Reduced." And if the paint is not used in a reasonable period of time (such as several months), throw it out.

REVIEW QUESTIONS

1. What is a solvent?
2. What is a latent solvent?
3. What is a diluent?
4. What is a thinner?
5. What is a reducer?
6. Explain how solvents are made for the automotive refinishing trade.
7. Give the purpose of and describe the following solvents:
   (a) Slow-drying solvent
   (b) Medium-drying solvent
   (c) Fast-drying solvent
   (d) Retarder
8. Explain how various solvents can be blended by the painter for mist coating and for other spray paint applications.
9. Explain how retarder prevents blushing.
10. Explain how to premark a paint paddle and how to use it as a guide for reducing automotive color accurately in a paint cup.
11. What is the purpose of a viscosity cup, and how it is used?
12. Give a general description of the chart of variables (Table 7-2) that affect the shade of metallic colors.
13. List several spray painting variables over which a painter has direct control.
14. Name the three spray painting variables over which a painter has no control.
15. Explain how the painter can overcome uncontrollable variables through selection and use of solvents.
16. When the label directions on a can of paint state "Reduce 125%," to what does the percentage figure apply, the solvent or the color?
17. What is meant by the term "conventional reduction"?
18. What is meant by the term "modified-conventional reduction"?
19. What is a good rule to follow when purchasing solvents?
20. Why isn't a thinner or reducer all pure solvent?
21. What is vaporization?
22. What is a good way of telling a good solvent from a poor one?
23. What happens when a painter uses the wrong company's solvent?
24. Should leftover reduced material be poured back into the original container?

8

Undercoat Materials and Application

INTRODUCTION

Automobiles are painted for two primary reasons: **appearance** and **protection. Appearance** is one of the main things that helps to sell cars, and all car owners like to have their cars looking in good repair. The smallest pinhole or any deep scratch in paint over steel results in a rust spot. So the steel needs **protection.**

In general, paint finishes are made up of two parts: color and undercoats. The color coat is formulated to produce lasting beauty, but it requires undercoats to provide the required durability through good adhesion and protection to the metal. Undercoats are designed to protect and to adhere to the metal. Also, they provide the proper surface to which color can adhere (Fig. 8-1). Color alone will not adhere to bare metal properly.

To provide its intended usefulness under all weather conditions, a paint finish must be:

1. **Hard and durable:** To have excellent gloss and color retention and to withstand the elements over a long period of time.
2. **Water resistant:** To withstand continued exposure to water, rain, snow, dew, and high-humidity conditions without breakdown and to prevent moisture from reaching the metal surface.
3. **Adhesive:** To cling permanently with a strong bond to the surface to which it is applied.
4. **Elastic:** To expand and contract to an equal degree with the surface to which it is applied when exposed to hot and cold temperatures without breakdown.

214

Figure 8-1 Primer is required to make color stick to metal. (Courtesy of the DuPont Company)

5. **Chip-resistant:** To resist damage by flying sand, gravel, and other forms of contact without chipping under normal driving and usage conditions.
6. **Repairable:** To be able to be repaired efficiently and economically in a highly competitive market.

UNDERCOATS

Undercoats are divided into the following general categories:

1. Primers (one- and two-component types)
2. Primer-surfacers (one- and two-component types)
3. Sealers for acrylic lacquer system (one- and two-component types)
4. Sealers for enamel system (one- and two-component types)
5. Barrier coat (one-component systems)
6. Universal lacquer-type putties

Straight Primers: Description (Table 8-1, page 226)

The purpose of straight primers is to produce the best adhesion for the top coats and the best protection to the steel available. Straight primers offer the best protection to steel because they are mostly a thin liquid that penetrates into the valleys and cavities of sand scratches and surface irregularities most completely. When applied wet, as it should be, primer is drawn into the valleys of sand scratches and surface irregularities by capillary attraction. This superior wetting action is achieved when primer is applied in **thin, wet coats** (Fig. 8-2). Straight primers are very tough and flexible.

Primer

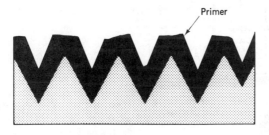

Figure 8-2 Straight primers are drawn into valleys and irregularities of surface. (Courtesy of Ditzler Automotive Finishes, PPG Industries, Inc.)

Capillary attraction is the attraction of the liquid primer by the molecular forces of the metal as the fluid is drawn into 100% firm contact with all the metal surface.

Primer-Surfacers: Description (Table 8-1)

The purpose of acrylic primer-surfacer is to do a twofold job for the lacquer and enamel paint systems as follows:

1. To **prime** the bare metal.
2. To **fill** small surface irregularities quickly so that, when sanded, the surface is smooth and ready for color application (Fig. 8-3).

Desirable characteristics of a good primer-surfacer are (Fig. 8-4):

1. **As a primer:** It should have excellent adhesion to all automotive finishes and very good anticorrosion protection for steel.
2. **As a surfacer:** It should have good filling and rapid buildup of film thickness.
3. **Sanding:** It should be easy to sand.
4. **Drying:** It should dry in 30 to 60 minutes.
5. **Holdout:** The holdout should be good and not porous.
6. **Settling:** It should not settle in the gun between jobs. Moderate settling should be stirred back into solution quickly.

Film Thickness for Primer-Surfacers. For best results, the thickness of primer-

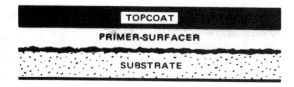

Figure 8-3 Primer-surfacer is a primer that also fills small flaws. (Courtesy of the DuPont Company)

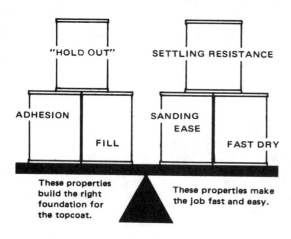

Figure 8-4 Good primer-surfacer is a balance of many properties. (Courtesy of the DuPont Company)

Undercoat Materials and Application   Chap. 8

surfacer, **after sanding,** should be about $1\frac{1}{2}$ to 2 mils to be on the safe side. Excessive thickness of primer-surfacer, beyond 2 mils or more, under refinish acrylic top coats could lead to premature crazing and/or cracking conditions (see Chapter 17).

Sealers: Description (Table 8-1, Figs. 8-5 and 8-6)

A sealer is used in the automotive refinishing trade for one of two purposes:

1. To provide adhesion between the paint material to be applied and the repair surface. Sanding of the surface may be required before application.
2. To act as a barrier-type material that prevents or retards the mass penetration of refinish solvents from the color and undercoats being repaired.

Sealers also provide the following desirable benefits:

1. Improve adhesion of repair color to very hard undercoats and enamel surfaces
2. Retard sand-scratch swelling
3. Improve gloss
4. Improve color holdout

Figure 8-5 A sealer bonds the topcoat and the old finish. (Courtesy of the DuPont Company)

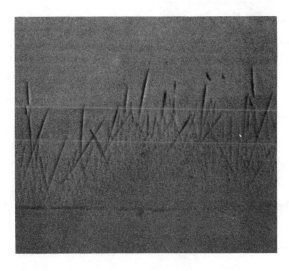

Figure 8-6 Sealers reduce sandscratch swelling problems. (Courtesy of the DuPont Company)

5. Prevent bleeding (when designed for this purpose)
6. Can be used on small, clean bare metal surfaces

Two general types of sealers are available:

1. One type of sealer is designed **for acrylic lacquer paint systems.** This sealer, when so stated on the label, is not to be top-coated with enamel finishes.
2. A second type of sealer is designed **for air-dry enamel paint systems.** This sealer, when so stated on the label, is not to be top-coated with acrylic lacquer finishes.

Because of differences in refinish paint systems and the severe hardness of most factory paint finishes, particularly the basecoat/clearcoat finishes, special sealers are needed for the proper repair of all the finishes on the road. No single sealer can serve all purposes. It is very important that painters be thoroughly familiar with the popular paint systems and the sealers required for their repair.

Table 8-1 describes and lists several sealers of five leading paint suppliers that are recommended for the repair of basecoat/clearcoat finishes, acrylic lacquers, acrylic enamels, and acrylic urethanes. When painters stray too far from label directions, serious problems can and often do develop.

Putty: Description (Table 8-1, Figs. 8-7 and 8-8)

The purpose of putty is to fill pits, deep scratches, file marks, and other isolated irregularities on the surface of the metal that cannot be filled satisfactorily with primer-surfacer. Putty is designed for application to spot locations rather than over a large area. Also, putty should always be applied over primer-surfacer.

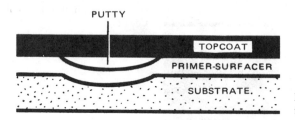

Figure 8-7 Glazing putty fills small flaws. (Courtesy of the DuPont Company)

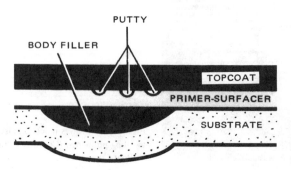

Figure 8-8 Body filler is used to fill large flaws. (Courtesy of the DuPont Company)

Undercoat Materials and Application   Chap. 8

In composition, putty is made up of a very high solids material of the same nature as surfacer, but with a low thinner or solvent content. Therefore, it has greater filling qualities.

Two types of putty are available: a "PX" lacquer type and an acrylic type. Lacquer and acrylic putties are the most popular and are shown in Table 8-1. Most paint companies have more than one brand of a given type of putty, which reflects varying degrees of filling qualities. The lacquer and acrylic putties are satisfactory for use in all acrylic lacquer and all enamel refinish paint systems as long as they are used in a spot application.

> **CAUTION:** After sanding putty, it is important to recoat the putty with a thin sealing coat of primer-surfacer or sealer before applying the final color coats.

The characteristics of putty are:

1. **As a primer:** It has excellent adhering quality to compatible paint materials.
2. **As a surfacer:** It builds up film thickness rapidly.
3. **Sanding:** It is easy to sand.
4. **Holdout:** The holdout is poor; requires sealer before top coating.
5. **Film thickness:** Putty can be used on depressions up to $\frac{1}{16}$ inch deep if the depressions are localized. If the depressions in the metal are deeper than $\frac{1}{16}$ inch and/or if there is a great number of them, it is better practice to fill the depressions with solder or plastic filler or to straighten the metal properly.

UNDERCOAT APPLICATION

All surface preparation operations up to this point must have been completed. This includes:

1. All washing and cleaning
2. All sanding and/or paint removal
3. All masking
4. All metal conditioning as paint company recommended

Although metal conditioning was covered in Chapter 6, Table 6-2, it should be done just before primer application. It is a surface maintenance operation that should never be neglected. Some primers in the trade do not require metal conditioning. Follow label directions.

Primer Application

1. Prepare primer according to label directions. In cold weather, check with viscosity cup.

2. Apply thin, wet coat of primer to bare metal surfaces.

    a. Apply with spray equipment to large surfaces.

    b. Apply with brush to very small or tiny spot surfaces.

3. Allow to dry before applying primer-surfacer. See label directions.

> **CAUTION:** Most good primers are of enamel base. **Never sandwich enamel primer between coats of lacquer** as lifting will result. Keep primer confined to bare metal by careful application. Wipe off any smears from lacquer surfaces if the next coat is lacquer type and apply primer-surfacer before topcoating.

Most quality paint shops have a top-quality primer (and brush) ready for use at all times everyday for small spot area applications.

Primer-Surfacer Application

Follow the label directions to reduce and prepare primer-surfacer. Label directions usually stress the following important operations:

1. Stir the material thoroughly at package viscosity to obtain homogeneous mixture before reduction. A material on the shelf for several weeks or months requires several minutes of mixing by hand or on a paint shaker.

2. Select the proper thinner for weather conditions. For average temperature conditions (65°F and up), use medium-evaporation thinner. Use a premarked container or paddle for fast and accurate reduction of primer-surfacer according to label directions. It is better to use a little more thinner in primer-surfacer than an insufficient amount. In cold weather, below 65°F, use fast-evaporating thinner. Spraying in too cold weather (below 55°F) is not recommended.

3. Reduce material, stir it thoroughly in a mixing container, and strain it through a coarse strainer into a paint cup.

4. Usually, label directions stress that material should be applied with shop and metal temperature at least 65°F. Use a low air pressure, not over 40 or less psi (at the gun).

Application (Fig. 8-9)

1. a. Check the spray gun adjustment with a flooding test pattern and adjust the spray gun as required.

    b. Check application of primer-surfacer on a spray stand or other suitable object before applying primer on a car.

    c. Spray a thin, wet, first coat as the primer coat. Allow to flash.

    d. Spray up to three or more thin-to-medium wet coats for additional film buildup. Allow each coat to flash off before applying succeeding coat. Never speed up flash-off by blowing air on wet film. Normally, for spot repair, apply each medium coat of primer-surfacer with 30 to 35 psi (at the gun). For panel repair,

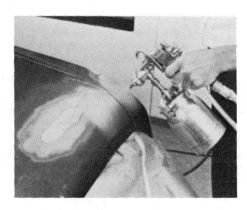

Figure 8-9 Primer-surfacer is best applied in medium-wet coats. (Courtesy of Ditzler Automotive Finishes, PPG Industries, Inc.)

use a suitable air pressure between 35 and 40 psi (at the gun). The average application of primer-surfacer is about 0.6 mil thick per coat **when dry. The film thickness of undercoats should total between 1 and 2 mils after sanding.** The film thickness (four coats × 0.8) may be **3.2 mils before sanding.**

2. Allow to air-dry. A normal application of primer-surfacer (2.4 to 3.2 mils **before sanding**) will dry in 30 minutes or less. The thickness of the film, the thinner used, and the temperature of the shop will influence the drying time.

3. Do not apply extra-heavy coats of primer-surfacer in one pass or in many passes of the spray gun to speed up the operation. Primer surfacer applied in this way requires more time to dry. The film will appear hard at the surface but will not be dry next to the metal. This condition can lead to difficulty in sanding, poor holdout, pinholes, mud cracking, and crazing.

4. Water-sand the surface with No. 400 sandpaper for best results. Use a sanding block when sanding large flat surfaces and a sponge pad on concave surfaces. For power sanding, use No. 320 or No. 360 sandpaper. Water sanding is preferred over dry sanding as a general rule. However, there are times when it is quicker and more convenient to dry-sand. Guard against cut-throughs at all edges, high ridges, and crease-lines. Do not press normally hard at these locations. Just wipe across them carefully or stay away from them completely. Repair cut-throughs when dry with additional primer-surfacer or primer-sealer. Check the progress of work with a squeegee. Clean up as required when finished.

Guide-coat Filling and Sanding

The purpose of a guide-coat system is to "fill and sand" a featheredged repair in a manner that assures a level surface and avoids a low spot from showing through the final color. This system is particularly helpful when filling one or more featheredged spots during the repair of enamel finishes.

"**Undercutting**" (Fig. 8-10) (removing too much primer-surfacer when sanding) happens between two hard surfaces of original enamel when sanding is done and the softer surface (new primer-surfacer) is removed accidentally and unknowingly. Guide-

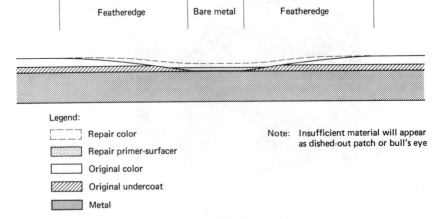

Legend:

⌐ ¬ (dashed)	Repair color
▓	Repair primer-surfacer
▭	Original color
▨	Original undercoat
▓	Metal

Note: Insufficient material will appear as dished-out patch or bull's eye

Figure 8-10 Causes of low spots in refinishing. (Courtesy of General Motors Corporation)

coat sanding advises the painter **when to stop sanding or when to become extra cautious.** All surface preparation operations before this must be completed.

Procedure

1. Using light (or dark)-colored primer-surfacer;
   a. First apply two medium-wet coats to the area within a sanded featheredge. Allow flash time between coats.
   b. Next apply two coats **slightly beyond** the first two coats. Allow each coat to flash before applying the next coat.
2. Use dark (or light)-colored primer-surfacer (of **contrasting color**) and reduce 200%:
   a. Apply one wet coat of primer-surfacer within the sanded repair area.
   b. Apply next wet coat to extend slightly beyond the previous coat. Allow each coat to flash before applying the next coat.
3. Allow primer-surfacer to dry about 30 minutes under normal conditions (70° to 80°F).
4. Water-sand the primer-surfacer with No. 400 sandpaper and a suitable sanding block as follows:

   a. If sanding on adjacent acrylic lacquer, keep off the lacquer as much as possible.
   b. Start sanding at the perimeter and use plenty of water. Continue sanding toward the center as the last-applied primer-surfacer is removed.
   c. Finish sanding across the center of the repair spot using uniform, light sanding strokes. Stop and check the progress of sanding frequently with a squeegee.

CAUTION: Do not sand the center of the repair too much. As soon as the orange peel is removed across the center of the spot, stop sanding.

5. Clean up and allow to dry before the next operation.

Improper Uses of Primer-surfacer

Condition. The excessive application of primer-surfacer over an entire car that has a good surface. This can cause excessive film thickness, which can lead to checking and cracking.

Remedy. Apply primer-surfacer only to damaged areas that are being repaired. A single coat of highly reduced primer-surfacer may be used as a sealer over the original acrylic lacquer color to minimize sandscratch swelling **if the final film thickness does not go over 8 mils.**

Condition. Application of primer-surfacer over poorly prepared or cleaned surface. This results in poor adhesion, poor drying, and other problems.

Remedy. Remove all foreign matter, visible and invisible, from the surface before the application of primer-surfacer. This is done by using paint finish cleaning solvent and metal conditioner with approved sanding practices.

Condition. Insufficient reduction of primer-surfacer when the painter attempts to obtain **greater filling** over **heavy file marks.** In those cases, the painter uses insufficient solvent in reduction and higher air pressure to get thicker material through the gun. This condition causes excessive orange peel, rough surface, and sandscratches to show up after the lacquer color is applied. Application of primer-surfacer in this manner usually traps air and vapor at the base (in the valley) of sandscratches as shown in Fig. 8-11a and b.

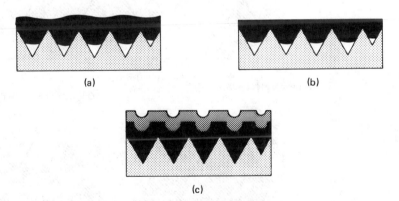

Figure 8-11 A common cause of sandscratches (cross section through painted file marks): (a) Insufficiently reduced primer-surfacer bridges sandscratches. (b) After sanding, bridges and voids remain. (c) Solvent in color coats rewets the primer-surfacer, which sinks into sandscratch valleys. Scratches are now visible. (Courtesy of Ditzler Automotive Finishes, PPG Industries, Inc.)

Undercoat Application   **223**

When color is applied, the solvent penetrates and resoftens the primer-surfacer, which then sinks into the sandscratch valleys (Fig. 8-11c). This condition becomes most visible when paint films shrink upon drying.

When correctly reduced and applied over coarse file marks, the file marks become very evident as the primer-surfacer dries (Fig. 8-12).

Remedy. Reduce the primer-surfacer according to the label directions. Apply the required amount of material in thin, wet coats with sufficient flash time between coats. **The best remedy is to remove all coarse file marks before painting is done.**

Condition. The use of an improperly formulated thinner in the primer-surfacer. In many cases, the painter uses leftovers from other paint work and/or paint system. This can cause any number of problems, depending upon the contamination of solvents used.

Remedy. Follow the label directions and use the correct brand of solvent for weather conditions.

Sealer Application

1. In the area to be color coated, clean finish thoroughly with paint finish cleaning solvent (Table 6-1)
   a. When topcoating over cured OEM enamels, use #400, 600, or Ultra Fine sandpaper plus cleaning solvent to wet-sand complete OEM color to be sealed.
   b. When topcoating over acrylic lacquer, compound and reclean the entire area to be sealed with paint cleaning solvent.

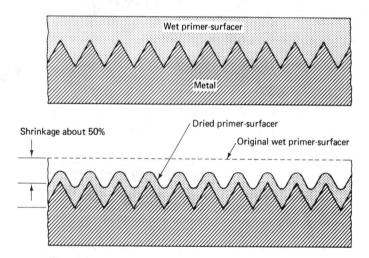

Figure 8-12 Coarse file marks require additional filling. (Courtesy of General Motors Corporation)

2. Using the correct sealer for the repair situation, apply one or two coats of sealer at the correct air pressure per label directions slightly beyond where color will stop.

3. Allow sealer to air dry 30 minutes or longer per label directions before applying color.

Putty Application

Surface Preparation.   Perform all necessary surface preparation operations through the application of primer-surfacer and allow to dry for at least 10 minutes. Putty is designed to be applied over primer-surfacer.

1. Apply putty to affected spots with a squeegee as follows:
   a. Apply putty from the tube to the edge of a squeegee in a small amount.
   b. Quickly press putty on the affected spot and flatten out with a fast scraping motion. Use moderate pressure to assure that putty fills the depression completely. A second fast pass may be made safely. Do not squeegee as putty begins to dry. This is evident when putty begins to "roll."
   c. Two or three thin applications of putty, allowing 15 to 20 minutes of air dry between coats, will produce better filling than one heavy coat.

2. Apply the balance of primer-surfacer if necessary.

3. Allow to air-dry hard before sanding. Drying time varies with the thickness of putty application and weather. Thin to medium coats (up to 10 mils) can usually be sanded in 1 hour under average temperature conditions (70° to 95°F). Heavier coats require a correspondingly longer drying time. Very heavy coats should be allowed to dry overnight before sanding.

   CAUTION: Force-drying putty applications is not recommended.

4. Seal visible putty with primer-surfacer or sealer before applying color coats.

If lacquer-type putty becomes hard in the container or tube, a small amount of slow thinner or retarder may be worked in to restore original consistency. Use a short section of welding rod to work in the thinner.

Improper Uses of Putty.   As mentioned earlier, putty is designed for an occasional spot application and not for a large-area application. Many body repair people and painters substitute putty as a correction for poor metal work. Putty was never designed to replace the bumping hammer, the body file, or proper metal straightening operations. A painter should never use putty to fill a deep "ding," as the repair is very apt to crack and fail prematurely (see Fig. 17-21). The application of putty in extra-heavy thicknesses and then force-drying leads to shrinking and cracking conditions. Always apply putty in thin coats, allowing sufficient drying time between coats.

Table 8-1 shows in lines 1 through 5 an outstanding anticorrosion system available from each of five leading paint suppliers. These products were selected from many available because they are easy to use while offering the most outstanding durability properties.

TABLE 8-1 SELECTED PRIMERS, PRIMER-SURFACERS, SEALERS, AND PUTTIES

Purpose of product	Rinshed-Mason	DuPont	Ditzler	Martin-Senour	Sherwin-Williams
1. PRIMER: primes bare steel, galvanized steel, zinc-coated metals, fiberglass, aluminum	(No metal cond.) 834	(No metal cond.) 615S +616S	(Metal cond.) DP-40/401	(Metal cond.) 8827	(Metal cond.) E2G973
2a PRIMER-SURFACER: primes and fills surface irregularities:	HP-100	181S	K-200 + K-201	5100 + 5150	P6H49 + V6V79
2b do not exceed label film build to avoid cracking and splitting	or 831 +	or 131S +	or DZ-3 +	or 3254 +	or P2A43 +
3. SEALER: improves adhesion and minimizes solvent penetration	CS150, 870, RS200, or PS-19	1984S or 1985S	DL-1970 or DAS-1980	5105 + 5150 + 5110	E6H59 + V6V79 + R7K89
4. ADHESION PROMOTER: This factory recommended sealer is required for adhesion of acrylic lacquer to original BC/CC finishes	811	222S	DSX-1900	3061	P1C48
5. OPTIONAL COLOR SYSTEM: beautifies and protects the metal	+ A/L; A/E; BC/CC	+ A/L; A/E; BC/CC	+ A/E; A/L; BC/CC	+ A/L; A/E; BC/CC	+ A/L; A/E BC/CC
6. SEALER: Improves adhesion of repair acrylic lacquer over original acrylic lacquer; minimizes sandscratches	PS-19 or 870 CS150 or RS200	1984S or 1985S	DL-1947 or DL-1970	3060	P1A38
7. PRIMER-SEALER: for use under acrylic enamel topcoats	PS-19, CS150, PS-21, RS200, 870	1984S or 1985S	DAS-1980	8823 or 8098	E2A52 or E2A28
8. BARRIER COAT: a primer-surfacer for use over cracked or crazed finishes; can seal air-dried enamel for lacquer top coats	HP-100 or 806 Must be sealed with PS-19 or PS-21 before top coating with Miracryl-2.				
9. LACQUER-BASE PUTTY: requires sealing with primer-surfacer	76	2286S 2288S	DFL-1 DFL-17	6390 6394	D3R7 D3A2737

NOTE: Many additional primers, primer-surfacers, sealers, and undercoat items are available for refinishing from all paint suppliers. The products shown here exhibit outstanding quality and durability under field testing and service conditions. Check with the paint jobber for specific use of specific products.

The following describes Table 8-1 by line number.

1. R-M's 834 and DuPont's 615S/616S are two primers that do not require metal conditioning. All others do. 834 is rich in zinc phosphate and is a one-component primer. Other primers shown on Line 1 are two-component primers. All primers shown are enamel base and should be topcoated with primer-surfacer or sealer before topcoating with acrylic lacquer.

2a. The most advanced primer-surfacers in refinishing are on line 2a. R-M's HP-100 is a one-component waterborne primer-surfacer with two-component qualities. HP-100 comes ready to spray, so no reduction is necessary. Three paint suppliers have a two-component acrylic urethane primer-surfacer: Ditzler's K-200/K-201, Sherwin-Williams' P6H49/V6V79, and Martin-Senour's 5100/5150. These primer-surfacers appear to have the greatest durability of any on the market.

2b. This line shows each paint supplier's acrylic lacquer primer-surfacer. Only one is shown, but more are available.

3. The reason several sealers are shown for R-M, DuPont and Ditzler is because some sealers are for acrylic lacquer and some are for acrylic enamel or acrylic urethane topcoating. Sherwin-Williams and Martin-Senour have available a very durable and universal two-component sealer of acrylic urethane construction. Sherwin-Williams' E6H59/V6V79 and Martin-Senour's 5105/5150 can be used under any acrylic lacquer color or under any enamel topcoat system.

4. Adhesion promoter is designed for use on scuff-sanded OEM enamel finishes; all OEM basecoat/clearcoat finishes; Ford, Chrysler, AMC, GM high solids; and water-based enamel, as well as most vans, trucks, and imported cars.

5. The selection of the top coat is up to the painter: A/L (acrylic lacquer), A/E (acrylic enamel), A/U (acrylic urethane), and BC/CC (basecoat/clearcoat).

6. Sealers are repeated as a reminder that repairs of acrylic lacquer systems with acrylic lacquers require this type of sealer.

7. Sealers are repeated as a reminder that they are under acrylic or urethane enamel topcoats.

8. R-M's Barrier Coat (806) and (HP-100) are the only waterborne primer-surfacers available that make possible the application of acrylic enamel, acrylic urethane, or acrylic lacquer over moderately cracked and crazed finishes. After application and sanding, the barrier coat should be sealed with an appropriate sealer before topcoating with color. Barrier Coat can also be used over fresh enamels and urethanes.

9. All five paint suppliers have two types of lacquer base putty available for the repair of automotive finishes. One putty is for glazing and the other is for spot use.

REVIEW QUESTIONS

1. What are the two primary reasons why cars are painted?
2. List six qualities that are built into a paint finish.
3. What does "repairability" mean?

4. What is the purpose of a straight primer?

5. What is a durable primer available from each paint supplier?

6. What is the purpose of a primer-surfacer?

7. What is the most durable primer-surfacer shown in Table 8-1?

8. Give several characteristics (good points) of a primer-surfacer.

9. When should the metal conditioning operation be done in a repair sequence?

10. How thick should a film of primer-surfacer be after sanding?

11. What is the best recommended method for sanding primer-surfacer?

12. What is meant by guide-coat filling and sanding, and how is this repair technique done?

13. Why should application of excessive thicknesses of primer-surfacer be avoided?

14. Why is it unwise to underreduce primer-surfacer to obtain faster filling over deep file marks?

15. What is the purpose of glazing putty?

16. What is a safe maximum depth beyond which putty should not be used?

17. Describe how to apply glazing putty.

18. What is the purpose of a sealer?

19. What basic types of sealer are used in the automotive refinishing trade?

20. Name a top-quality DuPont primer and primer-surfacer.

21. Name a top-quality Ditzler primer and primer-surfacer.

22. Name a top-quality Rinshed-Mason primer and primer-surfacer.

23. Name a top-quality Sherwin-Williams primer and primer-surfacer.

24. Name a top-quality Martin-Senour primer and primer-surfacer.

9

Automotive Colors:

Description and Behavior

The purpose of color in a paint finish is to beautify the surface painted and, with the help of undercoats, to protect the metal against corrosion.

The appearance of a car is important to every car owner. The single most important thing that makes a car appealing to the owner is the beauty and gloss of the paint finish. A paint job in good repair makes a car look its very best. The appearance of every factory-produced car, van, and truck is vital to the sale of that vehicle. People know that a good paint finish is essential to the lasting beauty and durability of a car.

Almost every car passing from one car owner to another needs paint repairs of one form or another. The painter plays a key role in the sale of used cars because making every used car paint finish look like new is a routine part of used car reconditioning.

WHAT IS COLOR?

Pigments have the ability to reflect and to absorb light rays. When a person sees **blue,** the pigment absorbs all the light rays with the exception of blue ones, which it reflects. When a person sees **red,** the pigment absorbs all light rays except red ones, which it reflects. The eye is like a tiny radio receiver and picks up these waves of light as they are reflected.

When a person sees **white**, all the colors of the spectrum are being reflected. When a person sees **black,** all the colors of the spectrum are being absorbed.

Color is described in three terms or dimensions:

1. **Hue:** What the color is; red, blue, green, and so on.
2. **Value:** Lightness or darkness of color; how black or white it is.
3. **Chroma:** Color intensity, how bright the color is.

COMPONENTS OF AUTOMOTIVE COLOR

Automotive colors are made up of the following ingredients:

Resin or Binder

Resin is the principal film-forming part of a paint system into which all the other film-forming ingredients are added. The resin system of a paint is the primary ingredient that determines the identity or type of paint. The resin system provides the following qualities in a paint material:

1. Hardness
2. Durability
3. Gloss
4. Adhesion
5. Water resistance
6. Chip resistance

Added features of urethane enamels:

7. Super high gloss
8. Chemical stain resistance
9. Greater chip and scratch resistance

Solvents

After a resin is made, the resin must be reduced with solvent to a degree for two reasons:

1. The resin must be pumped through large-diameter pipes from the location where it was made to the location where paint materials are formulated.
2. Paint materials must be brought to proper viscosity when packaged.

Pigments

Pigments do two important things for a paint film:

1. They provide the color to the paint.

2. They make a paint film more durable to the extent to which they screen out ultraviolet light of the sun.

Plasticizer

Plasticizer, available in several types, is a special oily chemical that is added to acrylic lacquers for **elasticity** and **flexibility** purposes. Without plasticizer, a paint film would be very brittle and would crack as the metal expanded and contracted in hot and cold weather conditions. Plasticizer also assists in the **flow-out** of a paint material.

In enamel paint materials, plasticizer is **unitized** with the resin system during the (cooking) manufacturing process as enamel resins are made. Thus, enamels have more built-in elasticity and flexibility and can be applied more heavily than lacquers.

Paint finishes are designed to work best on car surfaces within **certain limits of thickness.** Normally, the maximum limit of thickness for automotive lacquers is about 7 to 10 mils. Extra-thick lacquer films are likely to crack when subjected to excessively hot and cold temperatures because paint is a poor conductor of heat. Also, paint does not heat or cool uniformly through its thickness from top to bottom.

If the top surface of a lacquer film is hotter than the bottom (at the metal), the paint at the surface tries to expand while the underneath does not. The result is **stress** at the area where warm paint expands and cool paint does not. When the stress is great enough, a slight crack, often invisible to the eye, may develop. Once a crack starts, like in a pane of glass, it becomes larger when exposed to the same stress conditions (see "Micro-Checking," "Crazing," and "Checking and Cracking" in Chapter 17).

Metallic Particles

Metallic particles are most often of aluminum flake construction and are used in metallic colors to achieve more glamorous colors with the effect of depth. Chopped mica, Mylar, and other plastics may be used in current and future automotive color formulations.

Ultraviolet Screener

The purpose of a screener, as the name implies, is to stop ultraviolet light at the very point of contact with the paint film. Without a screener of this type, a paint film suffers fading, chalking, crazing, and general paint film breakdown much more quickly.

Other Additives

Other additives are used in the manufacture of automotive colors depending upon the color. Metallic colors sometimes use "antimottling" agents. These agents make possible a more trouble-free paint material by preventing the mottling condition when the paint is applied. Sometimes special agents are used to prevent gloss. These are called "**flattening**" compounds and are used when repainting interior parts of cars in certain locations.

HOW AUTOMOTIVE COLOR IS MADE

The following is a description of how automotive color is made (Fig. 9-1).

1. In the upper left of Fig. 9-1, chemical liquids are brought in and stored in large tanks at the paint factory.
2. In a special cooking process, chemical liquids such as methyl methacrylate and a catalyst are cooked. It is amazing how a waterlike liquid transforms into a heavy syruplike material. This is "resin," the backbone of a paint material.
3. As shown at step 3 in Fig. 9-1, a paint resin gives the following properties to a paint film:
   a. Hardness
   b. Durability
   c. Gloss
   d. Adhesion
   e. Water resistance
   f. Chip resistance
   g. In the case of urethane finishes, greater gloss, chemical resistance, and film hardness is achieved.
4. Solvents or thinners are added to the newly made resin.
5. The newly made resin is filtered.
6. The new resin solution is kept in a large holding tank.
7. Pigments are mixed with resin solution to form a pigment paste.
8. Plasticizer and other additives are added to the pigment paste.
9. The pigment paste is prepared to go to the ball mill or sand mill.
10. At this location, all the ingredients of the paint are thoroughly dispersed. "**Dispersion**" means to mix the pigments, the resin, and all paint ingredients very thoroughly. This is a key step in making paint. Each pigment particle is coated with resin. A ball mill or a sand mill is a special device used to disperse or to cover pigments and other paint ingredients with resin.
11. Aluminum particles that have been specially treated with a chemical coating are added to the final color as required.
12. Acrylic color is ready for packaging, which means "**canning**" in the paint industry (Fig. 9-2). The term "**vehicle**" in Fig. 9-2 means the liquid portion of the paint consisting of the resin (also known as "**binder**") and volatile solvents. These ingredients help the paint in storage and in application: therefore, the name "vehicle."

Figures 9-3 to 9-7 tell a graphic story of how automobile paints are made. The pictures and story are furnished through the courtesy of R-M Automotive Products BASF Inmont Corporation, of Detroit, Michigan.

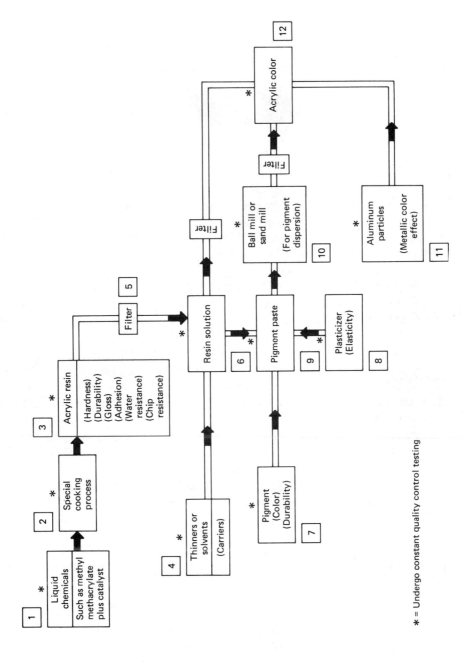

Figure 9-1 Composition of acrylic color. (Courtesy of General Motors Corporation)

* = Undergo constant quality control testing

233

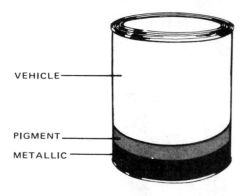

VEHICLE

PIGMENT

METALLIC

Figure 9-2 Can of factory-packaged color. Failure to thoroughly mix pigment, metallic flake, and vehicle may result in a color mismatch. (Courtesy of the DuPont Company)

Resin Processing

Figure 9-3 shows the modern automotive paint resin processing equipment, which is representative of many such complete systems at R-M plants. Resins are the **film-forming substances of paint** and are a major factor in the durability of every paint product. The following is a description of Fig. 9-3:

1. **Solid materials** are weighed into hopper scales.
2. **Electronic controls** automatically pump and measure liquids from storage to weigh tanks. The liquids are then metered to reaction kettles. (This is where the important cooking process takes place.)
3. A 7000-gallon reaction kettle is heated or cooled by three independent peripheral Aroclor jackets, controlled by a panel board. This is a giant pressure cooker into which various chemicals and catalysts are placed and cooked for a prescribed period of time at a prescribed temperature. Everything is electronically and automatically controlled.
4. The reflux condenser receives water and solvent vapors from the kettle, separates and decants (removes) the water, and returns solvent to the kettle, maintaining a constant solvent content in the resin batch.
5. After the reaction is completed (cooking is done), a 10,000-gallon thinning tank (not shown) receives resin from the kettle for thinning and filtering before final processing.

Rinshed-Mason's modern synthetic resin plant is a totally enclosed, gravity-flow system. This is a five-story building. The thinning tanks (not shown) are on the second floor and protrude into the third floor. The tops of the kettles (Fig. 9-3) are on the fourth floor and the bases of the kettles extend to the third floor.

All types of resins are produced here, such as acrylics, alkyds, epoxies, urethanes, and other types. Automated controls, electronic measuring, and pneumatic modulating temperature regulators are used in paint processing. Resins are checked continuously during processing. Final tests check resins for clarity and chemical and physical properties. When completed, resins are pumped to mixing tanks (Fig. 9-4).

Automotive Colors: Description and Behavior   *Chap. 9*

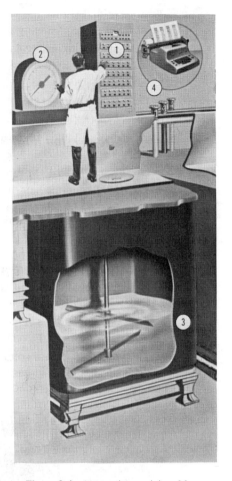

Figure 9-3 Cross section of cooking kettle. Paint resins are made by cooking. (Courtesy of R-M Automotive Products, BASF Inmont Corp.)

Figure 9-4 Automatic premixing. Many paint ingredients are mixed by computer method. (Courtesy of R-M Automotive Products, BASF Inmont Corp.)

Automatic Premixing (Fig. 9-4)

Automatic premixing of solvents, resins, and pigments helps to achieve closely controlled paint processing, speeds up the continuous dispersion operation, and contributes to uniform quality of the finished R-M paint product. Here is how the automatic premixing works:

1. The electronic batching unit has eight digital preset positions that govern the formula to be processed and control the sequence of additions. Each digital preset unit can handle up to 11 different materials. After numbers are punched, everything, such as filling and processing, takes place automatically.

How Automotive Color Is Made   235

2. A scale dial shows the weighing progress of each ingredient. The total of each addition is automatically recorded on the batch card.

3. An agitator tank rests on an integrated scale mechanism. Stainless steel shielding above the tank contributes to better housekeeping and cleanliness in processing.

4. A recording typewriter produces a final record of time, the amount of each ingredient, and the tank and batch numbers.

Sand Mill Dispersion (Fig. 9-5)

Sand mill dispersing at R-M represents a most efficient method for volume production of clean, bright, intermediate base colors used to produce automotive color finishes. Using a controlled premix of resins, pigments, and solvents, sand mills make possible the consistent high-quality results of continuous dispersion. This is how continuous dispersion works:

1. A pump feeds premix under pressure into the bottom of the sand unit.

2. A water-cooled sand unit contains hardened steel discs rotating at high speed in Ottawa sand, dispersing and coating all pigment and paint additives with resin.

3. Sand is retained by a screen at the top of the unit and the dispersed intermediate base color flows to the receiver.

4. The intermediate base color is screened in the receiver before it is used in finished color processing or in base color storage.

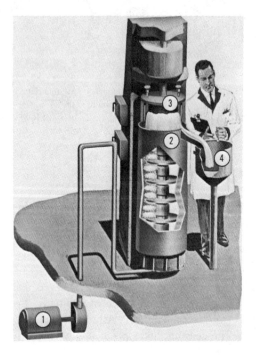

Figure 9-5 Sand mill dispersing. This mill mixes color paint ingredients thoroughly. (Courtesy of R-M Automotive Products, BASF Inmont Corp.)

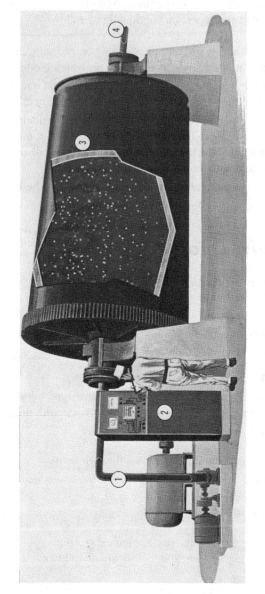

Figure 9-6 Ball mill dispersing. This mill mixes undercoat ingredients thoroughly. (Courtesy of R-M Automotive Products, BASF Inmont Corp.)

Ball Mill Dispersion (Fig. 9-6)

Ball mills are generally used in the dispersion of primer coats and darker colors. The above R-M mill, one of the largest in use in the paint industry, measures 8 by 12 feet, and is designed for **continuous dispersion. Material is fed and discharged without interruption.** The ball mill operates continually as follows:

1. A premix of solvent, resin, and pigment is pumped into the mill through the trunnion. (A trunnion is a hollow axis or axle on which the ball mill rotates.)
2. A control cabinet regulates the flow of material in and out of the mill, controls the mill temperature, and records the number of revolutions.
3. The premix is dispersed through the action of steel balls in a continual cascade as the mill turns or rotates. The steel balls fall and flow continuously like a waterfall as the mill rotates. **The fundamental objective of dispersion is to coat each pigment particle with resin.**
4. Completely dispersed material is discharged through the trunnion and is pumped to tanks.

TYPES OF AUTOMOTIVE COLORS

All automotive colors are divided into two general classes:

1. Solid colors
2. Metallic colors

Solid Colors

Solid colors are made with a high volume of opaque-type pigments. Opaque pigments block the rays of the sun and absorb light in accordance with the type of color they are. Features of solid colors are:

1. Opaque pigments do not let light pass through them.
2. Ultraviolet light is kept out of the paint film.

Metallic Colors (Fig. 9-7 and 9-8)

Metallic colors are designed with special pigments, a high volume of metallic particles, and a clear resin. Features of metallic colors are as follows:

1. Metallic colors have more sales appeal and more depth.
2. Metallics allow light to penetrate beyond the surface.
3. This light penetration, reflecting off the aluminum flake and passing around pigment particles of varying density, produces the final color shade and effect.

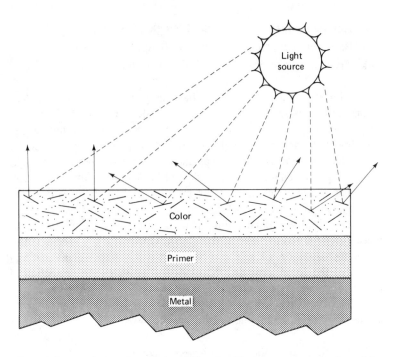

Figure 9-7 Description of standard metallic color. The bars represent aluminum flakes and the specks represent pigment particles. (Courtesy of General Motors Corporation)

4. Metallics change in color when viewed under different types of light.
5. Metallics change in color when viewed from different angles.

Transparency is characteristic of many metallic finishes, which allows rays of light to penetrate beyond the surface so that the metallic particles can be seen distinctly (Fig. 9-7). Some custom metallic flakes are ''hex''-shaped (six-sided), some are round, and others are square. Custom metallic flakes are also much larger than the flakes used in conventional colors. Some custom metallic flakes are multicolored and are available in many sizes.

Translucence is the property of allowing rays of light to penetrate into the paint film without permitting the metallic particles to be distinctly seen. Translucence is semi-transparency.

AMERICAN CAR FACTORY PAINT USAGE

Millions of factory painted cars on the roads in the United States have been painted with one of the following paint systems:

1. Acrylic enamel color (standard, single phase type)

2. Acrylic lacquer color (standard, single phase type)
3. Basecoat/clearcoat acrylic enamel (two phase color)
4. Tri-coat special enamel (a BC/CC type, three-phase color)

Almost all cars on the road have acrylic enamel finishes. Acrylic lacquers rate second and the basecoat/clearcoat finishes rate third. The U.S. car companies are using more basecoat/clearcoat finishes each year. If the trend continues as projected, it appears that almost all cars on the road one day will be painted with basecoat/clearcoat finishes.

The term **standard color,** as used in this book, refers to the old or early conventional lacquer or enamel finish as used in the factories for years.

The term **single phase color** means that the color was designed to be used over undercoats with no clear coating over it.

The term **two phase color,** as used in this book, Fig. 9-8 means that two parts or phases are required to make up one finish. One part is the special color coat that provides the pigmentation or color. The second part is the special clear coating that brings out the beauty of the color, provides the gloss and provides the protection of the finish. Two-phase colors are the basecoat/clearcoat finishes.

The term **three-phase color,** as used in this book, means that three parts or phases are required to make up one finish. See Fig. 9-9.

1. The first part is the special basecoat color.
2. The second part is the special pearl lustre or tinted clearcoat. This is known as the sandwich coating.

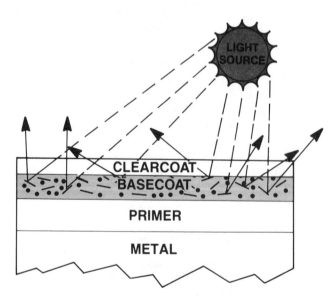

Figure 9-8 Description of basecoat/clearcoat metallic color. The bars represent aluminum flakes and the specks represent pigment particles. (Courtesy of General Motors Corporation)

3. The third part is the special clearcoating that brings out the beauty of the color, provides the gloss, and provides the protection to the finish.

Three-phase colors are known as **tri-coat** finishes. They are the most advanced form of basecoat/clearcoat finishes.

In addition to showing the differences between the basecoat/clearcoat and tri-coat color systems, Fig. 9-9 shows a typical comparison of the thicknesses of factory coatings that make up these finishes. Thus, Fig. 9-9 gives the painter a general idea of how much repair material may be needed in a repair situation.

Ford, Chrysler, and A.M.C. passenger cars have been painted with standard acrylic enamel for many years.

GM Truck and Coach have painted vans, buses and trucks with acrylic enamels for many years. Other car companies, like V.W. and Nissan, etc., also used acrylic enamels from the start.

Since the early 1980s, all U.S. car companies have introduced and have increased their usage of basecoat/clearcoat acrylic enamel finishes.

More than half of GM passenger cars on the road are finished with acrylic lacquer. The rest are painted with acrylic enamel. Over the last several years, GM has converted

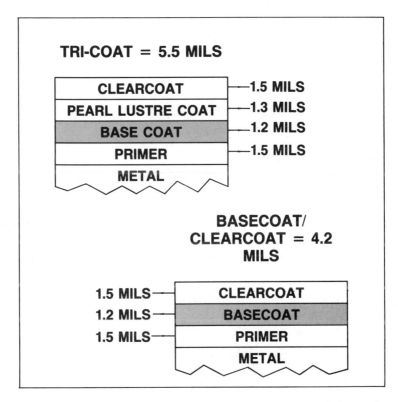

Figure 9-9 Film thickness comparison of factory basecoat/clearcoat and tri-coat color finish. (Courtesy of General Motors Corporation)

American Car Factory Paint Usage

more than half of its factories to using acrylic enamel specializing in basecoat/clearcoat finishes.

General Motors Paint Evolution

GM used five different types of paint on millions of cars in the U.S. from the 1950s to the present. A question often asked is: "Why did GM use so many different types of paint?" The answer follows.

In the late 1950s, all GM passenger cars were painted with solution acrylic lacquer. When California experienced "smog" problems in the 1960s, the federal government's Environmental Protection Agency (EPA), established "Rule 66" (a short name for a regulation to help clean up the air; the law is still in effect).

GM developed and used a "waterborne acrylic enamel" to meet Rule 66 requirements which allowed production of cars in California. Later, GM developed and used a "high-solids acrylic enamel" to meet Rule 66 in other areas of the country. To combat pollution nationwide, almost all GM plants that were using "solution lacquer" switched to using "dispersion lacquer," which is a much cleaner paint.

In recent years, to combat pollution and to improve the quality and appearance of cars, more than half of GM's car factories are using the high solids basecoat/clearcoat acrylic enamel paint system. Apparently, plans are that all of GM's car factories will one day use basecoat/clearcoat finishes.

The five types of GM paint finishes and their identities are as follows:

Type of Paint	Body Number Plate Designation
1. Solution lacquer	L
2. Dispersion lacquer	L
3. High-solids acrylic enamel	E
4. Waterborne acrylic enamel	W
5. Basecoat/clearcoat acr. enamel	BC/CC

Factory Thermosetting Acrylic Enamel Colors

Although each car factory identifies its acrylic enamel under different company names, the basic enamel system as used by the American car factories is thermosetting acrylic enamel. This is how a factory thermosetting acrylic enamel system works:

1. Car bodies (or complete car shells) are painted as required with acrylic enamel. On basecoat/clearcoat finishes, the color is applied and, after a short interval, the clearcoating is applied.
2. The bodies then proceed through a factory high-bake oven system.
3. At a certain temperature, some solvents are driven out of the paint.
4. At a higher temperature, surface tension is created on the paint surface, similar to that on a glass of water, producing a high gloss.
5. At this temperature, the paint film sets up or hardens and cures very quickly and the gloss remains. This paint cannot be redisolved.

Description of Basecoat/Clearcoat Finishes (Fig. 9-8)

Basecoat colors are specially formulated and require a durable, clear topcoating to complete the finish. Basecoat/clearcoat finishes have been used in Europe for many years.

1. In refinishing, basecoat colors are available in two qualities:
   a. Acrylic lacquer
   b. Acrylic enamel (or acrylic urethane enamel)

   Each major paint company which is an OEM supplier has its own paint formulations for OEM use and for field refinishing. See Table 9-1.
2. Basecoat color pigments and metallic particles are much smaller than standard finishes. Thus, basecoat colors allow more homogeneous and random positioning of pigments and metallic particles. This feature allows for better color control and color quality.
3. Basecoat colors are designed to achieve full hiding in two color coats for most colors. Some colors may require a third coat. Full hiding of basecoat colors is achieved with less than one mil of color. Standard colors require almost two mils of color for full hiding. Tri-coat sandwich colors require more coats than do basecoat colors.
4. Basecoat colors dry to a flat finish and require the proper clear topcoating for proper depth of color, appearance, gloss, and durability.
5. Figure 9-9 is a film thickness comparison of a typical factory basecoat/clearcoat finish and a factory tri-coat paint finish.

Description of Tri-coat Paint Finishes (Fig. 9-9)

The tri-coat paint finish is basically a basecoat/clearcoat paint system that is made up of three layers of special topcoating materials as follows:

1. The first coating is a specific basecoat color.
2. The second coating is a special-effects color such as a pearl lustre color coat or a tinted clearcoating. The second coating is known as a sandwich coating.
3. The third coating is the final tough clearcoating for gloss, durability, and ease of finish maintenance. These are the most glamourous colors in automotive use.

FIELD PAINT REPAIR MATERIALS

Standard Acrylic Lacquers (Table 9-1, Item 1)

Acrylic lacquers rate as the principal refinish color coat material for spot and panel repair of standard acrylic lacquers and acrylic enamels. Over 95% of all cars in the world are painted with original factory acrylic lacquers or acrylic enamels. Field-repair acrylic lacquers rate as good field-repair materials for the following reasons:

TABLE 9-1 EXTERIOR CAR COLOR REFINISH SYSTEMS AND CLEAR COATINGS

Product description	Rinshed-Mason	Ditzler	DuPont	Martin-Senour	Sherwin-Williams
1. Acrylic lacquer color (Standard type)	Alpha-Cryl	Duracryl	Lucite	Acrylic Lacquer	S-W Acrylic Lacquer
2. Acrylic lacquer color (BC/CC type). Must be topcoated with clear. See label directions.	Alpha-Cryl Basecoat Color	Duracryl Basecoat Color	Lucite Base Color Coats	Acrylic Lacquer Basecoat Color	Acrylic Lacquer Basecoat Color
3. Clear acrylic lacquer for standard & BC/CC colors	727 or 827	DCA-468	380-S	3072	T1C275
4. Clear urethane enamel for topcoating standard & BC acrylic lacquer colors	893 2-K Clear	DAU-75 DBC-420	580-S	3073	T1C276
5. Hardener for above urethane enamel	894	DXR-80 DBC-421	582-S	3083	V6V376
6. Acrylic lacquer mist-coat material	890	DXA-100	300-S	3080 3081	T1C296 T1C259
7. Acrylic enamel color (Standard type). Use of hardener optional. See label.	Miracryl-2 Plus use of MC-5000 (optional).	Delstar DAU-75 or DAU-82 (optional)	Centari 780-S (optional)	Acrylic Enamel 8853 (optional)	Acrylyd Acrylic Enamel V2V398 (optional)

	MH-1 MH-2	DXR-79 DXR-80	792-S 793-S	8850 8870	V6V-241 V6V-247
8. Hardener for standard acrylic enamels: For spot use For overall					
9. Urethane or enamel color (BC/CC type). Must be top coated with clear. (For proper use, see label)	Miracryl-2 Basecoat Color	Deltron Basecoat Color DBU Prefix	Centari Basecoat Color	Acrylic Enamel Basecoat Color	Acrylic Enamel Basecoat Color
10. Clear acrylic urethane (for topcoating above enamel BC/CC colors). See label directions.	MC-1000	Option: DBU-670 DAU-82 DBU-88	780-S	8853	V2V398
11. Hardener for clear acrylic urethane and acrylic enamel BC colors	894	DBU-89	782-S	8850	V6V241
12. Acrylic urethane colors (Standard type)		Deltron DAU-82 (Optional)		Nitram	Sunfire 421 T1C1000 (optional)
13. Polyurethane enamel colors (Standard type)	Mirathane	Starthane Durethane DU-1000	Imron 500-S (optional)	Ureglo	Acrylyd Plus
14. Prevents fisheyes in catalyzed enamels	809	DX-77	259-S	87	V3K780
15. Prevents fisheyes in standard acrylic lacquers	809	DX-66	FEE 1, 2, 5, & 10, 259-S	77B	V3K265

Note: Alkyd enamels are omitted from this chart and book to conserve space. However, they are still available through your local paint jobber.

1. They possess good flexibility in color matching all solid and metallic colors.
2. They have good durability and gloss.
3. As an option, clear acrylic lacquer may be applied over the color, **providing finish thickness limitations are observed.** Two to three coats should be the maximum. As indicated in Table 9-1, item 4, a clear urethane enamel is also optional for use over standard acrylic lacquers. For further information, contact your local paint jobber.

Standard Acrylic Enamels (Table 9-1, Item 7)

The most popular enamel paint systems are the acrylic enamels. Acrylic enamels are considered the principal refinish color for complete paint jobs and are gaining in popularity for spot and panel repair. Overall acrylic enamel finishes are applied in less time than other types of finishes. Use of the urethane catalyst adds a measure of durability, gloss, and stain resistance that car owners have come to accept.

As an option and as indicated in item 7, Table 9-1, a clearcoating may be applied over standard acrylic enamel. For further information, contact your local paint jobber.

Types of Basecoat/Clearcoat Finishes (Table 9-1)

For the repair of OEM basecoat/clearcoat finishes, two types of repair systems are available:

1. Acrylic lacquer basecoat color (Table 9-1, Item 2)
   Two systems of clearcoating are optional:
   a. Clear acrylic lacquer (Item 3)
   b. Clear acrylic urethane enamel (Item 4)
2. Acrylic enamel or acrylic urethane basecoat color (Item 9)
   One system of clearcoating is available from most paint suppliers. (Item 10). Ditzler has three systems.

Figure 9-9 is a film thickness comparison of a typical factory basecoat/clearcoat finish and a factory tri-coat paint finish. This illustration gives the painter an idea of how much material is on the car on which repairs may be required.

Standard Acrylic Urethane Enamels (Table 9-1, Item 12)

Acrylic urethane finishes have been gaining in popularity in the refinish trade in recent years. These finishes are applied as easily as lacquers; they result in an excellent high gloss upon drying; and no compounding is required. Acrylic urethanes are harder, more durable, more chip resistant, and more chemical resistant than acrylic enamels or lacquers. They can be recoated at any time after drying and they can be lightly sanded and compounded to remove dirt and scratches. Acrylic urethanes are available in a variety of automotive colors. As an option, clear coatings may be applied over the color as indicated in Table 9-1.

Standard Polyurethane Enamels (Table 9-1, Item 13)

Polyurethane enamels, used considerably on trucks and aircraft, have the greatest durability of all refinish products even under excessive sun, humidity, and cold temperature conditions. The toughness of the finish makes it scratch, abrasion and chip resistant. Because it is the smoothest, least porous and hardest finish, ordinary dust, dirt and road grime wash off easily. Polyurethane enamel is the most chemical resistant finish in the trade. It applies as easily as standard lacquer or enamel. Polyurethane finishes are used almost exclusively on the big-track race cars. A wide variety of polyurethane colors are available for use on cars. As an option, a specific clear coating may be applied over the color as indicated in Table 9-1.

> **WARNING:** When applying any catalyzed paint systems, the painter is cautioned to use a NIOSH-approved charcoal or air-supplied respirator as required in catalyst label directions.

Items 14 and 15 of Table 9-1 are a listing of products that prevent **fisheyes** when applying catalyzed or noncatalyzed finishes. For proper use, follow label directions.

NOTE: Due to text space limitations and the increase in factory use of basecoat/clearcoat finishes, alkyd enamels are not covered in this book. However, alkyd enamels are still available through your regular paint jobber.

DRYING OF ACRYLIC LACQUERS

All acrylic lacquers in the refinish trade are designed to air-dry. Air-drying means that all lacquer materials dry simply by the evaporation of solvents. **Evaporation** is the changing of a solvent to a **vapor** or a **gas** to be carried away by the moving air. In time, all paint solvents evaporate from lacquers and the paint hardens.

DRYING OF ACRYLIC AND/OR URETHANE ENAMELS

All enamels in the refinish trade are designed to air-dry in two stages:

1. The first stage is **evaporation.** Certain solvents, when used, must evaporate from the film as the first stage of drying.
2. **Oxidation** or **polymerization** is the second stage of enamel drying. In this stage resin combines with oxygen of the air and a chemical change takes place in the resin. The liquid resin becomes a tough, flexible, and durable film and cannot be redissolved into resin again. The use of a urethane catalyst in a resin makes the film still tougher, more durable, more chip resistant, and more chemical stain resistant.

DESCRIPTION OF STANDARD TYPE METALLIC COLORS

Standard Shade of Standard Type Metallic Colors

Figure 9-10 is a picture of uniform dispersion of aluminum flake and pigments. The small dots in the picture represent pigment particles. The lines that look like little logs are a cross section of metallic particles. The concept of metallics is easier to explain in this manner.

Each metallic particle is like a tiny mirror. Note that the metallic particles are positioned in different directions. They are about equally spaced. On any given line, the metallic particles rotate. They point in all directions of a 360° circle. While this is occurring, it will be noted that the pigment particles are distributed very uniformly throughout this film. **This is what is considered a standard color shade of metallics.**

Light Shade of Standard Type Metallic Colors

Figure 9-11 shows the flat orientation of metallics. Notice that the metallic flakes are mostly in a flat orientation. They lie in a plane almost parallel to the surface. Metallic

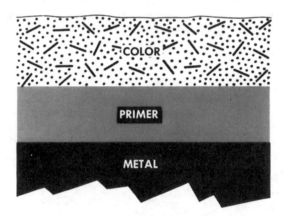

Figure 9-10 Standard color shade of standard metallic color. The uniform dispersion and density of aluminum flake and pigment particles shown result in a standard color shade. (Courtesy of General Motors Corporation)

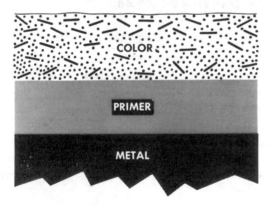

Figure 9-11 Light color shade of standard metallic color. An accumulation of aluminum flake dispersed nearly horizontally at top of paint film and obscuring most pigment particles beneath results in light color shade. (Courtesy of General Motors Corporation)

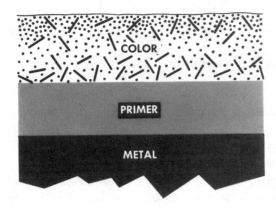

Figure 9-12 Dark color shade of standard metallic color. Dense flotation of pigment particles near surface combined with aluminum flake dispersed nearly perpendicularly results in dark color shade. (Courtesy of General Motors Corporation)

flakes oriented as shown reflect the greatest amount of light, like tiny mirrors, and thereby produce the lightest shades of that color. Another factor that helps to produce light shades of color is that the metallic particles, because they are flat, cover a high percentage of the pigments.

Dark Shade of Standard Type Metallic Colors

Figure 9-12 shows the perpendicular orientation of metallics. In **wet coat application** of standard metallic colors, the metallic orientation may be described as shown. Notice that a high percentage of particles lie in a plane almost perpendicular to the surface. This condition causes a maximum of light penetration into the film and less metallic reflection. This condition exposes a higher-than-normal percentage of pigments at the surface, and this produces more richness or darkness of color shade.

PAINT COMPATIBILITY

Paint compatibility means the ability of paint coating to work well with other coatings when applied on them or under them during refinishing. Automotive paint coatings and solvents are designed by a paint supplier for a specific purpose. Some products are designed to be used in several different lines of paint made by the same paint company. This does not mean that the products can be used universally with other company products. The modern automobile requires a number of different paint systems to service the paint on the complete car.

In the refinish trade the painter cannot always tell just by looking at a car what type of finish it has. Sometimes painters encounter cars that have been repainted since production.

The Importance of Paint Finish Identity. It is very important that a painter identify the type of paint on a car before attempting repairs. **Non-basecoat or standard colors and basecoat paint repair systems are not interchangeable. This means**

standard refinish colors should not be used to repair basecoat/clearcoat finishes, and basecoat colors should not be used to repair standard colors.

Three things must be known by a painter to identify a proper paint repair procedure for a given car:

1. **Model year, type of car, and series**
2. **Paint code and/or WA number** (if GM)
3. **Type of paint on car**

To find the body number plate and color identity, see Chapter 2. If in doubt about the paint type and code, check with the paint jobber, or perform the "Test to Determine Type of Finish" in this chapter.

NOTE: As a reminder to the painter, basecoat colors are marked very **BOLDLY** on the container as follows: **THIS IS A BASECOAT COLOR.**

Test to Determine Type of Finish

Generally, the painter can determine the type of finish on a car with the following test. Using acrylic lacquer removing solvent (or a good grade of lacquer thinner), soak a section of clean cloth with the solvent and rub a spot in an area to be repaired.

1. If color washes off readily onto the cloth, the finish is **acrylic lacquer.**
2. If the finish does not wash off, even with vigorous rubbing, the finish is **enamel.**
3. To determine if the finish is a single-phase enamel or an OEM basecoat/clearcoat finish, perform a sanding test as follows:
    a. Use a No. 220 or 320 sandpaper and dry sand over a small spot in the area to be repaired.
    b. Check the sanding residue particles:
       (1) If the sanding residue is colored, like the surface, the finish is a **single stage enamel color.**
       (2) If the sanding residue is **whitish, powdery** and **clear,** the finish is a **basecoat/clearcoat finish.**

PAINT THICKNESS LIMIT

Most painters do not realize that automotive finishes should be applied only up to certain limits. A paint finish applied beyond these limits is subject to various cracking conditions. After determining the type of paint on a car, the next important thing to determine is **how much paint is on the car.**

Every paint shop should be equipped with at least one good paint thickness gauge. Before any panel or complete paint job is repainted, every car to have paint work done on it should have written on the paint order the current paint thickness on the subject parts. In many cases, paint shops would turn paint jobs away or charge extra to remove excess paint before repainting. **Excess paint** is a job that has been repainted once or twice already and has in the area of 8 to 12 mils of paint on it, if not more, and the job is in the paint shop for more paint repairs. A job of this type requires stripping most of the paint before paint repairs are started.

When paint shops must redo cars that have cracked paint, the expense of stripping the finish and repainting could be considerable. Applying paint to cars "in the blind" without knowing how much paint is on the car is considered "working in the dark" with an **unknown** that may come back to haunt the paint shop. The painting of cars is the responsibility of the paint shop, unless the car owner knowingly cannot afford a proper job to be done and signs away his or her legal rights.

The paint finish on a car is designed to be safe from cracking if applied at the recommended paint thickness. A safe paint thickness range is 6 to 8 mils maximum for standard lacquer finishes.

> Generally, *any factory car can be repainted one time if painted according to factory or paint supplier recommendations with no danger of paint cracking.* This refers to *line checking* (see "Checking and Cracking," Chapter 17).

Paint Thickness of Standard Refinish Lacquer Coats

In terms of film thickness, when standard acrylic lacquers are reduced 150%, applied in a medium-wet coat, and then dried fully and measured, they measure about 0.3 mil. When acrylic lacquers are reduced 125% and are applied and measured in the same way, they measure about 0.4 mil. That is why to achieve 2 or more mils of color, label directions usually advise application of six to eight *single* coats, or three to four **double** coats.

> **NOTE: Complete lines** of paint products from paint suppliers are guaranteed against major problems such as cold cracking or line checking on steel surfaces when the products are applied according to paint supplier recommendations. See the paint product label directions.

Paint Thickness Gauge (Tinsley Gauge)

A very commonly used paint thickness gauge, and the least expensive, is the Tinsley gauge, which works on a magnetic principle and is very easy to use. Figure 9-13 shows how the gauge is held when checking paint thickness on a surface. Figure 9-14 shows how the gauge is constructed.

Description (Fig. 9-14)

1. The protective cover has a clip that holds the gauge in a pocket.
2. The gauge housing is of aluminum alloy construction.
3. The window in the housing aids visibility of the measuring red magnetic rod.

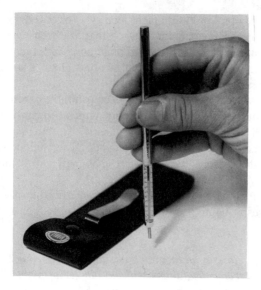

Figure 9-13 Tinsley paint thickness gauge. (Courtesy of James G. Biddle Co.)

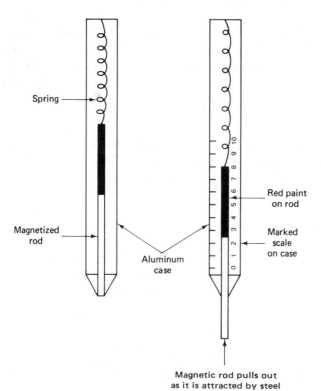

Spring

Magnetized rod

Aluminum case

Red paint on rod

Marked scale on case

Magnetic rod pulls out as it is attracted by steel

Figure 9-14 How Tinsley gauge is constructed.

4. The rod is a permanent Alcomax magnet, which is not normally affected by temperature or vibration.
5. The rod is attached to the end of the housing by a special spring.
6. The gauge window is marked with a scale on each side:
   a. A scale in thousandths of an inch (so indicated on the housing) is used for measuring paint thickness on ferrous metals.
   b. A scale on the opposite side is used for general purposes.

Procedure for Use

1. Remove the cap and place on the opposite end of the gauge.
2. Hold the gauge at **right angles** to the surface to be tested (flush, not at an angle).
3. The test surface should be free of oil, grease, sticky paint, or magnetic particles, such as chips or grinding dust.
4. Touch the magnet end of the gauge to the surface; then lift the gauge away slowly, smoothly, and steadily, without sliding the tip sideways. On bare or thinly coated metal, the attraction of the magnet is at a maximum, and it takes considerable lift and extension of the spring to overcome the magnetic pull. On heavily coated metal, much less lifting action overcomes the weaker magnetic force.
5. After one try to find the approximate pull-off point, repeat as necessary, moving slowly and watching the scale closely as the pull-off point is approached.
6. The proper reading is the farthest point to which the red rod of the magnet extends on the scale before pull-off or **at pull-off.**

The availability of the Tinsley gauge in any area of the country can be determined by contacting either of the following sources:

Gardner Laboratory, Inc.
P.O. Box 5728
5521 Landy Lane
Bethesda, Md. 20014

James G. Biddle Co.
Township Line and Jolly Roads
Plymouth Meeting, Pa. 19462

REVIEW QUESTIONS

1. What is color?
2. What is the principal film-forming part of a paint system?
3. What is the purpose of solvents in paint manufacturing?

4. What are two primary functions of pigments in a color?
5. What is the purpose of a plasticizer?
6. Of what material are most metallic particles made?
7. Describe briefly how automotive color and undercoats are made at a paint factory as follows:
   (a) How is resin made?
   (b) What is sand mill dispersion?
   (c) What is ball mill dispersion?
8. Describe solid colors, and list several of their characteristics.
9. Describe metallic colors, and list several of their characteristics.
10. What is transparency?
11. What is translucence?
12. What does the word "thermosetting" mean?
13. With what basic color systems are American-made cars painted at the factory?
    (a) American Motors
    (b) Chrysler
    (c) Ford
    (d) G.M.
14. How do acrylic lacquers dry?
15. How do acrylic enamels dry?
16. Explain the orientation of metallic particles and pigments in a standard color shade.
17. Explain the orientation of metallic particles and pigments in a light color shade.
18. Explain the orientation of metallic particles and pigments in a dark color shade.
19. What is the ideal temperature range for spraying automotive finishes?
20. What is the lowest temperature below which spray painting is not recommended?
21. What is meant by "paint compatibility" in automotive refinishing?
22. Explain how to determine if original paint being tested is acrylic lacquer, acrylic enamel, or basecoat/clearcoat type finish.
23. What durability problem can be expected when an exterior car color is applied on flexible exterior plastic parts at the same time that the car color is applied?
24. What is the safe maximum limit (in thousandths of an inch) to which a lacquer paint finish can be applied and still be safe from cold cracking or checking?
25. What is a Tinsley paint thickness gauge, and how does it work?
26. What is a single-phase color?
27. Describe a two-phase color.
28. What is a three-phase color and what are its components?

10

Automotive Colors: Preparation and Application

INTRODUCTION

Before preparing colors for application, certain basic preparation operations should be done first so that the spray painting operation can proceed smoothly from start to finish without interruption. First, all tools and equipment for mixing paint, handling paint, straining paint, and refilling the paint cup should be ready, as follows:

1. Have a large container with a sufficient supply of reduced paint ready for use.
2. The car must be inspected and approved as ready for paint.
3. The spray booth must be clean and ready for use.
4. The spray gun and all equipment must be ready.
   a. The air regulator should be checked to see that it works properly.
   b. Check the regulator drain to assure that no water is in the unit.
   c. Check the spray gun vent cleaning tool (wire or pointed tool).
   d. Have a place to hang the spray gun while refilling the paint cup.

TOOLS AND EQUIPMENT NEEDED IN THE PAINT MIXING ROOM

1. Mix paint in a room or area that meets OSHA standards.
2. Clean the workbench; a metal surface (unpainted) is easy to keep clean and is easy to maintain.

255

3. The room or area should be properly lit.
4. The room should be continuously ventilated.
5. All metal benches and shelves should be grounded.
6. A trash container for paper and throwaway rags.
7. A container for clean shop towels and a second container for soiled shop towels.
8. A trash container for empty cans should be outside the paint mixing room.
9. A special container for throwaway solvents.
10. A 1-gallon container for semisoiled solvent that could still be used.
11. Special tools should hang at the front of the workbench:
    a. Pliers (for opening thinner cans, etc.).
    b. A hanger for hanging the spray gun while refilling the paint cup with primer, etc.
12. A supply of clean shop towels and a roll of paper towels.
13. A cleanup tray 4 by 4 by 10 inches minimum; larger one preferred.
14. A small glass or cup for soaking and cleaning the air cap.
15. A 1-inch paintbrush for spray equipment cleanup.
16. Another 1-inch paintbrush cut down to $\frac{5}{8}$ inch in length. This is needed for additional cleanup.
17. A woven plastic scouring pad for cleanup.
18. A 3-gallon plastic container to hold reduced paint materials.
19. A supply of paint strainers.
20. A paint strainer stand.
21. A paint shaker should be outside the paint mixing room. (This is a great time saver. Every paint shop should have one.)
22. A supply of paint paddles. These should be about $1\frac{1}{2}$ inches wide by $\frac{1}{8}$ inch thick and 12 inches long. Aluminum or brass paddles are best. They should be flat-bottomed.
23. Masking tape.
24. A screwdriver and a hammer.
25. A pointed tool such as a scratch awl.

Every paint shop should be well stocked with medium-grade thinner, which is used as the primary cleaning solvent, whether painting in lacquer or enamel. Other solvents are usually more costly, and medium thinner is ideal for the universal-type primer-surfacer that is used in most paint systems. Medium-grade thinner should be purchased in 30- or 50-gallon drums.

Other thinners that should be kept on hand for immediate use by the gallon are (Table 7-1):

1. Slow-grade color thinner
2. Fast-evaporating thinner
3. Retarder

Acrylic enamel reducers that should be kept on hand for immediate use by the gallon are (Table 7-1):

1. Slow-grade color reducer
2. Medium-grade color reducer
3. Fast-evaporating reducer
4. Acrylic enamel retarder

The best-grade primer (and catalyst), the best-grade primer-surfacer, and glazing putty should also be on hand ready for use (see Table 8-1).

All the items listed should be stored in a paint mix room for immediate use. When these items are not on hand they must be procured from a store, and this takes time. Time cuts down on jobs, and time is money in a paint shop.

CHECKLIST FOR PREPARING A CAR BEFORE COLOR COATING

Check, Repair, and Complete All Masking

Before giving the final go-ahead for masking, inspect **all** masking with a careful eye to quality. Start at a given point on the car, make a complete circle around the car, and end up in the spot where inspection started. Look over every inch of masking. Make sure by visual inspection and by feeling specific joints that they are down tightly, flush, and smooth. Be sure that all masking on the side windows, windshield, and back window is sealed, with no open joints.

Check and Prepare the Spray Booth as Required

There are two basic ways to spray paint. Spraying enamel finishes requires much cleaner sanitation conditions than does spraying lacquers.

Lacquer Application. Spraying acrylic lacquers does not require as clean a spray booth as for spraying enamels. However, the spray booth should be kept as clean as possible because less booth preparation is required when an enamel job is to be done. Floors should be kept clean by sweeping and watering down periodically.

Enamel Application. For enamel application, the walls, ceiling, and floor should be cleaned by hosing them down and blowing them dry. All booth intake filters should be blown clean and vacuumed (if not replaced). All openings in filter doors, walls, ceiling, and all booth joints should be checked with a positive air flow and sealed as required. All door seals lose their sealing qualities as they age and should be repaired or replaced as required. Air exhaust filters should be replaced according to OSHA standards. **No flying dirt particles whatsoever** should enter the booth when an enamel job is being sprayed.

The previously mentioned maintenance operations do not have to be done with every paint job but should be done as part of a regular maintenance program two or three times each year. However, the spray booth should be hosed down before every enamel paint job.

PREPARATION OF COLOR

Automotive colors are prepared in two basic ways for refinishing:

Hand Mixing

The most thorough way to mix the paint by hand is as follows:

1. Open the can carefully (Fig. 10-1). Use the proper can opener.
2. Make a pouring spout on the can with masking tape (Fig. 10-2). Use several sections of $\frac{3}{4}$-inch tape if wider tape is not available.
3. Pour about half of the paint into a second clean container.
4. Mix each half of the container thoroughly using a wide, flat-bottomed paddle (Figs. 10-3 and 10-4).
5. Combine both halves in the original container and mix them thoroughly. Remove the tape spout when finished, and the can is clean.

This method results in a faster and more thorough way of mixing paint with less mess.

Machine Mixing (Use of a Paint Shaker)

Not many painters do this, but they should:

1. Open the can of paint and, with a flat-bottomed paddle, loosen all pigments at the bottom, including pigments trapped at all corners. Use the edge of the paddle to scrape pigments loose at the lower corner edges.

Figure 10-1 Opening can of paint with friction lid. (Courtesy of the DuPont Company)

Figure 10-2 Making pouring spout on can with masking tape. (Courtesy of the DuPont Company)

Figure 10-3 Stirring paint thoroughly with flat-bottomed paddle. (Courtesy of the DuPont Company)

Figure 10-4 Automotive colors must be sprayed. Do not expect wet paint in can to match color on car, especially metallic colors. (Courtesy of R-M Automotive Products, BASF Inmont Corp.)

2. Using a suitable clean paintbrush, return paint from the paddle to the container. Install the cover on the can by positioning the cover, covering the can with a suitable cloth, and tapping the cover down tightly with **light** hammer blows.

3. Put the can of paint on a paint shaker and secure firmly in place. Check the shaker operation for 1 or 2 seconds, and stop the machine. Recheck the tightness of the clamps, can, etc., and when all is in order, turn the shaker on for the required amount of time. About 5 to 10 minutes of shaking does a thorough job.

Loosening the hard, settled paint in the can before shaking cuts down mixing time considerably.

To speed up mixing time even more, some painters throw a small amount of **solvent-washed** tacks, small screws, or bolts into the can before putting it on the shaker. The objects are caught later in a paint strainer. The painter washes and rinses them in thinner and saves them for the next use.

COLOR REDUCTION (CONVENTIONAL METHOD)

Reducing color by the conventional method means reducing color according to **label directions**. Label directions change every so often because paint technology changes. In early years, when acrylic lacquers were first used in the refinish trade, the standard reduction for refinishing was 150%. Rinshed-Mason over the years has recommended a 125% reduction. But in recent years, because of millions of cars-worth of experience, the label directions have changed in favor of matching metallic colors. Since factories use about a 125% reduction, the refinish trade conventional reduction has also become about 125%. This is 5 parts solvent to 4 parts color. However, because of variables that can affect the shade of metallics at the factory, the label directions now include: "Reduce from 100% to 150%." This is why the viscosity cup discussed in Chapter 7 has achieved more prominence in color matching.

If a person cannot read label directions for any reason, he or she should have someone read the directions out loud. Sometimes the printing size of label directions is very small.

If preparing 1 quart or less of reduced paint material, prepare the reduction in an extra container, mix it thoroughly, and then strain the reduced material into the regular paint cup.

USE OF URETHANE HARDENER (CATALYST) IN ACRYLIC ENAMEL (Table 9-1)

Chapter 9 explains the growth and increasing popularity of catalyzed acrylic enamels. All paint companies are uniform on the amount of catalyst to use per gallon of acrylic enamel, which is 1 pint, before reduction. A gallon has 8 pints, so the ratio is 8 to 1. Follow label directions.

What most painters do is catalyze only the required amount of enamel to be used. Then they reduce and use the amount prepared. Painters reduce more paint only as required. Once acrylic enamel is catalyzed, it must be used within the required time indicated in the label directions. Otherwise, it spoils.

PROCEDURE FOR REDUCTION

1. Prepare a mixing paddle with suitable "sharp" markings on the tape and/or on the paddle as described in Fig. 10-5.

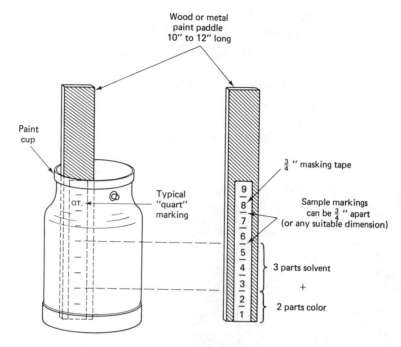

Wood or metal
paint paddle
10" to 12" long

Paint
cup

Typical
"quart"
marking

QT.

$\frac{3}{4}$ " masking tape

Sample markings
can be $\frac{3}{4}$ " apart
(or any suitable dimension)

9
8
7
6
5
4
3
2
1

3 parts solvent

+

2 parts color

Figure 10-5 Prepare marked paddle for reducing paint.

Figure 10-6 Pouring solvent from a square can. (Courtesy of the DuPont Company)

Procedure for Reduction

261

2. Prepare the reduction **by first pouring the color into the container to the proper line on the paddle** (see Table 7-4).

3. **Add the proper solvent** (Fig. 10-6) according to label directions. Use care not to overreduce or underreduce.

4. Mix the reduction thoroughly with a flat-bottomed paint paddle.

5. Check the viscosity of the reduced paint (Fig. 10-7).

6. Position a clean strainer over the paint cup or on a strainer stand, and strain the reduced paint into the paint cup (Fig. 10-8).

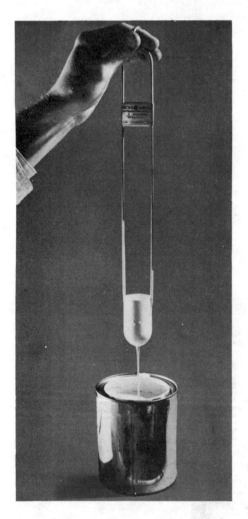

Figure 10-7 Checking viscosity of reduced paint (see Table 7-2). (Courtesy of General Electric Company)

Figure 10-8 Straining reduced paint into paint cup. (Courtesy of the DuPont Company)

NOTE: This is for preparing 1 cup of reduced material. When painting a complete car, the required amount of material is prepared all at once in a suitable container. Then, as each quart (or two) is refilled, the reduced paint is strained at that time. Each reduction is made in accordance with the size of the job; that is, size of the car, type of paint, and amount.

CHECK THE SPRAY OUTFIT BEFORE PAINTING

1. Attach the cup to the spray gun and tighten the attachment securely.
2. Check the cup lid vent hole with a pointed tool to make sure that it is fully open.
3. Check the spray gun by holding it horizontally as when spraying a roof panel to determine if it will leak at the gasket. If the cup is the old type and even remotely liable to leak, install a "diaper" around the cup lid. Simply wrap a several-inch-wide band of cloth or absorbent paper towel around the cup lid and secure with masking tape.

   NOTE: Various modern spray guns have special gaskets and leak-proof lids that make possible spraying on horizontal surfaces without dripping. This precaution is not required on vertical surfaces.

4. **Adjust the spray gun for a full-open spray fan.** Check a flooding test pattern on a vertical wall. (This could be a section of the wall or spray stand suitably masked off for this purpose.) See "Spray Gun Adjustments," Chapter 4.
5. Check and adjust the air pressure as follows:
   a. **For acrylic lacquers,** use 30 to 40 psi (at the gun). Allow for pressure drop (see Table 5-4). This could be plus or minus about 5 psi. The complete range is 25 to 45 psi.
   b. **For enamels,** use 50 psi for most acrylic enamels unless otherwise recommended in the label directions. The complete range is 50 to 70 psi for other types of enamels.

The best air pressure for any paint system is one that provides the best atomization at the lowest air pressure. The proper spray gun adjustment is one that provides a level and uniform flooded test pattern.

Before starting to apply color, be sure the following are in the booth or are easily accessible outside the booth:

1. Reduced color and paint paddle
2. Paint strainers and strainer stand
3. Cleaning solvent (medium thinner)
4. Cleaning equipment (pan, brush, and wiping rags)

5. Diaper material and masking tape
6. NIOSH-approved respirator

NOTE: When a painter wears a NIOSH-approved respirator according to the manufacturer's directions, the painter's lungs are fully protected.

HOSE CONTROL WHEN SPRAYING EXTRA-WIDE SURFACES

An item that a painter must be able to control at all times and that is not covered in Chapter 4 is hose control. This involves handling the hose and controlling it so that the hose does not interfere with the spray painting operation. Simply holding the hose with the opposite hand is not sufficient control, particularly when spraying the roof, the hood, or any large area. The best way to control the hose is to run it under one armpit, over the neck, and allow the hose to extend to the spray gun being held by the other hand. In this fashion, the hose is prevented from scraping on the edge of the roof or car panel when making an extended reach during paint application.

SILICONE ADDITIVES (Table 10-1)

The purpose of a silicone additive is to speed up the completion of a refinishing operation after all surface preparation operations have been completed, and when fisheyes appear after the first color coat is applied. The purpose of a silicone additive is not as a substitute for the usual surface preparation operations. Silicone additives should not be used freely in every color application. Use the product only when necessary.

Surfaces to be refinished may be contaminated with silicone, which may come from one of the following in a shop: car polishes, rubber lubricants, oil, grease, and shop towels. Silicone is very slippery. When used in car polishes, it results in less dirt and road film sticking to the finish.

When a surface is contaminated with silicones and is painted, this is how fisheyes are caused:

1. The fresh paint solvent dissolves a particle of silicone that is on the paint finish.
2. The silicone, being quite light, floats to the surface on horizontal surfaces. On

TABLE 10-1 ADDITIVES FOR PREVENTION OF FISHEYES

Description of product	DuPont	Ditzler	Rinshed-Mason	Sherwin-Williams	Martin-Senour
For all acrylic lacquer and enamel colors	FEE	DX-66	809	V3-K-265	77B
For all urethane and urethane-catalyzed finishes	259-S	DX-77	809	V3K-780	87

vertical surfaces, the circulation of solvent as it evaporates carries silicones with it.

3. Silicones, being very slippery, cannot hold the surface tension of the new color coat as it is applied wet. The lack of surface tension at the silicones opens up and causes fisheyes, which are always round in shape and appear as small craters.

Use

Before applying color coats to a surface, perform all the required surface preparation. This includes washing with paint finish cleaning solvent, sanding with No. 500, 600, or finer sandpaper and recleaning with solvent. This is the best way to remove silicones. Silicones are sometimes very difficult to remove. See Table 10-1.

Active particles of silicone may still remain on the surface, which would not affect adhesion of newly applied color but could cause fisheyes. It is prevention of fisheyes under these circumstances that has led paint companies to provide silicone additives to the refinishing trade. When a silicone additive is used in repair color, the new color becomes 100% saturated with silicones. This causes a uniform tension on the surface of the new color coat, thus preventing fisheyes.

Application

For best results, follow the label directions. Using too much silicone additive leads to other refinishing problems. Also, use proper additive for the specified paint system (see Table 10-1).

Fisheye Prevention (without a Silicone Additive). If a painter encounters a fisheye problem upon spraying the first coat, the problem can be remedied without a silicone additive by proceeding immediately using the following technique:

1. Adjust the spray gun for dry-spray application (see "Spray Gun Adjustments," Chapter 4).
2. Apply the equivalent of one full dry-spray coat of color on areas where fisheyes occurred and on other surfaces to be painted. It will be noted the fisheyes practically disappear because of only one coat of paint. Allow the dry-spray application to dry for 10 to 15 minutes.
3. a. If applying acrylic lacquer color, proceed with medium to light color coats before applying the final two coats of color extra wet.
   b. If applying acrylic enamel color, apply two *very light* coats (which together would make up the first coat). Allow full flash-off between coats. Then apply a final extra-wet color coat.

In effect, the dry-spray color coats act as a sealer and prevent the covered silicones from reaching the surface. An appropriate sealer applied on the semidry side would serve the same purpose.

PAINT APPLICATION PROCEDURE

The final operation before spray painting is to use an air blow gun and a tack rag to blow off and to tack-wipe the entire car (Figs. 10-9 and 10-10).

1. With the spray booth exhaust on, start blowing off each surface, starting at the rear of the car and working forward.
2. Blow off, then tack-wipe each panel, overlapping each wiping area with the next one. Use new sections of the tack rag as the operation progresses.

Many methods of doing complete paint jobs are available to painters. Most veteran painters have their own favorite ways of painting complete cars. The author's favorite sequence of doing a complete paint job is shown in Fig. 10-11 (two methods are shown).

NOTE: A suitable bench or stable boxes should be on hand in the spray booth for painters who need them to reach all areas of passenger car roofs. Also, special ladders or scaffolding is required to paint van roofs and other high vehicles.

Roof Panel (Fig. 10-12). With the paint spray cup full and a respirator in place:

1. Apply a banding coat at the windshield and back window.
2. Apply the first coat, starting at the near edge of the roof, by making a pass from left to right *and* from right to left with a medium wet application. Always start edges like this.
3. Then, because of the limited angle of a *full* spray gun cup, overlap 60% to 70% and apply each succeeding pass working toward the center of the roof. As each pass is made, observe the paint for the proper gloss to show. This is done by

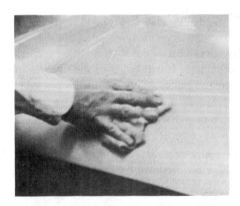

Figure 10-9 Dusting surface with compressed air and cloth. (Courtesy of the DuPont Company)

Figure 10-10 Tack-wiping surface with tack rag for final dusting just before painting. (Courtesy of Ditzler Automotive Finishes, PPG Industries, Inc.)

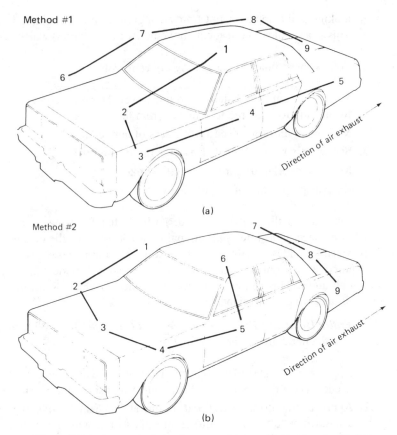

Method #1

(a)

Method #2

(b)

Figure 10-11 Sequence of spraying a complete car: Method 1 and method 2.

Figure 10-12 Spray painting a roof panel. (Courtesy of Ditzler Automotive Finishes, PPG Industries, Inc.)

looking at the applied paint from an angle with proper lighting in the background. This is an indication of medium wetness of application, which is desired.

Follow these fundamentals as rigidly as possible:

1. Maintain a uniform distance; do not waver the arm inconsistently. **Stay parallel to the surface.** Keep 6 to 8 inches from the surface.
2. Maintain a uniform speed for wetness of application.
3. **See** what is being applied. Do not spray **in the dark.**
4. Keep the overlap uniform, stroke to stroke.
5. Keep as perpendicular as possible without dripping.

When one side of the roof is finished, go immediately to the opposite side and, with benches in place, **continue applying paint, working from the center to the near side.** This system provides a wet-on-wet application that minimizes overspray. Apply banding as required at the front and rear. When a roof is painted in ideal fashion, it is uniformly wet in all areas. This can be seen from the reflected gloss. Refill the cup for spraying the next area. Check the diaper, if necessary.

Entire Hood and Tops of Front Fenders (Fig. 10-13). **With no blowing of air,** tack-wipe the hood area to be painted.

1. Apply a banding stroke along the base of the windshield. No banding stroke is needed along the front of the hood unless it is short and reachable.
2. Apply the first medium-wet coat starting at the near edge over the fender by making a pass from left to right **and** from right to left with a medium-wet application. Always start edges like this.
3. Then, because of the limited angle of a **full** spray gun, overlap 60% to 70% and apply each succeeding pass working toward the center of the hood. Observe each pass for the proper gloss to show.
4. Working from the opposite side, start the spray application along the center of the hood and continue the application toward the near side of the hood.

Figure 10-13 Spray painting a hood panel. (Courtesy of Ditzler Automotive Finishes, PPG Industries, Inc.)

5. The application of sound fundamentals is what produces best-quality results.
6. Then proceed to the front of the car and, starting at one side, complete the application of a single coat to the front of the car. Use about a 4-inch overlap when applying color to new areas. Apply color to valance panels if present below the bumper.

Entire Rear Deck Area. Work in a similar fashion to painting the roof and hood. Tack-wipe but do not air-blow the rear deck area. Check and refill the spray gun cup as required. Check the diaper.

1. Apply a banding stroke along the base of the back window to the center.
2. Standing at the side of the rear fender, apply the first medium-wet coat, starting at the near edge. Make a medium-fast pass from left to right and from right to left as the first pass.
3. Continue applying single coats with 60% to 70% overlap because of the gun tilt to the center of the rear deck.
4. Switch sides and, continuing from the center, apply single coats as directed toward the near side of the car. Observe the reflection of the applied paint to keep it wet at all times. Move only as fast as the reflection shows wetness of application.
5. Proceed to the rear of the car and, starting at one side, complete the application of a single coat to the rear of the car. Use about a 4-inch overlap when blending color to previously applied color. Apply color to valance panels below the bumper, if present.

Sides of the Car (Fig. 10-14). Tack-wipe but do not air-blow the sides to be painted. Check and refill the spray gun cup as required. A diaper is not needed.

1. Apply banding strokes vertically down the sides at a comfortable distance toward the front of the car.
2. Starting at the top or bottom, apply a double pass, from left to right and from right to left, to start an edge. Continue to apply a single coat (this is a 50% overlap) to the reachable area until the area is fully coated.

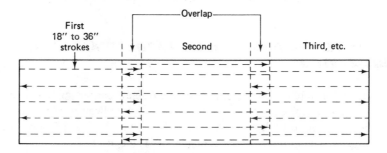

Figure 10-14 How sides of car are spray painted.

3. Move to the next forward area and make another vertical banding pass at the area that can be reached comfortably. Using a 4-inch overlap, fill this area with a single-coat paint application, making sure that the paint is applied wet and that what is applied is "seen."

CAUTION: When in doubt as to whether to apply another coat of paint to a questionable area, it is best **not** to apply it. The reason is that too much paint will result in a run. A missed area can always be color-coated later when it is determined that more paint is needed. It is up to the painter to know specifically and exactly where color was last applied. When necessary, provide proper, safe lighting.

4. Painting wheel-opening flanges:
   a. Reduce the fan size as required, or do as veteran painters do: use 50% or less trigger pull.
   b. Position the gun at the center of the opening and at right angles to the surface.
   c. Apply color lightly to the flange while pivoting the gun at the center of the opening. Avoid flooding. This is done with "feel." Color can always be applied. When applied too heavily, it is too late.
   d. First do one-half of the wheel opening, then position the gun and do the opposite half of the wheel opening, overlapping a few inches at the center.

5. Painting rocker panels (if convenient, raise the side of the car several inches with a car jack, or set the wheels on 4-inch wooden blocks):
   a. Use a medium-size fan and controlled trigger pull as required. This is an area where the painter must improvise and deviate from standard practice.
   b. While leading in one direction with the wrist, allow the hand and gun to trail to obtain the best possible application angle. Apply color to the rocker panel carefully with this motion. Strive for a medium-wet application. Avoid flooding. "See" what is being applied. This is an operation that must be done with "feel" and care, and good lighting.

6. Painting windshield pillars and sedan door headers:
   a. Use a small fan and controlled trigger pull as required.
   b. Apply color lightly with several passes until the proper wetness of color is seen.

7. When one side of the car is painted, paint the opposite side in the same sequence.

DIFFERENCES BETWEEN ACRYLIC LACQUER AND ENAMEL PAINT SYSTEMS

The color application system covered in detail earlier applies to both paint systems, acrylic lacquers and enamels. The same basic application procedure and spraying techniques apply to both paint systems. But there is a big difference between both paint systems. The differences are explained in Table 10-2.

Even though acrylic enamels and acrylic lacquers are totally different paint sys-

TABLE 10-2 DIFFERENCES BETWEEN APPLICATION OF ACRYLIC LACQUERS AND ACRYLIC ENAMELS

	Acrylic lacquers	Acrylic enamels
Reduction (see label directions)	From 100% to 200% (125%[a])	Sometimes no reduction Normally 25%; 33%[b]; 50%
Air pressure (at gun)	Normal: 40 psi May be 20 to 30 psi May be 45 psi	Normal: 60 psi[b] May be 50 psi May be 35 psi (mist)[b]
First coat	Medium-wet coat (0.3 to 0.4 mil)	Medium-wet coat ($\frac{3}{4}$ to 1 mil)[b]
Second coat	Medium-wet coat (0.3 to 0.4 mil)	Extra-wet coat ($1\frac{1}{4}$ mils or more)[b]
Total coats needed	6 to 8 coats needed; 4 to 6 coats to go	2 enamel color coats[b] completed
To produce final gloss	Lightly sand; compound and polish	Gloss comes up automatically
Recoating (e.g., repairing next day)	Can be recoated or repaired anytime	Catalyzed coating can be recoated anytime[b] Uncatalyzed coating requires *recoat sealer* in sensitive period[b]
Dirt control	Not too much of a problem	Greatest problem[b]

[a]Most popular for acrylic lacquer system.
[b]Applicable to acrylic enamel system.

tems, the refinishing principles of (1) surface preparation (cleaning, sanding, primer, and primer-surfacer application) and (2) color preparation and application of first color coat are highly similar. Basic refinishing principles that apply to both paint systems have been covered just once. The principles that are different are so labeled and explained. The basic differences between acrylic lacquers and acrylic enamels (which also includes alkyd enamels) are shown in Table 10-2. The differences in lacquer and enamel refinishing operations are explained next.

APPLYING STANDARD ACRYLIC AND URETHANE ENAMEL PAINT SYSTEMS

1. Apply a second coat of enamel when the first coat has dried sufficiently.
   a. This is when the painter can rub the back of a forefinger (between the first two knuckles) on the corner of a panel section painted with the first coat and the paint does not rub off.
   b. This usually takes place by the time the painter completes application of the first coat when painting a complete car.
   c. Apply a second coat extra wet, which is much heavier than the first coat. The

heavier second coat will not run, as the first coat helps to absorb much of the solvent.

d. Three typical ways a painter can apply a wetter application of paint are as follows:

(1) Slow down each stroke the required amount. Make slow, deliberate passes, but do not make them too slowly.

(2) Use about a three-quarter overlap pass instead of a 50% overlap.

(3) Cut down slightly on the distance from the surface. The painter must become very good at using any of the above systems before attempting to combine any two of them. In enamel painting this could lead to a run very quickly.

Important: If an uneven gloss or overspray problem is encountered, it can be remedied by careful application of mist coating. The painter must remember that excessive mist coating of enamels can affect the gloss and durability of enamels in the long run. Excessive mist coating tends to wash the protective resin off the pigments.

2. If mist coating is required, proceed as follows:

a. Use 95% solvent and 5% color, or use straight 100% reducer of the same type as that used in the reduction.

b. Use reduced air pressure of about 20 to 30 psi at the gun.

c. Adjust spray gun in midrange adjustment and check spray pattern. (See "Spray Gun Adjustments," Chapter 4).

d. Apply uniformly wet mist-coat material to affected surfaces to remedy the problem. Avoid application of too much solvent. Allow a little flash time for condition to clear as solvent levels surface and evaporates.

3. Allow the finish to become dust-free before removing the paint job (30 to 60 minutes) from the spray booth. Never place the car in the hot sun to dry, whether acrylic lacquer or enamel. Ideal drying conditions include plenty of fresh, warm air. Avoid polishing new paint jobs with sealer type polishes for at least 30 days.

APPLYING THE STANDARD ACRYLIC LACQUER PAINT SYSTEM

1. Apply a second medium-wet coat of acrylic lacquer to the car. Follow the same sequence outlined for applying the first coat.

2. When a complete car is being painted, color coats are applied continually, as complete flash-off takes place between coats.

3. Apply the third through eighth coats (or the number of coats per the label directions) until complete hiding is achieved (see Table 10-2). **Proper hiding** means that when a color is applied to a thickness of 2 mils (when dry) the color will effectively and equally cover and hide a light **and** a dark shade of undercoat.

NOTE: Painting an acrylic lacquer car takes many more coats than painting an enamel car. This requires many more refills of the paint cup, each of which must be strained. One strainer can be reused several times on the same color on the same day. The use of a diaper by the painter on large flat horizontal surfaces is an option that, if used, must be redone with each refill. That is why having all reduced color and sufficient strainers in the paint booth saves time.

4. Allow the car to dry sufficiently before moving it to another location.
5. Remove masking as follows:
   a. On catalyzed enamel jobs, after 2 hours
   b. On uncatalyzed enamel jobs, wait until next day
   c. On acrylic lacquer jobs, after 1 hour
6. Clean up the car as required: windows, front and rear ends, and bumpers and wheels. Also clean up the interior as required.
7. Allow the finish to air-dry several days, preferably 1 week, before compounding. Or force-dry the finish with banks of infrared heat lamps at 180°F for 30 minutes or 160°F for 1 hour.
8. Compound and polish as required (see Chapter 11).

REPAIRING PROBLEMS DURING LACQUER AND ENAMEL PAINT APPLICATION

A condition that may occur when wet spraying any metallic color is called **mottling.** Mottling is a condition that appears as dark-shaded or off-color areas or streaks within a paint finish. Mottling is described more fully and discussed in Chapter 17.

If a mottling condition appears during the final color application, the condition can be remedied with the following fog-coating technique:

1. Move the spray gun back 18 to 24 inches from the affected surface.
2. Use the same reduction as in applying color on a car.
3. Use a three-quarter to full pull on the trigger, and apply a fog coat to the entire affected area as follows:
   a. Maintain the gun at 18 to 24 inches from the surface.
   b. Keep the trigger pulled and hold it open continually over the affected area while swirling the spray gun in a continuously moving circular motion. After several seconds of fog coating, observe the appearance of the mottling condition, which gradually disappears with an application of fog coating.
   c. As the mottling or streaking condition disappears, stop the application and move to another affected area.
4. Allow the repair application to air-dry in the spray booth with the air exhaust on for 30 to 45 minutes.
5. Then apply a final mist coat with a high-volume solvent for final gloss on enamels or lacquers.

6. Allow the repair to dry in the booth until it is dust-free (30 to 60 minutes) before removing the paint job from the spray booth.

Insect or Dirt Lands on Wet Paint

If a flying insect or a large piece of dirt lands on wet paint during a painting operation, pick it off within 30 to 90 seconds as follows:

1. Apply a short section of masking tape in reverse on a pencil or a section of wire. Sometimes a painter will reverse-roll a short section of tape by itself, with the adhesive side out.
2. Quickly, but carefully, press the tape lightly on the insect or dirt and pick it off. Expertly done, the damage to the finish is negligible.
3. If tape does not work and the finish is setting up, use suitable tweezers to pick off the dirt.

Accidental Hose or Clothing Contact on Fresh Paint

If an accidental smudge occurs on a fresh paint finish during paint operations, most conditions can be remedied as follows:

1. Apply a dry spray (see "Spray Gun Adjustments," Chapter 4) to the affected area for several seconds to attempt flattening and coating the spot. When very dry, a coating can be applied continually with a circling motion.
2. With midrange spot-repair spray gun adjustments, apply two color coats and allow to flash 5 to 10 minutes.
3. Apply a mist coat solvent to the repair and surrounding areas to blend in the gloss.

REVIEW QUESTIONS

1. List several important items that should be done before spray painting starts so that operation can proceed smoothly from start to finish without interruption.
2. List tools, equipment, and containers that should be in a paint mixing room (or equivalent area) to speed up the preparation of paint materials before painting starts.
3. What solvent is used most in a paint shop for cleanup purposes?
4. List the basic solvents that should be in a paint mixing room (or equivalent area) to do paint work on a year-round basis.
   (a) Acrylic lacquer system solvents
   (b) Acrylic enamel system solvents
5. What primers and primer-surfacers should be on hand for immediate use?
6. On a complete refinish, what is the procedure to check out masking before painting starts?

7. What is the procedure for checking out a paint spray booth before spraying an enamel job?

8. Explain the procedure for mixing a can of paint by hand.

9. Explain the procedure for mixing a can of paint on a paint shaker.

10. Explain how to check a spray gun for adjustment and for air pressure setting to apply:
    (a) Acrylic lacquer
    (b) Acrylic enamel

11. What should the air pressure setting (at the gun) be for applying a 95% to 100% mist-coat solvent?

12. Explain how to control the hose during spray application when painting a roof, hood, and rear deck of a car requiring an extended reach.

13. What is the purpose of a silicone additive?

14. What is the procedure for using a silicone additive?

15. Explain how silicones cause fisheyes to occur.

16. Explain how to prevent a fisheye condition by the dry-spray method in the event that no silicone additive is on hand.

17. Explain the method for spray painting a roof panel (starting, etc.).

18. Explain the method for spray painting the hood and tops of the front fenders (starting, etc.).

19. Explain the method for spray painting the rear deck of a car (starting, etc.).

20. Explain the method for spray painting the complete side of a car when the air exhaust in the spray booth is at the front of the car.

21. How many single coats are generally required when applying a complete recolor coating with:
    (a) Acrylic lacquer system
    (b) Acrylic enamel system

22. In mils, or thousandths of an inch, how much thickness of color coat gives complete hiding when applying **standard** acrylic lacquers?

23. Explain the remedy for correcting mottling that appears during final heavy color application.

24. Explain how and when to pick off a large dirt nib or insect that lands on wet paint during a painting operation.

25. Explain how to repair quickly an accidental hose or clothing smudge on fresh paint during painting operations.

11

Compounding and Polishing

The purpose of compounding and polishing is as follows:

1. To make acrylic lacquers glossy as a final operation after paint application.
2. To remove sandscratches from acrylic lacquer blend areas before making spot repairs.
3. To compound acrylic enamels in areas where spot repairs are to be make; or to remove minor paint problems without repainting on **BC/CC** finishes.
4. As a service repair operation:
   a. To restore appearance of older lacquer and enamel cars that have chalked and faded.
   b. To remove minor scratches from new and used cars.
   c. To increase the gloss of car finishes.
   d. To remove road grime from a car before polishing.
   3. To remove various paint conditions described in Chapter 17.

NOTE: On acrylic lacquer finishes, water sanding with No. 500 or 600 sandpaper before compounding speeds up the surface leveling and gloss operation.

DESCRIPTION OF RUBBING COMPOUNDS

Rubbing compounds are made of abrasive powders that are mixed with water, solvent, oils, and other liquids. The abrasive powders are available in different sizes. The largest or coarsest abrasives have the fastest cutting speed, but they also result in limited gloss because of the coarser scratches. In general, the abrasive sizes are coarse, medium, fine, and extra fine. Abrasives are made up of one or a combination of the following: pumice, talc, and tripoli. Each of these abrasives breaks down to a smaller size on use.

Generally, compounds with coarse particles are called **rubbing compounds.** When the particles break down to a smaller size, they are called **polishing compounds.** Rubbing compounds work two ways. When first used, the abrasive particles cut and smooth the surface. As abrasives break down to smaller size, they then work as a polish. The lubricant serves to ease the rubbing operation and prevents excessive scratching.

The main difference between hand and machine compounds is in the vehicle.

Hand Compounds

1. Hand compounds are much slower drying because they use more slowly drying oils.
2. For this reason, they remain in paste form longer.
3. When used with a machine polisher, the hand compound clogs up the bonnet and loses cutting efficiency.
4. Generally, hand compounds are composed of the finest grade of abrasives.

Machine Compounds

1. Machine compounds are designed for fast drying and become powdery quickly for ease of cleanup.
2. The use of a machine compound by hand usually results in less gloss.
3. Machine compounds are made of a combination of coarse, medium, and fine abrasives.

Each rubbing compound is characterized by a particular cutting speed and quality of gloss for which it is designed, and for the method of rubbing, hand or machine. Painters find out quickly by experience which compounds work best for them. Selecting and using a slow and poor gloss compound slows a painter down and he or she learns quickly which are the most efficient compounds.

Newly sprayed lacquer finishes should not be rubbed and polished until the solvents have evaporated completely and the film is thoroughly dry. Painters can usually tell that a paint finish is ready for compounding when there is no pronounced odor from the film. This may require at least one and possibly several days. When necessary, catalyzed enamels can be compounded the next day. But, generally, the compounding of enamel finishes is not recommended. If lacquer finishes are compounded too soon,

TABLE 11-1 HAND AND MACHINE-RUBBING COMPOUNDS

Description of product	Dupont	Ditzler	Rinshed-Mason	Sherwin-Williams	Martin-Senour
Fast-cutting hand compound	101-S	DRX-45	851	D1T13	6360
Fast-cutting hand compound	202-S	DRX-55	853	D1T271	6356
Light-cutting hand compound	606-S	DRX-25	852	D1T273	6358
Machine rubbing compound (for No. 2 or 5 carpet pad)	808-S, 303-S	DRX-16	854, 858	D1T122	6361

hazing or a dulling back will result. Rubbing and polishing methods are divided into two categories: hand and machine. See Table 11-1 for the availability of rubbing compounds from the leading paint suppliers.

HAND RUBBING PROCEDURE

Before starting, agitate the compound in a container before use for uniform homogenized mixture.

1. Apply the compound sparingly to a rubbing ball (Fig. 11-1a) made of a water-dampened and wrung-out clean, soft cloth. Flannel cloth is excellent for this purpose. Do not apply hand compound to the job.
2. Rub with straight back-and-forth motions in one direction (Fig. 11-1b) until the desired smoothness and gloss are obtained. Work small areas at a time, about 8 to 12 inches long by 4 to 6 inches wide. Use moderate pressure on a rubbing ball. As gloss begins to appear, ease hand pressure and polishing action until a final gloss is attained. The amount of compound on the cloth is determined by the size of the area worked.
3. With another clean cloth, wipe the surface clean by removing all traces of rubbing compound.
4. Use a small ($\frac{1}{2}$ or 1 inch) soft-bristled paintbrush to aid in removing compound from gap spacings, crevices, and tight corners.

MACHINE RUBBING PROCEDURE

Machine rubbing involves the use of a power polishing machine that should have an rpm (revolutions per minute) rating of 1400 to 2200 or higher **under load** (Fig. 11-2). The lightweight, high-rpm machines are most popular on acrylics because of the higher degree of gloss they produce. A polisher in this range could also be used effectively with modern-design sanding pads now available for use with them (see Table 6-5).

Machine compound is applied most effectively with a plastic squeeze bottle (Fig. 11-3). A short-tufted, carpet-type pad is designed for machine rubbing and polishing.

(a)

(b)

Figure 11-1 (a) Apply hand-rubbing compound directly to hard rubbing ball made of flannel-type cloth. (b) Hand compounding is done with moderate pressure over small area with straight back-and-forth strokes. (Courtesy of the DuPont Company)

Heavy-duty rubbing pads, such as Amcor No. 2 or 5, or equivalent, are designed with shorter tufts and provide faster cutting and a better polishing effect.

A carpet-type pad is secured to a polisher much the same as a sanding disc is secured to a sander. It is secured by a clamp nut (see Fig. 6-7, item C).

Lamb's-wool bonnets (Fig. 11-4) are ideal for polishing with liquid polishes. However, they can also be used with polishes or rubbing compounds containing mild or extra-fine abrasives. Most lamb's-wool bonnets are designed to fit over a rubbing pad and are secured to the pad with a strong lace in a listing pocket on the back side of the bonnet (Fig. 11-4).

The use of a power polisher is the fastest method of bringing out the final smoothness and gloss on a newly applied lacquer finish. However, a certain amount of **hand rubbing and polishing** is required in certain inaccessible areas such as behind the outside rear view mirrors, at sharp corners, and under U-shaped outside door handles. Also,

Figure 11-2 Machine compounding is done as shown after compound is applied and spread uniformly on surface. (Courtesy of Ditzler Automotive Finishes, PPG Industries, Inc.)

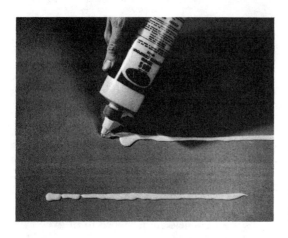

Figure 11-3 Machine compound is best applied and controlled with plastic squeeze bottle. The same is true for most car polishes. (Courtesy of the DuPont Company)

hand polishing is advised over all raised panel edges, all sharp creaselines, and all sharp panel corners.

The cutting action of a power polisher is very fast and requires skill and a certain amount of experience on the part of the painter to achieve the difference between perfection and just a good job. It is wise practice to apply masking tape to all raised panel

Figure 11-4 Polishing of car surface can be done with wool bonnet as shown or with carpet-type pad. (Courtesy of the DuPont Company)

edges such as creaselines, sharp corners, and misaligned or high panel edges to prevent cut-throughs.

Extreme care must be used when rubbing out and polishing standard metallic colors because removal of excess material in one spot can result in a condition known as **scaling.** In this case, removing too much color from one spot causes the edges of the cut-through metallic color to show. When this condition occurs on panel edges, it is known as a **cut-through.** When it occurs in the middle of a panel, the condition is known as "scaling."

Observe the following precautions when using a power polisher:

1. Wear safety goggles.
2. Wear a dust-type respirator.
3. Check the pad or bonnet attachment by applying extra torque to the clamp nut or spanner nut with a wrench made for that purpose. A loose nut can loosen more and damage the finish.
4. Grip the polisher firmly when picking it up, starting it, using it, and laying it down.
5. **Keep the electrical cord away from the polishing pad at all times.** Also, keep the cord off the paint finish during the rub-out operation. This is done by running the cord over, but never around the neck, and allowing the cord to extend to the polisher.

   WARNING: If the cord gets caught in the polishing wheel, turn off the machine immediately.

6. Use a clean pad for best results. Also, clean the pad during use with a pad-cleaning tool or a suitably bladed tool.

Machine Rubbing Procedure

Procedure for Cleaning the Pad during Use

1. Go to a suitable location in the building, or outside the building if weather permits.
2. Lay the polisher on the floor with the pad up, grip the handle, and turn on the polisher.
3. Apply the bonnet cleaning tool or suitable tool to the right side of the pad as the polisher is running, and move the tool toward the center.
4. Work the tool from the center to the right edge and back in a straight line. Repeat this movement of the tool back and forth several times until the pad is clean.

How to Use Rubbing Compounds

1. Prepare the car by applying masking tape ($\frac{3}{4}$ inch) to the crease lines, raised panel edges, and sharp corners that will be contacted by the rubbing pad to prevent cut-throughs.
2. Prepare the rubbing compound by following the label directions. Usually, it is necessary to add water and agitate the mixture thoroughly.
3. Prepare the polisher with a recommended, clean, short-tufted, carpet-type pad. Have pad cleaner handy for occasional use during compounding to keep the pad clean.
4. Wear a suitable apron or shop coat to protect clothing. Rubbing compounds are thrown for some distance when compounding.
5. Apply rubbing compound to the surface with a suitable brush (2- to 4-inch) from a special container or from a suitable plastic squeeze bottle (see Fig. 11-3). **Never apply compound to the wheel. Avoid the use of too much compound.**
6. Use the polisher as follows:
   a. After the compound has been applied, **press the rubbing pad to the compound, in the flat, and generally distribute compound** to the area to be rubbed. Never press on the polisher. Let the polisher's own weight do the job. Always do a small area at a time, such as 2 feet by 2 feet square.
   b. Now turn on the polisher. Start with **left-to-right and right-to-left strokes. Lift the right half of the pad up slightly when moving to the right; and lift the left half of the pad up when moving to the left.** These strokes are equivalent to the **buffing** strokes described in Fig. 6-12.
   c. Overlap each left-to-right and right-to-left stroke by 50%.
   d. After 2 square feet have been covered going from left to right, change directions to move fore and aft. Use the upper half of the pad on the surface by raising the lower half to move toward the operator. Use the lower half of the pad on the surface by raising the upper half to move away from the operator.
   e. Overlap each fore-and aft stroke by 50%.
   f. Two times over with left-to-right strokes, and two times over with fore-and-aft strokes constitutes a complete compounding cycle.

7. If too much compound remains at the end of the compounding cycle, too much compound was used at the start.

8. If compound disappears sooner than two or three times over the surface, this is an indication that not enough compound is being used.

9. As each area is compounded, move to a new area. Overlap each area 3 to 4 inches.

10. Check the surface closely during operation to determine the progress of the desired cutting action. Reapply compound to the surface as necessary.

NOTE: The use of water or mineral spirits for wet sanding with No. 600 or finer sandpaper before compounding is determined by the condition of the surface, that is, the amount of dirt nibs, overspray, and/or amount of orange peel present. The objective of rub-out and polish operations is to match adjacent surfaces in terms of gloss and surface smoothness.

11. Remove masking tape from all crease-lines and panel edges. Rub out and polish these surfaces by hand. Also, do those areas that were inaccessible with the polishing wheel.

To complete a compounding and polishing job, wash the car completely, including all crevices, corners, chrome, glass, and exterior plastic parts. Using a chamois or equivalent cloth, wipe all surfaces, windows, and chrome parts. When doing a complete paint job, clean all windows inside and outside and vacuum the interior trim and floor carpets.

For a listing of problems that may arise during the compounding process, see Table 11-2.

TABLE 11-2 COMPOUNDING PROBLEMS, CAUSES, AND REMEDIES

Problem and cause	Remedy
1. Cut-throughs at panel edges and corners.	1. Clean and brush touch-up as required.
Cause: Excessive compounding without protection.	*Prevention:* Tape sharp edges.
2. Although polisher and pad are O.K., compounding is slow and gloss is poor.	2. Contact another paint jobber and change to a different brand.
Cause: Substandard compound.	
3. Compounding process slow due to excessive orange peel and overspray.	3. Water-sand surface with No. 500 or 600 sandpaper before compounding.
Cause: Poor solvents and poor spray technique.	
4. Rub-through in middle of panel; primer shows.	4. Spot- or panel-repair as required.
Cause: Apparently insufficient color applied or excessive compounding.	
5. Pad clogs up fast; poor results.	5. Clean or change pad as required; use proper compound.
Cause: Hand compound used with power polisher.	

REVIEW QUESTIONS

1. State the purpose of and describe hand rubbing compounds.
2. State the purpose of and describe machine rubbing compounds.
3. Describe how rubbing compounds work as cutting and as polishing agents.
4. Are all hand rubbing compounds alike? If not, what are the differences?
5. Are all machine rubbing compounds alike? If not, what are the differences?
6. How does a painter determine which rubbing compounds work best for speed and quality of finish?
7. Describe the hand rubbing procedure.
8. What is the rpm rating of machine polishers? Which polishers produce the best gloss?
9. What type of bonnet or pad is best for machine compounding?
10. Explain how to replace a pad on a power polisher.
11. What type of bonnet is ideal for polishing with liquid polishes?
12. What is a wise practice to avoid cut-throughs at high panel edges, sharp corners, and sharp crease-lines?
13. What is scaling?
14. List several precautions the painter should take when using a power polisher.
15. Give the procedure for cleaning a polishing pad during use.
16. Describe the machine-rubbing procedure.
17. Describe the process of water sanding with 500 or finer sandpaper to speed compounding and to improve the gloss.
18. What final car appearance cleanup operations should be done after compounding is completed?

12

Panel and Sectional Panel Repair

The purpose of this chapter is to review the basic fundamentals of panel and sectional panel repair. To do all types of panel repainting properly, the painter must be familiar with the following:

1. How to identify the paint finish on any car before starting repairs. **The standard and basecoat/clearcoat finishes are entirely different and are not to be inter- mixed.** (see Chapters 2 and 9).
2. The proper refinish paint systems and refinishing methods available.
3. Car factory recommendations for repainting panels on new and used cars.
4. Paint supplier recommendations for repainting panels on new and used cars.

Painters can become familiar with these paint requirements and procedures by continual communication with the following:

1. Car factory paint training schools
2. Insurance companies (when doing collision repairs and reviewing estimates with insurance companies before doing the work)
3. Paint jobbers (who are continually updated on new products and factory require- ments)
4. Car dealers (dealers who do not have their own paint shop work closely with in- dependent paint shops)

COMPLETE PANEL REPAIR—GENERAL DESCRIPTION

Two types of complete panel repairs are done in the refinish trade, and each involves a different amount of work, paint, and price.

1. Generally, when 50% or more of any outer panel requires color coating, and the panel has no moldings or natural breaklines, the entire panel should be color-coated (Fig. 12-1a).

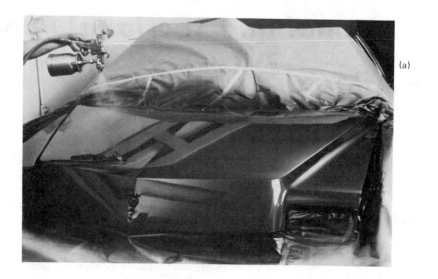

(a)

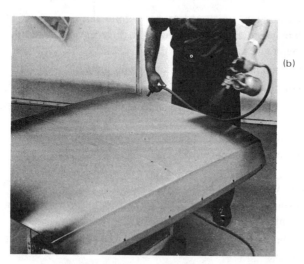

(b)

Figure 12-1 (a) Spraying a deck lid panel (on car) (Courtesy of Ditzler Automotive Finishes, PPG Industries, Inc.); (b) Spraying a deck lid panel (off car). (Courtesy of the DuPont Company)

Panel and Sectional Panel Repair   *Chap. 12*

2. When a major car panel is replaced with a service panel, such as a fender, door, deck lid, or hood, the complete panel should be painted before installation in a fashion similar to factory painting (Fig. 12-1b). This includes painting all panel facings and the inside and the outside surfaces. If the panel was rust-proofed or undercoated before, these operations should be reapplied on the replacement panel. This item should be included in the insurance estimate.

SECTIONAL PANEL REPAIR (Fig. 12-2)

Sectional panel repairs involve similar paint application as in a complete panel repair except that the color is confined to a smaller part or section of the panel. Sectional panel repairs are made possible because the repair color can be extended to natural breaklines made up of the following:

1. Panel creaselines
2. Moldings
3. Panel edges
4. Striping, decal, or two-tone-paint breakline

Sectional panel paint repairs are done in less time, using less paint material, and for much less labor cost than would be the case if complete panels were painted. Sectional panel paint repairs are very beneficial to all concerned because:

1. Insurance companies, by nature, like to keep paint repair costs down.
2. Car factories, because of simple, good business practice, are organized to keep paint warranty costs at a minimum.
3. Private passenger-car owners like to keep their paint repair costs down.

Figure 12-2 Small area of door panel is painted by sectional panel repair method. (Courtesy of R-M Automotive Products, BASF Inmont Corp.)

When a complete car is painted, color accuracy is no problem because the same color is used on all panels of the car. However, when only a single panel on a car is repainted, the need for color accuracy becomes very important. This is when color-matching problems are most likely to be encountered.

Panel-to-panel mismatches show up more readily than do spot-repair mismatches because a side-by-side comparison shows up color mismatches most vividly. The difference between two colors is noted most easily *when each color is cut off abruptly on each side of a line* (Fig. 12-3). In spot repairs, slightly mismatched colors could be blended into adjacent surfaces over a large area and they could be made to look acceptable. Spot-repair techniques are discussed in Chapter 13.

Before completing a panel repair, compare the repair color with the original color

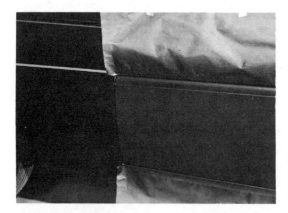

Figure 12-3 Panel repair mismatches show up more than spot-repair mismatches. (Courtesy of the DuPont Company)

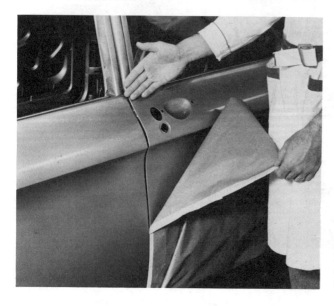

Figure 12-4 Raising masking to compare color match to adjacent panel. (Courtesy of General Motors Corporation)

by raising the masking on the adjacent panel and by comparing the repair color under good lighting conditions (Fig. 12-4).

1. If the color match is satisfactory, remask the adjacent surfaces and complete the panel repair.
2. If the color is a mismatch, determine the problem, adjust the repair color as required (see Chapter 14), and then blend the adjusted final color into the adjacent areas or panels.

CONVENTIONAL METHOD OF REPAINTING A COMPLETE PANEL

The following paint repair system will last for a number of years in any part of the country. The painter is often the "paint engineer" in the refinish trade who selects the refinish paint system to be used. Table 8-1 suggests a top-rated system from each of five paint suppliers for excellent durability. When proper metal conditioners and best primer systems are used, paint repairs are most durable when exposed to:

1. Road salts and cold environments
2. Salt air near ocean environments
3. Highly industrialized areas, particularly the coal and steel industries
4. High concentrations of air pollution in any part of the country

In this procedure, only highlights or key steps are mentioned. For complete details, see Chapters 6 to 11.

The term "conventional method" means applying color according to label directions. This procedure covers a complete panel repair as done on a door of a car (Fig. 12-5).

Figure 12-5 Cleaning surfaces with solvent after washing car. (Courtesy of R-M Automotive Products, BASF Inmont Corp.)

Analysis of the Panel to Be Repainted

Before starting repairs, examine the panel to be repainted to determine the following:

1. **Problem condition:** The problem condition, which is identifiable by *its* appearance and the appearance of the *paint*, tells the painter the extent of the problem and the type of repair required (see Chapter 17), for example, rust condition, showing rust deposits and blistering, causing paint to lift and peel. Rust is like cancer. **All rust** must be removed **completely** before repainting.

2. **Undercoats and color system to be used:** This is determined by the type and age of the car, factory recommendations, and the type of paint system to be used. Order paint from the jobber as soon as the job is written up and the type of repair system is determined.

   a. An acrylic lacquer system is the most popular and is factory recommended for spot and panel repair of standard colors on many domestic and imported cars that are basically new (and up to 2 to 3 years old). This includes repair of standard lacquer and enamel jobs.

   b. Catalyzed acrylic and urethane enamels are gaining in popularity for panel and overall repainting of passenger cars and vans.

   c. Basecoat/clearcoat and standard finishes are not to be intermixed.

   d. Use of clear urethane enamels over standard acrylic lacquers and enamels is gaining in popularity. See Table 9-1.

Repainting Procedure (Common Operations before Color Application)

1. Wash the car.
2. Clean and wash the repair panel and surrounding surfaces with paint finish cleaning solvent (Table 6-1 and Fig. 12-5).

   CAUTION: Keep solvent off plastic fillers; otherwise, blistering can occur.

3. Sand the surface as necessary to remove the problem condition. Where metal is exposed, featheredge all broken edges (Fig. 12-6). All original area to be repainted must be sanded thoroughly with No. 360 or 400 sandpaper.

   CAUTION: Reduce the existing original finish on the panel to 2 or 3 mils by thorough sanding as required. Keep the total film thickness, after all repairs are done, at 6 or 7 mils or less to prevent film overbuild, which leads to paint cracking.

4. Reclean the repair panel and adjacent surfaces with paint finish cleaning solvent after all sanding is completed.
5. Mask off the adjacent surfaces as required (Fig. 12-7).

   a. If acrylic lacquer color is used over acrylic lacquer surfaces and slow solvents

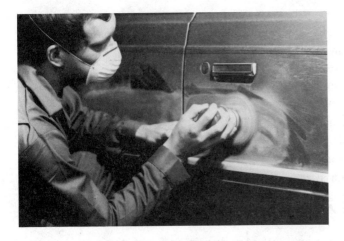

Figure 12-6 Featheredging after metal repairs. (Courtesy of R-M Automotive Products, BASF Inmont Corp.)

Figure 12-7 Application of primer-surfacer. (Courtesy of R-M Automotive Products, BASF Inmont Corp.)

are used in reduction, double-mask adjacent panels within a 6-inch distance of the repair panel.

b. If enamel color is used over acrylic lacquer or enamel surfaces, a single sheet of masking is sufficient to protect adjacent areas. However, it is necessary to cover all horizontal surfaces of the car. Use a large cloth or plastic covers.

6. Apply a two-part metal conditioner to the bare metal (Table 6-2) if necessary.

7. Apply the primer system (Fig. 12-7, Table 8-1).

8. Apply best-type primer–surfacer (Table 8-1). Sand the primer–surfacer as required.

9. Apply the proper sealer to the entire panel.

a. Use an enamel system sealer if the top coat is to be enamel (Table 8-1).

b. Use a lacquer system sealer if the top coat is to be lacquer (Table 8-1).

Color Application

The most popular color refinishing systems are as follows:

1. Acrylic lacquer system
2. Acrylic enamel system
3. Acrylic urethane enamel system
4. Polyurethane enamel system
5. Lacquer basecoat color system
6. Enamel basecoat color system

Acrylic Lacquer Color Application (Standard Type)

1. Reduce acrylic lacquer color 125% (4 parts paint to 5 parts thinner). Use proper thinner for temperature conditions. See Table 7-1.
2. Set the air pressure at 30 to 35 psi at the gun. Increase the air pressure if necessary.
3. Apply color to achieve a color match as follows (Fig. 12-8)
   a. Spray a small test panel with several coats, allowing proper flash time between coats.
   b. Adjust amount reduction, air pressure, and type of solvent to obtain a good color match.
   c. Spray test panel to full hiding for comparison. Fig. 12-10.
   d. If color mismatch still results, adjust the color as explained in Chapter 14 and apply sufficient color for hiding on car as required. Allow proper flash time between coats.
4. As an optional operation, apply two to four coats of clear acrylic lacquer per label directions or two coats of clear acrylic urethane per label directions (see Table 9-1).

Figure 12-8 Application of color. (Courtesy of R-M Automotive Products, BASF Inmont Corp.)

Figure 12-9 Compounding acrylic lacquer after thorough drying. (Courtesy of R-M Automotive Products, BASF Inmont Corp.)

5. If acrylic lacquer clear coat was applied, allow to dry at least 1 day and preferably 3 to 4 days before compounding and polishing (Fig. 12-9).

CAUTION: Painters are urged to use proper face-mask or hood-type respirators as specified in paint supplier's label warnings.

Acrylic Enamel Color Application (Standard Type)

Note: The use of a hardener in acrylic enamel is optional.

1. Reduce acrylic enamel according to label directions. Use proper reducer for temperature conditions. See Table 7-1.
2. To determine the correct spray technique for a color match, proceed as follows:
   a. Spray a small test panel with several coats, allowing proper flash time between coats. Start with 45 psi at the gun.
   b. Adjust amount of air pressure, reduction, and type of solvent to obtain a good color match.
   c. Spray test panel to full hiding for comparison. Fig. 12-10.
   d. If color mismatch still results, adjust the color as explained in Chapter 14.
3. Apply sufficient coats of color for full hiding. Some colors call for two to three coats, and others call for three to four coats. See label.
4. As an optional operation, apply two full wet-coats of clear coating according to label directions. Allow proper flash time between coats. For proper clear coating, see Table 9-1, line 7.
5. Allow the finish to dry to a dust-free condition (1 to 2 hours) before moving car from spray booth, or move the car to a drying room.

CAUTION: Painters are urged to use proper face-mask or hood-type respirators

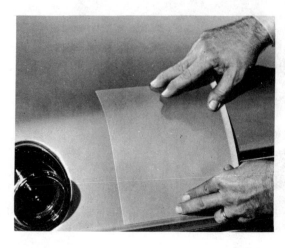

Figure 12-10 Comparing sample spray out for color match to car. (Courtesy of the DuPont Company)

as indicated in paint supplier's label warnings. The inhalation of the products of spray painting may be dangerous to your health.

Acrylic Urethane Enamel Color Application (Standard Type)

1. Reduce acrylic urethane color according to label directions. Use proper reducer for temperature conditions. See Table 7-1.
2. To determine the correct spray technique for a color match, proceed as follows:
   a. Spray a small test panel with several coats, allowing proper flash time between coats. Start with 40 psi at the gun.
   b. Adjust amount of air pressure, reduction, and type of solvent to obtain a good color match.
   c. Spray test panel to full hiding for comparison. Fig. 12-10.
   d. If color mismatch still results, adjust the color as explained in Chapter 14.
3. Apply sufficient coats of color for full hiding. Some colors call for two to three coats, and others call for three to four coats. See label.
4. As an optional operation, apply two full-wet coats of clear coating according to label directions. Allow proper flash time between coats. For proper clear coating, see Table 9-1, or check with paint jobber.
5. Allow the finish to dry to a dust-free condition (1 to 2 hours) before moving car from spray booth, or move the car to a drying room.

   CAUTION: Painter's are urged to use proper face-mask or hood-type respirators as indicated in paint supplier's label warnings. Inhalation of isocyanate vapors and/ or other byproducts of spray painting may be detrimental to your health.

Polyurethane Enamel Color Application (Standard Type)

1. Reduce polyurethane enamel according to label directions. Use proper reducer for temperature conditions. See Table 7-1.
2. To determine the correct spray technique for a color match, proceed as follows:
   a. Spray a small test panel with several coats, allowing proper flash time between coats. Start with 45 psi at the gun.
   b. Adjust amount of air pressure, reduction, and type of solvent to obtain a good match.
   c. Spray test panel to full hiding for comparison. Fig. 12-10.
   d. If color mismatch still results, adjust the color as explained in Chapter 14.
3. Apply sufficient coats of color for full hiding. See label.
4. As an optional operation, apply two full-wet coats of clear coating according to label directions. Allow proper flash time between coats. For proper clear coating, see Table 9-1, or check with the paint jobber.
5. Allow the finish to dry to a dust-free condition (1 to 2 hours) before moving car from spray booth, or move the car to a drying room.

CAUTION: Painters are urged to use proper face-mask or hood-type respirators as specified in paint supplier's label warnings. Inhalation of isocyanate vapors and/or other byproducts of spray painting may be detrimental to your health.

DESCRIPTION OF BASECOAT/CLEARCOAT REPAIR SYSTEMS (CHAPTER 9)

As shown in Table 9-1, two systems are available for the repair of basecoat/clearcoat finishes:

1. Acrylic lacquer basecoat color systems are shown in item 2.
2. Acrylic enamel and acrylic urethane enamel basecoat color systems are shown in item 9.

The lacquer basecoat color system of each paint supplier has two systems of clearcoating, which are optional;

1. Clear acrylic lacquer (line 3) is better for spot-repair blending.
2. Clear acrylic urethane enamel (line 4) is better for panel repair.

Item 10 of Table 9-1 shows each paint supplier with at least one clear-coating system for enamel basecoat colors, but Ditzler has three systems available. Check with the local paint jobber for the best clear-coating system for your particular situation.

Panel Repair of Basecoat/Clearcoat Finish with Acrylic Lacquer Basecoat Color (Figs. 12-11 and 12-12)

1. Wash panel with mild detergent and water, and then solvent clean the panel as required.

2. Repair and featheredge the damaged area. Treat bare metal with metal conditioner as required. Metal conditioner is not required if using R-M's 834 primer or DuPont's 615S/616S primer (see label.)

3. Apply straight primer to bare metal and allow to dry. Apply primer-surfacer to damaged areas; allow to dry and sand with No. 400 sandpaper to required smoothness (Fig. 12-11).

4. Sand all areas adjacent to the repair (Fig. 12-12, areas in **white**) with No. 400 sandpaper. Sand with No. 600 or compound the area shown in **mottled gray**. If there is no natural breakline, extend the sanding with No. 600 paper or compounding into the next panel, 4 to 6 inches, as shown. Reclean and tack wipe all repair surfaces.

5. Mask the job as required.

6. Apply one or two coats of **adhesion promoter** (Table 8-1) over the entire panel to be color and/or clearcoated. **This includes all the white and gray areas of the**

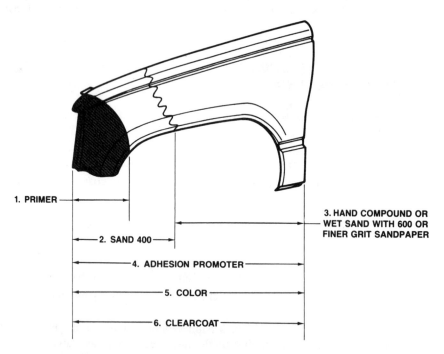

1. PRIMER

2. SAND 400

3. HAND COMPOUND OR WET SAND WITH 600 OR FINER GRIT SANDPAPER

4. ADHESION PROMOTER

5. COLOR

6. CLEARCOAT

Figure 12-11 Typical full panel repair (fender). Basecoat/clearcoat method. (Courtesy of General Motors Corporation)

Panel and Sectional Panel Repair   *Chap. 12*

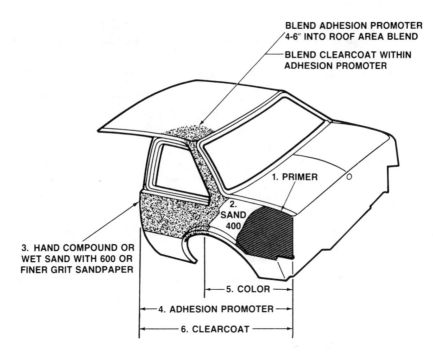

BLEND ADHESION PROMOTER
4-6" INTO ROOF AREA BLEND

BLEND CLEARCOAT WITHIN
ADHESION PROMOTER

1. PRIMER

2. SAND 400

3. HAND COMPOUND OR
WET SAND WITH 600 OR
FINER GRIT SANDPAPER

5. COLOR

4. ADHESION PROMOTER

6. CLEARCOAT

Figure 12-12 Typical spot/partial panel repair. Basecoat/clearcoat method. (Courtesy of General Motors Corporation)

quarter panel as shown, and extends into the roof panel (Fig. 12-12). Allow the sealer to dry at least 30 minutes before applying color.

7. Reduce acrylic lacquer basecoat color per label directions. Also, check the viscosity of the reduced color per label directions. See Chapter 7 for use of viscosity cup and Table 7-3. A proper viscosity reading is important to proper color match.

Note: If Zahn No. 2 cup is not available, use DuPont's No. 50 cup.

8. If a color problem is suspected, spray out a test panel as follows before applying color on car.

   a. Spray out a small test panel with two or three coats of basecoat color. Allow 5-minute flash time between coats. (Test panels are available through your local paint jobber.)

   b. Adjust amount of air pressure, reduction, and type of solvent until a good color match is obtained. These are paint variables over which a painter has control. See Table 7-2.

   c. Spray test panel to full hiding. Allow finish to dry per label directions. Then apply two to three coats of clear acrylic lacquer per label directions and allow to dry for a while. Compare test panel to car (Fig. 12-10).

9. If color match is acceptable, apply color to repair area using the same variables as used on the test panel that produced the acceptable match. Apply first coat of basecoat color and allow to flash.

10. Apply second coat of basecoat color extending it slightly beyond first coat.

11. While the color is drying, mix up some **special mist-coat material** as follows:
   a. Reduce clear acrylic lacquer about 150%.
   b. To 1 part of reduced acrylic lacquer, add an equal part of reduced basecoat color applied earlier.

12. Spray the mist coat with a feathering technique **from the outside in** to melt the overspray into the basecoat color. Apply the mist coat in medium-wet coats. Allow the basecoat color to dry according to label directions before applying the clear-coat.

13. If color match is not acceptable, adjust the color as explained in Chapter 14. Then apply the color to the car.

   NOTE: Basecoat color must not be sanded. If sanding is required, proceed as follows:
   a. Allow to dry and sand with ultra-fine sandpaper (see Table 6-3). Reclean and tack wipe.
   b. Apply one more coat of basecoat color.
   c. Allow to dry per label directions before applying the clearcoat.

14. Reduce acrylic lacquer clearcoat per label directions (Table 9-1).

15. Check and adjust viscosity of reduction per label directions.

16. Spray two or more medium-wet coats of reduced clear at 35 to 45 psi air pressure to the complete panel, including all areas that were sanded or compounded. Allow proper flash time between coats.

17. When blending repairs into an adjacent panel (Fig. 12-12) keep all spray application within the applied adhesion promoter. Blend with the paint supplier's ready-made mist-coat material (Table 9-1, item 6) or with clear acrylic lacquer reduced 200%. If additional leveling is desired over the entire panel, apply a final wet coat of paint supplier's mist-coat material at 20 psi at the gun.

18. Allow 24 hours air-dry, or force dry 30 minutes at 180°F. Compound lightly with hand rubbing or machine rubbing compound (see Chapter 11).

Panel Repair of Basecoat/Clearcoat Finish with Acrylic Enamel or Acrylic Urethane Enamel Basecoat Color (Figs. 12-11 and 12-12)

All surface preparation operations prior to color application are the same as for spot repair and complete panel repair. After sanding the primer-surfacer, **the complete panel should be sanded** with fine or ultra-fine sandpaper. See Table 6-3.

1. Apply enamel type sealer to panel per label directions. See Table 8-1.

2. Prepare and reduce enamel basecoat color per label directions.

3. Check viscosity of reduced color per label directions. Adjust viscosity of reduced color as required.

4. If a color problem is suspected, spray out a test panel as follows:

   a. Spray out a small test panel with two or three coats of basecoat color. Allow flash time between coats per label directions. Test panels are available through your local paint jobber.

   b. Adjust air pressure, reduction, and type of solvent until a good color match is obtained. These are paint variables over which a painter has control (See Table 7-2). This may take several tries.

   c. Spray test panel to full hiding. Allow finish to dry per label directions. Then apply two or three coats of label-directed clearcoat and allow to dry. Compare test panel to car (Fig. 12-10).

5. If color match is acceptable, apply color to repair area using the same variables as used on test panel. Apply first coat of basecoat color and allow to flash. Then apply second coat of color extending the color slightly beyond the first coat. Allow to dry per label directions before applying the clearcoat.

6. If color match is not acceptable, adjust the color as explained in Chapter 14. Then apply the color to the car.

   NOTE: Basecoat color must not be sanded. If sanding is required to remove dirt or sags, proceed as follows:

   a. Allow to dry and sand with ultra fine sandpaper. Reclean and tack wipe.

   b. Apply one more coat of basecoat color.

   c. Allow to dry per label directions before applying the clearcoat.

7. Prepare enamel clearcoat per label directions (See Table 9-1, item 10). Check viscosity of reduction. Up to 10% solvent may be added.

8. Spray two medium-wet coats of reduced clear at label-directed air pressure.

9. Allow to dry per label directions before putting car into service.

   WARNING: It is dangerous to inhale the isocyanates contained in catalyzed painting systems. Painters are cautioned to follow paint supplier's label instructions to the letter for using proper respiratory protection as recommended.

Optional Clear Urethane Enamel for Topcoating Basecoat or Standard Acrylic Lacquer Colors (Table 9-1)

Description. This clear urethane enamel mixed with a hardener results in a very glossy, durable and chemically resistant automotive finish when applied over acrylic lacquer (both standard and basecoat colors). The material provides increased gasoline resistance.

All surface preparation operations through the application of color are the same as

TRI-COAT PAINT REPAIR OPTIONS

Tri-coat paint finishes are an advanced form of basecoat/clearcoat finishes. The finishes are described on pages 240, 241, and 243. The tri-coat paint repair information in the following is based on the latest data available at the time of publication approval. Car factories reserve the right to make product or publication changes at any time without notice.

The successful repair of pearl lustre effects depends upon the painter's spray technique, the painter's experience with such colors and the color itself. While some painters may be able to repair certain pearl luster effects successfully, other painters could experience a great amount of difficulty with them.

Some pearl lustre effect colors are more difficult to repair than others. All colors are rated for repairability, ranging from "easy to repair" to "difficult to repair." However, all production colors are designed to be repairable.

Mica or pearl flake, a component part of pearl colors, weighs more than comparable aluminum flake. The use of agitator cups is highly recommended to keep the flake in suspension for consistent color match.

When Selecting and Using Tri-Coat Paint Materials:

1. Use only top quality materials.
2. Follow manufacturer's label instructions.
3. Do not mix different brands of materials.

The Success of a Tri-Coat Paint Repair Depends Upon:

1. An acceptable color match
2. A good blend with the original color
3. Proper build-up of the "sandwich coat"
4. A similar gloss and uninterrupted smoothness of the finish

TABLE 12-1 AFTER-MARKET TRI-COAT PAINT REPAIR MATERIALS

Manufacturer	Material Name
1. BASF (R-M Products)	Diamont
2. DuPont	Lucite or Cronar
3. PPG	Deltron
4. Sherwin Williams	Ultra Base
5. Sikkens	Auto-Base and Auto Clear

Which After-Market Paint and Application Procedure is Best?

The material and system that produces a good color match for the person making the paint repair.

After-Market Color Availability:
Paint materials are available from paint jobbers in the following ways:

1. Base Color—F/P(Factory Pak) or mix, depending on manufacturer.
2. Pearl Lustre Color—F/P(Factory Pak) or mix, depending on manufacturer.

Variables the Refinisher Can Control:

A good base color match and the proper number of applied "sandwich coats" (pearl lustre) are very critical in order to obtain a good color match.

Regarding Basecoat Color:

1. Apply only the number of coats necessary to achieve full hiding.
2. Do not substitute another product color for recommended base color coat.
3. The slightest change in the base color coat will be greatly magnified once the pearl lustre coat and the clear top coat finishes are applied.
4. Follow product manufacturer's label instructions.
5. It cannot be overstressed that tinting takes time and should be done as a last resort.

Regarding Pearl Lustre Coat: (Fig. 12-13)

Make a sample spray out panel, known in the trade as a "let-down" panel. Use this to compare the pearl lustre effect of the applied refinish material build-up to that of the O.E.M. applied material. See Fig. 12-13 and procedure for making sample panel.

Procedure for Making a Let-Down Sample Panel: (Fig. 12-13)

1. Prepare a suitably sized test panel with the same color undercoat as used on the job. Allow to dry, sand as required, and apply small check hiding sticker to ensure proper amount of base material. (Stickers are available through paint jobbers.)

DO NOT APPLY CLEAR TOP COAT	APPLY CLEAR TOP COAT
5	COATS PEARL
4	COATS PEARL
3	COATS PEARL
2	COATS PEARL
1	COAT PEARL
BASECOAT ONLY	

NOTE: APPLY SMALL CHECK HIDING STICKER
TO ENSURE PROPER AMOUNT OF
BASE MATERIAL.

Figure 12-13 Layout of Tri-Coat "Let-Down" Sample Panel (Courtesy of General Motors Corporation)

2. Apply basecoat color to complete panel to achieve full hiding and allow to dry. Use heat lamp to speed drying.

3. Divide and mark panel in six equal sections as shown, Fig. 12-13, to illustrate film build variations. Mark section numbers on both sides of panel.

4. Prepare and install five sections of premasked masking paper:

   a. Mask "BASECOAT ONLY" section.

   b. Then mask "BASECOAT ONLY" and #1 section.

   c. In overlapping fashion, continue masking through section #4.

5. Starting with section #5, apply first single medium-wet coat of pearl lustre color and allow to flash.

6. Remove first section of masking to uncover #4 section.

7. Apply another single medium-wet coat of pearl lustre over uncovered area of panel and allow to flash.

8. Repeat above steps until complete panel (except BC ONLY section) has been sprayed with pearl lustre material.

9. Place panel under heat lamp to dry.

10. After panel is dry, mask off one-half of panel lengthwise as shown.

11. Apply three single medium-wet coats of clear top coat material over unmasked side of panel, then remove masking paper and place panel under heat lamp until dry.

The above panel illustrates the effect each additional coat of material has on the lightness/darkness of the final top coat color.

A "let-down" panel should be used as an aid to determine the approximate number of pearl coats needed to achieve a color match by comparing the various film-build areas on the panel to an adjacent panel on the car prior to material application.

Mica or pearl flake weighs more than a comparable aluminum flake. The use of agitator cups is highly recommended to keep the flake in suspension for consistent color match.

WARNING

(ISOCYANATES)

It is MANDATORY that adequate respiratory protection be worn. Examples of such protection are: air line respirators with full hood or half mask. Such protection should be worn during the entire painting process. Persons with respiratory problems or those allergic to isocyanates must not be exposed to isocyanate vapors or spray mists.

Typical Tri-Coat Spot/Partial Panel Repair Procedure (Fig. 12-14 and 12-15)

1. Apply primer-surfacer as required. Follow label directions.
2. Wet sand with #600 grit sandpaper areas where basecoat will be applied.
3. Compound or wet sand areas of the vehicle to be painted using ultra-fine or finer sandpaper.
4. Apply adhesion promoter/bonding clear over the entire area to be painted.
5. Apply basecoat color to full hiding. Overlap each coat.
6. Apply pearl coats (as determined by the "let-down" panel) in the same manner as the basecoat. Overlap each coat but do not exceed the basecoat edge. The last coat of pearl should cover the entire basecoat area and be blended into the panel(s). A mist coat is recommended beyond the original repair for uniform appearance.
7. Apply clearcoat to panel(s) per label directions, blending where necessary.

NOTE: Remember to tack wipe between each coat to remove overspray and airborne dirt particles. Each coat of pearl and clear will be transparent. All dirt and dry spray will be noticed in the paint finish.

REMEMBER: As the film-build of the pearl lustre paint increases, the color becomes darker. Once color is acceptable, it may be necessary to apply one or more additional coats of pearl in the blend area to improve color match.

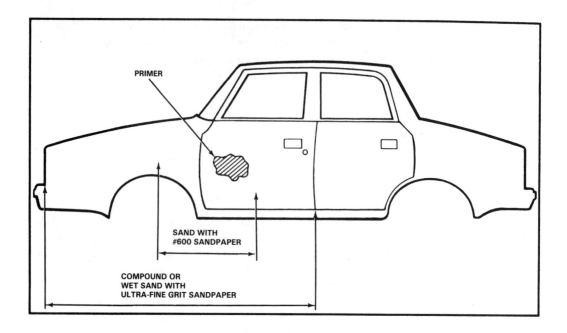

Figure 12-14 Typical spot/partial panel repair showing tri-coat finish preparation (Courtesy of General Motors Corporation.)

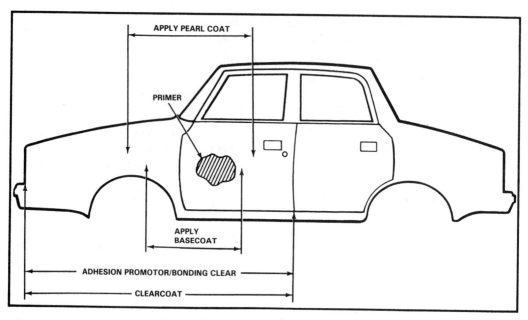

Figure 12-15 Typical spot/partial panel repair showing tri-coat finish application (Courtesy of General Motors Corporation.)

Use feathering and arcing techniques at end of strokes to minimize an excess film-build of pearl material which could result in a "halo" or "bull's eye" type repair.

Typical Tri-Coat Complete Panel Repair Procedure (Fig. 12-16)

To "picture frame" paint a panel that has an O.E.M. tri-coat pearl lustre finish is quite difficult. A suggested method of repair is to prepare the adjacent panel(s) or zone(s) to blend the "sandwich" coat.

1. Apply primer-surfacer as required. Follow label directions.
2. Wet sand with #600-grit sandpaper areas where basecoat will be applied.
3. Compound or wet sand areas of the car to be painted using ultra-fine or finer sandpaper.
4. Apply adhesion promoter/bonding clear over the entire area to be painted.
5. Apply basecoat color over complete panel to achieve full hiding. Remember to tack wipe between each coat to remove overspray and dirt particles. Each coat of pearl

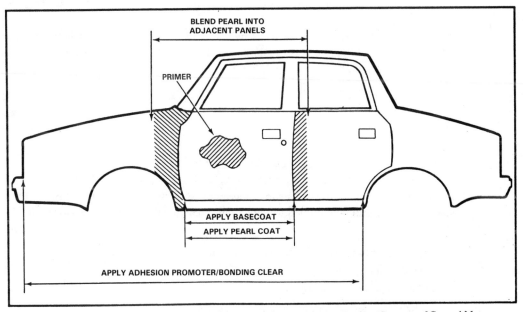

Figure 12-16   Typical tri-coat panel repair showing finish application (Courtesy of General Motors Corporation.)

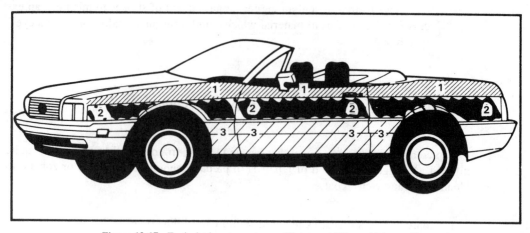

Figure 12-17 Typical tri-coat zone areas (Courtesy of General Motors Corporation.)

and clear will be transparent. All dirt and dry spray will be noticed in the paint finish.

6. Apply the number of pearl coats as indicated by your ''let-down'' panel to achieve color match. If the match is too dark, blend the pearl color into the adjacent panels using an arcing and feathering technique until an acceptable match is achieved.

7. Apply clearcoat to panel(s) per label directions, blending where necessary. Fig. 12-16.

Typical Tri-Coat Zone Repairs (Fig. 12-17)

Some vehicles may lend themselves to being repaired by the zone repair method. In these instances, repairs can be confined to very small areas for the following reasons:

1. These cars possess natural break lines which aid in their repair.
2. A repair can be accomplished without clearcoating the entire panel(s).
3. Only zones will be clearcoated.
4. Utilize body side moldings to contain the zone.
5. Utilize feature lines for the reverse masking technique.

PAINT STRIPING REPLACEMENT

If a car panel with OEM striping must be repainted, new striping to match OEM striping can be applied quickly with the following procedure.

1. Secure the proper **3-M Fine Line** striping tape, or equivalent, and the proper color from the paint jobber according to car series, model year, and type of stripe needed.
2. Clean the surface to be striped with paint finish cleaning solvent to remove any wax, grease, or other contaminants.
3. Cut a length of striping tape 2 to 3 inches longer than needed for the panel. Before cutting tape, place a piece of masking tape or paper to adhesive side of tape as shown in Fig. 12-18.
4. Align and temporarily apply the striping tape according to the OEM stripes on each side as a reference. If only one reference is available, obtain the needed reference markings from the opposite side of the car. Before sticking the tape down firmly, gunsight the tape for alignment from each end and correct any misalignment as required. Also, allow 2 to 3 inches of tape to protrude beyond the panel as shown (Fig. 12-19).

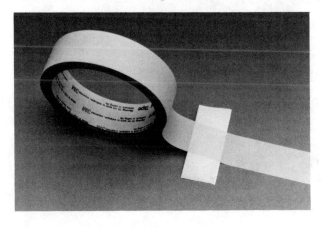

Figure 12-18 Securing tape on back side with paper or masking tape before cutting. (Courtesy of the 3M Company)

Paint Striping Replacement

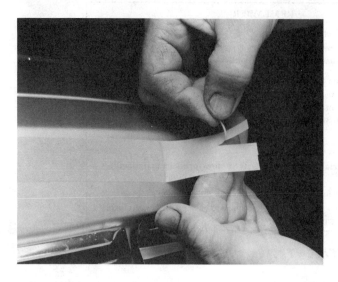

Figure 12-19 Striping tape protrudes at end to aid selection of proper insert. (Courtesy of the 3M Company)

5. After slicking down the rest of the tape firmly to the panel, remove the desired pull-out piece(s) (Fig. 12-20) to match the OEM stripe(s). Remove desired pull-out sections at a 90° angle with a moderate, steady, continuous motion (Fig. 12-20).

6. Lightly scuff the exposed paint stripe areas through the tape (Fig. 12-21) with **3M Scotch-Brite pad, No. 07447,** or equivalent, to ensure good paint adhesion.

7. Mask adjacent areas as required. Apply color with brush or spray equipment as required. If color is applied by brush (Fig. 12-22, add up to 5% retarder to package

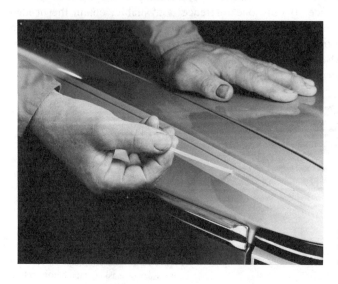

Figure 12-20 Removing tape insert at 90° angle to surface. (Courtesy of the 3M Company)

Figure 12-21 Scuffing paint through insert opening with 3M Scotch Brite Pad. (Courtesy of the 3M Company)

Figure 12-22 Application of paint stripe with touch-up brush. (Courtesy of the 3M Company)

viscosity color. Allow stripe(s) to dry partially: lacquer, 10 to 15 minutes); enamel, 15 to 20 minutes. Then remove outside tape first (if a double stripe) at 90° angle, pulling slightly away from edge. Remove remaining tape at 90° angle. Figure 12-23 shows the finished job.

NOTE: If working at front or rear end of stripe(s), duplicate striping design with sections of masking tape according to opposite side of car. If force-drying is required, remove tape before applying heat lamps.

Figure 12-23 The finished job with paint stripes applied. (Courtesy of the 3M Company)

SERVICE REPLACEMENT PANEL PAINTING

Generally, most service replacement panels are factory-coated with a high-bake enamel-type primer. This coating protects panels when in storage and serves as the primer system in the collision repair trade. To paint a service replacement panel, proceed as follows:

1. Repair any dings or dents in the panel as required.
2. Scuff-sand the complete panel with No. 400 or 500 sandpaper.
3. Clean the panel with paint finish cleaning solvent.
4. Apply metal conditioner and the best primer to the bare metal.
5. Apply the proper sealer system to the complete panel.
6. Apply the best primer–surfacer system and sand as required.
7. Select and apply an acrylic lacquer, enamel, or basecoat color system according to label directions.

   CAUTION: When factory service panels are not cleaned, scuff-sanded, and sealed before top coating, painters can expect a certain amount of peeling to take place. This applies to panels painted with a high-bake primer.

REVIEW QUESTIONS

1. How can the painter in the paint shop be advised of the following on a continuing basis?
   (a) Factory refinish recommendations
   (b) Latest paint supplier refinish procedures
2. In a general manner, describe a complete panel repair.
3. In a general manner, describe a sectional panel repair.

4. What are the advantages of a sectional panel repair over a complete panel repair?
5. Do color mismatches show up more readily on panel repairs or on spot repairs? Why?
6. List several natural breaklines that make sectional panel repairs possible.
7. Outline the procedure for painting a service replacement panel coated with factory high-bake primer.
8. Describe the procedure for applying an acrylic lacquer finish.
9. Describe the procedure for applying an acrylic enamel finish.
10. Describe the procedure for applying an acrylic urethane enamel.
11. Describe the procedure for applying a polyurethane enamel finish.
12. Describe the procedure for a spot/partial panel repair of an OEM basecoat/clearcoat finish with acrylic lacquer basecoat color system.
13. Describe the procedure for repainting an OEM basecoat/clearcoat finished panel with acrylic enamel basecoat color system.
14. Describe the procedure for repainting the OEM paint striping on a door panel.
15. What is meant by the side zone method of repairing a tri-coat paint finish?
16. Describe the procedure for repainting a complete panel with the tri-coat color system.
17. What is the principal difference between the basecoat/clearcoat and the tri-coat color systems?

13

Spot Repair Techniques

By definition, spot repairs are divided into two general categories:

1. **Standard color spot repairs**
2. **Basecoat/clearcoat finish spot/partial panel repairs.**

A **standard color spot repair** (Fig. 13-7) consists of repairing a paint finish at a spot location within a panel, or at a small area near an edge, and blending the repair color with the adjacent original color. A spot repair could consist of repairs to the color coat only or to the color and undercoats.

The **spot/partial panel repair system** has become the most popular method for repairing spot and/or partial panel sections on basecoat/clearcoat finishes. This system features blending the color at a spot location and then clearcoating the entire panel to the nearest breakline or, if no breakline exists, into the nearest adjacent panel (Fig. 13-12).

It is only through experience and spray testing that a painter in the field is able to judge beforehand whether to spot repair or panel repair to the nearest breakline. Any time a painter can match an adjacent panel with a color, the painter should be able to spot repair that same color, and vice versa.

All automotive colors are rated by each car company for "repairability" properties ranging from easy to spot repair to difficult to spot repair. Each production color falls into a rating category between these two limits. So all automotive production colors are designed to be repairable. The term "repairable" means a color can be spot or panel repaired successfully by an average painter using field repair materials. Color repairability is a very important factor that determines if a color is to be used in a production plant.

CHARACTERISTICS OF SUCCESSFUL SPOT AND/OR PARTIAL PANEL REPAIR

A successful spot repair has the following three repair characteristics:

1. **A commercially acceptable color match:** The color match, if not perfect, would be so close that it would be acceptable to a very high percentage of the motoring public.
2. **A good blend:** The repair blend should be smooth, gradual, and fully acceptable. There should be no telltale ring or pronounced shaded perimeter around the repair.
3. **Comparable gloss and surface texture:** The entire repair should have similar gloss and comparable smoothness to adjacent surfaces. Even the orange peel effect should be comparable.

SURFACE PREPARATION FOR SPOT REPAIRS

The identity and depth of a paint problem and type of paint system tells the painter the surface preparation required. For every paint problem or failure, there is a proper and a required surface preparation. To know what surface preparation to do for a specific paint problem, the painter should check the appropriate paint condition in Chapter 17. The main concern of the painter during surface preparation is to remove any affected paint as required and to prepare the surface as required before making a paint repair.

The following surface preparation operations and illustrations are designed to help an apprentice in doing top-quality work.

1. Wash the surface with water (Chapter 6).
2. Clean the surface with paint finish cleaning solvent (Table 6-1).
3. Sand and featheredge broken paint edges (Fig. 13-1).
   a. For details on featheredging, see Chapter 6.
   b. For lacquer removing solvent, see Table 6-3.
   c. For rust removal, see Chapters 6 and 18.

Figure 13-2 is a typical cross section of a sanded featheredge on metal. A cross section of a painted panel is a paint finish and metal panel cut straight through at right angles to the surface. Figure 13-2 shows the following:
(1) The factory standard color, about 2.5 mils thick
(2) The factory undercoat, usually about 1.00 mil thick

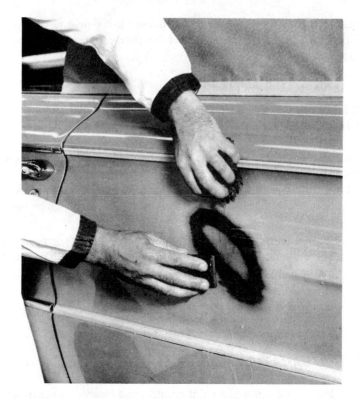

Figure 13-1   Featheredging technique around spot repair. (Courtesy of General Motors Corporation)

(3) The metal

(4) The sanded featheredge, several inches long

Figure 13-2 gives the painter an idea of how far back broken paint edges should be sanded. When rubbing the hand with the fingers extended across a repair area sanded correctly, the featheredge is hardly felt, or it is not felt at all. The surface should be very smooth to the touch. This is thorough and correct featheredging. This is an important key to successful spot repairing.

4. Treat bare metal surfaces with two-part metal conditioner (see Table 6-2 and Chapter 6). After treatment, wipe the metal-conditioned surfaces with a water-dampened cloth to remove excess metal conditioner from the surrounding surfaces. Allow to dry.

5. Apply the primer and primer-surfacer (see Table 8-1).

   a. Apply straight primer on the bare metal. Repair primer may overlap the original primer. **Avoid sandwiching enamel-type primer between lacquer coats.** Do this by applying straight primer directly to the bare steel with a brush, as necessary. Allow to dry according to the label directions. This is the best way to

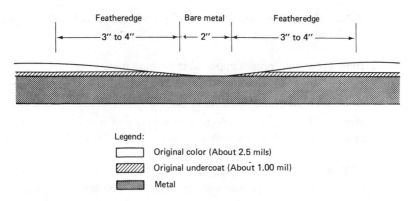

Legend:

☐	Original color (About 2.5 mils)
▨	Original undercoat (About 1.00 mil)
▦	Metal

Figure 13-2 Standard color spot-repair cross section: featheredging. (Courtesy of General Motors Corporation)

prime small-area spots. A best-type straight primer and brush should be handy for use in a paint shop every day.

b. Build up the featheredged area by spraying three to four light, wet coats of primer-surfacer (Fig. 13-3). (See also Table 8-1)

c. Allow the primer-surfacer to dry 30 minutes before sanding. A proper application of primer-surfacer, when dry, should feel like No. 400 sandpaper. If the surface feels like No. 320 or coarser sandpaper, adjustments are required in the:

(1) Primer-surfacer reduction

(2) Straining

(3) Air pressure, and/or

(4) Spraying technique

Figure 13-3 Application of primer–surfacer over spot repair. (Courtesy of General Motors Corporation)

Surface Preparation for Spot Repairs

Figure 13-4 shows a cross section of primer and primer-surfacer application before and after the undercoats dry.

Item 1: Straight primer application on bare metal.

Item 2: When first applied, wet primer-surfacer is shown by the upper broken line.

Item 3: Dried primer-surfacer is shown by the second broken line.

Item 4: The sanded primer-surfacer is shown by a solid line. Note how the sanded primer-surfacer **bridges** smoothly and uniformly across the original color coats.

6. Prepare the primer-surfacer and adjacent original color as follows (Fig. 13-4).

   a. Sand the inside primer-surfacer with No. 400 sandpaper and water.

   b. Remove the overspray on the adjacent original color with a hand compound. Allow rub-out to include the edges of the sanded primer-surfacer, as shown in Fig. 13-5.

   c. Also compound the complete blend area on standard colors.

   d. Clean the compounded surfaces with a cloth dampened with a small amount of water and paint finish cleaning solvent. Compounding acrylic lacquer surfaces prevents sandscratch swelling and prepares the adjacent surfaces for matching the final gloss. If sandscratches on lacquer are kept to a minimum, the need for compounding is lessened.

Figure 13-6 shows what happens when an insufficient amount of primer-surfacer is present in a spot-repair situation. Insufficient primer-surfacer shows up as a dished-out patch, bull's-eye, or low spot within a spot repair. The condition is caused by a lack of primer-surfacer application or by too much sanding after primer-surfacer application. Apprentices can prevent this problem by using the **guide-coat** filling and sanding technique covered in Chapter 8.

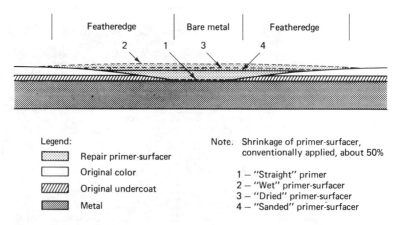

Legend:

▨ Repair primer-surfacer

▢ Original color

▨ Original undercoat

▨ Metal

Note. Shrinkage of primer-surfacer, conventionally applied, about 50%

1 – "Straight" primer
2 – "Wet" primer-surfacer
3 – "Dried" primer-surfacer
4 – "Sanded" primer-surfacer

Figure 13-4 Standard color spot-repair cross section: primer–surfacer application. (Courtesy of General Motors Corporation)

Figure 13-5 Compounding sandscratches around a featheredge. (Courtesy of the DuPont Company)

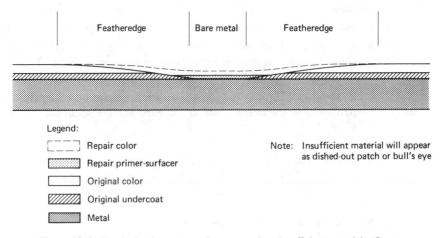

Featheredge	Bare metal	Featheredge

Legend:

⌐ ¯ ¯ ¯ ⌐ Repair color

▓▓▓ Repair primer-surfacer

☐ Original color

▨▨▨ Original undercoat

▓▓▓ Metal

Note: Insufficient material will appear as dished-out patch or bull's eye

Figure 13-6 Standard color spot-repair cross section: insufficient material. (Courtesy of General Motors Corporation)

The best precautions to follow when sanding primer-surfacer, especially when spot-repairing enamel finishes, are:

  e. Sand the inside overspray edge **around** the center of the spot using No. 400 sandpaper, a suitable sanding block, and water. Keep off the center area at first.

  f. When sanding over the center area, check the progress of the sanding frequently. **Stop sanding at the center area as soon as the surface is smooth and free of orange peel.**

 7. Finally, reclean the entire compounded area with a cloth dampened with water and very little finish cleaning solvent.

IMPORTANT: When spot repairing original acrylic enamels with acrylic lacquer, **for best adhesion, most factories recommend using an adhesion promoter at this stage of repair.** See Table 8-1. Follow label instructions. For more information, contact the paint jobber.

STANDARD ACRYLIC LACQUER SPOT REPAIRS

Color Preparation

Double-check certain key items to assure that the best equipment and color are being used, particularly when matching metallics.

1. Check the standard color on hand to be sure that it is correct as to color code.
2. Check for correct solvents.
3. If available, set up an agitator-type paint cup (Fig. 3-10), which makes spraying metallics as easy as spraying solid colors.
4. Be sure to agitate color thoroughly by hand or on a paint shaker.
5. Prepare acrylic lacquer color with a two-spray gun system as follows:
   a. In spray gun 1, prepare a conventional reduction of acrylic lacquer color. Use slow thinner in reduction for average temperatures (Table 7-1). Label the cup **"Color."**
   b. In spray gun 2, prepare a mist coat thinner made up of 1 part slow thinner, 1 part medium thinner, and about 5% clear acrylic lacquer. Label the cup **"Mist Coat."**

   NOTE: All ingredients in the mist coat solvent should be from the same paint supplier. Mark the cup "Mist Coat." As an optional mist-coating material, use ready-made material, as indicated in Table 9-1.

Standard Color Application (Fig. 13-7)

1. Set up the spray gun in the midrange adjustment (Chapter 4).
2. Spray out a small test panel with several coats, allowing proper flash time between coats. (See your local paint jobber for special black and white paper test panels.)
3. Adjust amount of reduction, air pressure, and type of solvent to obtain a good color match. See Table 7-2. These are variables in spray painting that are controllable by the painter.
4. Spray test panel to full hiding for comparison to car.
5. If color mismatch still results, adjust the color as explained in Chapter 14 before proceeding.
6. Apply a first coat over the primer-surfaced area (Fig. 13-7). Use a feathering technique at the beginning and end of each stroke. For technique, see Chapter 4. Apply mist coat solvent to the edges and allow to flash.

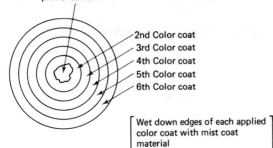

Apply first coat over spot filled with
primer-surfacer

2nd Color coat
3rd Color coat
4th Color coat
5th Color coat
6th Color coat

[Wet down edges of each applied color coat with mist coat material]

Figure 13-7 Blending standard acrylic lacquer into the old finish. (Courtesy of the DuPont Company)

7. Apply the second through the final coat in the same manner, extending each coat beyond the previous one as shown in Fig. 13-7. Mist coat the edges and allow each coat to flash. Application of color is complete when full hiding is achieved.

8. Allow the repair to dry at least 1 hour at normal temperature. Then, as an option, apply three coats of clear acrylic lacquer reduced 200% with slow-type thinner to the complete repair area. Blend the edges of the clear acrylic application with a mist coat of solvent.

   CAUTION: Application of clear acrylic lacquer before 1 hour of air drying will cause metallic colors to darken and affect the color match.

9. Allow the repair to dry at least 1 full day but preferably one week. Or force dry the repair with a heat lamp at 180° for 30 minutes.

10. Compound and polish the repair and adjacent areas as required. Figure 13-8 shows

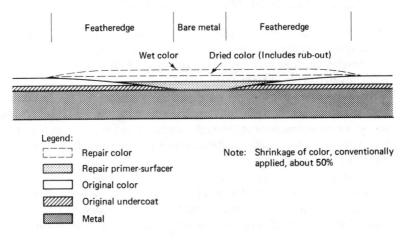

Featheredge | Bare metal | Featheredge

Wet color   Dried color (Includes rub-out)

Legend:
- Repair color
- Repair primer-surfacer
- Original color
- Original undercoat
- Metal

Note: Shrinkage of color, conventionally applied, about 50%

Figure 13-8 Spot-repair cross section: standard color application. (Courtesy of the General Motors Corporation)

the color application and amount of shrinkage in a dried acrylic lacquer. (Shrinkage of standard color, conventionally applied, is about 50%.)

Things to Remember When Spot Repairing with Acrylic Lacquers

1. Use a NIOSH-approved respirator at all times when spray painting.
2. Use recommended solvents in color reduction.
3. Measure reduction components carefully.
4. Check spray gun adjustments before starting.
5. Start application of metallic colors at about 30 psi (at the gun).
6. Increase air pressure 5 psi with each metallic color coat until a color match is achieved.
7. Apply color wet with correct feathering technique.
8. Blend edges with solvent after each color coat.
9. Check color match before applying color on car.
10. Do not apply a mist coat of solvent on freshly applied metallic colors.
11. See every spray painting application clearly.
12. Allow sufficient flash time between coats. **Do not rush!**
13. Do not apply clear acrylic lacquer over metallic colors too soon.
14. Allow sufficient flash time (at least 30 minutes) before applying force-drying equipment.
15. Use retarder in hot and humid weather conditions.
16. Allow finish to dry thoroughly before compounding.
17. Clean up equipment at the end of each day with medium thinner.

STANDARD ACRYLIC ENAMEL SPOT REPAIRS

Spot repairing over original acrylic enamel color with acrylic enamel color is recommended by most car factories. To gain adhesion of top coats without use of a sealer, it is necessary to clean and compound original acrylic enamel surfaces with a fine compound by hand (Fig. 13-5).

Most paint suppliers package enamel mostly by the gallon. Quarts and pints are not factory-packaged. Since quart quantities are the most used, the painter must depend on the jobber for an accurate mix. An accurate mix is more important with solid colors than with metallics because metallic colors can be controlled for degree of shade variation by spraying techniques.

Most paint suppliers (Ditzler, DuPont, Sherwin-Williams, Rinshed-Mason, and Martin-Senour) have hardeners available in the field (Table 9-1). All these acrylic enamels, including catalyzed enamels, can be compounded very lightly for gloss purposes after 24 to 48 hours if necessary. However, thorough compounding of enamel color is not recommended. When the need arises to do thorough compounding due to poor blending of spot repairs, it is better for durability purposes to redo the spot repair. To do so, simply wash off the enamel color with the appropriate reducer and do the repair over again—correctly.

Spraying acrylic enamels may appear complicated to the apprentice or beginner because everything in enamel refinishing takes place more slowly. The painter must learn to adapt and be very patient when working with these materials. With practice and experience, spot repairs can be made expertly as the painter becomes more familiar with the paint systems and products involved. Correct air pressure and spray technique with the correct materials are the key to top-quality workmanship.

Color Preparation

Double-check that the best equipment and color are being used, particularly when matching metallics.

1. Check the standard color on hand to be sure it is correct to color code.
2. Check for correct solvents for temperature conditions (Table 7-1).
3. If available, set up an agitator-type paint cup (Fig. 3-10), which makes spraying metallics as easy as spraying solid colors.
4. Be sure to agitate color thoroughly by hand or on a paint shaker.
5. Prepare acrylic enamel color with a two spray gun system as follows:
    a. In spray gun 1, prepare a conventional reduction of acrylic enamel color with proper reducer for the temperature. Label the cup "Color."
    b. In spray gun 2, prepare mist coat reducer. Use the same reducer as used in the color coat. Label the cup "Mist Coat."

Color Application (Fig. 13-7)

1. Set up the spray gun in the midrange adjustment (Chapter 4).
2. Spray out a small test panel with two coats of enamel color, allowing 5 to 7 minutes flash time between coats. (See your local paint jobber for special black and white paper test panels.)
3. Adjust the amount of reduction, air pressure and type of solvent to obtain a good color match. See Table 7-2. These are variables of spray painting that are controllable by the painter.
4. Spray two to three coats of color on the test panel for full hiding. Allow 5 to 7 minutes flash time between coats. Then compare the test panel to the car for color match (Fig. 13-9). If color matches satisfactorily, proceed with step 6. If color does not match, proceed with step 5.
5. If color mismatch still results, adjust the color as explained in Chapter 14 before proceeding.
6. Apply a first coat over the primer-surfaced area (Fig. 13-7). Use a feathering technique at the beginning and end of each stroke. For technique, see Chapter 4. Apply mist coat solvent to the edges and allow to flash.
7. Apply a second and, if necessary, a third coat in the same manner, extending each

Figure 13-9 Checking test panel for color match to car. (Courtesy of the DuPont Company)

coat beyond the previous one as shown in Fig. 13-7. Allow flash time between coats. Mist coat the edges as required.

Things to Remember When Spot Repairing with Acrylic Enamels

1. Read the label instructions before using any refinish products.
2. Use a NIOSH-approved respirator at all times, especially when spray painting with isocyanate hardeners.
3. Use the proper hardener or catalyst in the proper amount in acrylic enamel.
4. Use the recommended solvent for the prevailing temperature in reduction.
5. Measure the reduction components carefully.
6. Check the spray gun adjustments before applying color.
7. Start with low air pressure to achieve color matches on metallics.
8. Apply a mist coat of solvent to the edges with care.
9. Use a retarder in hot and humid weather.
10. Allow sufficient flash time between coats.
11. Allow sufficient flash time (at least 30 minutes) before applying force-drying equipment.
12. Clean up equipment with lacquer thinner at the end of each day.

REPAIRING BASECOAT/CLEARCOAT FINISHES WITHOUT REPAINTING

Some minor paint imperfections (Fig. 13-10) in the clearcoat can be repaired without repainting. They are:

1. Scratches (slight)

CHEMICAL SPOTTING

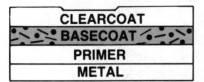

SAG

ORANGE PEEL

SCRATCH

DIRT

Figure 13-10 Minor paint defects that can be repaired without repainting. (Courtesy of General Motors Corporation)

2. Dirt
3. Chemical spotting
4. Runs or sags
5. Orange peel (slight)

If any of these conditions are not removed with the following procedure, no time is lost because the repair operations simply prepare the surface for repainting.

Procedure

1. **Wash** repair area with mild detergent and water.
2. **Clean** surface with paint finish cleaning solvent.
3. **Compound** repair area with mild compound, such as R-M's 854 or equivalent, with the polisher running at about 2,700 rpm. Keep the pad flat and use light pressure. Check the repair area often and, if necessary, add more compound.
4. If compounding removes the defect, finish by **polishing** the repair and adjacent areas with 3-M's Final Glaze, or equivalent.

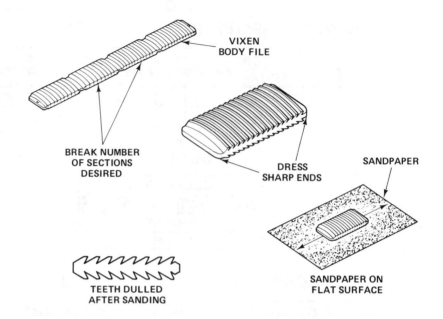

VIXEN BODY FILE

BREAK NUMBER OF SECTIONS DESIRED

DRESS SHARP ENDS

SANDPAPER

SANDPAPER ON FLAT SURFACE

TEETH DULLED AFTER SANDING

FABRICATION OF DIRT–NIB FILE

1. SECURE A 1-1/2″ TO 2″ LONG PIECE OF A VIXEN FILE BLADE.

2. DRESS OFF SHARP ENDS.

3. PLACE 400 TO 500 GRIT SANDPAPER ON FLAT SURFACE AND DRAW FILE IN FORE–AFT MOTIONS TILL FILE TEETH ARE SMOOTH (A LIGHT MACHINE OIL HASTENS THE OPERATION). CHECK FILE ON A PAINTED SURFACE; IT SHOULD REMOVE THE NIB AND LEAVE NO SCRATCHES.

Figure 13-11 (Courtesy of General Motors Corporation)

5. If condition is not removed by compounding, **sand** to remove the condition with ultra fine, 1200, or 1500 sandpaper and water. Sanding removes scratches, dirt, chemical spotting, and light orange peel. Use of a sanding block aids in a uniform cutting action.

6. **Compound** the repair area as in step 3.

7. *Polish* the repair area as in step 4.

8. Remove sags with a sag removal file. Use care. (See paint jobber for file availability; or make one as shown in Fig. 13-11.)

9. Sand surface as in step 5.

10. Compound surface to bring up uniform gloss as in step 3.

11. Polish the surface as in step 4.

BASECOAT/CLEARCOAT SPOT/PARTIAL PANEL REPAIR SYSTEMS

Two basic systems are available to the painter for the repair of basecoat/clearcoat finishes. See Table 9-1.

1. Acrylic lacquer basecoat color system with two optional clearcoating materials
2. Acrylic enamel or urethane base-coat color system with one or more clearcoating materials.

A certain number of painters may be able to spot repair basecoat/clearcoat finishes while keeping all repair materials within a small portion of the panel or inside the boundaries of a given panel. Research has found that most average and good painters feel it is easier and much quicker and that better results are achieved by a **combination of spot and partial panel repair methods,** as follows:

1. **Blend the repair color** into the adjacent original color as done in the usual spot repair method. This is done after achieving a good color match.
2. Then apply the clearcoat to the complete repair panel within natural breaklines. If no natural breaklines are present, carry the clearcoat into the next adjacent panel as shown in Fig. 13-12. The clearcoat must end and be blended into the adjacent original color while keeping within the **adhesion promoter** (sealer) application.

Basecoat Color Application Procedure: (Acrylic Lacquer Type) (Fig. 13-12)

1. Finish sanding primer-surfacer with No. 400 sandpaper and sand into the adjacent color for a short distance with the same sandpaper (Fig. 13-12).
2. Hand compound or wet sand with No. 600 or finer sandpaper the entire panel to the nearest breakline. If no breakline or crease-line is present, extend the sanding or compounding into the adjacent panel for a short distance (Fig. 13-12).
3. Clean the complete compounded or sanded area with paint finish cleaning solvent.
4. Apply **adhesion promoter** (Table 8-1) per label directions to the complete sanded or compounded area as shown (Fig. 13-12). Allow to dry 30 minutes to one hour.
5. Prepare spray gun with acrylic lacquer basecoat color according to label directions. Check the viscosity of color reduction according to label directions. This is a key that helps to arrive at a proper color match. For checking viscosity, see Chapter 7.
6. If a color problem is suspected, spray out a test panel as follows before applying color on car:
   a. Spray out a small test panel with two or three coats of basecoat color. Allow flash time between coats per label directions. Test panels are available through your local paint jobber.

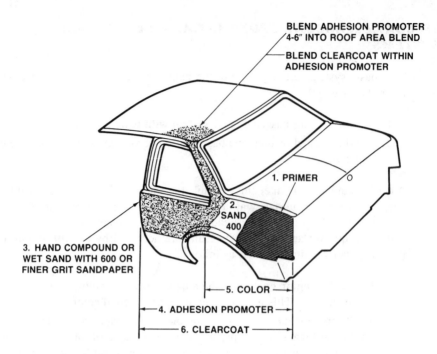

BLEND ADHESION PROMOTER
4-6" INTO ROOF AREA BLEND

BLEND CLEARCOAT WITHIN
ADHESION PROMOTER

1. PRIMER

2. SAND 400

3. HAND COMPOUND OR
WET SAND WITH 600 OR
FINER GRIT SANDPAPER

5. COLOR

4. ADHESION PROMOTER

6. CLEARCOAT

Figure 13-12 Typical spot/partial panel repair: basecoat/clearcoat repair method. (Courtesy of General Motors Corporation)

b. Adjust the amount of air pressure, reduction, and type of solvent to obtain a good color match. These are paint variables over which a painter has control. See Table 7-2.

c. **Spray test panel to full hiding. Allow to dry and apply two to three coats of clear acrylic lacquer per label directions.** Allow to dry and compare test panel to car (Fig. 13-9).

NOTE: Whenever spraying a test panel, include on the back side of the test panel:

Date	Type of solvent used
Paint code	Temperature
WA number (if GM)	Air pressure
Mix ratio (viscosity if known)	

The painter should keep a personal record of all test cards or panels for future color-matching reference.

7. If the color match is acceptable, apply color to repair area using the same variables as used on the test panel that produced the acceptable match. Apply the first coat of basecoat color over primer-surfaced area using a feathering technique at the beginning and end of each stroke. For technique, see Chapter 4.

8. Apply a second coat of basecoat color in similar fashion extending the color slightly beyond the first coat. Allow the color to dry according to label directions before applying clearcoat. In most cases two full wet coats achieve hiding. At times it may be necessary to apply a third coat.

9. If the color match is not acceptable, adjust the color as explained in Chapter 14. Then apply the color to the car.

   IMPORTANT: Basecoat color should not be sanded. If basecoat color must be sanded for any reason, proceed as follows:

   a. Allow color to dry. Sand with ultra-fine or finer wet-or-dry sandpaper. See Table 6-3.

   b. Reclean and tack wipe.

   c. Apply one or more coats of basecoat color to achieve hiding.

   d. Allow to dry according to label directions before applying clearcoat.

Clearcoat Application Procedure: Acrylic Lacquer Type (Fig. 13-12)

1. Prepare one spray gun with clear acrylic lacquer reduced according to label directions. Check the viscosity of reduced clear according to label directions. Prepare a second spray gun with mist coat material. See Table 9-1. Mark one cup "**Clear**" and one cup "**mist coat.**"

2. Spray clearcoat at 35 to 40 psi gun pressure.

3. Apply two to three medium-wet coats, allowing 15 to 20 minutes flash time between coats.

   a. Blend clearcoat into adjacent panel if necessary while staying within **adhesion promoter** application (Fig. 13-12).

   b. Apply mist coat solvent to clearcoat blend area.

   c. Apply a final mist coat application to the entire clearcoated panel at 20 psi to reduce orange peel and to aid final compounding.

4. Allow to dry completely (at least 24-hour air dry) before compounding.

5. Rub out with a light cutting hand or machine polishing compound.

6. Polish out swirl marks using a nonsealing type car polish, like **3-M's Final Glaze**, part number 05988, or equivalent.

Optional Clearcoat Application Procedure: Clear Urethane Enamel Type for Topcoating Basecoat or Standard Acrylic Lacquer Colors (Fig. 13-12)

Description: Items 4 and 5 of Table 9-1 list the clear urethane enamels and the hardeners that may be used as an optional clearcoating system over basecoat or standard acrylic lacquer colors. Some painters like to use this clearcoat because no compounding is required after application and the clear dries to a super high gloss finish.

1. As a safety measure, during the preparation and application of urethane finishes, remember to use a NIOSH approved air-supplied or cartridge type respirator. See hardener label for additional warnings.

2. Prepare surface as follows before clearcoating:

   a. If OEM standard lacquer requires no repairs, simply wash the surfaces with detergent and water, and then clean the surfaces with a paint finish cleaning solvent before topcoating.

   b. Allow fresh standard acrylic lacquer to dry a minimum of 2 hours, and preferably 16 hours before topcoating.

   c. If necessary, OEM acrylic lacquers may be **lightly** compounded before clear application.

   d. **Do not compound** freshly applied acrylic lacquer before topcoating.

   e. **Do not sand** freshly applied acrylic lacquer before topcoating.

   f. If complete car is painted with acrylic lacquer, **do *not* sand** the lacquer before topcoating with clear urethane.

   g. Basecoat lacquer color may be topcoated with clear urethane after 30 minutes to 1 hour of drying.

3. Activate the clear urethane coating by carefully measuring and mixing together the specified amount of clear enamel and proper hardener as specified in the label directions. This mixture should be used in the specified amount of time as indicated in label directions. The pot life varies with the type of urethane and the paint supplier.

4. Using the correct air pressure (usually 50 psi unless otherwise specified in label directions), apply two or three medium wet coats over the entire area to be refinished. Allow 15 to 20 minutes flash time between coats. The number of coats varies with the paint supplier. To improve flow-out during hot weather, use 1 to 2 ounces of correct retarder to 1 quart of activated mixture (see Table 7-1). Allow to cure overnight.

5. If necessary to make a blend into an adjacent panel, use a solvent recommended by the paint supplier for the type of clearcoat used.

6. If necessary to remove dirt after application, allow clearcoat to dry at least 48 hours (or longer) before sanding and compounding.

RE-REPAIR OF CLEAR URETHANE APPLIED OVER BASECOAT OR STANDARD ACRYLIC LACQUER

1. Wash and clean area with paint finish cleaning solvent.

2. Repair damaged area as required, featheredge, and apply straight primer like 834 ZIP, or equivalent.

3. Apply five to six coats of HP-100 or 806 Barrier Coat per label directions to entire panel; sand Barrier Coat with No. 500 to 600 dry sandpaper. Do not over sand.

4. Apply acrylic lacquer to full hiding and at correct color match.

5. Allow color to dry at least 2 hours before topcoating.

6. Apply clear urethane per label directions. Allow to dry overnight or several hours before putting car into service.

THINGS TO REMEMBER WHEN MAKING A SPOT/PARTIAL PANEL REPAIR ON OEM BASECOAT/CLEARCOAT FINISH WITH LACQUER BASECOAT COLOR

1. **Compound or sand** complete area to which **adhesion promoter** is applied.

2. Apply **adhesion promoter** to area beyond where color and clearcoat ends.

3. Reduce basecoat color according to label directions.

4. Check reduced color and clearcoat with viscosity cup before application.

5. Use basecoat and clearcoating materials from the same paint supplier.

6. When a color matching problem is suspected, **spray out a test panel** with color and clearcoating for comparison to the car, and adjust the color as required before application on car.

7. **Apply** two to three full-wet coats for hiding.

8. **Do not sand** basecoat color before applying clearcoat.

9. **Reduce** clearcoat according to label directions.

10. **Keep application** of color and clearcoats **within** area sealed with adhesion promoter.

11. **Use proper respirator** according to label warnings when preparing and applying automotive finishes.

BRUSH TOUCH-UP REPAIRS (EDGES)

General Description

The purpose of brush touch-up is as follows:

1. To make paint repairs quickly without using the spray gun.

2. To make paint repairs good looking and commercially acceptable.

3. To make paint repairs at very low cost.

The term **brush touch-up** in refinishing means to make small paint repairs with a brush.

Brush touch-up repairs are done best when the chipped paint does not extend beyond $\frac{1}{8}$ inch from the edge. Paint damage that extends beyond $\frac{1}{8}$ inch should be repaired with conventional paint spray methods.

Procedure

1. Surface preparation
   a. Wash and clean the surface.
   b. Featheredge the damaged edge with suitable sandpaper. Dry sanding with No. 220 or 320 is fast and satisfactory. If working on acrylic lacquer finishes, featheredging with color removing solvent is fast.
   c. Completely remove all rust.
   d. Apply metal conditioner to bare metal (Table 6-2) as recommended.

2. Undercoat application
   a. Apply a thin coat of the best-type primer to bare metal with a brush. Allow to dry.
   b. Apply the best-type primer-surfacer with a brush. Allow to dry.

   CAUTION 1: Do not sand in the conventional manner. Simply wipe the primer-surfacer with No. 400 or 500 sandpaper very lightly to make it smooth. Avoid cut-through.

   CAUTION 2: Color applied directly to bare metal will not adhere properly to the surface.

3. Color application
   a. Mix the color thoroughly at package viscosity and transfer a small amount into a paper cup.
   b. Add a very small amount of retarder (5% to 10%) and mix thoroughly.
   c. Using a sword-type striping brush, apply color to the panel edge as follows:
      (1) Hold the striping brush by the specially contoured handle between the first two fingers and the thumb with the handle of the brush touching the palm. Extend the fingers lengthwise on the handle. This gives the painter a better "feel" for the brush.
      (2) Clean the brush bristles by dipping in the solvent cup and wiping on a cloth. This gives the painter a "feel" for the softness of the bristles.
      (3) Dip the brush in color, scrape off excess color at the cup edge, and apply color to the panel edge. Steady the striping hand by contacting the extended small finger against the panel; or steady the striping hand by resting it against the other hand, which, in turn, could slide along a panel edge as a reference.
      (4) After contacting the panel with the brush, apply color in a long, continuous stroke until the color on the brush runs out. Do each striping stroke with a medium-fast, long, continuous motion. Lacquers may require two or three coats. Enamels usually require one or two coats. Allow proper flash time between coats.

CAUTION: Do not rebrush over applied paint when it becomes sticky. Allow the proper short drying period and then reapply more color. To level a rough spot, use straight solvent.

4. Allow lacquer to dry thoroughly, usually overnight. Then compound lightly with a hand compound.

REVIEW QUESTIONS

1. Why are spot repairs necessary in automotive refinishing?
2. What does the term "paint repairability" mean?
3. Three things are required to make a successful spot repair. They are:
   (a) Color match
   (b) Blend
   (c) Gloss and surface texture
   Explain how good each should be.
4. What paint system has been used most popularly in the refinish trade for making spot repairs?
5. What single paint variable causes most painters problems when color matching metallic colors?
6. Explain the procedure a painter should follow to determine the correct air pressure when color matching metallic colors.
7. Why is compounding of adjacent surfaces required when spot repairing original acrylic enamel finishes?
8. What two thinners make up an excellent solvent combination for mist coating when repairing original acrylic lacquers with acrylic lacquer materials?
9. Name two types of solvents that are suited for blending the edges of freshly applied acrylic enamels in spot repairing.
10. When spot repairing acrylic lacquers or enamels, what spray technique is best for applying color coats?
11. Outline the procedure for spot repairing original standard (metallic) acrylic lacquers with an acrylic lacquer repair system.
12. Outline the procedure for spot repairing original standard (metallic) acrylic enamels with an acrylic enamel repair system.
13. Outline the procedure for spot repairing basecoat/clearcoat (metallic) finishes.
14. What is the purpose of brush touch-up repairs?
15. What is the maximum distance a chip can extend from an edge and still be repairable by brush touch-up?

16. Explain the procedure for making brush touch-up repairs.

17. Explain the procedure for making a spot/partial panel repair on a basecoat/clearcoat finish.

18. Name several paint problems that can be corrected on basecoat/clearcoat finishes without repainting.

19. What is the procedure for correcting problems in basecoat/clearcoat finishes without repainting?

14

Color Matching
Fundamentals
and Techniques

INTRODUCTION

When a color match problem is expected or encountered, the painter should spray out one or more test panels to full hiding for comparison to the car. By adjusting the variables under his or her control on additional test panels, the painter very often can achieve a good color match. When a good color match cannot be achieved under these circumstances, tinting is required. **Tinting most definitely should be done as a last resort.**

The basics on color matching and tinting as covered in this chapter should aid the novice or experienced painters in achieving color matches. Best results are achieved by working closely with paint formulas for specific colors being adjusted. If formulas are not available at a paint shop, check with the paint jobber of the paint material being used for answers to specific questions and specific tints required. If possible, take a painted car part to the paint jobber.

As paint technicians, painters need to know more about color and adjustment than ever before because of the ever increasing advances in automotive paint technologies and application methods. To adjust a color by tinting, the painter should have a fundamental knowledge of basic color theory. He or she should understand the basics as well as the tints themselves before picking up tinting colors in an attempt to "bring a color in." It is only through practice and experience, two important ingredients, that a painter becomes qualified as an expert in the art of tinting.

Because of their construction and behavior, metallic colors are very sensitive to the solvents with which they are reduced and the air pressure with which they are applied. A **variable** is a part of the spray painting environment (such as temperature, humidity, and ventilation) or a part of the spray painting process (such as amount of reduction, evaporation rate of solvents, air pressure and type of equipment). Table 14-1 is a chart of variables and their effect on the shade of a metallic color. As each variable changes during application, metallic finishes are affected accordingly.

Light penetrates the surface of the cured paint film, reflects off the aluminum flakes, and then passes around the pigment particles of varying densities thus producing the ultimate color shade. Figure 14-1 portrays a basecoat/clearcoat finish that produces the **ultimate color shade.**

Figure 14-2 portrays normal orientation of metallics and pigments. The uniform dispersion and density of aluminum flakes and the pigment particles produce a **standard metallic color shade.**

Figure 14-3 portrays flat orientation of metallics. To produce a **light metallic color shade** requires an accumulation of aluminum flake dispersed nearly horizontally at the top of the paint film, thereby obscuring most of the pigment particles beneath.

Figure 14-4 portrays perpendicular orientation of metallics. The dense flotation of

TABLE 14-1 VARIABLES AFFECTING THE COLOR OF METALLICS

VARIABLE	TO MAKE COLOR LIGHTER	TO MAKE COLOR DARKER
SHOP CONDITIONS:		
a. Temperature	Increase	Decrease
b. Humidity	Decrease	Increase
c. Ventilation	Increase	Decrease
SPRAY EQUIPMENT & ADJUSTMENTS:		
a. Fluid Tip	Use Smaller Size	Use Larger Size
b. Air Cap	Use Air Cap with Greater Number of Openings	Use Air Cap with Lesser Number of Openings
c. Fluid Adjustment Valve	Reduce Volume of Material Flow	Increase Volume of Material Flow
d. Spreader Adjustment Valve	Increase Fan Width	Decrease Fan Width
e. Air Pressure (at Gun)	Increase Air Pressure	Decrease Air Pressure
THINNER USAGE:		
a. Type of Thinner	Use Faster Evaporating Thinner	Use Slower Evaporating Thinner
b. Reduction of Color	Increase Volume of Thinner	Decrease Volume of Thinner
c. Use of Retarder	(Do Not Use Retarder)	Add Proportional Amount of Retarder to Thinner
SPRAYING TECHNIQUES:		
a. Gun Distance	Increase Distance	Decrease Distance
b. Gun Speed	Increase Speed	Decrease Speed
c. Flash Time Between Coats	Allow More Flash Time	Allow Less Flash Time
d. Mist Coat	(Will Not Lighten Color)	The Wetter the Mist Coat the Darker the Color

(Courtesy of General Motors Corporation.)

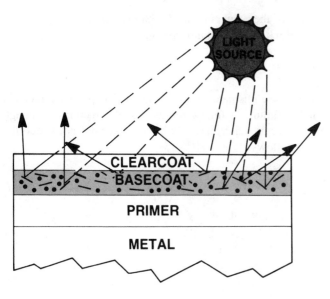

Figure 14-1 Ultimate color shade. (Courtesy of General Motors Corporation)

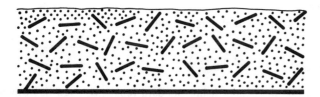

Figure 14-2 Normal orientation of metallics and pigments. (Courtesy of General Motors Corporation)

Figure 14-3 Flat orientation of metallics. (Courtesy of General Motors Corporation)

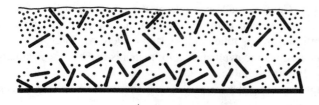

Figure 14-4 Perpendicular orientation of metallics. (Courtesy of General Motors Corporation)

pigment particles near the surface of the paint combined with aluminum flake dispersed nearly perpendicular results in a **dark metallic color shade.**

Other Causes of Color Mismatches

It would be untrue to state that all color mismatches are because of the paint technician's spraying techniques or his or her failure to follow product label directions, although many are. But there are any number of other reasons why the color did not match the car. Some of these causes are as follows:

Balling of the metallic flake
Bending of the metallic flake
Shearing and wearing of the metallic flake
Fading of the color pigments
Unstable tints
Thin paint
Wrong color
Underbaked finish (at OEM level)
Overbaked finish (at OEM level)
Ultraviolet breakdown
Portions of vehicle painted at different plants or other sources
Poor jobber mix
Unbalanced thinner (true, latent and diluent)

Factory-applied materials can be duplicated using standard repair techniques. In many cases, however, application alone may not correct all mismatches. No matter what the reason or who is to blame, the problem becomes the painter's.

GLOSSARY OF TINTING TERMS

Face: To look at a painted surface head on for color match.
Pitch or side tone: To look at a painted surface from a 60° to 45° angle.

LIGHTING CONDITIONS AND COLOR INSPECTION

Figure 14-5 is a graphic picture of the sun. All color, as the eye sees it, originates from the radiant energy of the sun. Color is made possible by the reflection of light from all that is seen. The white light of the sun is made up of all the colors of the spectrum, which are red, orange, yellow, green, blue, indigo, and violet. All these colors are available for reflection. The best way to evaluate a color match is to make the evaluation under the best daylight conditions available.

Figure 14-6 is a graph depicting the intensity at which all colors are seen clearly

Figure 14-5 Graphic picture of the sun. (Courtesy of General Motors Corporation)

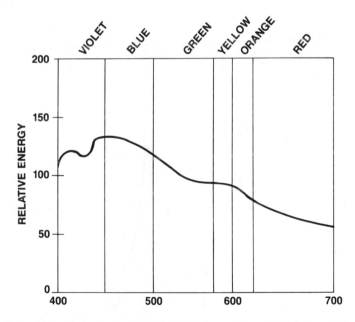

Figure 14-6 Graph of natural daylight. (Courtesy of General Motors Corporation)

Lighting Conditions and Color Inspection

in natural daylight. Natural daylight is variable. Lighting studies indicate that color analysts, artists, finishers, and the like, prefer the light from a natural moderately overcast north sky. The color of this light is shown in Fig. 14-6. Note that all colors are present in the light and there is a little more blue than in the others, which accounts for the bluish characteristics of the north sky daylight. Natural daylight then represents the ideal with which light sources are compared to determine how well the artificial source can be substituted for the natural one.

Figure 14-7 shows that a standard fluorescent light (with only blue, yellow, and red) contains only a portion of the visible light that is available for reflection. Figure 14-8 is a graph of average fluorescent daylight. This graph shows the abrupt changes of the fluorescent simulation versus the smooth flow of the natural daylight graph curve. Violet, green, and red show up much more under this type of light. Because of the emitting of high-energy peaks of certain colors, a person's judgment is misled.

Figure 14-9 is a picture of incandescent light, which contains only a portion of the visible light for reflectance (yellow and red). Figure 14-10 shows a graph of ordinary incandescent light. Note how low this light is in violet, blue, and green for reflectance.

Figure 14-7 Fluorescent light (blue, yellow, red). (Courtesy of General Motors Corporation)

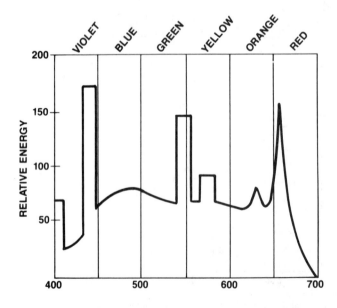

Figure 14-8 Graph of average fluorescent daylight. (Courtesy of General Motors Corporation)

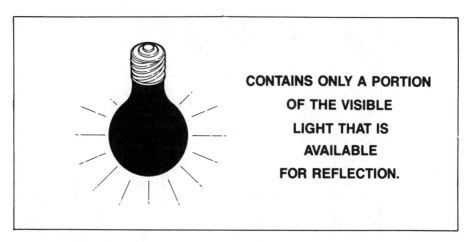

Figure 14-9 Incandescent light (yellow, red). (Courtesy of General Motors Corporation)

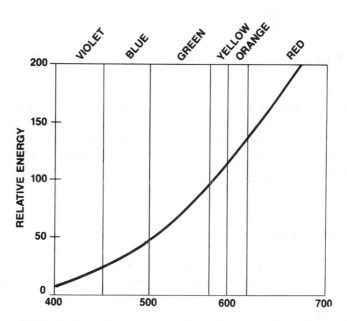

Figure 14-10 Graph of ordinary incandescent light. (Courtesy of General Motors Corporation)

Figure 14-11 shows that the color intensity of the Macbeth filtered daylight-type light is very close to natural daylight. The disadvantage of this type of light is that it will not show the amount of metallic sparkle in the color that the sunlight will. Therefore, the amount of metallic sparkle in a paint finish can only be matched in bright sunlight.

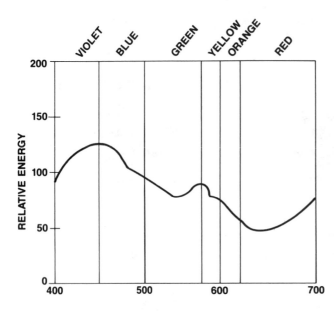

Figure 14-11 Graph of Macbeth filtered daylight, Spectralight.® (Courtesy of General Motors Corporation)

CONCEPT OF BLACK AND WHITE SPRAY-OUT PANELS

To be sure that there is adequate hiding for evaluation of a color match, the paint companies are making available black and white test spray-out panels to the after-market paint refinisher. These panels can be used to spray out a color prior to applying it on a car to check for a color match against an undamaged area. The black and white concept is to apply color over both areas of the test card or panel until black and white areas are no longer distinguishable. This ensures a proper film build and proper hiding of applied color. You can secure test cards at your local paint jobber.

THEORY OF COLOR

To perform color adjustment by tinting, the painter should have a fundamental knowledge of basic color theory. The painter should understand the basics as well as the tints themselves before attempting tinting operations. Tinting most definitely should be done as a last resort.

Pigments have the ability to reflect and absorb light rays. When a person sees **blue,** the pigment absorbs all the light rays with the exception of blue ones, which it reflects. When a person sees **red,** the pigment absorbs all light rays except red ones, which it reflects. The eye is like a tiny radio receiver and picks up these waves of light as they are reflected.

A particular color does not appear the same under different types of light. Figure 14-12 shows how the same color appears differently under sunlight and under an incandescent light. The reason is that the incandescent light has less wavelength reflectance due to less light components to reflect.

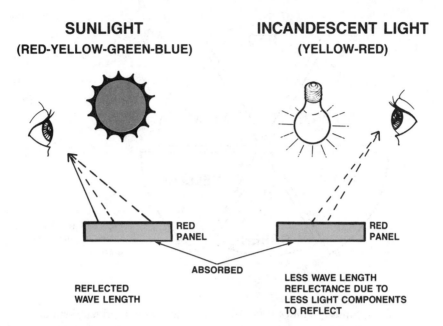

SUNLIGHT
(RED-YELLOW-GREEN-BLUE)

INCANDESCENT LIGHT
(YELLOW-RED)

RED PANEL

RED PANEL

ABSORBED

REFLECTED WAVE LENGTH

LESS WAVE LENGTH REFLECTANCE DUE TO LESS LIGHT COMPONENTS TO REFLECT

Figure 14-12 How we interpret color. (Courtesy of General Motors Corporation)

Metamerism is a phenomenon whereby the spectral reflectance curves in a color are such that they match under one light source, but do not match under a second light source. Metameric matches can occur when paint materials are formulated with different dyes or pigments.

HOW WE SEE COLOR AND WHY

To better communicate about color matching, we need to have a common language to describe color. Every color has three dimensions. The painter must understand each of them if he or she wants to adjust a color successfully. The three dimensions of a color are *hue*, *value*, and *saturation*.

Hue. Hue may be described as the excitation of the sense of sight created by beams of light that allow us to distinguish one color from another. **Hue is a specific shade of a given family of color.** An example of this is flame red. Flame red is a specific hue within the red color range. Hue is often referred to as **color** or **cast. Color is adjusted clockwise or counterclockwise, never across the axis of the color wheel.**

1. **Primary colors (Fig. 14-13)**
   Red
   Yellow
   Blue

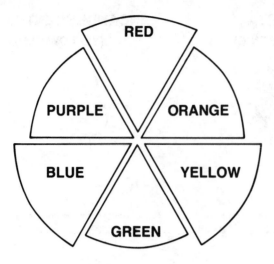

Figure 14-13 Primary and secondary colors. (Courtesy of General Motors Corporation)

2. **Secondary colors (Fig. 14-13):** mixture of two primary colors
   Orange
   Green
   Purple or violet
3. **Intermediate colors:** mixture of an adjacent primary and secondary color
   Red-orange
   Yellow-orange
   Blue-green
   Blue-violet or blue-purple
   Red-purple or red-violet

Using this same method we could have an infinite amount of colors. At present, paint manufacturers have worked with upward of 30,000 different color hues.

Value: LIGHTNESS or DARKNESS of a Color

White: highest in value
Black: lowest in value
Metallic: gray

Value may be described as the whiteness or blackness of a color. White and black are noncolors. **White is at the top of the neutral axis and black is at the bottom of the axis. Adding black or white does not change color hue. It changes value and saturation.**

Saturation.   All colors are most saturated with color intensity at the outer rim of the color wheel. As (1) black, (2) white, or (3) metallic are added to a color, it becomes (1) desaturated, (2) lighter, or (3) grayer. See Fig. 14-14. At position 1, the metallic color is a light blue metallic color. At position 2, it is a medium blue metallic color. At position 3, it is a rich dark blue metallic color. Another term used to describe the third dimension of a color is **chroma.**

As white is mixed with a color it becomes desaturated toward the light side. As black is added to a color it becomes desaturated toward the dark side. The addition of metallic to a color desaturates it toward the gray side.

Remember, if a color is rich in hue, it is saturated and it is located at the outer rim of the color wheel. As a color is desaturated, it is close to the center of the color wheel or neutral axis.

The three dimensions of a color are:

1. First, it is a **color.**
2. Second, it is either **light** or **dark.**
3. Third, it is either **Rich** or **Muddy.**

THE BRYG COLOR WHEEL (FIG. 14-14)

The BRYG color wheel is used to represent the position of each color family in regard to **hue** and **saturation** dimensions. The letters BRYG stand for blue, red, yellow, and green. **Hue dimension changes rotate around the wheel. Saturation dimension changes move from inside the wheel out.** The center of the wheel represents the neutral gray area. The farther away from the center, the more saturated the color becomes. For example, a slightly red blue metallic color would be plotted somewhere along the blue line as shown (Fig. 14-14).

Depending on its saturation, it would be plotted closer to the neutral gray center or farther out to the edge. Position 1 could be considered a light blue metallic, while 2 could be considered a medium blue metallic, and 3 a dark blue metallic.

Saturation changes can be adjusted by tinting with aluminum flake to desaturate the color or adding more of the primary blue to saturate the color. Hue changes can be adjusted by adding a greener blue (4) or green (5) or a redder blue violet (6) or red (7).

The color wheel is used in the same manner throughout the color families. BRYG on the color wheel is used in both metallic and solid color families.

Summary of the Dimensions of Color

Value of a color:	light or dark
Hue of a color:	is it bluer, greener, yellower, or redder?
Saturation/desaturation:	refers to purity; is color cleaner, brighter, or dirtier (grayer)?

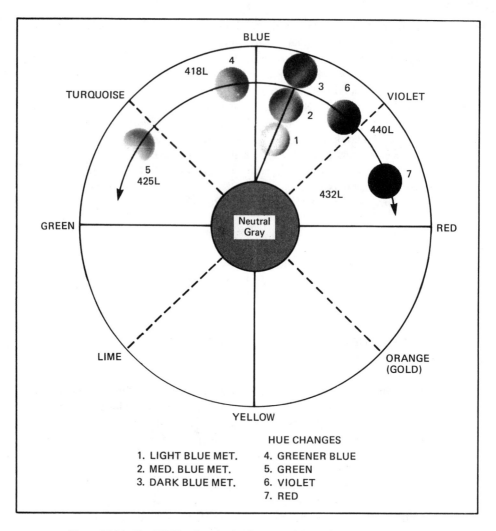

BLUE

TURQUOISE

418L

4

3   6

2

1

5
425L

VIOLET

440L

432L

7

GREEN

Neutral
Gray

RED

LIME

ORANGE
(GOLD)

YELLOW

HUE CHANGES

1. LIGHT BLUE MET.
2. MED. BLUE MET.
3. DARK BLUE MET.

4. GREENER BLUE
5. GREEN
6. VIOLET
7. RED

Figure 14-14   The BRYG color wheel. (Courtesy of General Motors Corporation)

MUNSELL COLOR TREE CONCEPT (FIG. 14-15)

The Munsell Color Tree was developed by Albert H. Munsell, an accomplished printer and art instructor, to create order in the world of color. He recognized that there was no generally accepted way of describing colors exactly. People made vague comparisons to colors in nature, such as sky blue, lemon yellow, or ruby red. There were endless arguments over colors and color names. Munsell identified the three basic qualities of color **(hue, value, and chroma)** and arranged them on numerical scales. The three qualities of color can be considered the three dimensions of a space in which colors are arranged in an orderly way. All perceptible colors relative to each other are located by means of their **hue, value, and saturation or chroma** on the color tree (Fig. 14-15).

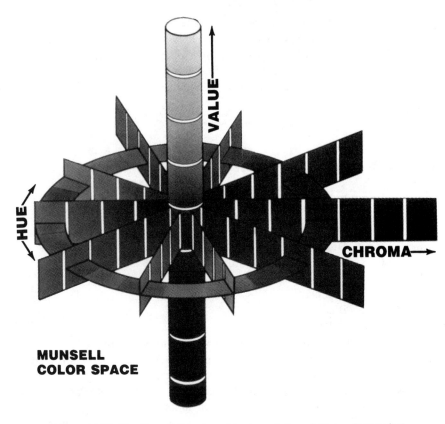

VALUE

HUE

CHROMA→

**MUNSELL
COLOR SPACE**

Figure 14-15 The Munsell color tree. (Courtesy of General Motors Corporation)

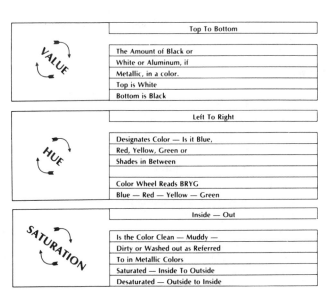

VALUE	Top To Bottom
	The Amount of Black or
	White or Aluminum, if
	Metallic, in a color.
	Top is White
	Bottom is Black

HUE	Left To Right
	Designates Color — Is it Blue,
	Red, Yellow, Green or
	Shades in Between
	Color Wheel Reads BRYG
	Blue — Red — Yellow — Green

SATURATION	Inside — Out
	Is the Color Clean — Muddy —
	Dirty or Washed out as Referred
	To in Metallic Colors
	Saturated — Inside To Outside
	Desaturated — Outside to Inside

Figure 14-16 Color dimension summary. (Courtesy of General Motors Corporation)

Munsell Color Tree Concept

Fig. 14-16 is a basic road map on color matching that isolates and summarizes the three dimensions of a color with tips on how to control each dimension in color matching. The tips are summarized at the right of the figure. The sequence of adjustment is important too: value, first; hue, second; and saturation, third. When each dimension is adjusted as directed in this chapter, the result is a very acceptable, if not perfect, color match.

HOW TO SOLVE COLOR-MATCHING PROBLEMS

I. **Learn to describe color correctly and in the proper sequence.**
   A. **Lighter or darker: value evaluation is first**
      1. Side-angle viewing
      2. Direct viewing
   B. **Cast or hue: color evaluation is second**
      1. Redder
      2. Greener
      3. Bluer
      4. Yellower
   C. **Brighter or grayer: saturation evaluation is third**
II. **Learn to compare the original paint to the color being sprayed.**
   This is done by asking these three questions:
   A. First, ask yourself, "Is the car's finish **lighter or darker** compared to the color being sprayed?" Come up with an answer.
   B. Then ask yourself; "Is the car's finish **redder or greener or bluer or yellower** compared to the color being sprayed?" Come up with an answer.
   C. Then ask yourself, "Is the car's finish **brighter (in color intensity) or grayer in color** compared to the color being sprayed?" Come up with an answer.
   When you can answer the three questions, you have a starting point for tinting the repair formula to match the car. Or if it is a good match already, you are ready to paint.
III. **General tinting procedure**
   A. The **first step** in tinting a color is to adjust for **lightness or darkness.** See Table 14-1 and steps IVA and B, which follow.
   B. The **next step** is to adjust the **cast or hue** of a color.
   C. The **last step** is to adjust for **brightness or grayness** when steps IIIA and B are OK.
IV. **Adjust the color for lightness or darkness as follows:**
   A. **Methods to lighten a metallic color**
      1. After spraying a wet coat, follow with a coat at half-trigger or with reduced fluid flow, while maintaining air pressure.
      2. Raise the air pressure at the gun (5 psi increments).
      3. Add more thinner. Use a faster drying thinner than what is in the mix.

4. Let the reduced color set for 10 minutes in the spray cup; pour off the top into a clean container, stir the remaining material, and spray.
5. Add additional metallic to the color.

B. **Methods to darken a metallic color**
1. Apply double-wet coats. Reduce gun fan size slightly.
2. Lower the air pressure at the gun (5 psi increments).
3. Add 2 ounces of retarder per reduced cup.
4. Let the reduced color set for 10 minutes in the spray cup; pour the top portion off into a clean spray cup; stir; attach gun and spray.
5. Add the predominant dark color to the mix (from formula).

C. **Spray test panel to full hiding after each step in steps IVA and B and check to car for color match.**

V. **After adjusting the color for lightness or darkness and the cast is off, tinting for correct cast is required.** The steps involved in tinting for correct cast are as follows:
1. Decide how the original finish is off as compared to the material sprayed on test panel. For example, the original finish may be redder than the test panel. A color can only be described in being off in cast as being redder, yellower, greener, or bluer.
2. See the proper color formula to determine which tinting color to use; or use a suitable company tinting guide as found in this chapter. Also, refer to Table 14-2 for a lead to a color.
3. Each color can vary in cast only in two directions. See Table 14-3 on color shifts.
4. Once the color necessary to adjust the cast correctly is determined, the amount must then be calculated.
   a. The first "hit" should be determined from the chart. Use the least amount necessary of the particular tint to effectively change the color. See Table 14-4.
   b. Mix the color thoroughly. Trigger the gun to clear the color passages. Spray the test panel to full hiding, allowing proper flash time between coats. Allow to dry and check with the OE panel. Add additional tint in the specified increments and repeat the process until the color match is acceptable.
   c. Record on the back side of test panel the color names and color amounts so the tinting can be duplicated for more of the same color when the need arises.

VI. **Final Adjustment (saturation)**
The final adjustment is made only after the color is correct in lightness or darkness and hue (cast). Emphasis in this color matching chapter is primarily on metallic colors.

A. **If saturation is required** (increasing color intensity), make the color more saturated by adding the primary family color noted in the formula. Use care and arrive at the proper saturation through test panel comparison.

B. **If desaturation is required** (making color grayer), add the proper aluminum

TABLE 14-2 IF A COLOR IS "TOO SOMETHING IN CAST," DO THE FOLLOWING TO CHANGE THE CAST

COLOR	ADD	TO CHANGE A CAST OF
Blue	Green	Red
Blue	Red	Green
Green	Yellow	Blue
Green	Blue	Yellow
Red	Yellow	Blue
Red	Blue	Yellow
Gold	Green	Red
Gold	Red	Green
Maroon	Yellow	Blue
Maroon	Blue	Yellow
Bronze	Yellow	Red
Bronze	Red	Yellow
Orange	Yellow	Red
Orange	Red	Yellow
Yellow	Green	Red
Yellow	Red	Green
White	Yellow	Blue
White	Blue	Yellow
Beige	Green	Red
Beige	Red	Green
Purple	Green	Red
Purple	Red	Green
Aqua	Blue	Green
Gray	Blue	Yellow
Gray	Yellow	Blue

Courtesy of the Sherwin-Williams Company.

pigment and/or other tint noted in the formula. Again, use care and arrive at the proper desaturation through spraying out a test panel for comparison.

C. **If color is slightly gray or dirty** spray on a wet color coat, followed by an additional coat applied from a slightly greater distance at half-trigger and same air pressure to lay the metallics flatter at the surface. If basecoat color, apply clear per label directions, allow to dry, and check against original finish.

D. **To make a color more gray,** if the formula is not available, add a small amount of white mixed with a very small amount of black. Spray out test panel, let it dry, and check for color match to OEM panel.

E. **To lighten the pitch depth of a color,** add white. Use the proper white in the proper volume. If in doubt, check with the paint jobber. The following are general guidelines for 1 pint of reduced paint:

1. For light metallics, use $\frac{1}{2}$ teaspoon white.

TABLE 14-3 COLOR SHIFTS

- Colors either greener or redder in cast
  1. Blues   4. Purples
  2. Yellows   5. Beiges
  3. Golds   6. Browns
- Colors either yellower or bluer in cast
  1. Greens   4. Blacks
  2. Maroons   5. Grays
  3. Whites and off-whites
- Colors yellower or redder in cast
  1. Bronzes
  2. Oranges
  3. Reds
- Colors bluer or greener in cast
  1. Aqua
  2. Turquoise

Remember
A color can only be described as being off in cast or hue, as being redder, yellower, greener, or bluer. Each color can only vary in two directions. To decide what tints should be used to adjust a color, refer to the formula mix for that color.

Courtesy of General Motors Corporation.

TABLE 14-4 TINTING MEASUREMENTS

- Trace: 0–1 gram
  - 25 drops = approximately 1 gram
  - $\frac{1}{8}$ teaspoon = approximately $\frac{3}{4}$ gram
- Small: 1–4 grams
  - $\frac{1}{4}$ teaspoon = approximately 1.5 grams
  - $\frac{1}{2}$ thinner cap = approximately 4 grams
- Medium: 4–10 grams
  - $\frac{1}{2}$ teaspoon = approximately 3 grams
  - 1 teaspoon = approximately 6 grams
  - 1 thinner cap = approximately 8 grams
- Large: 10–20 grams
  - $1\frac{1}{4}$ thinner caps = approximately 10 grams
  - $2\frac{1}{2}$ teaspoons = approximately 15 grams
  - 3 teaspoons = approximately 18 grams
  - 1 tablespoon = approximately 19 grams

NOTE
The above chart is a guide to assist you in determining an equivalent amount measurement when the indicated amount of tint to add to a given color is indicated in grams.

Courtesy of General Motors Corporation.

How to Solve Color-Matching Problems

2. For medium metallics, use $\frac{1}{4}$ teaspoon white.

3. For dark metallics, use $\frac{1}{8}$ teaspoon white.

F. **A flattening agent** can be used in a metallic color to increase metallic sparkle. As much as 15% to 20% may be used.

G. For further information on saturation, check with the paint jobber. Also, refer to the paint supplier's tinting guide.

H. When color is acceptable for blending, blend the repair color into the panel to achieve an acceptable color match. Allow to dry. If base-coat color, apply two to three coats of clear coat per label directions over the complete panel. Allow to dry. If acrylic lacquer, rub out and polish as required.

IMPORTANT: It is impossible to make a color brighter without throwing the two previous corrections off, which are **value** (lightness or darkness) and **hue** (color).

UNDERSTANDING THE PAINT FORMULA INGREDIENTS

All major and popular paint formulas are usually a part of a paint shop if it is equipped with a paint mixing setup from any particular paint company. If a paint shop is without a paint mixing setup, questions on paint formulas can be answered by the paint jobber.

There are two important things to remember when examining paint formulas.

1. Various tints make up a color in terms of certain percentages of each particular tint that are in the formula.

2. The mixing formula is an important tool to the refinisher when tinting of a color is required. Each formula provides the identity and specific amount of each component that makes up the formula.

The hue of pure tints can change drastically when mixed or "let down." All paint manufacturers make available to the after-market a list of their formula mix tints on color chip cards. These cards show the tint colors in their pure state, as well as how each reacts when "let down." The formula mix tints include the following information:

1. Name of tint

2. Product identity number

3. Strength of tint

A rule of thumb when examining the formula mix ingredients is that, if the quantity of a given tint in the formula is **minimal,** it most probably is **very high in strength.** Adding a very small quantity of the tint to a mix would make a very noticeable color difference. Become familiar with the strength of each tint. **Basecoat color tints are among the strongest available.** Extreme care must be exercised in their use.

HOW TO USE A COLOR TINTING GUIDE (SEE TABLE 14-5 OR 14-7)

The first pages of a tinting guide generally list those procedures that should have been tried before you decide to tint the color.

1. Gun technique
2. Color mixed properly
3. Color properly reduced
4. Proper blending techniques

Once You Have Determined You Need To Tint

1. Find the color family closest to the car color you are working with.
2. Under good lighting conditions (preferably daylight), compare the dried refinish color and the car to be refinished.
3. Determine what the color problem is. If the color requires a hue adjustment, does it need red or green, blue or yellow? If one of the hue directions is off, add trace amounts of the tinting color noted in the formula to correct it. If a formula is not immediately available, the painter can be guided by the tinting guides in this chapter. Use only trace amounts of the tinting colors noted. (See Table 14-5, p. 360, or Table 14-7, p. 364).
4. If hue direction appears to be OK, then evaluate lightness and saturation in the same manner. If lightness is the problem, add trace amounts of white or black. If saturation is the problem, make the color more saturated by adding the primary family color noted. If desaturation is needed, add aluminum or other tint noted in the formula mix. Check findings with Table 14-5 or 14-7.
5. Once you have determined what color to tint with, be careful not to add too much. Add small amounts and check the match after each ''hit'' under the same lighting conditions, at full hiding after it is reasonably dry. Remember, wet materials will often dry down to a different shade. You can always add more tinting color. But if you have added too much, you may find it impossible to tint your original color back. When this occurs, it often requires starting over with fresh color.

Keep an accurate record of each color tinted and the amount of tinting color used. Record this information on the backside of each spray test panel so that more of the same color can be made quickly when the need arises.

HINTS FOR COLOR MATCHING

Before tinting a color, be certain that a color variation is not due to:

1. Incomplete agitation
2. Incorrect reduction

3. Incorrect air pressure
4. Insufficient number of coats
5. Poor spray technique

Painters should get the idea out of their minds that they can achieve a perfect panel-to-panel color match. There is no such thing as a perfect panel-to-panel match. There are too many variables, both in the refinish situation and at the OEM level that can cause variations in color match. That is why blending into adjacent panels with the same color has become the most sensible thing to do. Go for **commercial acceptability** in a color match. **This is a color match that, although not perfect, would be acceptable to a very high percentage of the motoring public.**
    A car should be viewed from the following angles to check for color match:

1. 45° to 60° (side tone)
2. Head on (face)

The head-on appearance is the least important. A painter cannot blend a color with a bad side tone and lose it properly.

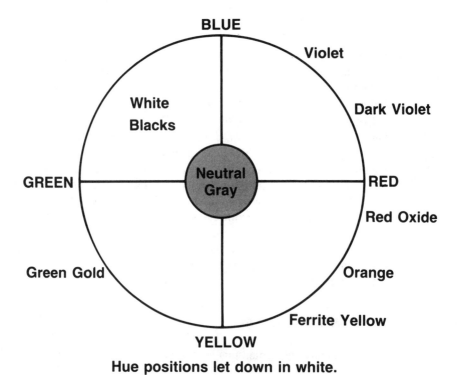

Hue positions let down in white.

Figure 14-17 Tinting colors used in solid color families. (Courtesy of General Motors Corporation)

If you have tried painting the car with a number of products prior to deciding to tint, sand the material off. Many colors applied over a color tend to oversaturate side tones. Always spray out a test panel with the repair color and check it to the car if problems with a color match are suspected.

Use only half of the repair color; keep the other half untouched. A record should be kept of what is done to the original formula when tints are added.

Before attempting to tint any color, all variables should be tried, including more paint or even a different batch of paint. **It cannot be overstressed that tinting takes time and should be done as a last resort.**

Tinting Colors Used in Solid Color Families (Fig. 14-17)

Solid colors are those that contain no metallic flakes. They are harder to tint to match as well as blend to match. To tint a solid color, no variables can be modified in order to blend and vary color effect. A solid color has to be tinted within the confines of a color hue and to near exactness. Figure 14-17 portrays a color wheel showing the most popular colors that are used when the tinting of solid colors is required.

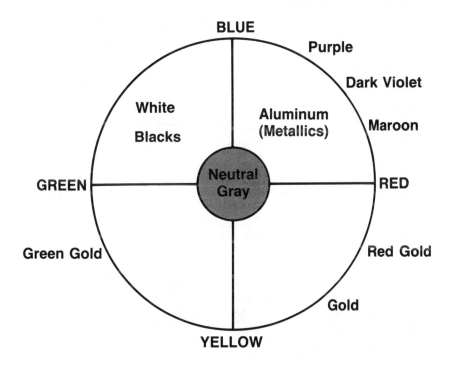

Hue positions let down in aluminum.

Figure 14-18 Tinting colors used in metallic color families. (Courtesy of General Motors Corporation)

Tinting Colors Used in Metallic Color Families (Fig. 14-18)

Metallic colors are paints that can be tinted to within what is commonly known as a "ball-park" match, knowing that gun techniques can often compensate for any minor color mismatches.

To lighten a metallic color, add more metallic flakes. The addition of white to a metallic color can result in distorted side-tone effects. It might match head on, but the side tone could be off-color and generally to the light side. The side tone would not be a mismatch from the metallic standpoint, but from the color itself and the lack of metallic sparkle.

COLOR PLOTTING

Figure 14-19 shows a color plotting example. A color wheel is used to represent the position of each color in regard to **hue** and **saturation**. Hue dimension changes **rotate around the wheel,** while saturation changes move **from inside the wheel out.** The center of the wheel represents the neutral gray area. The **further from the center, the more saturated** the color will become.

The color being plotted is a light yellow, code 50. There is no aluminum in the formula; therefore, it is a solid color. There is a large quantity of white and light tints

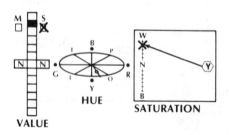

VALUE   HUE   SATURATION

COLOR: LT. YELLOW CODE: 50			
CODE	MOVEMENT	SCALE	TOTAL
402	WHITE	336	336
452	YELLOW	385	49
451	LT. YELLOW	398.5	13.5
457	YELLOW/RED	407.5	9
405	BLACK	419	11.5
465	BINDER	790.5	371.5
485	BALANCER	975	184.5

Figure 14-19 Color plotting example.
(Courtesy of General Motors Corporation)

PLOTTING CHART

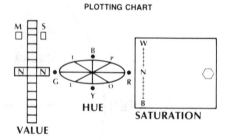

VALUE   HUE   SATURATION

COLOR		CODE	
CODE	MOVEMENT	SCALE	TOTAL

Figure 14-20 Color plotting chart.
(Courtesy of General Motors Corporation)

called out, therefore, it is **high in value**. The *hue* would fall between the yellow and red dimension of the color wheel, closer to the yellow area. The color is highly **desaturated** almost on the white side.

Figure 14-20 is a blank color plotting chart and Figure 14-21 is a blank color evaluation sheet; they could be reproduced in any size and number by a print shop for use by paint jobbers, paint shops, vocational training schools, and individuals.

COLOR EVALUATION

Color Code _____ Color Name _____ WA # _____

Compared to Vehicle Color, Sprayed Material is: _____

LIGHTNESS:

☐ Light   ☐ OK   ☐ Dark

SATURATION:

☐ Desaturated   ☐ OK   ☐ Saturated

HUE:

☐ Blue   ☐ Green   ☐ Yellow   ☐ Red   ☐ OK

TINT ADDED*	AMOUNT**
_____	_____
_____	_____
_____	_____
_____	_____
_____	_____
_____	_____

AIR PRESSURE AT GUN _____

AMOUNT OF THINNED MATERIAL _____

SOLVENT USED _____

VISCOSITY READING _____

*MUST BE CLEAR COATED TO GAIN COLOR MATCH IF BC/CC MATERIAL
**AMOUNT OF TINTS USED MAY VARY DEPENDING ON BUILD DATE OF VEHICLE

Date: _____   Signed _____

Figure 14-21 Suggested record for spray out test panel color evaluation. (Courtesy of General Motors Corporation)

A painter who can make an accurate color evaluation as outlined in Figure 14-21 has in front of him or her a blueprint for the proper adjustment of any color. This is a real help to the painter.

DITZLER COLOR-BLENDING SYSTEM FOR REPAIR OF STANDARD METALLIC COLORS

If a painter experiences a problem of color matching a standard (single-phase) metallic color that is a slight mismatch and is not too objectionable, the problem could be solved satisfactorily with the Ditzler Color-Blending System. This is an acrylic lacquer repair system that is suitable for the repair of all single-phase automotive finishes. The system consists of applying the problem color to a complete panel and then blending the same color into adjacent panels according to the following procedure. For products needed, see Table 9-1.

> NOTE: Although this is a Ditzler-developed system, this principle of color blending is not entirely new to the trade. The same procedure can be used with other leading paint suppliers' equivalent products. However, successful repairs involve **a color that is not too far off-color,** a good color eye, and expert blending techniques.

Procedure

1. Prepare a complete panel, such as a door or front fender, for color coating. Before masking:
    a. Clean, compound, and reclean all adjacent panels for a distance of 1 or more feet (Fig. 14-22). This will be the blending area. Use paint finish cleaning solvent (Table 6-1) and a wheel or hand-rubbing compound (Table 11-1). Clean surfaces with solvent before and after compounding.
    b. Mask off adjacent panels (Fig. 14-23).

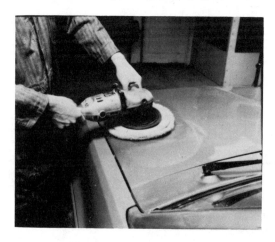

Figure 14-22 Compounding adjacent surfaces for color blending. (Courtesy of Ditzler Automotive Finishes, PPG Industries, Inc.)

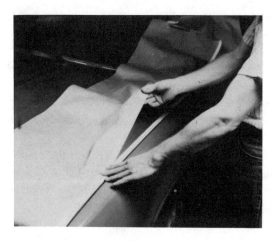

Figure 14-23 Masking for complete panel painting. (Courtesy of Ditzler Automotive Finishes, PPG Industries, Inc.)

2. Agitate, reduce, and apply color according to label directions with conventional spray technique for complete hiding.

3. Remove the masking from adjacent panels and check the color match.

4. Using the same spray gun, color reduction, air pressure, and spraying technique, **blend two to three wet coats** of the same repair color into adjacent panels as follows:

  a. Always spray **toward** new paint (Fig. 14-24).

  b. **Feather** the color application **at the beginning of each stroke** a convenient distance away and apply wet color coats up to the newly painted panel.

  c. Start each color coat beyond the previous coat.

  d. Leave an uneven outer edge by staggering the start of each coat.

  e. **Do not use a banding technique at blend areas.**

5. Prepare blending clear as follows:

  a. **Use 1 part original reduced color.**

Figure 14-24 Initial blending of repair color on adjacent surfaces. (Courtesy of Ditzler Automotive Finishes, PPG Industries, Inc.)

    b. Add an equal amount of clear acrylic lacquer (see Table 9-1).

    c. Add 200% of acrylic lacquer mist coat material (DXA-100) (see Table 9-1). Mix thoroughly.

6. Apply blending clear coats to the outer edges of the complete repair (Fig. 14-25), not too dry and not too wet, until a mismatch of any type disappears. This involves enlarging the repair area slightly. Allow flash time between coats.

7. Reduce clear acrylic lacquer 200% with acrylic lacquer mist coat material (DXA-100) (see Table 9-1).

8. Apply two to three full wet coats of reduced clear over the entire area. Apply reduced clear beyond the edge of the newly painted area (Fig 14-26).

9. Allow a normal drying time (overnight or force-dry 30 minutes at 180°F). Compound and polish. Figure 14-27 shows the completed job.

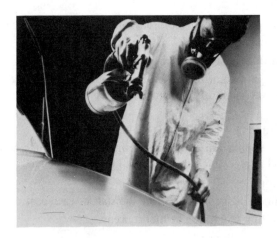

Figure 14-25 Application of tinted clear on adjacent surfaces. (Courtesy of Ditzler Automotive Finishes, PPG Industries, Inc.)

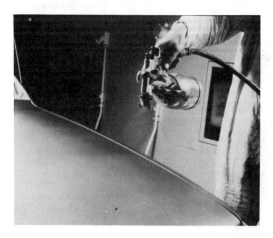

Figure 14-26 Application of clear acrylic lacquer to entire repair area. (Courtesy of Ditzler Automotive Finishes, PPG Industries, Inc.)

Figure 14-27 Final job after compounding. (Courtesy of Ditzler Automotive Finishes, PPG Industries, Inc.)

REVIEW QUESTIONS

1. What is the best way to check out a refinish color when color matching problems are suspected?
2. Before going to the trouble of tinting a color, the painter must be certain that the color variation is not due to what four common items over which he or she has control?
3. Name three variables over which a painter does not have control. (It is assumed in this case that the painter does not own the shop.)
4. Name five common causes of color mismatches.
5. Inspection of a paint finish is done in proper lighting conditions from what two angles?
6. Explain how a person sees color.
7. What are the three primary colors?
8. Name three secondary colors.
9. Describe the **VALUE** of a color.
10. Describe the **HUE** of a color.
11. Describe **SATURATION** of a color.
12. Describe the BRYG wheel.
13. Describe the Munsell Color Tree.
14. When tinting a color, what is the first quality that should be adjusted?
15. When tinting a color, what is the second quality that should be adjusted?
16. What four major colors will adjust the hue of any color mismatch?
17. Pair up each description number with the proper color dimension that it describes:

    Hue _____ 1. The strength or intensity of a color

    Value _____ 2. A specific shade of a given family of color

    Saturation _____ 3. The lightness or darkness of a color

TABLE 14-5 RINSHED-MASON TINTING GUIDE

Color to be tinted	Color is too light — To make color darker, add:		Color is too dark — To make color lighter, add:		Color is too yellow — To make color bluer, add:		Color is too red — To make color greener, add:	
	Acrylic lacquer	Acrylic enamel	Acrylic lacquer	Acrylic enamel	Acrylic lacquer	Acrylic enamel	Acrylic lacquer	Acrylic enamel
Gray								
Metallic	AT-141	MB-451	AT-114	MB-081	AT-122, AT-125	MB-212, MB-251	AT-136	MB-335, MB-351
Solid	AT-141	MB-451	AT-190	MB-961	AT-122, AT-125	MB-212, MB-251	AT-136	MB-335
Blue								
Metallic	AT-141	MB-451	AT-114	MB-081	AT-122, AT-125	MB-212, MB-251	AT-136	MB-335
Solid	AT-141	MB-451	AT-190	MB-961	AT-122, AT-125	MB-212, MB-251	AT-136	MB-335, MB-351
Green								
Metallic	AT-141	MB-451	AT-114	MB-081	AT-125	MB-212, MB-251	AT-136	MB-355, MB-351
Solid	AT-141	MB-451	AT-190	MB-961	AT-125	MB-212, MB-251	AT-136	MB-355, MB-351
Red								
Metallic	AT-141	MB-451	AT-114	MB-081	AT-151, AT-163	MB-633, MB-643	—	—
Solid	AT-141	MB-451	AT-170	MB-961	AT-151, AT-163	MB-633, MB-643	—	—
Maroon								
Metallic	AT-141	MB-451	AT-114	MB-081	AT-151, AT-163	MB-643	—	—
Solid	AT-141	MB-451	AT-170	MB-961	AT-151, AT-163	MB-643	—	—

Color	Finish							
Yellow								
	Metallic	—	—	—	MB-081	—	—	AT-133	MB-335, MB-351
	Solid	AT-141	MB-431	AT-190	MB-961	—	—	—	MB-335, MB-351
Gold, tan								
	Metallic	AT-141	MB-431	AT-114	MB-081	—	—	AT-133	MB-335, MB-351
	Solid	AT-141	MB-431	AT-190	MB-961	—	—	AT-133	MB-335, MB-351
Orange								
	Metallic	AT-141	MB-431	AT-114	MB-081	—	—	—	—
	Solid	AT-141	MB-431	AT-172	MB-961	—	—	—	—
Brown, beige								
	Metallic	AT-141	MB-451	AT-114	MB-081	—	—	—	—
	Solid	AT-141	MB-431	AT-190	MB-961	—	—	—	—
White, cream								
	Metallic	—	—	—	—	—	—	—	—
	Solid	AT-141	MB-431	AT-190	MB-961	AT-125	MB-233	AT-136	MB-335

Courtesy of R-M Automotive Products, BASF Inmont Corp.

Note: This tinting chart is a general guide to assist the user in the selection of tinting bases prior to tinting. However, specific reference should be made to the color chips on the tinting base comparison chart before final selection of bases is made. The color chips represent the strength and shade of each tinting base. See paint jobber for tinting guide with complete tinting base comparison chart.

Table 14-5 (continued)

Color to be tinted	Color is too green — To make color redder, add:		Color is too blue — To make color yellower, add:		Color is too clean — To make color Grayer, add:		Color is too dirty — To make color brighter, add:	
	Acrylic lacquer	Acrylic enamel	Acrylic lacquer	Acrylic enamel	Acrylic lacquer	Acrylic enamel	Acrylic lacquer	Acrylic enamel
Gray Metallic	AT-153	MB-557, MB-633	AT-174	MB-711, MB-765	AT-114, AT-141	MB-083, MB-431	AT-117	MB-085
Solid	AT-153	MB-553, MB-643	AT-174	MB-722, MB-711	AT-141, AT-190	MB-431	AT-190	MB-961
Blue Metallic	AT-120 AT-153	MB-553, MB-643	—	—	AT-114, AT-141	MB-083, MB-431	AT-117	MB-085
Solid	AT-120 AT-153	MB-553, MB-643	—	—	AT-141, AT-190	MB-431	AT-122, AT-125	MB-251 MB-253
Green Metallic	—	—	AT-174	MB-711, MB-765	AT-114, AT-141	MB-083, MB-431	AT-117	MB-085
Solid	—	—	AT-174	MB-711, MB-722	AT-141, AT-190	MB-431, MB-961	AT-136	MB-351, MB-355
Red Metallic	AT-162 AT-153	MB-551, MB-557	AT-172	MB-711, MB-763	AT-114, AT-141	MB-083, MB-431	AT-117	MB-085
Solid	AT-153	MB-553	AT-172	MB-568, MB-722	AT-141, AT-190	MB-568, MB-931	AT-153	MB-553, MB-557
Maroon Metallic	AT-151 AT-153	MB-557	AT-176	MB-711, MB-763	AT-114, AT-141	MB-083, MB-431	AT-117	MB-085
Solid	AT-153	MB-553	AT-176	MB-722, MB-733	AT-141, AT-190	MB-431, MB-643	AT-153	MB-763, MB-568

Color				
Yellow Metallic	AT-170	— / MB-731, MB-763	AT-180 / MB-711, MB-765	— / MB-431	AT-117 / MB-085
Solid	AT-170 / MB-731, MB-733, MB-566	AT-170 / MB-733, MB-566	AT-172 / MB-711, MB-718	AT-141, AT-190 / MB-431, MB-722	AT-172 / MB-714, MB-718
Gold, tan Metallic	AT-176 / MB-731, MB-763	AT-186 / MB-711, MB-765	AT-114, AT-141 / MB-431, MB-083	AT-117 / MB-085
Solid	AT-179 / MB-566	AT-186 / MB-711, MB-722	AT-141, AT-190 / MB-431, MB-566	AT-184 / MB-711, MB-763
Orange Metallic	AT-170 / MB-557, MB-763	AT-180 / MB-711, MB-765	AT-114, AT-141 / MB-083, MB-431	AT-117 / MB-085
Solid	AT-170 / MB-553, MB-566	AT-172 / MB-718, MB-722	AT-141, AT-190 / MB-431, MB-568	AT-184 / MB-731, MB-733
Brown, beige Metallic	AT-176 / MB-557, MB-763	AT-184, AT-174 / MB-711, MB-765	AT-114, AT-141 / MB-083, MB-431	AT-117 / MB-085
Solid	AT-179 / MB-566	AT-174 / MB-711, MB-722	AT-141, AT-190 / MB-431, MB-568	AT-184 / MB-711, MB-722
White, cream Metallic	— / —	— / MB-711	— / MB-431	— / —
Solid	AT-179 / MB-566	AT-174 / MB-722	AT-141, AT-190 / MB-961	AT-190 / MB-961

Courtesy of R-M Automotive Products, BASF Inmont Corp.

Note: This tinting chart is a general guide to assist the user in the selection of tinting bases prior to tinting. However, specific reference should be made to the color chips on the tinting base comparison chart before final selection of bases is made. The color chips represent the strength and shade of each tinting base. See paint jobber for tinting guide with complete tinting base comparison chart.

Note: Where two colors are shown for a given tint, the second color is much stronger than the first. Use proper caution.

TABLE 14-6 SUGGESTED RINSHED-MASON BASIC TINTING COLORS (1 QUART EACH)

ACRYLIC LACQUER SYSTEM (For Alpha-Cryl colors)	ACRYLIC ENAMEL SYSTEM (M-2) (For Miracryl 2 colors)
AT-111 Fine Iridescent	MB-083 Medium Aluminum
AT-112 Sparkle Iridescent	MB-085 Coarse Aluminum
AT-129 Bright Blue	MB-251 Green Blue
AT-138 Green Toner	MB-355 Blue Green
AT-142 Ebony (black)	MB-431 Black
AT-153 Astral Red	MB-551 Brick Red
AT-165 Rich Maroon	MB-553 Bright Red
AT-170 Moly Orange	MB-714 Yellow
AT-171 Yellow Toner	MB-722 Ferrite Yellow
AT-174 Ferrite Yellow	MB-733 Bright Yellow
AT-176 Red Gold	MB-763 Red Gold
AT-192 Pale White	MB-952 White

Notes: These tinting bases are available through paint jobbers so that tinting may be done in shops. Other tinting bases may be added to the basic kits as required. A No. 996 quart hand agitator and pour spout should be supplied for each tinting base to assure color uniformity and to make dispensing easier. Courtesy of R-M Automotive Products BASF Inmont Corp.

TABLE 14-7 DITZLER TINTING GUIDE

Basic Tints needed to do various jobs	Deltron	Delstar	Duracryl
WHITES to lighten	646	401	311
to brighten	610	410	342
to muddy or brown up	623 or 644	476 or 487	382 or 383
YELLOWS, GOLDS AND COPPERS			
to lighten nonpoly colors	646 or 643	401 or 484	311 or 322
to lighten poly colors	631 or 636	431 or 435	323 or 349
to brighten or make deeper color	637, 623 or 644	440, 476, 487	309, 382, 383
to brighten sparkle	635 or 636	435, 436	323, 325
to gray up or fade color	631 or 648	431 or 491	349 or 346
GREENS to lighten nonpoly colors	646, 643 or 644	401, 484, 487	311 or 322
to brighten or lighten poly colors	635 or 636	435, 436	323, 325
to darken or make greener	637 or 648	440 or 491	309 or 346
to darken or make bluer	610	410	342
to darken or make yellower-browner	623 or 644	476 or 487	382 or 383
BLUES to lighten nonpoly colors	646	401	311
to lighten poly colors	631 or 635	431 or 435	323 or 349
to brighten poly colors	635, 636 or 610	435 or 410, 436	323 or 342, 325
to darken or make greener	637 or 644	440 or 487	317 or 382
to darken or make bluer	610 or 648	410 or 491	342 or 346
to darken or add red cast	625	451	360
REDS to lighten or brighten nonpoly colors	646, 643 or 644	401, 484, 487	311 or 322
to lighten or brighten poly colors	631, 635 or 644	431, 435, 487	323, 349, 382
to make orange nonpoly colors	643	484	322
to make orange poly colors	644	487	382
to darken	625 or 623	451 or 476	360 or 383

Courtesy of Ditzler Automotive Finishes, PPG Industries, Inc.

TABLE 14-8 DITZLER BASIC TINTING TONERS

TONERS NEEDED FOR DELSTAR

401	Weak White	410	Organic Blue
431	Poly	435	Large Poly
436	Fine Bright Poly	451	Dark Permanent Red
440	Organic Green	484	Yellow
476	Transparent Red Oxide	491	Weak Black
487	Organic Yellow		

TONERS NEEDED FOR DURACRYL

309	Thalo Green	317	Organic Green
311	White	323	Large Poly
322	Yellow	325	Fine Bright Poly
342	Organic Blue	346	Weak Black
349	Poly	360	Dark Permanent Red
382	Transparent Yellow	383	Transparent Red Oxide

TONERS NEEDED FOR DELTRON

610	Pthalo Blue	637	Pthalo Green (Yellow Shade)
623	Transparent Red Oxide	643	Light Chrome Yellow
625	Quindo Violet	644	Indo Yellow (Red Shade)
631	Fine Aluminum	646	Weak White
635	Very Coarse Aluminum	648	Weak Black
636	Regency Aluminum		

Courtesy of Ditzler Automotive Finishes, PPG Industries, Inc.

15

Identifying and Painting Interior Plastic Parts

HOW PARTS ARE SERVICED

Most automotive interior plastic parts are serviced in one color or in a prime coat to keep the inventory of service parts to a minimum. When these parts are replaced in service and require a different color, they must be repainted. Plastic parts on cars in

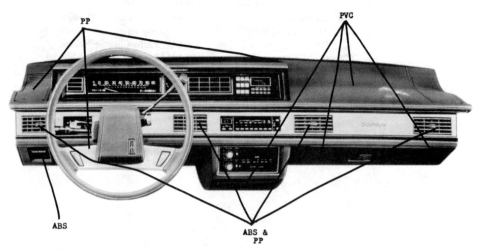

Figure 15-1 Typical use of different plastics on car interiors. **PP**, polypropylene; **ABS**, acrylonitrile-butadiene-styrene; **PVC**, vinyl, also known as polyvinyl chloride. (Courtesy of Oldsmobile Division, General Motors)

service need repainting for many reasons. The most frequent reasons are collision damage involving parts replacement and fading due to excessive exposure to the elements.

A painter must be able to identify each major type of plastic and be familiar with approved paint systems and materials for each plastic in order to do refinish work properly and with maximum durability. Painters become familiar with plastic parts best by working with them over a period of time. Figure 15-1 shows how several different plastics are used on car interiors.

HOW TRIM PARTS ARE COLOR KEYED

The painting of all interior body components is color keyed by the trim combination number on the body number plate (see Chapter 2 for location and description). The first two numbers of trim combination indicate the basic color. Sometimes a basic color is

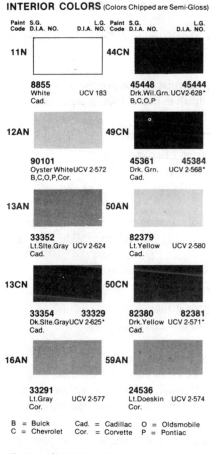

INTERIOR COLORS (Colors Chipped are Semi-Gloss)

Paint Code	S.G. D.I.A. NO.	L.G. D.I.A. NO.	Paint Code	S.G. D.I.A. NO.	L.G. D.I.A. NO.
11N			44CN		
	8855 White Cad.	UCV 183		45448 Drk.Wil.Grn. B,C,O,P	45444 UCV2-628*
12AN			49CN		
	90101 Oyster White B,C,O,P,Cor.	UCV 2-572		45361 Drk. Grn. Cad.	45384 UCV 2-568*
13AN			50AN		
	33352 Lt.Slte.Gray Cad.	UCV 2-624		82379 Lt.Yellow Cad.	UCV 2-580
13CN			50CN		
	33354 Dk.Slte.Gray Cad.	33329 UCV 2-625*		82380 Drk.Yellow Cad.	82381 UCV 2-571*
16AN			59AN		
	33291 Lt.Gray Cor.	UCV 2-577		24536 Lt.Doeskin Cor.	UCV 2-574

B = Buick   Cad. = Cadillac   O = Oldsmobile
C = Chevrolet   Cor. = Corvette   P = Pontiac

*Instrument Panel Color must be sprayed with UCV-69 Low Gloss Clear.

Figure 15-2 Sample portion of Ditzler color chart, showing several GM passenger car interior colors. Actual colors are not shown as this black and white illustration is used only as an example of available material. **Trim code** is shown as "**Paint Code**"; **D.I.A.**, Ditzler interior acrylic color number; **S.G.**, semigloss; **L.G.**, low gloss; **UCV**, Ditzler vinyl color (all vinyl colors are **S.G.**); stock numbers at left of each chip are **S.G.**; stock numbers at right of each chip are **L.G.** (Courtesy of Ditzler Automotive Finishes, PPG Industries, Inc.)

made up of two colors. The third and/or fourth numbers or letters, when used, indicate the trim type and trim design, which is usually one of the following:

1. Cloth and vinyl
2. All vinyl
3. All leather

An example trim combination number is **19 N**. The **19** could mean that the trim color is black. The letter **N** could indicate an all-vinyl interior.

Before using any color on the interior of a car, be sure that the color complies with the trim number as shown on the body number plate and on the paint supplier color chart (Fig. 15-2). Also note if the color chart calls for colors to be low gloss or semi gloss. Color charts sometimes show color chips of trim colors to help the painter identify interior colors more quickly and accurately.

FEDERAL AND FACTORY PAINT STANDARDS

Painting of interior autobody parts is quite different from painting the exterior of a car for several reasons:

1. A federal regulation requires that all components in a driver's vision area be painted with a low-gloss or flat finish to prevent sun glare or sun reflection into the driver's eyes. The parts affected are:
   a. Instrument panel upper section cover
   b. Instrument panel at front of cover
   c. Radio front speaker grilles
   d. Windshield pillars and other parts at the front end

   NOTE: The same principle applies to components around the back window that could reflect sunlight indirectly through the inside rear view mirror. These parts are:
   a. Back window side and lower finishing moldings
   b. Radio speaker grilles
   c. Rear window de-fogger grilles
   d. Rear package shelf trim foundations

2. All other interior painted parts are usually finished with a semigloss finish, which is about a 25- or 30-degree gloss finish, unless otherwise specified, in a color and gloss matching fashion. Normally, when an interior acrylic lacquer is applied in a conventional manner with a medium solvent, the finish is very close to semigloss. Interior semigloss parts are as follows:
   a. Door, headlining, and side wall trim, including parts attached
   b. Arm rests

c. Seat cushions and seat backs, including parts attached

d. Head rests

e. Station wagon and hatch-back-style rear load floors

TESTING QUALITY AND DURABILITY OF PAINT PRODUCTS

Each painter is the paint engineer in his or her particular paint shop. Use only proven and fully tested products in the paint shop. Following this commonsense rule helps paint shops to avoid substandard paint work due to faulty products. The painter usually has enough problems when he or she works with approved materials.

As a reminder to painters, the following are the key properties built into each refinish material as used on the interiors of cars:

Wear and Abrasion Resistance

A painted trim part should look well, clean well, and be normally wear resistant. This means continued durability when exposed to normal service use and continued cleaning without paint failure.

One common failure of a poor paint finish is called **crocking.** Crocking is the wearing off or transfer of paint pigments from the paint to a person's clothing. The condition is caused by poor paint and by a combination of rubbing, pressing, heat, and perspiration. Applying color over a wax surface also contributes to the problem. The condition happens, for example, when a person takes a trip on a hot day and sits on a newly painted vinyl seat cushion. If color transfers onto the clothing, staining or discoloring it, the paint is no good.

Crack Resistance: Flex Test

Good service paint finishes are built to withstand cracking in all types of weather, just as original finishes do. The test for this paint property is:

1. Subject the painted flexible trim part to a temperature of 5° to 20°F **below freezing** for about 30 minutes.

2. Flex the part by bending it in half, if possible, or stretch the part the normal distance that it should stretch.

3. If the paint finish cracks on being flexed in cold temperatures, the paint finish is no good.

Color Fade Resistance

Painted trim parts should show a similar performance to an original car paint finish with respect to fade resistance. One of the greatest enemies of a paint finish is the ultraviolet portion of sunlight. A good paint product has an ultraviolet screener added that cuts off ultraviolet light at the surface so that paint finishes last longer. Upon excessive exposure, both service paint and original finish should fade uniformly. This is a sign of good service paint. If service paint fades excessively before the original color, this is a sign of poor paint.

Proper Adhesion

Equally important to the appearance and color of a finish is its adhesion. A paint finish should not be removable with masking tape. In fact, one test for adhesion is with the use of masking tape.

Adhesion Test. Perform at all edges and at the center of the panel being tested. **Perform the test when the paint is fully dried.**

1. Apply a good grade of masking tape to each area being tested. Apply tape to an area 4 inches wide and 6 inches long, with sufficient tape raised at the edge for a good grip.
2. Pull to remove tape in one fast motion at right angles to the surface, while the panel is supported as required.
3. **If no paint is removed with the masking tape, the adhesion is proper.**

If tiny bits of paint are removed where the finish was **damaged, chipped, or cut,** this is normal. Test labs usually make tape-pull tests over an "X" that has been cut into the paint finish on the panel. However, if large sections of paint, one inch square or larger, are peeled up from the surface, **the paint adhesion is poor.**

Proper OEM Appearance Standards

Service paint finishes should match, look like, and wear like the original paint finish. Good appearance and durability qualities are built into a good paint finish. Therefore, whenever a paint finish is factory approved, the painter knows that the product can be used worry free.

The factors that make up good appearance in a repair situation are:

1. Color match and good blend if spot repair
2. Matching gloss level
3. Matching orange peel level

INTERIOR PLASTIC TRIM PARTS FINISHING

Most paintable plastic interior trim components as used by the automobile industry can be divided into three general categories:

1. Polypropylene plastic

2. ABS plastic, which comes from the words acrylonitrile-butadiene-styrene
3. Vinyl plastic, better known in the chemical trade as polyvinyl chloride or PVC

Almost all plastics as used for automotive interior purposes are made up of these three plastics. Excluding the soft vinyl seat cushion and seat back trim cover assemblies, the plastic used most widely on the interior of auto bodies is polypropylene plastic. It is very important for a painter to be able to identify each plastic in order to paint it satisfactorily. Each plastic requires a different repainting or repair procedure.

Tests for Plastic Identification

The purpose of the following tests is to determine the identity of a given plastic so that proper paint procedures and materials can be used.

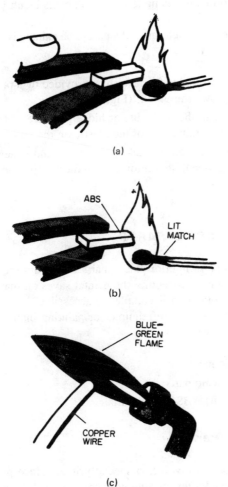

Figure 15-3 Flame test identifies type of interior plastic before painting. (a) Polypropylene. (b) ABS. (c) Vinyl.

Test for Polypropylene and ABS Plastic.   The following is known as a **burn test.** To determine if a particular service part to be painted is polypropylene or ABS plastic, perform the following burn tests:

1. From a hidden back-side portion of the part, remove a sliver of plastic with a sharp blade.
2. While holding the sliver of plastic with tweezers or laying it on a clean noncombustible surface (such as the bottom of a glass bottle or jar), ignite the plastic.
3. Observe the burning plastic closely:
   a. Polypropylene plastic burns with **no readily visible smoke.** It is a clean burn (Fig. 15-3a).
   b. ABS plastic burns with a **readily visible black smoke residue,** which hangs temporarily in the air (Fig. 15-3b). The smoke of ABS plastic looks like an oxyacetylene torch burning when the oxygen is cut off and only the acetylene gas is burning, so this is a definite indication of its identity.

Test for Vinyl Plastic.   To determine if a part to be painted is vinyl plastic (PVC), perform a copper wire test as follows:

1. Heat a copper wire in a suitable flame such as provided by a propane or equivalent torch until the wire glows (turns red) (Fig. 15-3c).
2. Touch the heated wire to the back side or hidden surface of the part being tested in such a manner as to retain some of the plastic on the wire.
3. Return the wire (and retained plastic) to the flame and observe for a green-turquoise blue flame. A flame in this color range indicates that the plastic being tested is vinyl.

PAINTING OF INTERIOR PLASTIC PARTS

The most practical way to paint interior plastic parts is to paint the parts before installation. By following this simple procedure, the painter saves on masking time and does the painting with ease while the part is completely accessible.

Three different paint systems are required for painting interior plastic trim parts, depending on the part and plastic type:

1. Polypropylene plastic parts
2. Rigid or hard ABS plastic parts
3. Vinyl and flexible (soft) ABS plastic parts

Polypropylene Plastic Parts

Painting polypropylene plastics involves a special primer. Since polypropylene plastic is hard, it can be color coated after priming with conventional interior acrylic lacquer.

CAUTION: It is essential that the service part be primed first with a coating of special polypropylene primer (Table 15-1) according to factory recommendations. Failure to use the required primer will result in the color coat lifting and/or peeling.

Painting Procedure

1. Wash the part thoroughly with paint finish cleaning solvent, such as Acryli-Clean, Pre-Kleano, Prep-Sol, or equivalent.
2. Apply a thin, wet coat of polypropylene primer (Table 15-1) according to the label directions. Wetness of the primer application is determined best by observing a gloss reflection of the sprayed primer in proper lighting. Be sure that the primer covers all edges. Allow the primer to flash-dry **1 minute minimum and 10 minutes maximum.**
3. During the flash-time period (1 to 10 minutes), apply conventional interior acrylic lacquer color as required and alow to dry before installing the part. Application of color during the flash-time period promotes best adhesion of color coats.

Rigid or Hard ABS Plastic Parts

Rigid or hard **ABS plastic requires no primer.** Conventional interior acrylic lacquers adhere satisfactorily to hard ABS plastics.

TABLE 15-1 PRODUCTS FOR PAINTING BODY INTERIOR PLASTICS AND OTHER TRIM PARTS

Product	Ditzler	DuPont	Rinshed-Mason	U.S. Body Products
Cleaner for vinyl and cleaning solvent	UK-403, DX-330	3919-S, 3939-S[a]	900	—
Vinyl conditioner	UK-405	—	—	VPC
Interior vinyl trim colors	Trim code and UCV number	Trim code and vinyl mix	Trim code and interior lacquer + 891	Trim code and Vynicolor number
Vinyl clear				
Nonglare	UCV-69	—	—	4000
Semigloss	UCV-71	—	—	—
Interior acrylic lacquer trim colors	Trim code and DIA number	Trim code and lacquer mix system	Trim code and acrylic lacquer number	—
Urethane flex agent for acrylic lacquer	DX-369	350-5	891	—
Polypropylene primer	DPX-800	329-S	864	PP-2250
Flattening compound for nonurethane	DX-265	4528-S (for lacquer)	850	—
Flattening compound for urethane	DX-685	—	—	—
Nonurethane flex agent	DX-1798	—	—	—

Note: Flatten interior colors as required to meet original equipment standards.

[a]Use on GM cars painted with LDL-type acrylic lacquers.

Painting Procedure

1. Wash the part thoroughly with paint finish cleaning solvent (Table 15-1).
2. Apply conventional interior acrylic lacquer color according to the trim combination and paint supplier color chart.
3. Allow the paint finish to dry and then install the part.

CAUTION: Apply only sufficient color for proper hiding. Avoid excessive color application, which could wash out the grain effect.

Vinyl and Flexible (Soft) ABS Plastic Parts

The outer cover material of flexible instrument panel cover assemblies is made of ABS plastic. The same is true of many padded door trim assemblies. The soft cushion padding under ABS covers is urethane foam plastic.

The most widely used flexible vinyls (polyvinyl chloride) are coated fabrics as used in seat trim, some door trim assemblies, headlinings, and sun visors. Most (all-vinyl interior) head rests are covered with flexible vinyls. Examples of hard vinyls are door and front seat back assist handles, coat hooks and exterior molding, and bumper inserts.

The paint system for vinyl and flexible ABS plastic involves the use of **interior vinyl color** and a **clear vinyl top coat. Note:** No primer or primer–sealer is required.

Painting Procedure

1. Wash the surface thoroughly with vinyl cleaner or with paint finish cleaning solvent (Table 15-1).
2. Prepare the vinyl surface for paint with vinyl conditioner according to the directions on the label or as given in this chapter (Table 15-1).
3. Using the proper vinyl color as recommended by the car factory, apply interior color (Table 15-1) according to the label instructions. Apply color in wet coats for complete hiding. Allow sufficient time between coats.
4. Before the final color coat flashes completely, apply one wet double coat of clear vinyl for proper gloss level according to the color chart.
   a. Use a nonglare clear vinyl as described in this chapter for instrument panel and rear window area parts.
   b. Use a semigloss clear vinyl for all other areas.
5. Allow the parts to dry as required before installing them.

NOTE: Apply only enough color for proper hiding and wear to avoid washout of the grain effect.

PRODUCTS FOR PAINTING BODY INTERIOR PLASTIC AND OTHER PLASTIC TRIM PARTS

Table 15-1 is a summary of paint products and systems that are car factory-and/or paint supplier-recommended for repair of all automotive interior paint finishes. Each product and its proper use is explained next. For the availability of each, check with the local paint jobber. If the nearest jobber does not handle a specific item, check with the next-nearest paint jobber. Nearby paint jobbers are contacted most efficiently through the *Yellow Pages* of the phone book.

Vinyl Cleaner (or Paint Finish Cleaning Solvent) (Table 15-1)

Vinyl cleaner is made up of a blend of solvents designed to clean dirt and foreign matter from vinyl painted surfaces. Always use this cleaner or a paint finish cleaning solvent before repainting automotive vinyl surfaces.

Cleaning Procedure

1. Apply the cleaner on the area to be cleaned and allow to set for 30 seconds to 1 minute, depending on soiled condition.
2. Wash the surface with cleaner and a water-dampened cloth as required. Wipe the surface dry with a clean cloth.
3. Use a soft-bristled brush to loosen deeply embedded dirt and to speed the cleaning action.
4. Repeat the cleaning operations if necessary.

Vinyl Conditioner (Table 15-1)

The purpose of vinyl conditioner is to prepare a vinyl surface to be repainted. Vinyl conditioner is made up of a blend of strong solvents that penetrate and soften original vinyl finishes and cause repair vinyl paint to fuse better into vinyl surfaces.

Vinyl Conditioning Procedure

1. Apply vinyl conditioner generously to the surface to be painted with a clean, lint-free cloth. Wipe the conditioner onto the surface with a one-directional wiping motion.
2. Allow the conditioner to remain on the surface for 30 to 60 seconds and wipe off with a clean lint-free cloth while the surface is still wet.

CAUTION: Always wipe in one direction by lifting the cloth on the return stroke and overlapping as required. **Rotate** the cloth as wiping progresses. **Do not rub back and forth.**

3. Repeat these operations as necessary to condition the surface. The surface can be repainted with vinyl color immediately after conditioning is completed.

Interior Vinyl Spray Colors (Table 15-1)

Vinyl spray colors are specially formulated for painting interior vinyl plastic trim parts. In addition to matching interior colors, factory-approved vinyl colors must match two levels of gloss: low and semigloss. Leading paint supplier color charts show how available interior vinyl colors are color controlled to match interior trim codes for repair of all American Motors, Chrysler, Ford, and General Motors cars for current and past model years.

The Rinshed-Mason interior vinyl painting system makes use of a flexible urethane additive, which has been used successfully for years in the refinish trade. It is a hard, flexible coating that needs no top coating with a clear, unless final gloss needs correction.

For availability of vinyl trim colors, check local paint jobbers and paint supplier color charts. Many paint suppliers in addition to those listed in Table 15-1 have vinyl colors on the market for the repair of automotive interiors. For best results in painting vinyl parts, follow the directives of the car factory or vinyl paint supplier.

Interior Clear Vinyl Finishes (Table 15-1)

Clear vinyl finishes are available in two gloss levels for painting interior trim parts: low gloss and semigloss. Instrument panel trim parts can be painted with semigloss vinyl paint and then be finished with a double coat of low-gloss vinyl clear to meet car factory specifications. However, most instrument panel-specified vinyl colors are available in the low-gloss finish.

Application Procedure for Clear Vinyls. Apply clear vinyl of the **proper gloss level** to instrument panel parts, seat cushions, seat backs, head rests, and arm rests as follows:

1. Allow the vinyl color to dry 20 to 25 minutes.
2. Agitate the clear vinyl thoroughly.
3. Apply two conventional wet coats of clear vinyl. Allow flash time between coats.
4. Allow to dry 2 to 4 hours before installing the part or putting into service. Allow to dry overnight before using seat cushions.

Interior Acrylic Lacquer Trim Colors (Table 15-1)

Interior acrylic lacquer colors are matched with the trim combination number. To determine the acrylic lacquer color, check the paint supplier color chart, interior color section. Find the trim combination number on the color chart. The trim number is listed next to or on the same line with the paint supplier color stock number. Note that some colors are designated as flat or LL, which means low luster. Other colors are designated SG, which means semigloss.

Interior acrylic lacquer colors are to be used for painting the following interior parts:

1. Properly primed polypropylene plastic parts
2. Rigid or hard ABS plastic parts
3. Properly primed or sealed metal parts

When used with R-M's No. 891 Urethane Flex Agent according to directions in this chapter, R-M's interior acrylic lacquers may be used to paint interior plastic soft trim parts.

For application of acrylic lacquer trim colors, see "Painting of Interior Plastic Parts."

No. 891 R-M Flex Agent (Table 15-1)

Application Procedure (for Use on Instrument Panel)

1. Prepare the following materials obtained from a R-M paint jobber:
   a. 1 part interior acrylic lacquer (see the trim code)
   b. 1 part No. 891 Flex Agent
   c. Add 10% to 15% (by volume) R-M No. 850 Flattening Compound
   d. $\frac{1}{2}$ part PNT 90 lacquer thinner
2. Mix thoroughly and strain into a paint cup.
3. Spray out several coats of color on a sample panel to achieve hiding. Allow the necessary flash time between coats.
4. Allow to dry 20 minutes to $\frac{1}{2}$ hour and check for a gloss match to the car. Adjust to a final flat gloss, if necessary.
5. Apply necessary coats to the instrument panel cover for complete hiding and color match, as required.

   NOTE: Use the same procedure for painting semigloss side wall trim parts with one exception: use only up to 5% flattening compound.

Polypropylene Primer (Table 15-1)

Polypropylene primer is an **essential primer** that was specially developed for use on polypropylene plastic parts for adhesion purposes. **Essential means that it must be used or there will not be proper adhesion of paint.** There is no substitute primer for use in painting polypropylene plastic surfaces.

Application Procedure

1. Wash the surface to be painted thoroughly with paint finish cleaning solvent.
2. Agitate the primer thoroughly, as required. A steel ball in aerosol containers helps to speed agitation. Primer is also available in 1-quart and 1-gallon containers.

3. Apply two thin but wet coats of primer to the entire panel at package viscosity. No reduction is required. If an aerosol can is used, hold the can 10 to 12 inches from the surface. Check the spray pattern before applying. After use, turn the can upside down and spray for several seconds to clean primer from the valve and fluid feed tube to prevent clogging.

Gloss Flattening Compound (Table 15-1)

Gloss flattening compound is available in two types through leading paint suppliers and jobbers. One type is for nonurethane finishes and the second is for urethane finishes. These compounds can be used to reduce gloss on interior repair colors to match adjacent trim parts.

Procedure for Use

1. Prepare according to the label directions by agitating the compound thoroughly.
2. After color-coating the part and determining that flattening compound is required, add in small amounts, such as 5% at a time, to reduced color and stir thoroughly.

   CAUTION: Some paint materials can take only a certain amount of flattening agent. After that, the paint material loses its durability.

3. Spray out a small sample panel and allow to dry several minutes. Check for the proper gloss level with adjacent parts. Adjust the color with additional flattening compound as required.
4. Apply final one or two color coats to the part as required.

LUGGAGE COMPARTMENT SPATTER FINISHES

For refinishing, the side wall and floor finishes for luggage compartments are made up of a special latex finish and a lacquer color material of one or more colors. The material is water reducible and can usually be applied in one coat. Before applying this color finish, complete all metal repair work and all priming as required.

Application Procedure

1. Keep agitation of the material at a minimum. **Do not shake on a paint shaker.** Some mixing with a paddle may be necessary if the material was on the shelf for a long period of time. Follow the label directions. Also, use a proper respirator.
2. Mask off the car, as required.
3. Open the fluid feed wide open. Open the fan only three-quarters of full open. Also, use the lowest air pressure that causes a spatter spray pattern. This is the opposite of good atomization. This is how the paint is designed to be applied.
   a. For larger spatters, reduce the air pressure.
   b. For smaller spatters, increase the air pressure.

4. Apply one heavy or two medium coats of spatter finish for full hiding. Allow several minutes of flash time between coats. Allow to dry before putting the car into service.

When ordering spatter finish from a paint jobber, two things are important: (1) make of car and (2) model year of car.

REVIEW QUESTIONS

1. In how many colors are paintable plastic parts serviced, as a general rule?
2. How are interior colors of a car identified?
3. At what gloss level are driver's-vision-area trim parts painted?
4. At what gloss level are interior side wall trim parts painted?
5. What is crocking?
6. Describe the flex test that painted interior flexible plastic parts must pass for the plastic paint finish to be acceptable.
7. What chemical ingredient is added to interior and exterior paint finishes to make them color-fade-resistant?
8. Describe the adhesion test that paint finishes on interior plastic must pass to be commercially acceptable.
9. What does the term "factory approved" mean?
10. To paint interior plastic parts, a painter must be able to identify them. Explain the burn test and how it helps to identify the following plastics:
    (a) Polypropylene plastic
    (b) ABS plastic
    (c) Vinyl plastic
11. Describe the procedure and materials required for painting polypropylene plastic.
12. Describe the procedure and materials required for painting rigid or hard ABS plastic parts.
13. Explain the procedure and materials required for painting vinyl and flexible (soft) ABS plastic parts.
14. Explain how to use a vinyl conditioner (Table 15-1).
15. What is the purpose of a clear vinyl finish? In what gloss levels are they available?
16. How are interior vinyl trim colors controlled to match the interiors of cars?
17. Name three categories of parts that can be painted with interior acrylic lacquer colors.
18. Explain how R-M (No. 891) Flex Agent is mixed with color and what interior parts can be painted with this system.
19. What is the procedure for applying polypropylene plastic primer?

16

Painting Flexible Plastic Parts and Vinyl Tops

This chapter deals with (1) **painting flexible exterior plastic parts** according to factory and/or paint supplier recommendations and (2) **painting vinyl** tops according to factory and/or paint supplier recommendations.

PAINTING FLEXIBLE EXTERIOR PLASTIC PARTS

This part of the chapter deals with how flexible exterior plastic parts are designed, how they are painted at the factory, and how they should be painted in the refinish trade.

Design of Flexible Exterior Plastic Parts

Certain car parts are made of flexible plastic to prevent damage to the car or parts whenever these parts are normally flexed under very low speed driving conditions, such as 5 to 10 mph. This incidental contact occurs frequently in heavy city traffic conditions when two cars touch or bump, bumper to bumper, very lightly. The condition also occurs commonly in parking lots when car bumpers lightly contact a barrier post or a wall upon parking.

Location of Flexible Exterior Plastic Parts

Flexible plastic parts are used in the following locations on cars and are painted in car color:

Filler panels.   These are located between the bumper and car. These parts were called filler panels from the beginning because they filled the space between the bumper and the car (Fig. 16-1). Filler panels improve the appearance of a car. Most filler panels are designed to be flexible.

Rear Quarter Extension Panels.   On certain car styles these panels are formed to the contour of the body and attach to rear sections of quarter panels. On many cars, quarter extension panels also house tail lamp assemblies.

Flexible Front End Panels.   These are large, formed flexible panels that finish off the partial or complete front end design on certain sports-style cars.

Urethane and Polypropylene Covered Bumpers.   The steel base bumpers on Corvette and other sports car styles are covered with a flexible, formed urethane or polypropylene plastic and the complete bumper is painted in the car color with elastomeric enamel. This forms a most beautiful and eyecatching styling design.

Elastomeric Paint Finishes

Most original paint finishes on flexible exterior plastic parts are baked elastomeric enamels. The word elastomeric has the same meaning as flexible, rubberlike, and elastic. These words mean that something can be bent, creased, and stretched; and then it can recover its original size and shape without cracking or injury of any type. Flexible plastics are designed to do the same thing without cracking or breaking. Also, elastomeric paint finishes are designed to do the same thing while firmly attached to flexible plastics.

An elastomer is a man-made compound with flexible and elastic properties. The resin system of elastomeric enamels and lacquers is made of these elastomeric compounds.

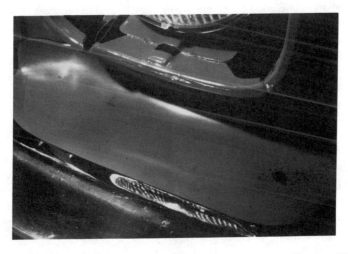

Figure 16-1   Filler panel at front of car with damaged finish shown. (Courtesy of R-M Automotive Products, BASF Inmont Corp.)

Requirements of Flexible Exterior Plastic Paint Repairs

Flexible plastic paint repairs must pass the following tests:

1. **Color match:** The color match between painted flexible parts and the car should be commercially acceptable.
2. **Gloss:** The gloss of the repair panel should match adjacent panels reasonably well.
3. **Crack resistance:** Repair paint finishes should be resistant to cracking as original finishes in all types of weather (see "Crack Resistance: Flex Test," Chapter 15).
4. **Proper adhesion:** Once applied and thoroughly dried, the paint finish should not be removable with masking tape (see "Adhesion test," Chapter 15).
5. **Proper OEM appearance standards:** Service paint finishes should match, look like, and wear like original paint finishes. Good appearance and durability qualities are built into a good paint finish. Therefore, whenever a paint finish is factory approved, the painter is assured that the product can be used worry free.

How Flexible Plastic Parts Are Serviced

Most automotive exterior plastic parts are serviced in one color or in a prime coat to keep the inventory of service parts to a minimum. When these parts are replaced in service and require a different color, they must be painted. Plastic parts on cars in service need repainting for many reasons. The most frequent reasons are collison damage involving parts replacement and fading due to excessive exposure to the elements.

Selection of the Correct Paint Repair System

There are many good elastomeric paint finishes on the market. Table 16-1 shows five of the best systems available. All five are factory approved by most car factories. There are other equally good products available on the market. Unfortunately, there are many substandard products on the market that have a tendency to crack when flexed in cold or even normal temperatures. The painter, as the paint engineer in his or her shop, makes an important decision when selecting a particular paint system. Equally important to selecting a high-quality product is the application of that product.

Exterior Flexible Plastic Parts Finishing

Painting flexible exterior plastic parts can be done with a paint system selected from Table 16-1. All plastics painted at the factory are paint repairable in service. It is best to paint full sections of panels to the nearest breakline, because thorough sanding and cleaning are required to promote adhesion of the repair paint system. Thorough sanding means to remove all gloss.

CAUTION: **Spot repair** of flexible plastic parts **is not recommended.**

TABLE 16-1 PAINT SYSTEMS FOR PAINTING FLEXIBLE EXTERIOR PLASTIC PARTS

Products needed for flexible paint system	Ditzler	Rinshed-Mason	Martin-Senour	Sherwin-Williams	Du Pont
ADDITIVES to make paint flexible	DX-369[a]	891[a]	3084[a]	V2V299[a]	365-B[a] + 792S or 350S
For STANDARD acrylic lacquer or enamel cars	Mix standard acrylic lacquer and flex agent per label directions.				
For STANDARD, baked OEM finishes (optional)	Mix standard acrylic enamel and flex agent per label directions.				
For BASECOAT finishes APPLY STRAIGHT BC COLOR (this includes lacquer and/or enamel basecoat colors)	Do not mix basecoat colors with flex agent.				
FLEX AGENT IS NEEDED IN ALL BASECOAT CLEARS per label directions	Mix clear coating (for BC colors) with flex agent per label directions.				
For TOP-COATING BC lacquer	DCA-468	727	3072	T1C275	380S
Optional	DBC 420/421[a]	893/894[a]	3073[a]	T1C276[a]	580S[a]
For TOP-COATING BC enamel	DBU-60[a]	MC-1000/894[a]	8853[a]	V2V398[a]	780S[a]
Optional	DAU-82[a]				
Optional	DBU-88[a]				
PRIMER for polypropylene plastic	DPX-800	864	6242	P3C24	329S
Primer/surfacer/sealer for flexible plastic parts	DPX-844	HP-100	3061	P1C48	222S

[a]Contains isocyanates. Use recommended respirator protection.
Note: To repair damage extending beyond surface of flexible parts, use **3-M Flexible Parts Repair Material, Part No. 05900.** The repair procedure is in this chapter. Flexible **putty** is **05903**; and flexible **primer–surfacer–sealer is 05905.** 3-M's **polypropylene primer is No. 05907.**

Rinshed-Mason System for Painting Flexible Plastic Parts (Table 16-1)

The painter should order the following to be on hand from a Rinshed-Mason paint jobber:

1. 1 pint Alpha-Cryl or Miracryl-2 color per car paint code
2. 1 pint No. 891 Urethane Flex Agent
3. PNT-90 color thinner or M-2 reducer

Note the damaged and faded condition of the paint before repair (Fig. 16-1).

R-M Application Procedure. Normally, parts are painted before installation. However, if painting is done on the car, it is important that the car be masked off as required.

1. Mask off the car as required (Fig. 16-2).

2. Thoroughly clean the flexible part(s) to be painted with No. 900 Pre-Kleano, a wax and grease remover. An equivalent cleaner may be used (Fig. 16-2).

3. Sand surfaces to be painted with No. 360 or 400 sandpaper (Fig. 16-3) to remove **all gloss from the surface.** Sand the complete panel. Failure to do so impairs adhesion. Spot repairing is not recommended.

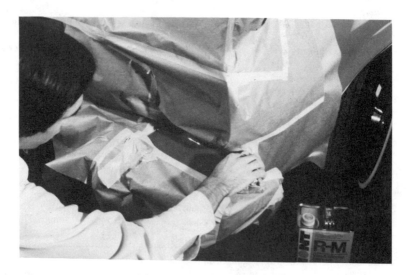

Figure 16-2 View of left front corner of car showing masking and cleaning at filler panel. (Courtesy of R-M Automotive Products, BASF Inmont Corp.)

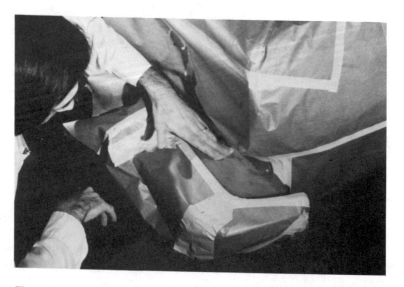

Figure 16-3 Sanding filler panel to remove all gloss. (Courtesy R-M Automotive Products, BASF Inmont Corp.)

4. Reclean the surface with finish cleaning solvent and allow to dry.

5. Prepare R-M flexible paint system as follows (Fig. 16-4):

   a. 1 pint Alpha-Cryl or Miracryl-2 color

   b. 1 pint No. 891 Urethane Flex Agent

   c. $\frac{1}{2}$ pint PNT-90 color thinner

Figure 16-4 Preparing flexible paint material by R-M. (Courtesy of R-M Automotive Products, BASF Inmont Corp.)

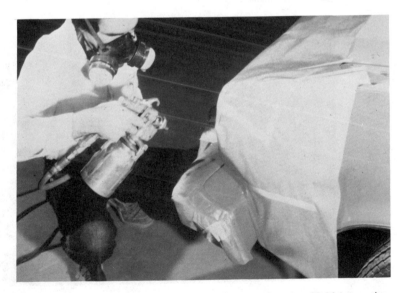

Figure 16-5 Application of flexible color on filler panel. (Courtesy of R-M Automotive Products, BASF Inmont Corp.)

Painting Flexible Exterior Plastic Parts

d. Prepare sufficient volume of color for job. Mix thoroughly and strain into a paint cup.

6. Wearing a NIOSH-approved respirator, apply sufficient color for hiding and color match. Use 25 to 35 psi air pressure at the gun (Fig. 16-5). Allow sufficient flash time between coats.

7. Remove masking after 1 hour (Fig. 16-6). If time permits, allow to dry overnight

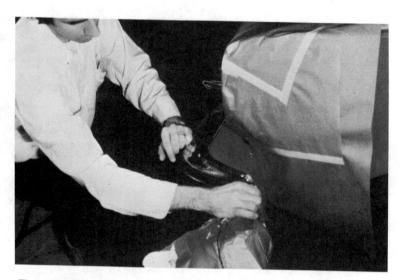

Figure 16-6 Removal of masking at front of car. (Courtesy of R-M Automotive Products, BASF Inmont Corp.)

Figure 16-7 Filler panel at front of car after completion of paint repairs. (Courtesy of R-M Automotive Products, BASF Inmont Corp.)

before putting into service. Figure 16-7 shows the final job after removal of the masking.

8. Clean up the spray gun and cup immediately after use.

NOTE: Reduced material cannot be stored. If a color-matching problem develops, achieve a match as described in Chapter 14.

REPAIR OF CUT OR DAMAGED BUMPER COVER BEFORE PAINTING (A 3M System of Plastic Repair)

When the smooth painted surface of a bumper cover is cut or damaged, the cover can be repaired successfully. Most bumper covers are made of plastics that can be divided into two general categories. Each category requires a special repair system. **System I** is for the repair of **polyurethane (PUR)** and similar plastics. **System II** is for the repair of **polypropylene (PP), ethylene propylene (EP),** and other plastics designated by the initials **TPO** and **EPDM.** The 3M Company's development of Polyolefin Adhesion Promoter (No. 05907) makes possible System II and the repair of previously unrepairable and unpaintable plastic parts. **To identify the type of plastic in a bumper cover so that you can follow the proper repair system use one of the following methods.**

Consult the car manufacturer's zone office service manager or major paint company representative giving the model year, car name, and car series name. Contact the paint jobber for phone numbers to these people.

Locate and read the plastic identification mold marking on the back side of the plastic. This is usually a set of circled initials. For example, **PUR = polyurethane; PP = polypropylene.**

Sand a small area around the damage. **PP plastic has greasy sanding properties.**

Burn a small piece of the plastic. Obtain one or two slivers of plastic from the back side of the part with a sharp blade. **PP type plastic burns smoothly and cleanly** with no noticeable smoke.

System I for Polyurethane and Many Other Plastics

1. Clean the repair area with soap and water, and then clean the complete repair surface with paint finish cleaning solvent. Mask as required.

2. Sand away the damaged area to create a tapered, smooth featheredge (Fig. 16-8). First taper the damage with 36 grit disc. Finish the rough featheredge with 180A grit disc (Fig. 16-9).

3. If backup aid is needed, clean the back side of the plastic and apply a suitable tape, like 3M's Auto Body Repair Tape No. 06935, or equivalent (Fig. 16-10).

4. Mix equal parts of FPRM (Flexible Parts Repair Material) 3M No. 05900 or 05901, Parts A & B) according to label instructions (Fig. 16-11).

5. Apply material to repair area with a squeegee (Fig. 16-12). First, apply a tight

skin coat to the surface. Then build FPRM slightly higher than the undamaged areas. Allow mixture to cure 30 minutes at 60° to 80°F until firm.

6. After curing, rough featheredge the plastic with grade 180A (Fig. 16-13).

7. Apply Flexible Parts Putty, 3M No. 05903, as needed to fill pinholes and sand-scratches (Fig. 16-14). Allow putty to dry 15 to 30 minutes.

8. Sand putty with grade 240A on a soft hand block (Fig. 16-15). Then, using grade 320 (by machine) or 400 (by hand), sand the complete OEM finish on the flexible plastic part to remove 80% to 90% of all gloss to the nearest breakline.

9. Wipe and blow off the repair panel (Fig. 16-16). Mask to paint the complete panel to the nearest breakline. **Spot repair of flexible plastic parts is not recommended.**

10. Apply a double wet coat of Flexible Parts Coating, 3M No. 05905, or R-M's HP-100 to the repair area (Fig. 16-17). Allow 10 to 15 minutes of flash time. Apply a second double coat to the entire panel section. Allow to dry 45 minutes to 1 hour and then sand to desired smoothness with 320A or 400 sandpaper (Fig. 16-18).

11. Clean up spray gun immediately after use; first with water, then with lacquer thinner.

NOTE: If flexible primer/surfacer/sealer product recommended in step 10 is not available, prepare and use a primer-surfacer compatible with a flex agent as recommended by the paint jobber. Mix the primer-surfacer with a suitable flex agent (see Table 16-1) according to label directions. Apply two to three coats to repair area and allow to dry. Sand to desired smoothness with No. 400 sandpaper. **If using a Ditzler system, apply Ditzler's DPX-844** to the repair area and to the complete panel prior to topcoating with color.

12. Prepare color for application as follows (Table 16-1; Fig. 16-19):

    a. **Mix flexible additive with standard acrylic lacquer or enamel** according to label directions.

    b. **Do not use a flex agent in basecoat colors.**

    c. If color match problem is expected, spray out and color match a test panel as explained in Chapter 14 before applying color on car.

    d. **If a basecoat color, apply clearcoat** according to label directions **that includes a flex agent.**

13. Complete the job by cleaning the spray gun and removing the masking.

System II for Polypropylene (PP), EP, TPO, and EPDM Plastics

1. Prepare the surface in the same manner as in steps 2, 3, and 4 of System I.

2. After the initial cleaning, sanding, and masking steps, apply Polyolefin Adhesion Promoter, 3M Part No. 05907, to repair area and allow to dry for 10 minutes.

3. Then mix and apply FPRM (Flexible Parts Repair Material, 3M No. 05900) over

Figure 16-8 Tapering damaged area.
(Courtesy of the 3M Company)

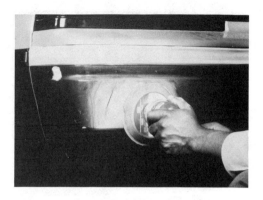

Figure 16-9 Initial featheredging.
(Courtesy of the 3M Company)

Figure 16-10 Backup material. (Courtesy
of the 3M Company)

Figure 16-11 Mixing FPRM A and B.
(Courtesy of the 3M Company)

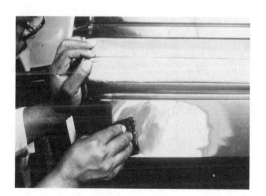

Figure 16-12 Applying FPRM.
(Courtesy of the 3M Company)

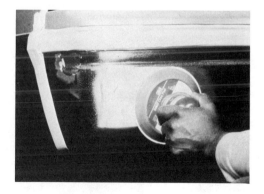

Figure 16-13 Final featheredging.
(Courtesy of the 3M Company)

Repair of Cut or Damaged Bumper Cover Before Painting

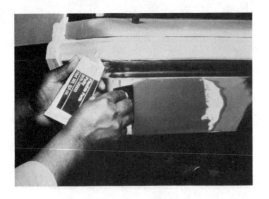

Figure 16-14 FP putty application. (Courtesy of the 3M Company)

Figure 16-15 Sanding the putty. (Courtesy of the 3M Company)

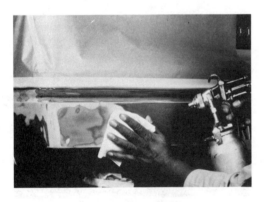

Figure 16-16 Wiping and blowing off repair area. (Courtesy of the 3M Company)

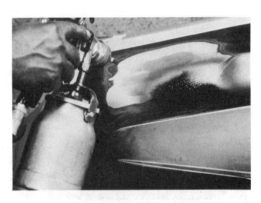

Figure 16-17 Application of flexible primer–surfacer–sealer. (Courtesy of the 3M Company)

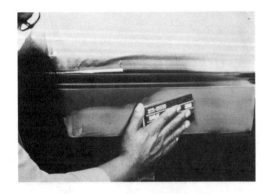

Figure 16-18 Sanding primer–surfacer–sealer. (Courtesy of the 3M Company)

Figure 16-19 Final color application. (Courtesy of the 3M Company)

the Adhesion Promoter in the repair area. Allow the material to cure per label directions and shape the material to contour with 180A. Apply FPRM material as in steps 4, 5, and 6 of system I procedure.

4. Apply a second application of adhesion promoter to the sanded repair area and allow to dry.

5. Apply an additional skin coat of FPRM to the repair to fill any low spots, pinholes, or sandscratches as needed and allow to cure.

6. Sand FPRM with grade 240A sandpaper to desired smoothness. Then thoroughly scuff-sand the complete OEM finish on the plastic part with NO. 320 or 400 sandpaper to remove 80% to 90% of all gloss to the nearest breakline. **Spot repair of flexible plastic parts is not recommended.**

7. Apply a third application of Adhesion Promoter to the plastic-filled and sanded area, and allow to dry.

8. Apply **one double wet coat of Flexible Parts Coating**, 3M No. 05905, **or R-M's HP-100 to the repair area** (Fig. 16-17). Allow 10 to 15 minutes flash time. **Then apply a second double coat to the entire panel section.** Allow to dry 45 minutes to 1 hour. Sand to desired smoothness with No. 400 sandpaper.

9. Clean up spray gun immediately after use: first with water, then with lacquer thinner.

NOTE: If flexible primer/surfacer/sealer product recommended in step 8 is not available, prepare and use a primer-surfacer compatible with a flex agent as recommended by the paint jobber. Mix the primer-surfacer with a suitable flex agent (see Table 16-1) according to label directions. Apply two to three coats to repair area and allow to dry. Sand to desired smoothness with No. 400 sandpaper. **If using a Ditzler system, apply Ditzler's DPX-844** to the repair area and to the complete panel prior to topcoating with color.

10. Prepare color for application as follows (Table 16-1; Fig. 16-19):
    a. **Mix flexible additive with standard acrylic lacquer or enamel** according to label directions.
    b. **Do not use a flex agent in basecoat colors.**
    c. If color match problem is expected, spray out and color match a test panel as explained in Chapter 14 before applying color on car.
    d. **If a basecoat color, apply clearcoat** according to label directions **that includes a flex agent.**

11. Complete the job by cleaning the spray gun and removing the masking. Allow the new finish to dry per label directions before putting the car into service.

TWO IMPORTANT CAUTIONS:

1. **Do not use Polyolefin Adhesion Promoter,** a System II item, **on Polyurethane plastic parts,** a System I item.

2. **Do not use Flexible Parts Putty, 3M No. 05903, on Polypropylene plastic parts.** Putty is for use with System I plastics only.

PAINTING VINYL TOPS

This part of the chapter deals with how to paint vinyl tops in the automotive refinishing trade according to factory and/or paint supplier recommendations.

How Vinyl Tops Are Color Coded

For color identification, factory-installed vinyl tops are color coded on the body number plate (see Chapter 2). Black-and-white tops are self-explanatory for color identification. Production vinyl tops are often color matched to the body color. However, if a vinyl top was installed by a dealer or trim shop after production, the color of the top can be matched in vinyl color paint material by the paint jobber for repair or repainting purposes.

Figure 16-20 is a typical section of a paint supplier color chart showing how a vinyl top color code ties in with paint supplier vinyl color numbers.

How to Order Vinyl Top Colors (Table 16-2)

To order vinyl top color for a car, two things must be known:

1. Make and model year of car
2. Code for vinyl top color (if included on body number plate)

If the code is not known, black and white can be ordered by phone. However, if the vinyl top color is not known, the paint jobber can determine the vinyl color for the car by examining the vinyl top and checking a color chart book.

American Motors does not show vinyl top colors on the body number plate. Use the paint supplier color charts as a comparison reference to determine the color of American Motors vinyl tops. Ford, Chrysler, and General Motors number plates do show vinyl top color codes.

Major Vinyl Top Paint Systems (Table 16-2)

Four of the leading vinyl top paint systems available in the refinishing trade are supplied by (in alphabetical order):

1. Ditzler (part of PPG Corporation)
2. DuPont
3. Rinshed-Mason (part of BASF Inmont Corporation)
4. U.S. Body Products Co. (a privately owned firm)

VINYL ROOF COLORS

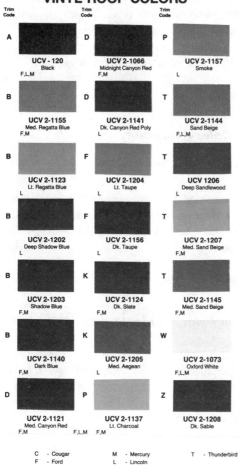

Trim Code		Trim Code		Trim Code	
A	UCV - 120 Black F,L,M	D	UCV 2-1066 Midnight Canyon Red F,M	P	UCV 2-1157 Smoke L
B	UCV 2-1155 Med. Regatta Blue F,M	D	UCV 2-1141 Dk. Canyon Red Poly L	T	UCV 2-1144 Sand Beige F,L,M
B	UCV 2-1123 Lt. Regatta Blue L	F	UCV 2-1204 Lt. Taupe L	T	UCV 1206 Deep Sandlewood L
B	UCV 2-1202 Deep Shadow Blue L	F	UCV 2-1156 Dk. Taupe L	T	UCV 2-1207 Med. Sand Beige F,M
B	UCV 2-1203 Shadow Blue F,M	K	UCV 2-1124 Dk. Slate F,M	T	UCV 2-1145 Med. Sand Beige F,M
B	UCV 2-1140 Dark Blue F,M	K	UCV 2-1205 Med. Aegean L	W	UCV 2-1073 Oxford White F,L,M
D	UCV 2-1121 Med. Canyon Red F,M	P	UCV 2-1137 Lt. Charcoal F,L,M	Z	UCV 2-1208 Dk. Sable F,M

C - Cougar   M - Mercury   T - Thunderbird
F - Ford   L - Lincoln

Figure 16-20 Sample of Ditzler color chart showing Ford Motor Company passenger car vinyl top colors. (Courtesy of Ditzler Automotive Finishes, PPG Industries, Inc.)

TABLE 16-2 PRODUCTS FOR PAINTING VINYL TOPS

Product	Ditzler	DuPont	Rinshed-Mason	U.S. Body Products
Paint cleaning solvent	DX-330	3919-S and 3939-S[a]	No. 900	—
Vinyl prep conditioner	UK-405	—	—	VPC
Vinyl colors for vinyl tops	Exterior color code + UCV number	Exterior color code + vinyl mix number	Standard color code acrylic lacquer or M-2 enamel + 891 + proper solvent	Exterior color code + Vyni-color number

[a]Use on GM cars painted with LDL-type acrylic lacquers.

Painting Vinyl Tops

Usually, one or more of these vinyl top paint systems are available through the local paint jobber. Many additional paint suppliers produce vinyl top colors of equivalent quality to those listed in Table 16-2. Unfortunately, a number of vinyl top paint systems on the market have proved not to be of factory standard quality. It is up to the painter to use good judgment in determining which paint system to use. The paint jobber that provides the best-quality materials and the best service to a paint shop is usually the paint jobber doing the most business.

Vinyl Top Paint System Color Availability

Black and white vinyl top colors are usually available in factory-packaged form ready to use from Ditzler, DuPont, and U.S. Body Products. These colors can be obtained immediately. However, all other vinyl top colors are made up to match production vinyl colors by a mixing machine formula as each color is ordered. Although there may be some basic difference among paint suppliers' products, the suppliers use essentially genuine vinyl colors for vinyl tops.

CAUTION: Vinyl colors come ready to spray and should not be reduced.

Rinshed-Mason Vinyl Top Paint System (Table 16-2)

The Rinshed-Mason vinyl top paint system has been used successfully in the trade for a number of years and is factory-approved. The system makes use of Urethane Flex Agent (No. 891), which is added to R-M acrylic lacquer or M-2 enamel color. This combination makes an excellent vinyl top paint. No color matching is required because the top color already matches the car color. No special primer is required. Once a simple color preparation is completed, the material is as easy to apply as any vinyl top colors. The R-M system produces a flexible, hard film with excellent durability.

Vinyl Top Painting Procedure (for All Paint Systems)

1. Wash the old top with bleach-type household cleanser, a brush, and plenty of water. Rinse the top and car thoroughly in clean water. Figure 16-21 shows a vinyl top before painting. Note the blemishes.
2. Mask off moldings and car as required (Fig. 16-22).
3. Clean the top thoroughly with paint finish cleaning solvent (Fig. 16-23).

NOTE: If using Ditzler or U.S. Body Products system, prepare the top with vinyl prep conditioner (Table 16-2) according to label directions.

4. Prepare vinyl top paint material by mixing thoroughly and by straining into a paint cup (Fig. 16-24).

Figure 16-21 View of vinyl top with problems before painting. (Courtesy of R-M Automotive Products, BASF Inmont Corp.)

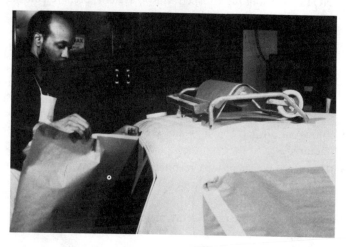

Figure 16-22 Masking off car before painting vinyl top. (Courtesy of R-M Automotive Products, BASF Inmont Corp.)

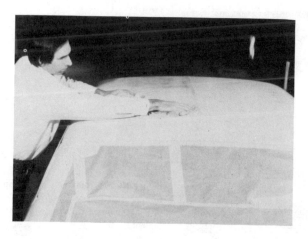

Figure 16-23 Washing and precleaning vinyl top. (Courtesy of R-M Automotive Products, BASF Inmont Corp.)

Painting Vinyl Tops

Figure 16-24 Preparing flexible paint material by R-M. (Courtesy of R-M Automotive Products, BASF Inmont Corp.)

NOTE: If using the Rinshed-Mason system, prepare color as follows:

a. Mix:
1 pint R-M acrylic lacquer or acrylic enamel color
1 pint No. 891 Flex Agent
$\frac{1}{2}$ pint PNT-90 lacquer thinner or M-2 solvent

b. Agitate thoroughly and strain into a paint cup. This preparation will do a complete vinyl top. Follow the label directions. The material has a limited pot life.

5. Blow out all gap spacings and crevices around the top and tack-wipe the top as required.

6. Use a NIOSH-approved respirator when applying the color. With a very small spray fan, apply a small, wet banding coat along all the edges around the complete top.

7. Using a full, wide-open spray pattern, apply a first full-wet coat of vinyl color as follows:

a. Use precautions as required to prevent dripping.

Figure 16-25 Applying vinyl top color from near edge to center of roof. (Courtesy of R-M Automotive Products, BASF Inmont Corp.)

Painting Flexible Plastic Parts and Vinyl Tops *Chap. 16*

b. Control the hose by positioning it over the shoulders and back.

c. Start the color application along the near side and proceed to the center of the top (Fig. 16-25).

d. On the opposite side of the car, start at the center and maintain wet application of color to the near side (Fig. 16-26).

e. Keep the application wet with a full and uniform 50% to 75% stroke overlap.

f. Keep the spray gun as perpendicular to the surface as possible (Fig. 16-26).

g. Apply color to the "sail" and rear quarter areas as required.

Figure 16-26 Applying vinyl top color from center to near edge of roof. (Courtesy of R-M Automotive Products, BASF Inmont Corp.)

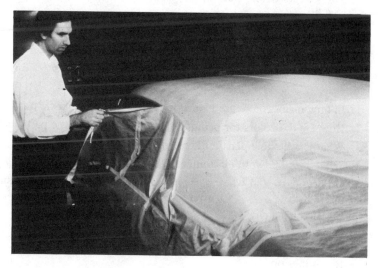

Figure 16-27 Removing masking materials after drying period. (Courtesy of R-M Automotive Products, BASF Inmont Corp.)

Painting Vinyl Tops

Figure 16-28 View of vinyl top after painting is completed. (Courtesy of R-M Automotive Products, BASF Inmont Corp.)

8. Apply a second full-wet coat, starting over as in step 7, for complete hiding and uniformity of wetness.

   NOTE: Any remaining streaks can be removed with an application of mist coat solvent, such as PNT-90 or equivalent reducer, immediately after painting the top.

9. After 1 hour of drying, remove the masking (Fig. 16-27). Allow to dry a minimum of 4 hours before putting the car into service. The finished job is shown in Fig. 16-28.

REVIEW QUESTIONS

1. In how many colors are paintable flexible exterior plastic parts serviced?
2. How are the colors for painting flexible exterior plastic parts identified?
3. What is a flexible plastic filler panel?
4. What does the word elastomeric mean?
5. On new cars, and when painted in service, flexible plastic paint repairs must pass the following tests. Describe each.
   (a) Color match
   (b) Gloss
   (c) Crack resistance
   (d) Adhesion
   (e) OEM appearance standards

6. Explain Rinshed-Mason's system for painting flexible plastics (Table 16-1).
7. What happens when conventional car exterior colors are applied on flexible plastic parts at the same time that the car panels are painted?
8. What happens when flexible plastic paint is applied on car metal panels at the same time that the filler panels are painted?
9. Where are vinyl tops color coded on cars?
10. Explain how to order vinyl top colors for a car.
11. In what forms are vinyl top colors available from paint jobbers?
12. Explain how to prepare the Rinshed-Mason vinyl top paint materials for application.
13. Explain the procedure for painting vinyl tops.
14. Explain the 3M System for repainting **polyurethane** plastic bumper covers after a deep cut damage has been repaired.
15. Explain the 3M System for repairing a cut and damaged **polypropylene** plastic bumper cover before paint operations are done.

17

Paint Conditions

and Remedies

The purpose of this chapter is to familiarize the painter with the identity and description of the more common paint conditions and problems that a painter encounters in the refinish trade. Painters are expected to repair these problems and conditions in a top-quality fashion.

Each paint condition and problem is described and, where helpful, is illustrated. Understanding the cause of a paint problem or condition is vital to the selection of correct repair procedures. Essentially, each paint condition and problem has its own specific repair requirements. The identity of any particular paint problem tells the painter the required repair procedure that must be followed to make a quality repair. The more a painter learns about refinish products, repair systems, and the common problems that are encountered, the more qualified a painter becomes.

A remedy for each paint condition and a prevention system for avoiding paint problems are included where applicable in the following pages. Type of finish affected is shown in parentheses.

ACID AND ALKALI SPOTTING, Fig. 17-1 (Lacquer and Enamel)

This condition can occur on solid or metallic colors in both the acrylic lacquer and enamel finishes, and on basecoat/clearcoat finishes. The condition appears as stained spots appearing in the finish and affects flat or horizontal surfaces mostly. On standard red metallics, spots are darker red; on blue metallics, spots are darker blue; and so on.

400

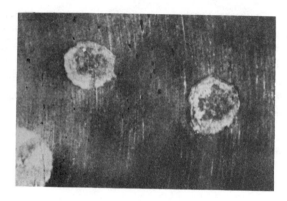

Figure 17-1 Acid and alkali spotting.
(Courtesy of General Motors Corporation)

On solid colors, discoloration spots may be of any color, depending on specific contaminants.

Cause. On metallic colors, the condition apparently is caused by fall-out or moisture in the form of rainwater containing acid or alkaline materials which attack the aluminum flake or clearcoat. On solid colors, specific pigments may be affected by specific materials from fall-out.

Remedy. In mild cases, rub out and polish. In severe cases, sand to remove the condition *completely* and color-coat as required.

Prevention. To prevent recurrence of the condition, apply clear acrylic lacquer or clear urethane enamel to the affected surfaces in accordance with factory specifications (see Table 9-1). Also, keep the paint finish clean and polished.

BLISTERING, Fig. 17-2 (Lacquer and Enamel)

Blistering is the appearance of a number of small, dome-shaped blisters formed in the paint finish. They can range in size from $\frac{1}{16}$ to $\frac{1}{4}$ inch or larger. Blisters are usually grouped together as shown.

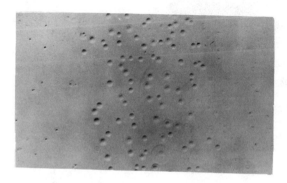

Figure 17-2 Blistering. (Courtesy of General Motors Corporation)

Blistering

Cause.   Blistering is usually caused by moisture becoming trapped within the paint film and then expanding between the metal and the undercoat, or between the undercoat and the color coat, causing different-size blisters to form. The depth of the condition is determined by cutting off a number of blisters and inspecting them and the spots from which they were removed. Inspection determines whether the finish blisters off the undercoats, or if the color and undercoat come off the metal. The painter is guided by knowing the color of the factory and service undercoats.

Remedy.   In minor cases, blisters may be sanded out, resurfaced, sanded, and color-coated. In severe cases, the finish must be removed down to the metal before refinishing.

BLUSHING, Fig. 17-3 (Lacquer)

Blushing is an off-color, milky, or dull mist formation on the surface of freshly applied color.

Cause.   Blushing is caused by a mixture of water with fresh paint as it is applied. The condition is brought about when highly humid air condenses on the surface during spray painting and water mixes with the paint material, causing a kick-out in the paint binder. Rainy or highly humid weather during spray painting is the usual cause of this condition.

Remedy.   *In most cases*, spraying a coat of slow-evaporating solvent with 10% to 20% retarder immediately over the affected area will dissolve the blushed condition and restore the normal appearance of the finish. *If blushed color dries*, add retarder to the reduced material and apply a final extra-wet color coat as required.

Prevention.   Keep the paint and car at room temperature. Use good-quality thinner. Use the required amount of retarder when spraying in high humidities and warm temperatures.

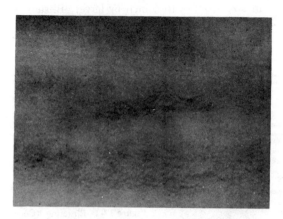

Figure 17-3   Blushing. (Courtesy of General Motors Corporation)

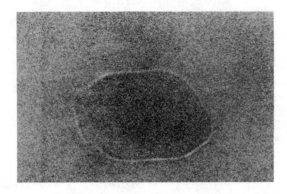

Figure 17-4 Bull's-eye. (Courtesy of General Motors Corporation)

BULL'S-EYE, Fig. 17-4 (Lacquer and Enamel)

This appears as a spotted, ringed outline or low area in the color coat. It often gives the illusion of a different color, depending on the reflection of light and shadows in the area. The primer might show.

Cause. A bull's-eye is the result of poor featheredging and/or poor spot-repair technique. Contributing causes are poor primer-surfacer sanding technique and/or undercoat shrinkage after the color was applied.

Remedy. In very minor cases, sand with No. 500 or 600 sandpaper, rub out, and polish. In severe cases, on standard colors, sand and featheredge the area correctly; build up the surface with primer-surfacer as required; and spot-blend color to match the adjacent surfaces.

Prevention. Use the guide coat sanding system (see Chapter 8), particularly when sanding small spots on enamels. Also, use the correct spot repair technique.

CHALKING (Lacquer)

Chalking appears as a loss of gloss and a powdery surface on standard colors. Eventually, the surface becomes flat and powdery.

Cause. Chalking is the natural breakdown of paint film by prolonged weathering. Ultraviolet light from the sun, together with moisture, are the greatest enemies of a paint finish. Breakdown of any paint binder system starts at the outer surface.

Remedy. Remove a light chalking condition simply by polishing the car to restore the original gloss. If chalking is severe, compound and polish the surface to restore gloss and appearance. If chalking returns abnormally quickly, re-color-coat the car as required; or compound color and apply suitable urethane clear coating.

Prevention. Agitate the paint thoroughly and use balanced solvents when applying color. Keep the car on a regular cleaning and polishing schedule. Use clear urethane coating.

Chalking **403**

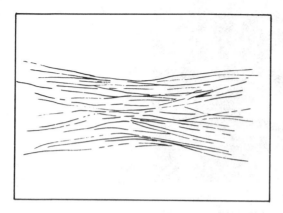

Figure 17-5 Checking and cracking. (Courtesy of General Motors Corporation)

CHECKING AND CRACKING, Fig. 17-5 (Lacquer and Enamel)

This condition is also known as line checking and/or cracking. The condition appears as a series of long, straight lines, usually traveling with the direction of a panel. Sometimes lines are curved, going in various directions. Depending on the thickness of the color and the severity of the condition, the lines may be quite short or as long as 18 inches.

Cause. The condition is usually due to excessively thick color coats or application of a new color over an old color that was cracked and not completely removed.

Remedy. Remove the cracked color coat from the affected area to the original undercoat and recolor coat as required. On standard acrylic lacquer colored cars, original undercoats are not affected by line checking.

Prevention. Paint shops should know how much total paint thickness is applied to every paint job. This can be determined with a paint thickness gauge described in ''Paint Thickness Limit,'' Chapter 9.

MICRO-CHECKING, Fig. 17-6 (Lacquer)

When observed normally, micro-checking appears as severe dulling of the paint finish, with little or no gloss. However, when examined with a magnifying glass, 5× to 7× power, the condition appears as a high volume of very small cracks in the paint surface. The cracks do not touch one another.

Cause. Micro-checking is the beginning of paint film breakdown. The condition apparently is caused by the ultraviolet rays of the sun.

Remedy. Completely remove the affected color coat and re-color-coat as required.

Prevention. If primer-surfacer is required in a repair situation over a finish with

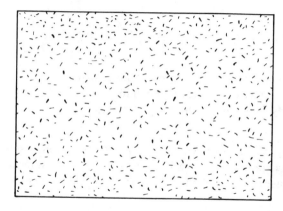

Figure 17-6 Micro-checking (magnified seven times). (Courtesy of General Motors Corporation)

micro-checking or very fine crazing, use a water-base primer-surfacer like R-M's 806 Barrier Coat or HP-100 Nova-Prime. This solves the checking problem.

CRAZING, Fig. 17-7 (Lacquer)

Crazing usually appears as a fine spider-web type of cracking in the color coat. The cracks may vary from very fine (requiring a magnifying glass to see) to relatively coarse. The crack lines connect to each other. Crazing sometimes occurs immediately after repairs are attempted.

Cause. Crazing occurs when excessive stresses, which occasionally may be set up in a paint color film during the time it cures, are suddenly released. The condition may occur when repairing acrylic lacquer that was used in a previous repair and has gone through a curing process for a period of time.

Prevention. Before repairs are attempted, test the acrylic lacquer color **(to be repaired with acrylic lacquer)** as follows:

1. Apply a *drop of repair lacquer thinner* to the surface to be repaired.

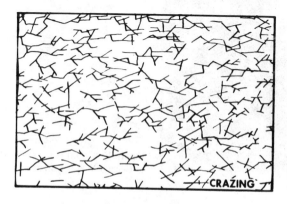

Figure 17-7 Crazing. (Courtesy of General Motors Corporation)

Crazing

405

2. Allow the thinner to evaporate.

3. Inspect the *paint surface within the thinner ring* for crazing.

A lack of crazing indicates that the paint surface **can be color-coated** or blended into normally. The **appearance of crazing within the thinner ring indicates the color cannot be repaired directly with the acrylic lacquer system.**

Option 1: If repairing with acrylic lacquer, use a water-base primer-surfacer like R-M's 806 Barrier Coat or HP-100 Nova-Prime according to label directions. After sanding, acrylic lacquer can be applied with no problem. This solves the stripping problem.

Option 2: To avoid removal of acrylic lacquer that would craze with a lacquer repair, make the panel repair with catalyzed acrylic enamel or acrylic urethane finish.

Remedy. If a panel surface to be repaired already has the crazing condition severely, remove the complete affected color coat from the factory undercoat and color-coat as required.

DIRT IN THE FINISH, Fig. 17-8 (Lacquer and Enamel)

Freshly painted surfaces with this condition show an uneven grittiness from flying dirt particles, foreign matter, and lint that have landed **on** or **in** the paint during spray painting.

Figure 17-8 Dirt in the finish. (Courtesy of General Motors Corporation)

Cause. Generally, the condition is caused by dirt coming from one or more of the following sources:

1. The car is dirty.
2. The paint is dirty.
3. The atomizing air is dirty.
4. The working area is dirty.
5. Poor spraying techniques.
6. Lint on clothing.
7. Static electricity.
8. Improper operation of the paint booth.

NOTE: For an in-depth look at the cause, see the special Binks summary on the causes of dirt in the finish at the end of the chapter.

Remedy. To repair the surface in minor cases, compound and polish as required. In severe cases, water-sand lightly with No. 500, 600, or finer sandpaper, then compound and polish.

DRY SPRAY (Fig. 17-9) (Lacquer and Enamel)

This condition is easily distinguished by a certain uniform, fine grittiness and dullness. It is usually in a linear pattern or in the direction of spray gun travel.

Cause. The condition is usually caused by holding the spray gun on an angle or too far from the surface. The condition can also be caused by insufficient solvent, excessive air pressure, a dirty spray gun, or spraying in a draft.

Remedy. In minor cases, rub out and polish as required. In severe cases, water-sand with No. 400 and/or 500 sandpaper and color-coat as required.

Figure 17-9 Dry spray. (Courtesy of General Motors Corporation)

ETCHING (Lacquer)

Etching is a very severe form of water spotting in which the entire paint surface within the periphery of each spot is etched or eaten away. The condition may appear as small or large water spotted areas and usually appears on the flat or horizontal surfaces. Etching penetrates much more deeply into the finish than in water spotting.

Cause.   The condition may be caused by bird droppings, insects, or contaminants, in which case a strong chemical deposit is allowed to react with the finish for a prolonged period of time.

Remedy.   If the condition is mild, sand to remove the condition and color-coat as required. If the condition is severe, sand to remove the condition, and apply undercoats and color coats as required.

Prevention.   The best prevention against this condition is to keep the paint surface clean and polished. A double coating of clear urethane enamel offers excellent protection against this condition.

FISHEYES (Fig. 17-10) (Lacquer and Enamel)

The appearance of small, round, craterlike openings in the finish immediately after it has been applied.

Cause.   Application of color coats over a surface contaminated with silicones.

Prevention

1. Clean the surface with wax and a silicone-removing agent such as Prep-Sol, Pre-Kleano, Acryli-Clean, or equivalent (see Table 6-1).
2. Sand the surface as required.
3. Reclean the surface with a silicone-removing agent.
4. Proceed with the color coat application.
5. If the preceding prevention steps are not successful and fisheyes appear upon ap-

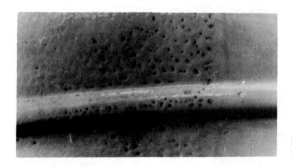

Figure 17-10 Fisheyes. (Courtesy of the DuPont Company)

plication of the first coat, add fisheye eliminator, known as Fish-Eye-Preventor, Fish-Eye-Eliminator, or equivalent, (see Table 10-1) to the reduced color according to paint supplier directions, and continue color-coating immediately.

Remedy. To repair a paint surface with a dried fisheye condition, sand the surface smooth and color coat as required, incorporating the previous prevention steps.

LIFTING OF ENAMELS (Fig. 17-11)

1. Raising and swelling of the wet film
2. Peeling when surface is dry

This condition also looks like puckering and crinkling.

Cause. Lifting is caused by solvents in a refinish paint attacking a previously painted surface. The following are additional causes:

1. Improper drying of previous coating
2. Sandwiching enamel between two lacquer finishes
3. Recoating improperly cured enamel
4. Spraying over unclean, incompatible surfaces

Remedy. Remove the lifted paint finish and refinish as required.

Prevention

1. Clean old surfaces thoroughly.
2. Allow all subcoats full drying time.

Figure 17-11 Lifting of enamels.
(Courtesy of the DuPont Company)

Lifting of Enamels

3. Seal old finishes.
4. Avoid the use of acrylic lacquers over uncured air-dried enamels.
5. Avoid the sandwiching of an enamel coat between two lacquer coats.

MOTTLING (Fig. 17-12) (Lacquer and Enamel)

Mottling appears as dark, shaded, or off-color spots and streaks in the paint finish. This condition occurs primarily in metallic finishes. A moderate amount of mottling is to be expected in metallic finishes as a standard condition.

Cause. Metallic colors are made from a combination of different pigments and aluminum flakes that have different weights and particle sizes. When the film is sprayed extra wet, the paint ingredients have a natural tendency to separate and float into groups when the film is in a liquid state. Under normal conditions, this tendency is small in magnitude and cannot be seen by the naked eye.

Certain conditions aggravate this to a point where the separation of the pigments and metallic flakes becomes visible. The conditions are caused by using solvents that dry too slowly; allowing pigment particles to migrate; applying color on a cold surface or in a cold room; or applying color coats too wet.

Remedy. In minor cases, no correction is required. In severe cases, perform the following operation:

1. Allow the applied color to flash thoroughly.
2. Apply additional color to the affected area in a *fog-coat* fashion to remedy the condition as follows (see "Fog Coating," pages 76 and 95).
   a. Apply color from 18 to 20 inches distance with a full spray fan and continually swirling movement until the condition disappears.
   b. Apply a mist coat solvent as required to bring the repair to the proper gloss. Use the same solvent as used in the painting operation.

Figure 17-12 Mottling. (Courtesy of General Motors Corporation)

OFF-COLOR (Lacquer and Enamel)

The color is off shade or does not match.

Cause. There are any number of reasons why a repair color does not match a car. Three conditions that can cause off-color at the factory are **balling, bending,** or **shearing** of the metallic flakes. Other causes at the factory are **overbaking** or **underbaking** of the finish and breakdown of the ultraviolet screener. Off-color due to field repair problems are poor jobber mix, unstable tints, improper spray techniques, and the spray painting variables (temperature, humidity, and ventilation). There are additional causes.

Remedy

1. Determine the specific color-matching problem according to Chapter 14.
2. Make the necessary color adjustments through spray technique or tinting to achieve the best color match on a spray-out test panel.
3. Make the same acceptable color-match repair on the car.
4. If necessary, blend the best developed or tinted color-matching material into the adjacent areas or panels with the Ditzler Color Blending System described in Chapter 14.

EXCESSIVE ORANGE PEEL (Fig. 17-13) (Lacquer and Enamel)

Orange peel is a natural occurrence in refinishing in which the resultant finish has uneven formations on the surface similar to those of an orange. A certain amount of orange peel occurs in normal refinishing and is acceptable. When a surface becomes extra coarse or rough with orange peel and becomes a distraction, this is considered excessive orange peel.

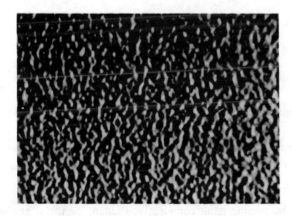

Figure 17-13 Excessive orange peel. (Courtesy of the DuPont Company)

Cause. Excessive orange peel is actually a defect of flow or leveling. This condition is brought about by any one or a combination of the following:

1. Using the wrong type or a poor grade of solvent
2. Insufficient reduction of color
3. Too high an air pressure
4. Improper adjustment of spray gun
5. Poor spray gun technique: holding gun too far from or too close to the surface
6. Spraying in a draft
7. Coats applied too dry and thin
8. Cold shop or metal temperatures.

Remedy. If the condition is slight, no remedy is necessary. If the condition is excessive, clean, sand (with fine sandpaper), compound, and polish the affected area.

OVERSPRAY (Lacquer)

The appearance of a rough or dull paint finish, similar to dry spray.

Cause. Overspray is caused by the settling of semidry paint particles on adjacent finished and unprotected surfaces during spray painting operations.

Remedy. If the condition involves the same color, compound and polish the affected area when dry. If the condition involves two colors but is slight, compounding and polishing may eliminate the condition. If the condition is severe, sand and color-coat as required.

Prevention. Proper masking and/or covering.

PEELING (Fig. 17-14) (Lacquer and Enamel)

Peeling is the separation of a paint film from the surface in sheet form.

Cause

1. *Not cleaning and sanding* original factory acrylic enamel thoroughly before painting
2. *Not using recommended sealer* on original factory acrylic enamel before color coating
3. *Not cleaning and sanding* flexible exterior plastics thoroughly before color coating
4. *Not using required primer* on polypropylene plastic parts before color coating
5. Incompatibility of the repair coat with the previous coat

Remedy. Remove the peeling paint completely. Prepare the metal and/or other surfaces as required to correct the cause, and refinish with a compatible paint system.

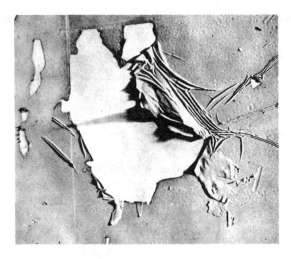

Figure 17-14 Peeling (poor adhesion). (Courtesy of R-M Automotive Products, BASF Inmont Corp.)

Prevention

1. Thoroughly clean and treat old surfaces.
2. Use the required primer and/or sealer.
3. Follow the recommended refinish practices.
4. Use compatible repair systems.

PINHOLING (Fig. 17-15) (Lacquer and Enamel)

Pinholing is a series of tiny, fine holes or pits that give the surface a spotty, dull, or off-shade appearance.

Cause. This condition is usually caused by trapping solvent or air in the paint film and then subjecting the paint to sudden high temperatures such as in force-drying.

Figure 17-15 Pinholing. (Courtesy of General Motors Corporation)

Remedy.   Sand down the surface with appropriate sandpaper to remove the problem, and then color-coat as required.

Prevention.   Allow plenty of flash time before subjecting freshly painted parts to force-drying. This depends on the solvents used and the shop temperatures.

RUB-THROUGH (THIN PAINT) (Fig. 17-16) (Lacquer)

Rub-through or thin paint conditions are easily evident because the undercoat shows through the top coat.

Cause.   The usual cause of this condition is excessive compounding that removes the paint film. Too coarse a compound and/or negligent use of the polishing wheel is often the cause of this condition. The condition may be caused by insufficient color application in a repair situation. Most rub-through conditions occur at panel edges when panel edges protrude above the surface.

Remedy.   For panels, clean the affected panel and color-coat as required. If edges or creaselines are thin, touch up with a brush as required.

Prevention.   Before compounding, apply $\frac{1}{2}$- or $\frac{3}{4}$-inch masking tape to all high panel edges and sharp panel creaselines. After compounding, remove the tape and rub out these areas very carefully by hand.

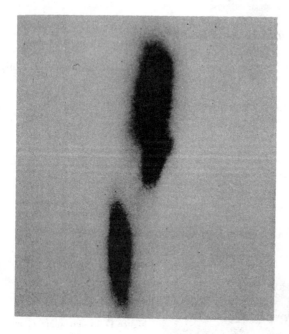

Figure 17-16   Rub-through (thin paint). (Courtesy of C.I.L. Paints, Inc., of Canada)

RUNS OR SAGS (Fig. 17-17) (Lacquer and Enamel)

Extra-heavy spray application of paint results in flooding the surface. Excess paint will first sag like a curtain and then turn into narrow runs that flow with gravity until excess paint runs out (see "Spray Gun Adjustments," Chapter 4).

Cause. This condition is caused by one or a combination of the following:

1. Spray gun out of adjustment.
2. Holding the spray gun too close to the surface.
3. Not triggering the spray gun properly on the return stroke.
4. Not observing the applied color (due to poor lighting) and reapplying color to the same spot, flooding it.
5. Forgetting where clear coating was last applied and reapplying clear to the same spot, flooding it. Poor lighting also contributes to this condition.

Remedy

1. If the circumstances are right, brush out a minor run problem with a suitable brush, and continue spraying.
2. If enamel, wash out the condition carefully. Blend the edges with a dry spray as required, and continue spraying (see Chapter 4).
3. If lacquer, allow to dry, sand out, and re-color-coat.

Prevention

1. Use the correct spray gun adjustment and application technique.
2. **Observe** the application of every spray painting stroke and follow the progress of spray painting closely to the completion of the job.
3. Allow sufficient flash time after each coat.

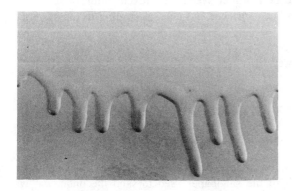

Figure 17-17 Runs or sags. (Courtesy of the DuPont Company)

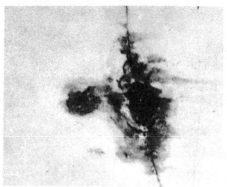

Figure 17-18 Rust spots and rusting. (Courtesy of C.I.L. Paints, Inc., of Canada)

RUST SPOTS AND RUSTING (Fig. 17-18) (Lacquer and Enamel)

Rust spots are usually accentuated by a rust-colored ring that forms at the affected area. Rusting beneath the film is usually made apparent by raised sections of film or blisters. After the film or blisters have broken, the rust begins to work back under the edges of the film. Since many primers are similar to rust in color, careful examination is necessary to identify minor rust conditions accurately. Major rust conditions are easy to identify.

Cause. Rust starts with moisture and chemicals attacking the metal through large or microscopic breaks in the paint film. An early stage of rusting is blistering, which, if unchecked, proceeds to peeling. Other causes are painting over rust that was not completely removed, painting over metal touched by bare hands, or painting over chemical deposits from sanding water.

Remedy. In minor cases where the paint is not blistered, wash the panel and clean the rust stain off with body polish or a mild rubbing compound, hand-applied; then protect the finish with an application of wax. In severe cases, remove the complete finish and rust from the affected area with sandblasting or a special cutting tool. **If surface rust, sand the metal clean and bright to remove all traces of rust.** Treat bare metal surfaces with a two-part metal conditioner according to label directions (Table 6-2). Prime the bare metal with the best primer system to prevent future rust (Table 8-1). Complete application of the primer–surfacer and color according to the system that is best for the car.

Prevention. See Chapter 18.

SAND OR FILE MARKS (Fig. 17-19) (Lacquer and Enamel)

After a metal and paint repair job dries, the surface is grained or scratched.

Cause. Coarse file, disc, or sandpaper marks in the metal, solder, or plastic filler before painting. Also, the grit of the sandpaper used to sand the undercoat was too

Figure 17-19 Sand or file marks.
(Courtesy of General Motor Corporation)

coarse. With present-day primer–surfacers, best results are achieved with No. 400 sand-paper.

Remedy.   Minor sand marks or scatches on the color coat may be lightly sanded with No. 500 or 600 sandpaper and water and compounded to achieve a repair. In severe cases, sand and refinish as required. See Figs. 8-11 and 8-12.

SANDSCRATCH SWELLING (Fig. 17-20) (Lacquer)

Sandscratch swelling appears as exaggerated sandpaper scratches and occurs mostly after spot repairs or panel refinishing are done over sanded original acrylic lacquer finishes. The condition is most apparent on dark colors.

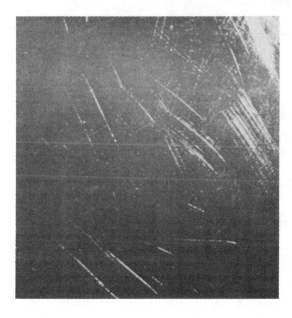

Figure 17-20   Sandscratch swelling.
(Courtesy of C.I.L. Paints, Inc., of Canada)

Cause. The condition is caused by sanding acrylic lacquer surfaces with too coarse a sandpaper preparatory to color coating. The thinner in the fresh color coats swells the scratches to an enlarged size.

Prevention. Do not sand acrylic lacquers unless required. When sanding with coarse sandpaper is required, finish sanding with extra-fine (No. 500, 600, Ultra Fine, 1200, or 1500) sandpaper. Other options: remove sandscratches by compounding, or apply an approved sealer (lacquer type, Table 8-1) according to label directions before color-coating.

Remedy. Remove minor sandscratches by rubbing and polishing. In certain instances, water sanding with No. 500, 600, or finer sandpaper may be necessary before rubbing and polishing. Remove severe sandscratches by employing the steps outlined in "Prevention," and then color-coat as required.

SHRINKING AND SPLITTING OF PUTTY (Fig. 17-21)
(Lacquer and Enamel)

This condition appears as a pulling away and splitting of the top coat and the undercoat layers from a repaired area.

Cause. Putty applied too heavily in thickness dries at the outer surface more quickly than at the under surface. As undercoats and top coats are applied, solvents

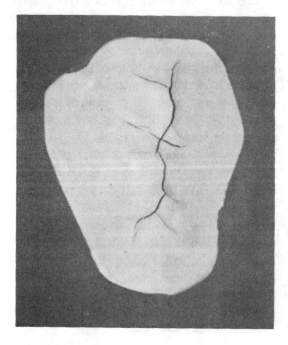

Figure 17-21 Shrinking and splitting of putty. (Courtesy of C.I.L. Paints, Inc., of Canada)

penetrate the complete paint film. Upon drying, the difference in shrinkage rates between the upper thickness and the lower thickness of the paint film causes the upper surfaces to split and crack open.

Remedy. Remove putty from the affected area and reapply in a series of thin coats with adequate drying time between coats (see the application section in "Putty," Chapter 8). If problem is considered deep, repair condition with plastic filler. See Fig. 8-8.

STREAKS IN THE FINISH (Fig. 17-22) (Lacquer and Enamel)

Dark or shaded streaks appear in the finish in the path of spray painting.

Cause. This condition is caused by any one or a combination of the following:

1. Unbalanced spray pattern
2. Poor spraying technique due to incorrect overlap
3. Spray gun dirty or needing repair
4. Spraying metallic colors too wet (mottling)
5. Spraying any color too dry
6. Substrate too hot or too cold

Prevention

1. Adjust the spray gun and check the spray pattern before starting each job (Chapter 4).
2. Use the correct spraying technique with sufficient overlap of strokes.
3. As necessary, clean the spray gun thoroughly.

Figure 17-22 Streaks in finish. (Courtesy of R-M Automotive Products, BASF Inmont Corp.)

4. As necessary, repair the spray gun.

5. Allow the metal to come to normal room temperature before spraying.

Remedy. Apply color according to the label directions while incorporating the previous prevention steps.

SWEAT-OUT OR BLOOM (DULLING) (Lacquer)

A dull-appearing paint repair after acrylic lacquer is applied and compounded and the repair has set for a day or two.

Cause. Compounding or polishing the color coat too soon after application, especially when retarder is used in the color coat. The condition is caused by film shrinkage, which wrinkles the smooth surface as final evaporation of solvents takes place.

Remedy. Compounding after the film dries is usually sufficient to bring the gloss to an acceptable level. In severe cases, where film shrinkage results in wrinkled or orange peel appearance, sand with No. 600 or finer sandpaper and water, and compound as required.

WATER SPOTTING (Fig. 17-23) (Lacquer)

This condition looks like tiny or small rings that surround each spot from which water has evaporated. These rings appear to be etched into the paint finish and cannot be removed by normal washing or polishing.

Cause. The condition is caused by the evaporation of droplets of water from a paint finish in a bright sun when the surface temperatures are over 150°F. The condition becomes more severe as the chemical content of the water and the temperature are in-

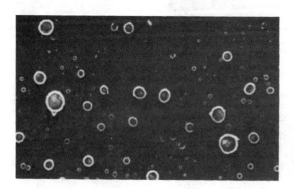

Figure 17-23 Water spotting. (Courtesy of R-M Automotive Products, BASF Inmont Corp.)

creased. A chemical reaction is believed to be caused by the evaporating water and the paint finish, resulting in the ring.

Remedy. In minor cases, rub out and polish as required. Use a very mild or fine abrasive compound. In more severe cases, lightly sand with No. 600 or ultra-fine sandpaper and water, and compound and polish.

WET SPOTS; FINISH DOES NOT DRY (Lacquer and Enamel)

The finish does not dry; it remains tacky in spots or on complete repair.

Cause. The condition may be due to any one or a combination of the following:

1. Application of finish over a surface contaminated with wax, silicones, oil, grease, fingermarks, or gasoline residue.
2. Poor ventilation in the drying room.
3. Air too humid and/or too cold.
4. Drier left out of the enamel when the color is prepared on the mixing machine.
5. The wrong type of thinner or reducer was used.
6. Extra heavy undercoats not properly dried.

Remedy. Sand or wash off the complete affected finish and refinish as required.

Prevention

1. Clean, sand, and reclean the surface as required with paint finish cleaning solvent.
2. Provide adequate ventilation and air movement in the drying area.
3. Allow the car to dry in average temperature conditions.
4. Include drier with the other ingredients when preparing color on the mixing machine.
5. Use the proper solvents.
6. Allow the undercoats to dry thoroughly.

WHEEL BURN (Lacquer)

A dark, often rough smear on a panel surface.

Cause. Holding the polisher too long in one spot.

Remedy. Rub out with a cloth treated with paint finish cleaning solvent, and hand polish. In severe cases, water-sand with No. 600 sandpaper, and then rub out and polish.

This is the wrinkling of an enamel paint finish that looks like the surface of a dried prune skin. The surface is wrinkled and puckered. At times, the wrinkling is so small that it cannot be seen by the naked eye. These surfaces appear dull and the wrinkling can be seen clearly with a magnifying glass.

Cause

1. Rapid drying of the top surface while the underneath remains soft
2. Application of excessively thick color coats
3. Spraying in hot sun, or exposing to sunshine before the enamel is thoroughly dry
4. Surface drying, trapping solvents
5. Fresh film subjected to force-drying too soon
6. Use of acrylic lacquer thinner in enamel

Prevention

1. Reduce enamels according to directions.
2. Apply as recommended.
3. Do not force-dry until solvents have flashed off.

Remedy

1. The best remedy is to remove the wrinkled film and repaint properly.
2. If the following operations can be done *while maintaining an 8- to 10-mil total film thickness*, this is an alternate remedy:
   a. Force-dry or allow wrinkled finish to harden thoroughly.

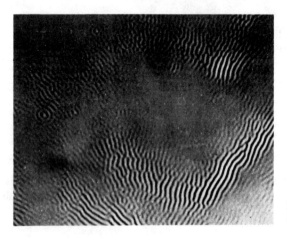

Figure 17-24 Wrinkling of enamels.
(Courtesy of the DuPont Company)

Paint Conditions and Remedies   Chap. 17

b. Apply two or more coats of enamel-type primer–surfacer. Allow to dry.

c. Thoroughly water-sand with No. 400 sandpaper or finer.

d. Apply color coats as directed under "Prevention."

BINKS SUMMARY ON DIRT IN THE FINISH*

This is one of the most prevalent problems encountered in the finishing industry today because it is just about the most elusive to solve. It is, therefore, important to look a little deeper into this problem.

Dirt in the finish may be a result of one or a combination of the following conditions:

1. **The product is dirty.**

   a. All loose dirt must be removed from the product prior to entry into the spray area by proper blowing off, tack-wiping, or steam or pressure cleaning. The additional cost of this operation is made up many times in the reduction of rework.

   b. When masking operations are performed, tack off the product again after masking to remove any paper, dust, or lint.

2. **The paint is dirty.**

   a. It is quite easy to contaminate paint during the mixing, thinning, and straining operation. Allowing dirt to build up on the mixing equipment and dirty containers add to this result.

   b. Some cheap materials may contain fillers that will not mix readily with the paint. Lumps, skins, and large particles must be strained out. Use paint supplier approved strainers (not cheesecloth or rags).

   c. Improper solvents may cause a precipitation in the paint that looks much like dirt. Use only the proper solvents recommended by the material supplier.

3. **The atomizing air is dirty.**

   a. Spray guns that are totally immersed in a solvent tank for cleaning quickly become "dirt generators." Dirty solvent leaves a residue in the air passageways, which will ultimately flake off into the air stream as the gun is used. Wash the outside of the gun with a solvent rag and flush the fluid passageways with solvent.

   CAUTION: Do not submerge a spraygun in solvent.

   b. Piping used in air lines will usually rust or corrode as a result of the moisture in the air. This rust will flake off and contaminate the air in the form of very fine particles and must be removed by filtration. These filters, called **oil and water extractors**, must be cleaned regularly.

*Courtesy of Binks Mfg. Co.

c. Check the condition of the air by holding a clean, white handkerchief over the end of the spray gun, with the air nozzle off and the fluid supply off. Trigger the gun so that the air will flow through the handkerchief for 1 minute. See the result in the handkerchief.

4. **The working area is dirty.**

Goodhousekeeping is a requirement for a dirt-free paint job. Remove dust accumulation from walls, floor, equipment, and the like, regularly. Wet down the floors to hold dust down. The spray booth should be of the proper type and size and equipped with an automatic damper to prevent back drafts. Do not grind, sand, or polish in the spray area.

5. **Improper operation of the booth.**
   a. The booth depends on clean air to function properly. Air intake filters must be kept clean to assure this supply. These are often overlooked.
   b. Exhaust filters must be cleaned or changed regularly to ensure proper air movement through the booth.
   c. A booth equipped with doors should have interlocks on them so that the booth will not operate unless all doors are closed. The exhaust air will obviously draw dirt into the booth area.

6. **Poor operator techniques.**
   a. The operator who sprays at excessive air pressure will contribute largely to the dust and overspray accumulation in the spray area. The resulting high air velocities will not only contaminate the paint job, but often dislodge other dirt and dust particles that normally would not be a problem.
   b. Always start spraying the area of the product farthest from the exhaust fan. This permits the overspray and offspray to move with the air flow over unpainted surfaces.

7. **Lint on the clothing.** Operators should wear starched lint-free clothing or clothing made of antistatic material.

8. **Static electricity.** Static electricity will attract dust particles like a magnet, especially when the humidity is low. Ground the product, the spray gun, and the operator when possible. For example, when painting a car, connect a wire from the ground terminal of the battery to a water pipe. The conducting air hose is available to ground the operator.

REVIEW QUESTIONS

1. What is the purpose of this chapter on paint conditions and remedies?
2. Why is it important to know the cause of a problem before repairs are made?
3. What is a prevention system?
4. What is meant by the **cause** of a paint condition?
5. What is meant by the **remedy** for a paint condition?

6. What is the remedy for excessive orange peel?

7. What is the remedy for a complete panel that has crazed severely all over and the panel must be repainted?

8. What is the remedy for rusting?

9. What is the primary cause of runs or sags?

10. What is the remedy for mottling?

11. Name several causes of dirt-in-paint problems.

12. What is the remedy for correcting blushing that has just occurred, and how can the condition be prevented from happening as the color-coating operation continues?

13. What is the remedy for correcting severe acid and alkali spotting?

14. What is the conventional procedure for the painter when fisheyes appear upon application of the first coat and the entire panel still has to be painted?

15. To prevent crazing, how can the painter test an acrylic lacquer paint finish before making spot or panel repairs over it?

16. What paint problems can be removed from basecoat/clearcoat finishes without repainting?

18

Rust Repairs and Prevention

INTRODUCTION

The purpose of this chapter is to familiarize automotive refinish trade and collision repair trade personnel with a sound approach and repair procedures for making rust repairs on cars that are guaranteeable. Making long-lasting high-quality repairs over rusted areas involves the following:

1. All rust must be removed completely from exterior car surfaces before paint operations are done. This is very similar to removing cancer from a person properly and thoroughly before an operation can be considered successful.
2. Using the best plastic-filling methods and materials that are water resistant and/or waterproof.
3. Using the best primer and primer-surfacer available for durability purposes.
4. Rust-proofing the reverse or hidden side of repairs to keep moisture and condensation off interior rust-repaired surfaces.

CAUSES OF RUST PROBLEMS

A number of factors contribute to the serverity of rust on cars:

1. Car environment
2. Lack of owner maintenance

3. Age of car
4. Design of car
5. Incorrectly repaired collision damage

A car may be affected by two or more of these factors, in which case the corrosion is that much more severe.

Car Environment

The environment is the single biggest cause of rust on cars. Highly industrialized areas aggravate and promote corrosion conditions. The smoke and pollutants from chimneys of coal-burning furnaces, as in steel mills, contribute heavily to corrosion conditions. The northeast quadrant of the United States, most of Canada, and other countries that use salt to melt snow and ice on streets and highways during cold weather have the most corrosion problems on passenger cars and trucks. Another rust-problem area is along the Florida and Gulf coasts, where the air is highly humid and salt filled.

Another factor that promotes rust conditions in these areas of the world are car-wash businesses that use recycled "salt" water. These businesses use recycled water as a means of cutting water costs and for national water conservation. As cars from salty streets are washed, the salty water runs into a water saving tank and is reused. Some of these car washes have a freshwater final rinse but many do not. Washing cars with salty water promotes corrosion, particularly in water-trap areas on cars.

Lack of Car Maintenance

Dirt, salt, chemicals, and water are the principal ingredients that cause rust on cars when these ingredients come in contact with the steel through microscopic or larger breaks in the paint finish. Any car that is not washed, cleaned, and waxed properly and periodically has a tendency to rust faster when exposed to rust-producing elements.

Age of the Car

Once started and not checked or repaired, rust conditions become more deeply embedded in the steel. The older the car, the more severe the corrosion.

Design of the Car

Many cars, by styling or incidental design, have water pockets or water traps built into them. A water trap is a location on a car so designed that it holds water against steel painted parts after runoff of water following a car wash, a rainfall, or heavy dew. Water traps invariably are the weakest spots on a car from a corrosion standpoint and are among the first to rust through for an unsuspecting car owner when the car is exposed to severe salt and chemical environments.

Incorrectly Repaired Collision Damage

Insurance companies pay collision repair shops to restore each collision-repaired car to the original condition. This includes application of rust-proofing and undercoating. However, due to speedy repair and/or negligence, some repair shops fail to rust-proof the interior construction of affected panels or areas of cars as written up on repair orders. This results in serious premature rust problems.

In some cases, collision repair persons use an improper panel-to-panel overlap joint, which results in an unprotected rust trap. In such cases, cars start to rust at the time of collision repair. In other cases, metal and paint repairs are made carelessly, as follows:

1. All known rust is not removed completely from the repair area before painting.
2. The metal is not cleaned or conditioned before painting.
3. A weak primer and/or primer–surfacer system is used before color coating.

TYPES OF RUST

Rust can be divided into three general categories.

Surface Rust

Surface rust is the first level of rust. This condition can be seen and repaired completely and satisfactorily on an exterior surface if done early with correct repair techniques. Figure 18-1 shows corrosion in the beginning stages. In a surface rust condition, rust is just getting started and there is no serious blistering. Surface rust is the beginning of corrosive pitting. The condition is mild and is not very deep. This is the easiest type of rust to repair because the condition can be corrected by sanding, metal conditioning, and painting.

Remedy. To repair surface rust:

1. Sand to shiny bright metal.
2. Apply a two-part metal conditioner (Table 6-2) to dissolve remaining rust in surface pits (Fig. 18-1).
3. Wash the surface with water; blow-dry with compressed air to dry the surface.
4. Apply the best primer and primer–surfacer system before color-coating (Table 8-1).

Corrosive Pitting and Scale Rust (Fig. 18-2)

Corrosive pitting is an advanced form of rusting. If left unchecked, rusting proceeds **laterally, under a paint film,** to cause rust blistering, as well as **in depth, into the thickness of the metal.** Rust deposits on a surface later turn into scale rust. Usually, a

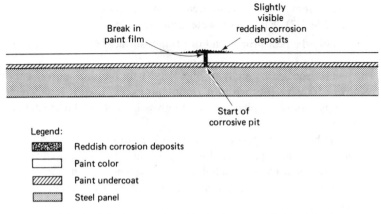

Figure 18-1 Cross section of beginning stages of corrosion.

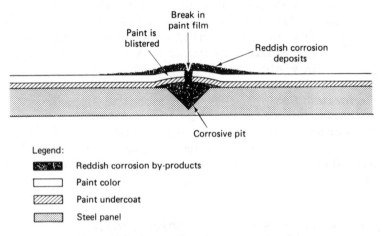

Figure 18-2 Cross section of severe corrosive pitting.

high number of pits are affected, which turns into scale on the surface as corrosion progresses.

Remedy

1. Remove rust from each pit thoroughly and completely.
   a. Sandblasting is the best and quickest method of rust removal.
   b. If sandblasting is not possible or available, use a pointed cutting tool and $\frac{1}{4}$-inch drill motor to grind out each pit completely, like the work a dentist does. Pointed abrasive tools are available through hardware and department stores and are fitted with a $\frac{1}{8}$-inch shank for use with a $\frac{1}{4}$-inch drill motor. If the number of corrosive pits is too great, the only answer is sandblasting or sectional panel replacement.

2. After removing the rust, treat each pit and surface area with metal conditioner (Table 6-2). Rinse with water and blow-dry.

3. Apply the best primer and/or primer–surfacer (Table 8-1), as required.

The painter can see by studying Fig. 18-2 why **hand or power sanding alone cannot remove corrosive pits without removing excess metal.** If not removed properly and completely, corrosive pits continue to grow in depth and diameter and the rust problem continues.

The best test to prove when corrosive pitting is removed completely is to tin the affected spot. Tinning is a metal repair operation that is required just before solder filling. **Solder will not stick to a rusted surface.** So when a spot area can be **tinned correctly,** the painter can be assured that there is no rust on the surface.

> **CAUTION:** Tinning on large flat surfaces should be done only by a technician experienced in this phase of metal repair. Improper tinning on a large flat panel will cause metal distortion and, in turn, will spoil the surface appearance of a panel. Before tinning a "spot" on a panel, the entire surrounding area must be heated uniformly by the gradual application of heat with a torch until a ballooning expansion is noted in the area metal. At this time, tinning can be done effectively and safely. Allow to air cool only. Do not quench.

Perforation Rust

Perforation rust is the most advanced form of rust and consists of complete perforation of a panel. The condition can originate on either side of a panel. This is also known as a **rust-through** or **rust out.** The repair of perforation rust involves repair or replacement of the affected panel section or panel.

HOW RUST REPAIR COSTS ARE DETERMINED

Straight-time work operations are estimated to make sectional metal repairs. Paint materials and labor are estimated and added to make up the total.

Panel replacement work operations are determined through flat-rate schedules. Also, paint material and labor are determined from flat-rate schedules. Both are added together to determine the total cost.

PROCEDURE FOR REMOVING RUST FROM A COMPLETE CAR (INCLUDING PATCH REPAIR FOR A PERFORATION CONDITION)

1. The most efficient way to remove rust, including corrosive pitting, is by sandblasting. As noted in Fig. 18-2, corrosive pitting and other advanced forms of rust cannot be removed efficiently by disc sanding or by other means of sanding because the depth of the condition causes too much metal to be removed.

2. If sandblasting is done in cold or rainy weather, below 50°F, the operation could be done safely and efficiently in a paint spray booth with the air exhaust on. Also, sandblasting could be done in a paint spray booth on a year-round basis.

3. If sandblasting is done in warm and dry weather, above 50°F, it can be done safely on a driveway or other suitable location outside the repair shop.

4. When sandblasting to remove rust at specific locations, perform the necessary parts removal operations. For specific removal and installation instructions, refer to the applicable car factory service manual.

    a. **Rust at moldings** (steel, aluminum, or plastic)

        (1) Remove moldings.

        (2) Store parts, clips, and screws for later installation.

    b. **Rust at nameplates**

        (1) Remove nameplates.

        (2) Store parts.

    c. **Rust at stationary glass windows**

        (1) Remove perimeter moldings and clips.

        (2) Store parts. When necessary, use emergency repair parts.

        (3) **Mask adjacent window glass with two to three thicknesses of cloth-back body sealing tape (2 inches wide, minimum).**

        (4) Where necessary, cut and remove glass adhesive sealant to expose the rust condition. Replace the sealant when the painting is done.

    d. **Rust along the edge of vinyl top**

        (1) Remove the moldings

        (2) Detach and fold back the vinyl top.

    e. **Rust under the vinyl top** (heavy, hard blisters push up the top cover)

        (1) Remove the vinyl top.

        (2) When installing a vinyl top, **use only factory-approved vinyl-top adhesive.**

5. Protect the adjacent area parts with several layers of masking paper.

6. Sandblast all rusted surfaces until the steel is bright and clean. No discoloration spots should remain. Adjust the air pressure for clean and thorough sandblasting as required. Observe the safety precautions outlined in **"Sandblasting,"** Chapter 6.

7. If the area being repaired is "blind" (no access to the back side), apply anticorrosion compound through the outer perforation(s) to protect the bared metal of the inner construction that is cleaned during the sandblasting operation. If the back side of the repair area is accessible, apply anticorrosion compound to the repair surfaces and the inner construction as the last step of the repair.

NOTE: For the availability of anticorrosion compound, check with the service department of the car dealer or zone office or with a local rust-proofing shop. Most sprayable, heavy-bodied anticorrosion compounds are basically similar in purpose, construction, and use. These compounds are designed to keep air and water away from the metal. Without water and air, steel does not rust.

8. Carefully "sink" metal (on an incline) around the edge of the perforation for a distance of 1 to $1\frac{1}{2}$ inches, as shown in Fig. 18-3.

9. Clean the exterior bare metal surfaces thoroughly by wiping with Part I of a metal conditioner.

10. Make a repair patch of suitable metal, such as aluminum, copper, or steel. Cut and fit the repair patch to bridge the perforation and secure temporarily in place with two or three screws. Check the patch alignment (Fig. 18-3). Be sure that the heads of the screws are positioned below the final surface line of the repair as shown. Do steps 11 and 12 before securing the patch permanently with screws or rivets.

11. Use one of the following products (or equivalent products) to make rust-proof plastic repairs:

   a. Alum-A-Lead, available through Ditzler paint jobbers

   b. Rust Out (No. ROF-1, Unican); see the paint jobber

   c. Duraglas (U.S. Chemical & Plastics, Inc.); see the paint jobber

   Alum-A-Lead hardener is a powder (DX-701). Alum-A-Lead resin is in a pour-spout container (DX-702). Both are prepared most efficiently in a suitable throw-away metal can or paper cup. Follow the label directions. Prepare to the desired consistency by using a greater or lesser volume of resin to a given volume of powder. Rust Out and Duraglas make use of cream hardeners and contain glass fibers that contribute to strength. For correct use and application, follow the label directions. All three products are moisture-resistant or moisture-proof and corrosion-resistant and are available in all parts of the country.

CAUTION: The ordinary or commonly available polyester fillers are not recommended for rust repairs because they tend to be water absorbent and promote rather than retard corrosion.

12. Remove the repair patch. Prepare a suitable amount of plastic. Apply about a

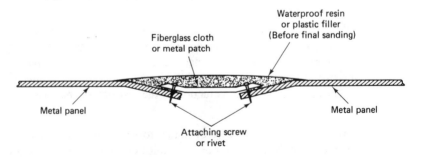

Figure 18-3 Patch repair of rust-through condition.

$\frac{1}{16}$-inch coating of plastic to the *back side* of the patch and install the patch with screws or suitable rivets. Wipe the repair surface smooth.

13. Prepare and apply the first coat of **plastic filler** to the complete repair area. Using a rubber or plastic spreader, apply an initial thin coating of plastic **very firmly** to the repair surface. Apply the remainder of the prepared plastic to the initial **fill** and level out for general smoothness.

14. Prepare and apply all additional plastic filler to complete filling the repair area.

15. As soon as the plastic becomes solidified to the touch, use a cheese-grater-type rasp and file the repair surface to the approximate exterior contour. This is done in the early stages of curing before the plastic hardens. Then sand the surface smooth to the approximate final contour with No. 80 sandpaper after the plastic cures. Finish sanding with No. 220 sandpaper.

16. If necessary, apply final glaze coat(s) of plastic to the surface to produce a final smooth surface free of imperfections. This may require more than one glaze coat to achieve final smoothness.

17. Allow to cure and sand smooth with No. 220 sandpaper.

CAUTION: Do not apply paint finish cleaning solvent on plastic filler. The solvent is absorbed by the plastic and dries very slowly. This leads to blistering of the paint finish.

18. Apply metal conditioner *to the bare metal* as described in Chapter 6 according to product label directions.

19. Apply the best primer system as explained in Chapter 8.

20. Apply the best primer-surfacer as explained in Chapter 8.

21. Apply color as required.

22. If access to the back side of the repair is possible, apply anticorrosion compound to the back side. Plug access holes as required.

CHIP-RESISTANT COATINGS (TABLE 18-1)

The purpose of chip-resistant coating is to protect the lower underside metal panels against stone and gravel chipping when cars travel on gravel roads. The tires pick up

TABLE 18-1 CHIP-RESISTANT COATINGS

Purpose of product	Rinshed-Mason	Ditzler	3-M Company	Martin-Senour	Sherwin-Williams
Chip-resistant material applied to low body panels prior to topcoating	891 (see label) + acr. lac. or M-2 enamel + proper solvent	DX-54	08874	6851 or 6850	G1W295

and throw stones against the car with great force. The abrasive action in this case is similar to sandblasting. While the paint may chip away, the protective coating remains and protects the metal (Fig. 18-4).

The early factory chip-resistant coating was made of a plastisol material similar to a vinyl top coating. The latest factory material is a tough urethane plastic, which has less orange peel than earlier materials. The thickness of a good protective material has been in the range of 15 to 20 mils. Table 18-1 lists several good chip-resistant coatings available to the painter. There are many more good ones on the market.

In event of collision damage to panels covered with chip-resistant coating, the coating must be removed to bare metal before metal repairs and repainting can be done. **The protective coating is designed for full panel repairs only.** The material is not suitable for spot repairs.

Repair Procedure

1. Remove the coating from the damaged panel.
   a. Some early-type coatings can be removed by using a heat gun on the product and then scraping the material off with a sharp putty knife.
   b. If the material is not readily removable in step 1a, the fastest method of coating removal is with a disc sander and a No. 36 or 40 grit disc. Finish with a No. 80 grit disc (Fig. 18-5).
2. Make all necessary sheet metal repairs according to current recommended procedures.
3. Clean the surface with paint finish cleaning solvent.

   CAUTION: Keep solvent off any plastic filler repairs.

4. Clean and mask the car for paint repair:
   a. If car is equipped with a lower body side molding, use it as the upper breakline. Keep masking off the sheet metal.

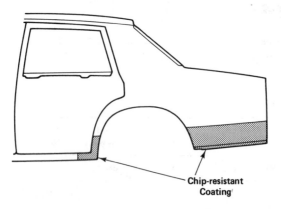

Chip-resistant
Coating

Figure 18-4 Location of chip-resistant coatings. Some styles include lower areas of doors. (Courtesy of General Motors Corporation)

Figure 18-5 Sanding off chip-resistant coating. (Courtesy of R-M Automotive Products, BASF Inmont Corp.)

    b. If car is not equipped with a lower molding, mask as follows:

      (1) Position masking paper and tape $\frac{1}{4}$ to $\frac{3}{8}$ inch above natural body crease-line.

      (2) Position $\frac{1}{2}$-inch 3-M Fine Line masking tape over the conventional masking tape and position the edge of the tape on the center of the crease-line. This tape edge forms the upper border.

NOTE: The center of a body panel crease-line is a good breakline for this purpose. Use Fine Line tape for this purpose because it leaves a sharp, clean edge with the thick vinyl coating.

    c. Mask balance of car, such as wheels and bumper.

5. Apply metal conditioner to bare metal as recommended by paint supplier and then apply straight primer.

NOTE: If R-M's 834 or DuPont's 615S primer is used, do not use a metal conditioner. Allow primer to dry per label directions.

6. Apply best type primer-surfacer, allow to dry, and scuff-sand (Fig. 18-6).
7. Secure chip-resistant coating according to Table 18-1, or secure an equivalent product.
8. Prepare the material and equipment per label directions.

    a. Prepare R-M products as follows:
      1 Part 891 flex agent
      2 Parts Alpha-Cryl lacquer or Miracryl-2 enamel
      DO NOT REDUCE BEFORE APPLICATION.

Figure 18-6 Spraying straight primer followed by primer-surfacer. (Courtesy of R-M Automotive Products, BASF Inmont Corp.)

  b. The following three companies' products are ready-for-use as packaged for application with a suction-feed spray gun:

  (1) Ditzler's DX-54, Road Guard

  (2) Martin-Senour's 6850 or 6851, Vinyl-Tex

  (3) Sherwin-Williams' G1W295, vinyl Gravel Guard

  c. 3-M Company's 08874, Rocker Schutz, is ready-for-use as packaged, but 3-M recommends that the product be applied with an undercoating gun as shown in Fig. 18-7.

9. Spray out sample test panel per label directions for full coverage and compare orange peel level to car. Make adjustments to air pressure (and material feed on guns so equipped) as follows:

  a. For coarse orange peel, apply with lower air pressure while leaving material feed wide open.

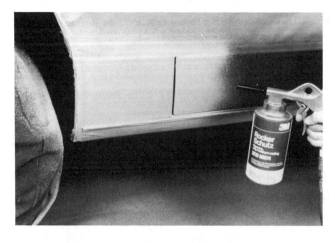

Figure 18-7 3M's Rocker Schutz product is applied with an undercoating gun. (Courtesy of the 3M Company)

b. For finer orange peel, apply with higher air pressure while reducing material feed slightly (if so equipped).

10. Apply protective coating to car (see Fig. 18-8) using same technique that produced acceptable finish on test panel. Allow to dry as follows:

   a. If acrylic lacquer topcoating is used, allow at least 1 hour for drying at normal temperature (70°F).

   b. If acrylic enamel topcoating is used, allow at least 2 hours for drying (70°F).

11. Apply the finish color as follows:

   a. If no molding bordered the upper area of the repair, remove the original strip of $\frac{1}{2}$-inch Fine Line masking tape before the protective coating dries. To remove tape, pull up and away from the panel.

   b. Place a new strip of Fine Line masking tape just slightly above, instead of "right on," the upper edge of the coating. This slightly relocated strip of tape ensures full coverage of the protective coating.

Figure 18-8 R-M's chip-resistant coating is applied with a conventional spray gun. (Courtesy of R-M Automotive Products, BASF Inmont Corp.)

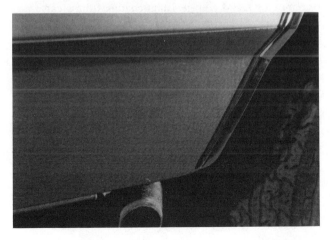

Figure 18-9 After drying period, apply color as required to achieve final color match. (Courtesy of R-M Automotive Products, BASF Inmont Corp.)

12. Apply final topcoats according to label directions or as directed in Chapter 12. Increased abrasion resistance is obtained by using a catalyst in standard acrylic enamel or by using a final enamel clearcoat that is catalyzed (Fig. 18-7).

13. Clean up equipment immediately after painting with medium lacquer thinner or equivalent. The finished job is shown in Fig. 18-9.

14. Allow paint finish to dry per label directions before putting car into service.

REVIEW QUESTIONS

1. What is the purpose of this chapter?
2. List several factors that contribute to the severity of rust on cars.
3. What is the single biggest cause of rust on cars?
4. Describe surface rust and give a remedy for its repair.
5. What is corrosive pitting?
6. Can corrosive pitting or other severe forms of rust be removed completely with conventional disc-sanding or hand-sanding methods?
7. What is the best method of removing corrosive pitting and all forms of rust completely?
8. What is the best test to use to prove that corrosive pits are removed completely?
9. What is perforation rust?
10. Where is the best place to do sandblasting inside a building in cold weather and still be in OSHA compliance?
11. Explain the procedure for repairing perforation rust by replacing a section of panel.
12. Name three different brands of plastic products, each of which can be used to make rust-proof plastic repairs.
13. Why are the commonly available polyester plastic fillers not recommended for rust repairs?
14. Explain the procedure for removing OEM chip-resistant coating from a car.
15. Explain the procedure for applying chip-resistant coating with a suction-feed spray gun.
16. How much time is recommended for drying of chip-resistant coating before applying standard acrylic lacquer or enamel?

19

Care of the Car
and Paint Finish

INTRODUCTION

The purpose of this chapter is as follows:

1. *To review how to keep a car looking its best at all times.* This involves keeping a paint finish clean and in good repair. This means getting the paint finish repaired as soon as possible when paint is damaged or affected in any way.
2. *How to reduce corrosion on a car.* This involves washing a car thoroughly as outlined in Chapter 6 and in this chapter and keeping the car clean (free of salts, chemicals, and pollutants) and protected with anticorrosion materials as outlined in this chapter.
3. *How to keep bright metal parts on a car looking their best.* Aluminum and plastic bright metal exterior parts require a different treatment than chrome-plated and stainless steel parts. Absolutely no abrasives or polishes with abrasives are to be used on aluminum or plastic bright metal parts.

Corrosion is a year-round problem everywhere in the country. Although some areas experience very little corrosion, other areas of the country experience severe amounts of corrosion.

As mentioned earlier, the purpose of a paint finish is (1) to protect the steel, and (2) to beautify the appearance of a car. But cars are continually exposed to the following environmental conditions, which have various effects on paint finishes.

1. Industrial fallout and pollution
2. Salts and sodium chloride from streets and highways
3. Salt air and high-humidity conditions along the Florida coast and in similar environments
4. Sunlight and moisture
5. Insecticides and insects

Among the most common conditions or problems that occur are:

1. Various types of corrosion: all cars
2. Chemical spotting: all cars
3. Chalking and fading: all older cars

A paint finish must be maintained properly on a year-round basis if the finish is to look its best and provide the durability expected of it.

WASHING THE CAR

The best way to keep a paint finish clean and free of problems is to wash the car frequently and to keep a good polish on the car. Some cars that are parked all day at coal mines or at steel mills require a car wash more often. Cars that are used in the average environment should probably be washed once a week. Some cautions to remember are:

1. Do not use hot water; warm water is OK.
2. Do not wash the car in the direct rays of the sun with the temperature over 85°F.
3. Do not use strong soaps or chemical detergents.
4. Promptly flush all cleaning agents from the surface.
5. Do not allow cleaning agents to dry on the paint finish.

Washing the Underside of the Car

Some car factories advertise on occasion that car owners should wash the *underside* as well as the *top side* of cars to reduce rust conditions. The worst rusting happens from the inside out. That is because salt, chemicals, slush, and mud tend to collect in the crevices underneath the car, in door and rear lid hemming flanges, and inside fenders. As moisture and chemicals get trapped in these locations, they cause rust unless the areas are rust-proofed.

This car wash procedure should be done at least once or twice each month if in a heavy salt environment. Otherwise, the procedure may be done each month or less often as conditions warrant. It would be a good idea if painters reading this book would pass this information on to car owners as they come in contact with them. The best place to do the operations is at a coin-operated car wash that provides pressurized (clean) water, detergent soap, and hot and cold water rinse. A person could do almost as good a job of rinsing the underside of the car with a garden hose.

Procedure

1. Wash and rinse each wheelhouse area:
   a. Around front wheels
   b. Around rear wheels
2. Wash and rinse inside the front fenders:
   a. Open the front door and clean out leaves, mud, and debris that accumulate inside the bottom at the rear of the fender. Use suitable tools and blow out with an air hose. Wear eye protection.
   b. Then flush out the area with pressurized soapy water, rinse with clear water, and allow to dry.
   c. Wash the back side of the headlamp area with pressurized soapy water; then rinse with clean water. Gain access to the headlamp from the top and/or bottom.
3. Wash the engine compartment components, including the dash or firewall and the side walls. Use hot soapy water; then follow with cool, clear water rinse.

CAUTION: If the car is not equipped with an electronic ignition system, cover the distributor and spark coil as required with a plastic cover or equivalent waterproof cover to avoid getting them wet. Electronic ignition cars are not affected by water in the engine compartment.

4. Wash and rinse the underside of the front and rear bumpers, and as much of the underbody of the car as is reachable safely, with a hose and water.

GARAGE PARKING AND RUSTING

Many people believe that parking a car in a garage helps to prevent rust. The opposite is true. Parking a wet or damp car in a garage with the doors closed reduces air movement, which, in turn, slows drying. Warm, wet, or humid slow-drying conditions promote corrosion. Allow the car to dry as required before putting it in a garage.

GLASS CLEANING

The best way to clean glass on cars is with a liquid glass cleaner containing ammonia. One of the most difficult things to clean from glass inside a car is an oily haze that accumulates on the glass. In many cases, the haze is a plasticizer type of oil that evaporates from interior vinyls or other coated parts under certain hot-temperature conditions and condenses on the glass. Many people believe this is an accumulation from cigarette smoking, but it is not. Ammonia or vinegar is required to "cut" and remove this oily substance.

Procedure

1. Wash window glass thoroughly with a water-dampened clean cloth or towel and glass cleaner containing ammonia.
2. Then wipe dry with a clean cloth or paper towel. Follow the label directions.

KEEP THE PAINT FINISH IN GOOD REPAIR

Paint that is damaged in any way, such as chipped, dinged, or scratched, should be repaired as soon as possible. Damaged paint leads to rust, which requires additional repair work. Minor damage can be touched up with a brush by the owner. Touch-up kits are available through car dealers. For major spray painting repairs, take the car to the dealer or to an independent paint shop.

ANTICORROSION PROTECTION FOR INTERIOR SURFACES OF THE CAR

The interior of major car panels is protected against corrosion by the factory and/or by the dealers. A similar treatment should be given to replacement parts when collision repairs are made. Anticorrosion compounds are designed for interior surfaces of cars and are available through applicable car dealers. All cars should have this treatment.

UNDERCOATING PROTECTION FOR THE EXPOSED BOTTOM OF THE CAR

This is a heavy anticorrosion material designed for application on the exterior bottom of the car. Replacement or repaired sections of an underbody should be undercoated with the equivalent of original equipment upon completion of metal repairs. Undercoating materials are available through applicable car dealers. All cars should have this treatment.

ANTICORROSION TREATMENT OF EXTERIOR BRIGHT METAL PARTS

Exterior bright metal parts are made of several different materials. Each material requires a special treatment for maximum durability of appearance. The materials are:

1. Stainless steel
2. Chrome-plated steel

3. Anodized aluminum
4. Bright metal and plastic combination

If necessary, check for the type of bright metal with a magnet. Stainless steel and chrome-plated steel react with a "draw" to an electromagnet. Aluminum and bright metal and plastic combination parts do not react to a magnet. If in doubt about a bumper's construction, check it with a magnet.

> **CAUTION:** When cleaning aluminum moldings or bumpers, *never use an abrasive* such as a rubbing compound, steel wool, or a car polish with abrasive in it. Harsh abrasives remove the fine anodized bright finish from aluminum and this finish cannot be replaced in service.

WAX TREATMENT FOR NONSTEEL BRIGHT METAL PARTS

Clean and protect anodized aluminum parts and combination bright metal and plastic parts with an occasional application of nonabrasive wax polish, as recommended in car owner's manual. This operation is best done at the time the car is polished.

OIL TREATMENT FOR CHROME-PLATED STEEL PARTS

One excellent treatment for keeping steel bumpers and other chrome-plated metal parts from rusting or corroding is to apply an oil treatment every 2 to 4 months. With this treatment, bumpers never rust, even in heavy salt environments.

When enlarged many times, chrome plating looks like a screen. A chrome-plated steel part usually has the following layers of elements on it:

1. *Steel:* base metal
2. *Copper:* sticks better to steel than nickel does
3. *Nickel:* the true protective coating; sticks better to copper
4. *Chrome* (or chromium, the proper name of the element)

Many automotive engineers use this oil treatment to keep chrome-plated steel on their cars looking new. The oil treatment seals off the base metals from water and corrosive elements. Even where scratched or dented, oil does a good job of protecting the steel.

Procedure

1. Apply suitable masking on a driveway or paint shop floor.
2. Using the same oil as used for the engine, apply oil to each chrome-plated surface

with a cloth or brush and allow to soak in for several minutes. Apply oil in sequence on all chrome-plated parts on the car.

3. With a clean wiping cloth, wipe off excess oil from each treated surface.

CAUTION ON SOLVENT CLEANERS AND CAR POLISHES

There are many solvent cleaners and car polishes on the market **that should not be used on all cars. Acrylic lacquers are softened and dulled by** what are known as **aromatic hydrocarbons;** examples are **benzene, toluene, and xylene.** Original baked enamel finishes are not so affected by these chemicals.

However, millions of cars on the roads with OEM acrylic lacquer and millions of additional cars **repaired** with acrylic lacquer are affected by these strong chemicals. Before using any product on your car, **read the label instructions and contents.** Apart from these exceptions, acrylic lacquer and enamel finishes may be polished or waxed with any reputable product.

USE OF SOLVENT CLEANER

Paint finish cleaning solvents are listed in Table 6-1. Use these solvents as required to remove foreign matter from paint finishes that water alone does not remove, such as road tar and oil. Read the label directions.

FINE RUBBING COMPOUND

Paint conditions not removable with water or paint finish cleaning solvent may require a fine abrasive compound for removal.

CAUTION: Do not use abrasives on aluminum parts

USE OF FINE SANDPAPER AND RUBBING COMPOUND FOR CLEANING PAINT

Experienced painters know that many paint conditions, such as mild chemical spotting and light surface scratching, are removable using this method. Sand with water and No. 600 or ultrafine sandpaper and follow with fine hand rubbing compound to restore the gloss (see Table 6-3). To complete the job, apply a good grade of polish to the areas cleaned.

CAR POLISHING AND WAXING

The purpose of car polishing is as follows:

1. To clean a paint surface by removing dirt, road scum, and foreign matter.
2. To beautify the appearance of a paint finish with more depth and a high gloss.
3. To remove minor scratches by filling them and leveling the surface.
4. To seal the pores of paint and make the finish more water repellent.

Car factories recommend polishing and waxing a car finish periodically to keep the car looking its best. Painters should know how to polish cars efficiently while removing a minimum of or no paint. Each car dealer offers several polishes that have proven value in maintaining the original finish appearance and durability.

One-Component, Solvent-Type Car Polish (with No Abrasive)

Features of a one-component car polish are as follows:

1. These polishes are designed **to clean and polish in one operation**. Each polish has its own secret blend of cleaning solvents. Purposely, there are no abrasives. Also, each polish has its secret formulation of wax application. Most liquid or solvent-type polishes are designed for hand use. Some liquid polishes are designed for machine and hand use.
2. The type of polish and application method determine how long a polish will last. Machine-applied polishes last the longest and are glossier. This is because the high rpm of the wheel causes a burnishing action that creates heat. The pad pressure and leveling of wax at a high temperature cause a harder and deeper wax film to form, which produces a high gloss.
3. *Liquid polishes do not rub through paint* at sharp crease-lines and edges unless abused severely. This is the outstanding feature of all liquid polishes.

A great number of one-component liquid polishes are available to the motoring public through car dealers, paint jobbers, auto accessory stores, and department stores. To determine which polish is best for a given car, contact the service manager of a nearby same factory car dealership. Generally, polishes with a trade name that includes the term "Poly" (like Poly-Shell, or Poly-Seal) are the best. They are the most glossy and durable. There are other equivalent polishes. Always follow label directions.

Many low-cost polishes are available. They are easy to apply by hand and provide a good gloss. But they do not last very long.

One-Component, Solvent-Type Car Polish
(with Abrasive)

To check the presence of abrasive in a polish, rub a small amount of polish between the thumb and finger or between two thumbnails. The presence of the abrasive and the size of the grit can be felt.

1. These polishes are designed to clean and polish in one operation. Because of the abrasive action, these polishes can cut through a paint film more quickly.
2. The type of polish and application method determine how long the polish will last.
3. These polishes are fast-acting but must be used with extreme care by an experienced technician to avoid cut-throughs at edges.

Two-Component Car Polish

Part 1 is a cleaner made of a blend of solvents and fine abrasives. The cleaner is designed to remove the outer portion of the paint film, together with road film, dirt, and contaminants.

Part 2 is a wax-type sealant that provides the gloss and beauty to the car. This is a special wax formula in a special solvent. This sealant wax, alone, could be used on aluminum parts. These polishes are usually available in smaller containers, such as 1 pint each. These polishes are usually the most expensive and they do a good job when used according to the label directions. However, repeated or excessive use of an abrasive cleaner on a car leads to rub-through problems. When rub-throughs occur, the only remedy is color-coating the affected areas.

Selection of Polishing Bonnets

The most popular commercial-type polishing bonnets are as follows:

Carpet-type Pad or Bonnet. A carpet-type pad is so named because the wool tuft construction looks like a carpet. These pads (such as Amcor No. 2 or No. 5) are ideal for compounding and excellent for polishing. The ideal combination for polishing is a carpet-type pad and a polishing machine that has a rating of 2000 rpm or higher under load. This combination produces the best burnishing action and the highest gloss. This same equipment combination is used for compounding (see Chapter 11). The pads are available through paint jobbers.

Lamb's-wool-type Bonnet. This bonnet, which looks like sheepskin, is ideal for applying nonabrasive and sealant-type wax polishes. The type of polish determines the final gloss. Some polishes are designed for application with this type of bonnet. See the label directions. The pads are available through paint jobbers.

Sponge-type Pad or Bonnet. These are specially designed sponge-type pad assemblies. The sponge pads are cement-bonded to a backing that is screw-attached to the polisher. Some polishes are designed for application with this type of bonnet. One feature of this type of pad is that the pad will polish a concave surface as uniformly as it will a flat surface. For additional information, see the paint jobber and the polish label directions. The pads are available through paint jobbers.

Car Polishing Procedure

The procedure for applying polish to a car is very similar to machine compounding. Each polish is designed for a particular method of application. Following are suggestions to incorporate into the polishing technique.

1. Condition the polishing pad by rubbing a slight amount of polish on it.
2. Use only the amount of polish specified in the label directions. Using too much polish gums up the polishing pad and slows the polishing operation.
3. Apply polish on the car with a suitable squirt bottle. Many polishes are available in ready-made squirt bottles. Plastic squirt bottles can be recleaned and reused.
4. Before turning on the polisher, spread the applied polish on the surface with the bonnet. This prevents wasting polish.
5. Work an area about 2 square feet at a time.
6. Use the method of "four times over" to produce a final gloss. The first two times over a surface involves cleaning and spreading the polish uniformly. The last two times over burnishes the surface and makes the polish glossy. If more than four passes are required:
   a. Too much polish is being used,
   b. The pad is gummed up and dirty, or
   c. The polishing machine is too slow.
   Make adjustments in any one or all three, as required.
7. Finish the polishing operation by hand at surfaces not reachable with the polisher.
8. Wash the car *last* to clean up excess polish trapped at gap spacings and crevices. Wipe the car with a water-dampened chamois.
9. Cleaning a carpet-type pad is required during polishing operations. Clean the pad with a pointed but not sharp tool, such as a putty knife, or with an air gun. Compressed air helps to clean and dry the pad. (For "Procedure for Cleaning Pad during Use," see Chapter 11.) Sponge and lamb's-wool pads can also be cleaned with an air gun.
10. Polishing pads should be laundered in an automatic washing machine and reused. They can be dried on a clothesline or in a drier.

CAUTION: To speed up polishing operations, **many polishing technicians add rubbing compound to a given polish or cleaner. This should never be done because it causes premature rub-throughs and thin-paint complaints.** This, in turn, leads to friction between the car owner and the paint shop. Excessive compounding also affects the durability of the finish because protective resins are removed to expose pigments.

REVIEW QUESTIONS

1. Why should the underside of cars be washed or rinsed periodically?
2. Does garage parking prevent or promote rust?
3. When cleaning windows, what type of cleaner is best suited to remove all types of oils and all forms of dirt from glass surfaces?
4. What is the best way to keep a paint finish in good repair?
5. What is meant by anticorrosion protection of a car? Should all cars be so treated?
6. What is the best way to care for the nonsteel bright metal parts on a car?
7. Describe a good way to care for chrome-plated steel parts to prevent corrosion.
8. Describe a one-component, solvent-type cleaner and car polish that consists of no abrasive.
9. Describe a one-component, solvent-type cleaner and car polish that contains an abrasive.
10. How can a painter tell quickly by examining a polish if the polish contains a harsh abrasive?
11. Explain the function of each component of a two-component car polish.
12. What types of polishes must be kept off all aluminum parts?
13. Name and describe three types of car polishing bonnets.
14. What is the best way to prevent cut-throughs when using abrasives over creaselines and sharp corners?
15. Describe how to polish a complete car:
    (a) With a machine polisher
    (b) By hand

Glossary of Terms

Abrasive (Aluminum Oxide): The toughest and most durable abrasive for use on metal surfaces; not quite as sharp as silicon carbide, but it does not break down as easily.

Abrasive (Silicon Carbide): The hardest and sharpest abrasive known; shiny black in color; best abrasive for sanding paint; breaks down fast on metal surfaces.

ABS Plastic (Acrylonitrile-Butadiene-Styrene):
1. The hard-type ABS is used on door arm rest bases and other areas where hardness is a factor.
2. The soft-type ABS is used in combination with vinyl (PVC) to form instrument panel covers and similar parts.

Acrylic Resin (Methyl Methacrylate): A very clear binder-type material that can be made into many forms by special chemical processing. One form is used in acrylic lacquers and another form is used in acrylic enamels.

Adhesion: The ability to stick to the surface due to interfacial forces.

Adhesion Promoter: A water-white, ready to spray lacquer material that provides a chemical etch to OEM finishes. Compatible under acrylic lacquer, enamel, and basecoat/clearcoat finishes.

Air Dry: The drying hard of a lacquer or enamel applied paint material at ordinary room temperatures and without the aid of artificial heat.

Arcing: Pivoting the spray gun at the wrist or by using an arm movement pivoting at the elbow. Causes an uneven (thin) application of paint at the beginning and end of each pass. Used in spot repairs and blending.

Atomize: The breaking up of a paint material into small droplets using a paint spray gun and compressed air by counteracting forces of air at the air cap.

Baking: The application of heat at temperatures of 200°F and higher. Technically, baking is not used in refinishing. At this temperature, glass would break and plastic parts would deform. *See* Force-Dry.

Basecoat/Clearcoat Enamel: A two-step OEM paint process composed of three coats of a highly pigmented enamel base color, plus two final coats of enamel clear paint. It is then baked. A similar material is available in lacquer and enamel for after-market application.

Binder: The resin portion of a paint that holds the pigments and other ingredients of a paint together.

Blending: To combine different varieties of materials by thoroughly intermingling so that a line of demarcation cannot be distinguished. To produce a harmonious effect. To mix.

Catalyst: A substance that causes or speeds up a chemical reaction when mixed with another substance but does not change by itself.

Chip Resistant: The ability to withstand chipping when exposed to normal stone and sand abrasion; and to withstand normal contact with a neighboring car when opening the door in a parking lot.

Chroma: The strength or intensity of a color. The departure from white, gray or black from the neutral axis of the color tree. Often referred to as saturation/desaturation.

Clear Acrylic Lacquer: A water-clear resin or binder with all the ingredients of a paint material (such as plasticizer and ultraviolet screener) but lacking pigments and metallic particles.

Clear Urethane Enamel: A water-clear urethane finish with plasticizer and ultraviolet screener, but lacking pigments and metallic particles. Clear urethane must be mixed with a catalyst before use.

Cold Cracking: Cracking of an excessively thick paint finish when subjected to cold and then to warm temperatures. As metal expands, paint does not expand with it, due to internal stresses in the paint, and the paint cracks. Also, flexing an improperly painted flexible plastic part in cool or cold temperature will cause cracking. See ''Plasticizer,'' Chapter 9.

Color: A color is determined by the light waves an object reflects, while it absorbs all other light waves. An object is blue if it absorbs all light waves except blue, which it reflects. An object is black when all light waves are absorbed and none are reflected. An object is white when all light waves are reflected.

Color Coat: To apply only the top color and no undercoat to a spot, large area, panel, or the complete vehicle.

Compatibility: The ability to become blended with other materials. For example, the color of one company is repairable with a similar type of material from another company.

Condensation: When a cold object, like a car, is brought into a hot, humid room, water condenses from the air on the cool surface. Fast-evaporating solvents lower the surface temperature on a car and cause condensation on humid days.

Crocking: The rubbing off or transfer of color from a painted object onto a person's clothing.

Diluent: A liquid that makes more liquid of the material to which it is added. In other words, it thins or dilutes. Diluents in lacquer thinner also serve as a solvent for the resin.

Dispersion: The fundamental objective of dispersion is to coat each pigment particle with resin. Pigments are light and resins are heavy. It takes considerable force to surround each pigment particle with resin. That is why the sand mill and ball mill are used.

Dispersion Lacquer: An OEM paint process that was the first transition stage of reducing solvent emissions at the assembly plants. The solid content of this material is between 17% to 27%. The paint hits the work at approximately 65% solids. Not available for after-market application.

Dissolve: To cause to pass into solution; to separate into component parts.

Double Coat: One sprayed single coat of paint followed immediately by another sprayed single coat.

Durability: The ability to maintain protection and appearance when subjected to the elements for long periods of time.

Elastomer: A man-made compound with flexible and elastic properties. The resin system of elastomeric enamels and lacquers is made of these elastomeric compounds.

Environmental Protection Agency (E.P.A.) Rule 66: Enacted by Los Angeles, California, concerning the quantities of photochemically reactive solvents that may be employed in paints that are sold in containers larger than 1 quart.

Evaporation: The escape of solvents from the paint into the air.

Evaporation Rate: Basically, the amount of time it takes for solvents to evaporate. Similar products from different companies evaporate at slightly different times. Generally, solvents are classed in four categories: fast, medium, slow, and retarder.

Fading: A gradual change in brilliance of a color.

Featheredging: The tapering of the broken edges of paint during sanding so that the featheredge is hardly felt or is not felt at all.

Feathering: Tapering to a very fine application of color at the beginning and end of a stroke by arcing and triggering. Color goes on like the cross section of a feather. An excellent technique for spot repair.

Film Build: The total thickness of the undercoat and top-coat finish of a painted panel, which is measured in mils.

Flash: Allowing solvents from a newly painted surface to evaporate from a glossy to a duller appearing surface.

Flattening Agents: A special combination of talc powder and/or other ingredients and solvents that can be added to paints to dull the gloss of the finish or to increase the metallic sparkle in base color of basecoat/clearcoat metallic paints.

Fluorescent Light: The emitting of visible light from a tubular electric lamp having a coating of fluorescent material on its inner surface and containing mercury vapor whose bombardment by electrons from the cathode provides ultraviolet light.

Fog Coat: Use in metallics. Following a wet coat in which mottling or streaking occur, move the gun back two or three times the normal distance and apply a fog coat with continuing fluid flow and circular motion until the condition is corrected. Then move to another area. This unifies the metallic and pigment orientation. If necessary in enamels, apply just enough mist-coat solvent to bring up the gloss.

Force Dry: The application of infrared heat to a painted surface to speed drying. Normally, temperatures up to 180°F maximum are safe on vehicles.

Gloss (or Luster): The brilliance of the reflection of a finish. Gloss is measured by percentage; 100% gloss is perfect. In general, there is high-gloss, gloss, and semigloss. Zero gloss is a flat finish.

Guide Coat: A reference coat. The color of the top coat is different from the color of the undercoat, and the system is used to serve as a guide coat in sanding to control the sanding depth. The system aids in determining when a smooth surface has been reached.

Hardener: *See* Catalyst.

Hiding: Has the same meaning as covering. Most standard colors achieve hiding at 2 to 2.5 mils. Proper hiding is important in color matching.

Hue: An excitation of the sense of sight created by beams of light that allow us to distinguish one color shade from another.

Humidity: Water vapor in the air. It is measured by percentage. High humidity slows the evaporation of solvents, and low humidity speeds evaporation.

Incandescent Light: The emitting of a white luminous glow created when an electrical current contacts the filament in a vacuum-sealed glass cylinder.

Increment: A minute increase in quantity. Gradual.

Ingredient: Something that is added to a compound or is a component part of any combination or mixture.

Intermediate Colors: A mixture of an adjacent primary and a secondary color. Red-orange, yellow-orange, blue-green, blue-violet or blue-purple, and red-purple or red-violet.

Iridescent: Rinshed-Mason uses this term to denote their metallic color lines.

Isocyanate Resins: This is a principal ingredient in urethane hardeners. Because this ingredient has toxic effects on the painter, the painter is always advised to wear a correct respirator approved by NIOSH (see Chapter 5).

Lacquer: A mixture of natural and/or synthetic resins that dries and hardens to form a film by evaporation of the solvent. Can be air-dried or force-dried.

Metallic Color: Acrylic paints are made by adding several sizes of metallic particles to the basic acrylic ingredients: acrylic resin, low opacity pigments, plasticizer, and solvent.

Metallic Particles: Most generally, aluminum flakes having iridescent and reflective properties are used in various combinations of sizes in paint colors. When added to the paint material it is commonly called a **metallic color.**

Metamerism: A term used to describe two or more colors that match when viewed under one light source, but do not match when viewed under a second light source.

Mil: A measure of paint film thickness equal to one one-thousandth of an inch.

Mist Coat: A light spray coat of high-volume solvent for blending and/or gloss enhancement.

Non-Photochemically Reactive Solvents: Generally composed of blends of different esters, primarily acetates, complex alcohols, and naphthenic hydrocarbons. Does not emit pollutants into the atmosphere.

OEM: Original equipment manufacturer.

Opaque: Impervious to light or not transparent; light cannot be seen through it.

Overlap: That specific area of coverage in which one spray pattern application is extended over and is partly covered by the next application.

Oxidation: The combining of oxygen from the air with the paint film. One principal cause of acrylic enamel drying.

Phosphate Coating: A chemical bond on a steel surface that provides the best adhesion for undercoats. Produced by a metal conditioner or a primer.

Photochemically Reactive Solvents: Common strong paint solvents such as aromatics, the branch chain ketones, diacetone alcohols, and trichlorethylene. Solvents may contain up to 20% toluene, 8% xylene, 20% methylisobutyl ketone, or 20% trichlorethylene. Emits pollutants in atmosphere that do not dissipate.

Pigment: A fine powdered, relatively insoluble substance that imparts black or white or color to coating materials. Some pigments are derived from natural sources and some are produced synthetically (man-made chemically).

Plasticizer: An oily type of substance that adds flexibility to an otherwise brittle substance. Used in acrylic lacquers but not in enamels. The resisn of enamels have a built-in quality of flexibility.

Polychromatic: Ditzler uses this term to denote their metallic color lines.

Polymerization: A change of state occurring chemically when certain ingredients are combined to form another compound with different physical properties, such as in making concrete. Ingredients cannot be returned to their original state. Enamels dry and form by this process. Lacquers do not, as they can be redissolved.

Polypropylene: A tough, lightweight rigid plastic made through a mechanical and chemical process. It is used extensively in the manufacture of interior trim parts. It is a very difficult plastic to paint and requires a special primer.

Polyurethane Resin: The resin system used in urethane products. *See* Urethane Enamel *and* Urethane Plastic.

Polyvinyl Chloride: A thermoplastic material composed of components of vinyl chloride. It has outstanding resistance to the elements. It can be made into a hard or soft plastic. PVC, as this plastic is known, is used in vinyl tops, instrument panel covers (with ABS), and exterior plastic filler panels. It has many other uses.

Pot Life: The amount of time a painter has to apply a plastic or paint finish to which a catalyst or hardener was added. Six hours is usually the pot life for catalyzed enamels. Follow label directions.

Pressure Drop: The difference in hose pressure at the transformer (on the wall) and at the spray gun (at the car). Caused by the size of the inside hose diameter. Friction caused by the walls of the hose and the length of the hose.

Pressure Feed Gun: A paint spray gun with the fluid nozzle being flush with the air nozzle. Paint material is force fed to the spray gun using a pressure cup, tank, or material pump.

Primary Colors: Red, yellow, and blue.

psi or PSI: Regarding air pressure, pounds per square inch.

Refinish: The replacement of undercoat and top color coat, the complete finish of a spot, large area, panel, or complete vehicle.

Repairability: The ability to be repaired satisfactorily in service.

Retarder: Prevents blushing. Slows down evaporation of solvents from paint material. Can be used for fine blending in enamels. Primarily, retarder makes possible the wet-on-wet painting system, which prevents overspray from showing on complete paint jobs.

Saturation/Desaturation: *See* Chroma.

Secondary Colors: Mixture of two primary colors: orange, green, and purple or violet.

Service Parts Identification Label: A paper decal with a protective plastic coating. Attached in designated locations of the vehicle. Provides the following for the painter: vehicle identification number, WA number, two-digit paint code number, and paint technology (type). (Used by GM since mid 1984.)

Settling: The gradual sinking of the heavier pigments, binders, and metallic particles that make up a paint material when allowed to remain in the liquid state.

Single Coat: Spray painting once over a surface with each spray pattern pass overlapping the previous pass by 50%.

Solids: Colors that contain no metallic flakes; must be tinted within the confines of a color hue and to near exactness. Consist of highly opaque pigmentation.

Solution: A homogenous mixture; when the solids are distributed evenly in a mixture of reduced paint.

Solvent: A liquid substance capable of dissolving or dispersing one or more other substances. Provides a solution.

Suction-feed Gun: A paint spray gun in which paint material is fed into the spray gun by atmospheric pressure due to a partial vacuum created by the design of the air and fluid nozzle.

(Tinting) Face of Metallic Color: The appearance of a color when viewed from the perpendicular (90°-angle).

(Tinting) Mass Tone: The color of a tinting base prior to mixing with other bases.

(Tinting) Pitch of Metallic Color: The appearance of a color when viewed from any angle other than "face" and usually 45° or less.

(Tinting) Under Tone: The color produced by a tinting base when it is mixed with white or aluminum.

Translucent: Having the property of allowing light to pass through but the objects beyond cannot be clearly distinguished; partly transparent. A property of metallic colors.

Transparent: Having the property of allowing light to pass through so that objects can be identified clearly through it. The opposite of opaque. A property of metallic colors.

Ultraviolet Screener: An ingredient added to paint finishes by paint manufacturers, which is designed to cut off or reduce ultraviolet light penetration into a paint film. This ingredient is needed primarily in metallics and in clears. Provides durability to paint.

Unstable Tints: A base color ingredient that lacks stability; subject to ready change in chemical composition.

Urethane Enamel: Requires an isocyanate hardener for curing. The ingredients have toxins that can affect a person coming in contact with them. Protective clothing and a NIOSH-approved respirator are required when applying materials containing isocyanate hardeners. The material is available in colors and in clear form. Glass-smooth finish approximately two and a half times harder than ordinary acrylic enamels.

Urethane Plastic: As used on bumpers, filler panels, and quarter extension panels, urethane plastic is of the thermoplastic type. It is very tough and flexible. This material can be plastic-welded. These parts require flexible plastic paint finishes.

Vacuum: The absence of air.

Value: The lightness or darkness of a color.

Vaporization: The conversion of solvents into gases during spray painting.

Vehicle: The liquid portion of a paint.

Ventilation: The correct movement of air during spray painting and drying of the finish. One of the variables of spray painting.

Vinyl: The common plastic name for polyvinyl chloride (PVC), as in "vinyl tops" and "vinyl trim." Vinyl plastics require a special type of paint in refinishing. For best refinish results, it is best to use factory-recommended brands of vinyl paints.

Viscosity: The flow characteristics of a paint material that determine how well it will atomize, how well it will "flow out" on the work, and the type of equipment necessary to move it.

Waterborne Enamel: An OEM paint process in which a special deionized, purified water is substituted as the solvent carrier instead of enamel reducer. Not available for field application.

Waterproof: Sheds water completely, none penetrates.

Water resistant: Sheds most water, but some penetrates.

Wavelength: The distance in the line of advance of a wave from any one point to the next point of corresponding phase.

Index

C

how to use, 206
need for, 205

W

Water spotting, 420
Wet sanding, 149
Wet spots, 421

Wheel burn, 421
Wiping towels, 139
Wrinkling of enamels, 422

Z

Zinc phosphate primer, enamel type, 227
Zinc stearate, 146